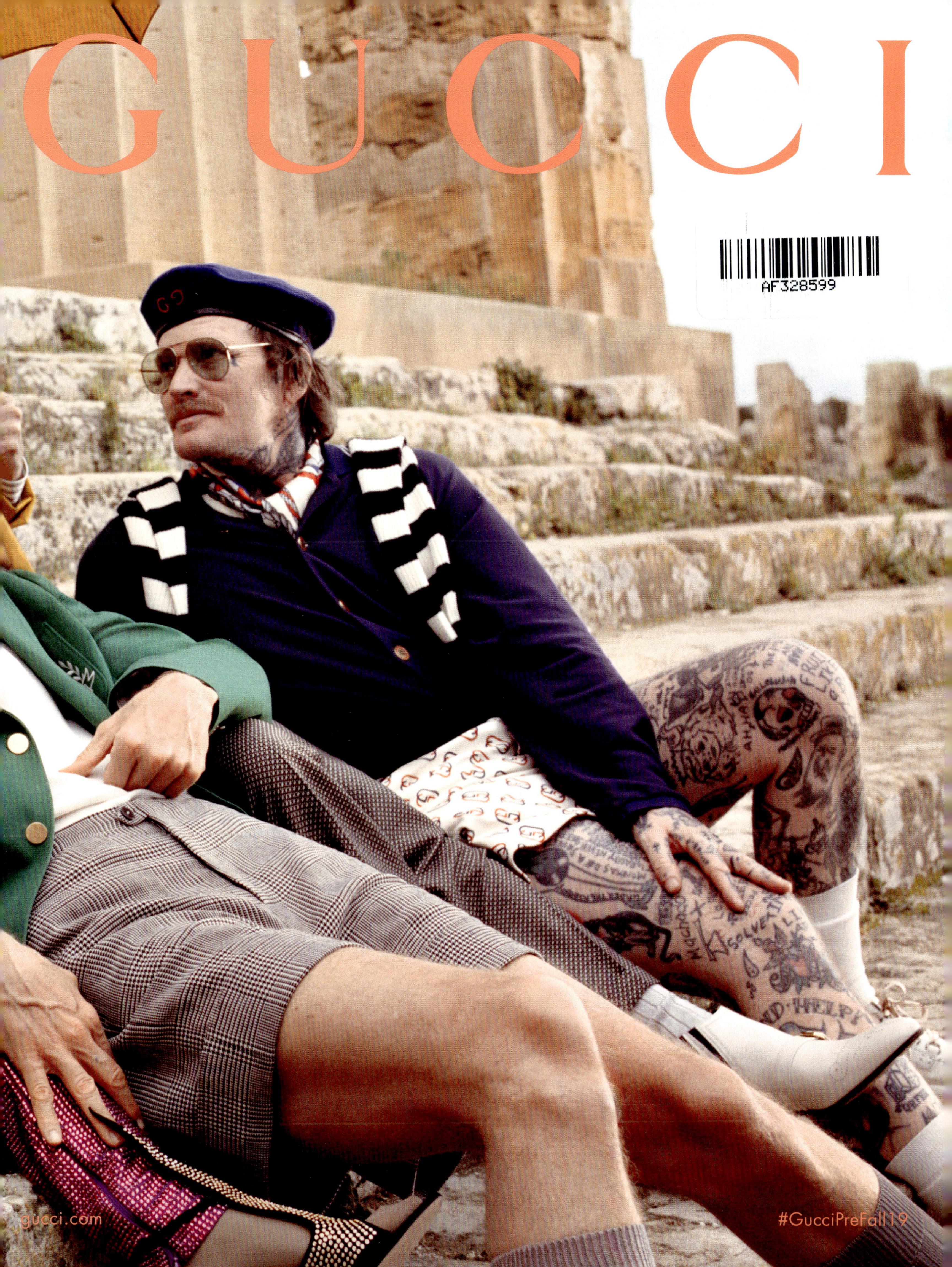

GUCCI
AF328599
gucci.com
#GucciPreFall19

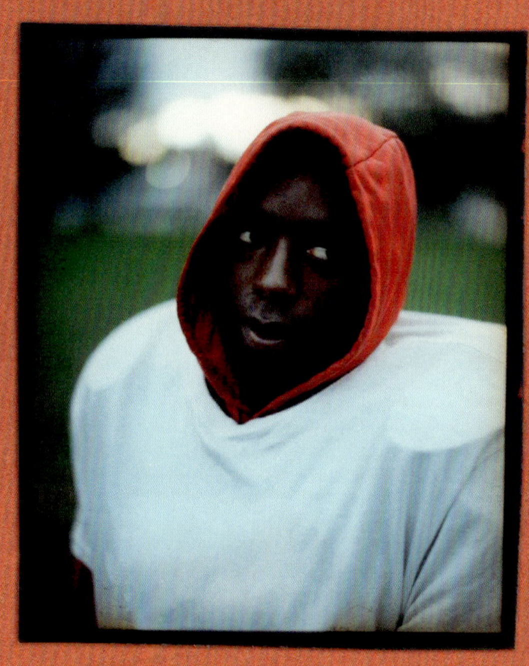

SEPTEMBER 2019
MACK

Brooklyn Museum   On View Now

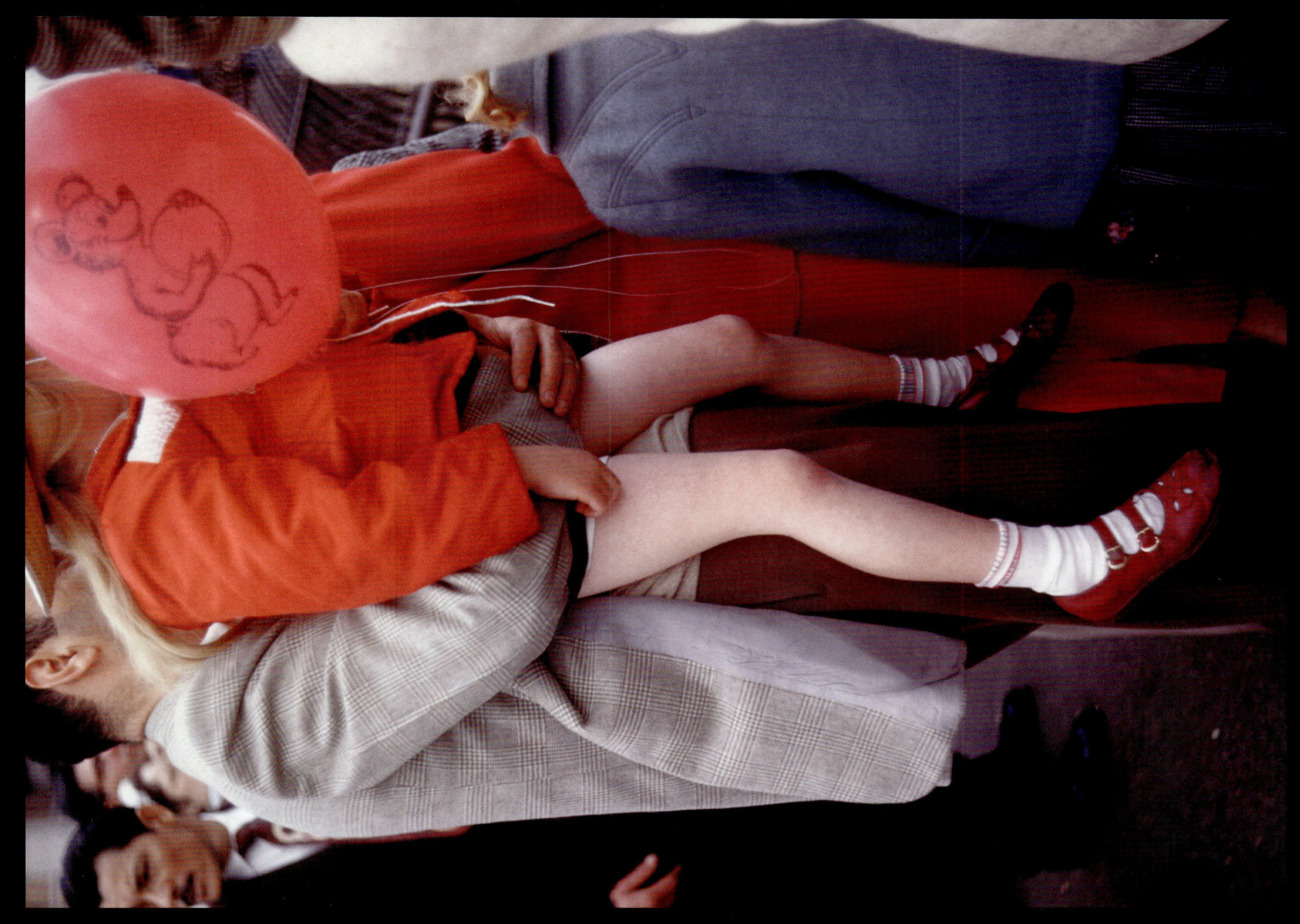

Garry Winogrand: Color
May 3–December 8, 2019

Garry Winogrand: Color is curated by Drew Sawyer, Phillip Leonian and Edith Rosenbaum Leonian Curator of Photography, Brooklyn Museum, with Michael Almereyda and Susan Kismaric.

Leadership support for this exhibition is provided by the Phillip Leonian and Edith Rosenbaum Leonian Charitable Trust.

Front cover:
**Iñaki Bonillas, *Adiós
fotografía* (Bye bye
photography), Mexico
City (detail), 2018**
Courtesy the artist and
Kurimanzutto, Mexico City/
New York

*Visita aperture.org para leer
una selección de artículos
de este número en español.*

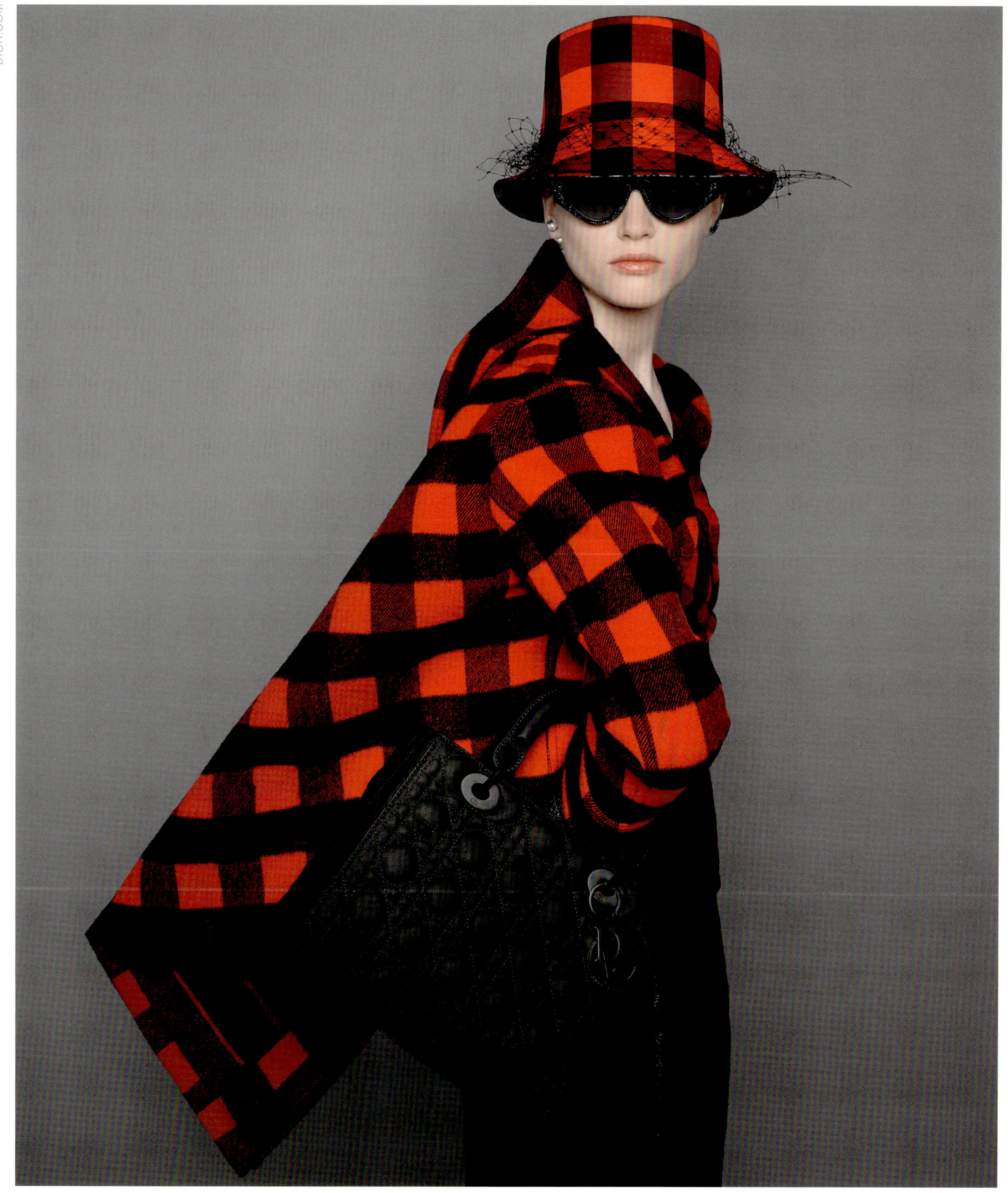

DIOR.COM
DIOR

Aperture, a not-for-profit foundation, connects the photo community and its audiences with the most inspiring work, the sharpest ideas, and with each other— in print, in person, and online.

Aperture (ISSN 0003-6420) is published quarterly, in spring, summer, fall, and winter, at 547 West 27th Street, 4th Floor, New York, N.Y. 10001. In the United States, a one-year subscription (four issues) is $75; a two-year subscription (eight issues) is $124. In Canada, a one-year subscription is $95. All other international subscriptions are $105 per year. Visit aperture.org to subscribe. Single copies may be purchased at $24.95 for most issues. Subscribe to the *Aperture Digital Archive* at aperture.org/archive. Periodicals postage paid at New York and additional offices. Postmaster: Send address changes to *Aperture*, P.O. Box 3000, Denville, N.J. 07834. Address queries regarding subscriptions, renewals, or gifts to: *Aperture* Subscription Service, 866-457-4603 (U.S. and Canada), or email custsvc_aperture@fulcoinc.com.

Newsstand distribution in the U.S. is handled by Curtis Circulation Company, 201-634-7400. For international distribution, contact Central Books, centralbooks.com. Other inquiries, email orders@aperture.org or call 212-505-5555.

Help maintain Aperture's publishing, education, and community activities by joining our general member program. Membership starts at $75 annually and includes invitations to special events, exclusive discounts on Aperture publications, and opportunities to meet artists and engage with leaders in the photography community. Aperture Foundation welcomes support at all levels of giving, and all gifts are tax-deductible to the fullest extent of the law. For more information about supporting Aperture, please visit aperture.org/join or contact the Development Department at membership@aperture.org.

Library of Congress Catalog Card No: 58-30845.

ISBN 978-1-59711-462-2

Printed in Turkey by Ofset Yapimevi

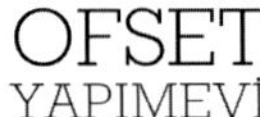

Aperture wishes to thank the following individuals for their ideas and guidance in assembling the magazine's "Mexico City" issue: Iñaki Bonillas, Miguel Calderón, Andrea Celda Laurent-Atthalin, Sarah Hermanson Meister, Elena Navarro, Pablo Ortíz Monasterio, Ramón Reverté, and Oswaldo Ruiz. Aperture also thanks FotoMéxico and Grupo Habita for supporting the launch of this issue in Mexico City, and Selina for supporting the launch in New York.

Significant support for *Aperture* magazine is provided by The Kanakia Foundation. Further generous support is provided in part by The Andy Warhol Foundation for the Visual Arts and the New York City Department of Cultural Affairs in partnership with the City Council.

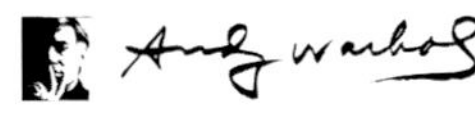

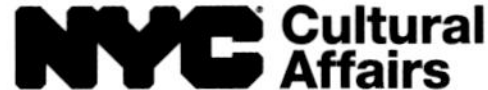

aperture

The Magazine of Photography and Ideas

Editor
Michael Famighetti
Contributing Editor
Elena Navarro
Managing Editor
Brendan Embser
Assistant Editor
Annika Klein
Copy Editors
Olivia Casa, Clare Fentress, Donna Ghelerter
Translators
Elianna Kan, Enrique Pérez Rosiles
Senior Production Manager
True Sims
Production Manager
Bryan Krueger
Work Scholars
Charis Morgan, Valeriya Pavlova, Ellen Pong

Art Direction, Design & Typefaces
A2/SW/HK, London

Publisher
Dana Triwush
magazine@aperture.org

Director of Brand Partnerships
Isabelle Friedrich McTwigan
212-946-7118
imctwigan@aperture.org

Advertising
Elizabeth Morina
917-691-2608
emorina@aperture.org

**Executive Director,
Aperture Foundation**
Chris Boot

Minor White, Editor (1952–1974)

Michael E. Hoffman, Publisher and Executive Director (1964–2001)

aperture.org

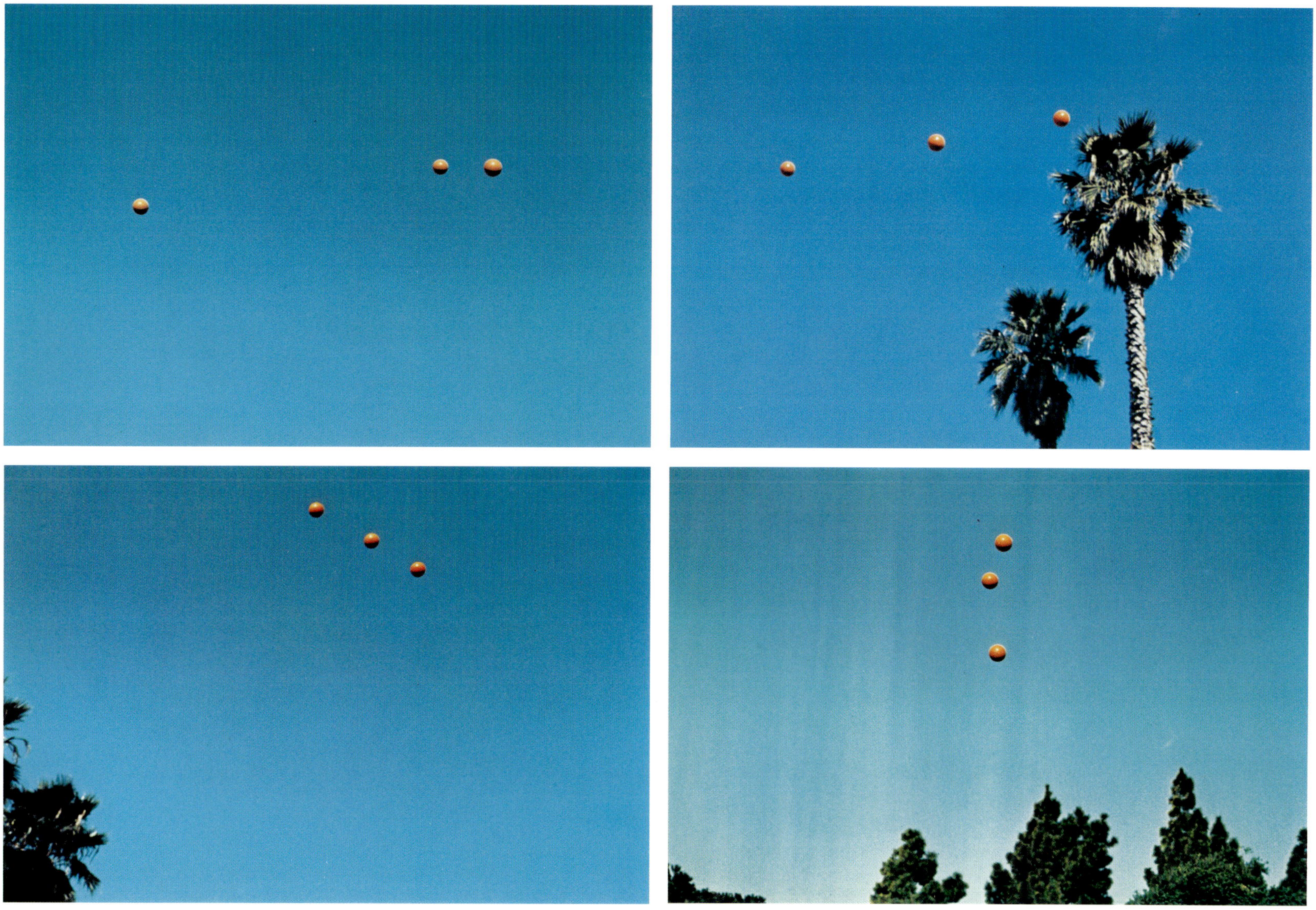

Agenda
Exhibitions to See

Alinka Echeverría

During a 2015 research residency at the Musée Nicéphore Niépce—a French museum devoted to Joseph-Nicéphore Niépce, who is often credited as the inventor of photography—Mexican British artist Alinka Echeverría employed an intersectional feminist lens to recontextualize the museum's colonial archives. With a background in social anthropology, she studies historical representations of women in photography, using collage to liberate and reframe these images. Echeverría's upcoming show at the Musée des beaux-arts de Montréal, *Simulacres*, revisits her work on Niépce to pose critical conversations between archival images of women and vases from the museum's collection. "Alinka's work not only addresses questions of the feminine but also the question of the 'other' as objects of colonial study," says María Wills Londoño, curator of the exhibition. "She works in collages—tearing images, taking objects, and making fragmentations—to question the semiotics of the feminine and how society and history are constructed."

Simulacres: Alinka Echevarría at the Musée des beaux-arts de Montréal, September 5–December 1, 2019

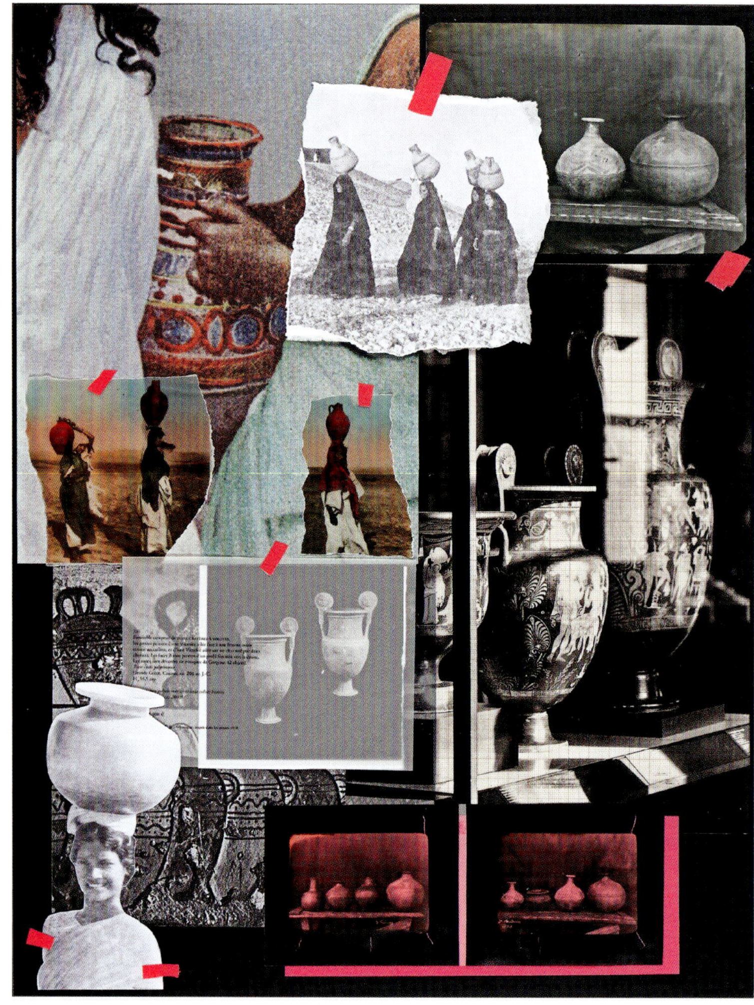

Alinka Echeverría,
Fieldnotes for Nicephora,
from the series *Nicephora*,
2015–ongoing
© the artist

Duane Michals

Duane Michals never really studied photography. When he started experimenting with pictures in the 1960s, he felt free to live and make work any way he wanted. He began to explore cinematic devices and multiple exposures, staging multipart photographic sequences that consider mortality and desire. He embraced technical errors. And he wrote in the margins of his prints. "Writing allowed Michals to find his voice in photography," says Joel Smith, curator of photography at the Morgan Library & Museum, which is presenting *Illusions of the Photographer*, Michals's first full-scale New York museum retrospective. Covering five decades of Michals's photography and short films, the exhibition will be accompanied by an artist's-choice show, selected by Michals from the Morgan's collection, featuring works by Eugène Atget, Auguste Rodin, and Joseph Cornell. "Illusions," Smith says of Michals's work, "allow a photographer to believe in the vision of the world he's got and make it real."

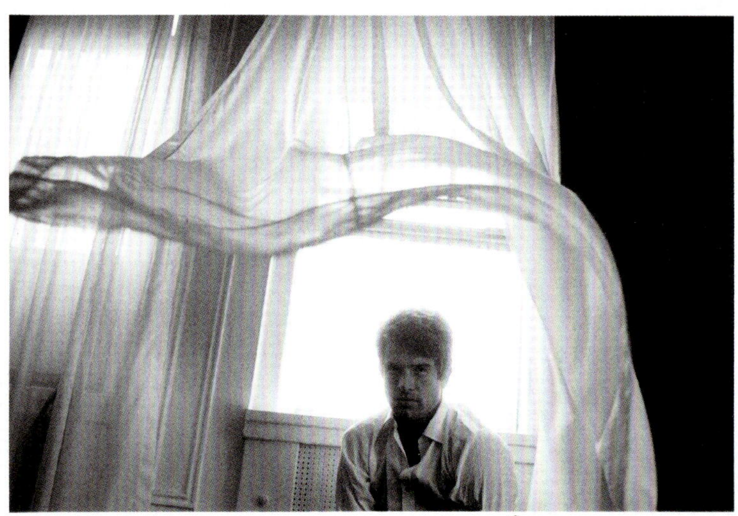

Duane Michals, *Warren Beatty*, 1966
© the artist and courtesy DC Moore Gallery,
New York

Illusions of the Photographer: Duane Michals at the Morgan at the Morgan Library & Museum, New York, October 25, 2019–February 2, 2020

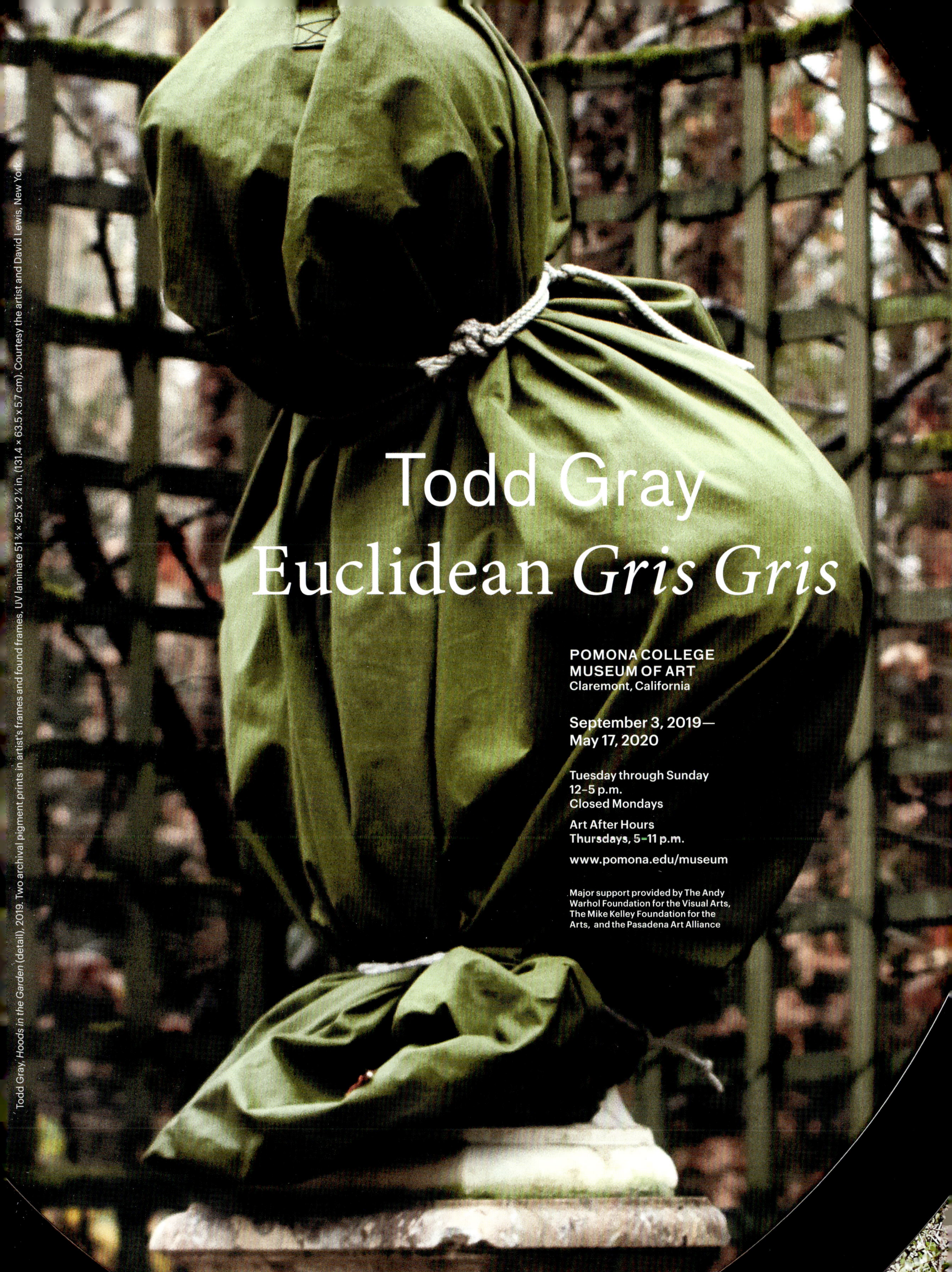

Todd Gray
Euclidean *Gris Gris*

POMONA COLLEGE
MUSEUM OF ART
Claremont, California

September 3, 2019—
May 17, 2020

Tuesday through Sunday
12–5 p.m.
Closed Mondays

Art After Hours
Thursdays, 5–11 p.m.

www.pomona.edu/museum

Major support provided by The Andy
Warhol Foundation for the Visual Arts,
The Mike Kelley Foundation for the
Arts, and the Pasadena Art Alliance

Todd Gray, 'Hoods in the Garden' (detail), 2019. Two archival pigment prints in artist's frames and found frames, UV laminate 51¾ × 25 × 2¼ in. (131.4 × 63.5 × 5.7 cm). Courtesy the artist and David Lewis, New York.

Jan Groover

"Formalism is everything for Jan Groover. It is a motto, true from the first work to the last work," says Tatyana Franck, director of the Musée de l'Elysée. Groover is best known for her kitchen still lifes from the 1970s and '80s, a body of work that became a postmodern classic and helped make the case for color photography as art. Two years after Groover's death in 2012, Franck visited the house in rural France that the artist had shared with her husband and was astonished to discover forty years of Groover's work there. In 2017, the museum acquired the archive, which contains some twenty thousand objects: sketches, Polaroids, negatives, contact sheets, test prints, technical equipment, and Groover's own photography collection. *Laboratory of Forms*, curated by Franck, is Groover's first survey in over thirty years and includes portraits, still lifes, and landscapes from 1967 to the very last negative Groover printed.

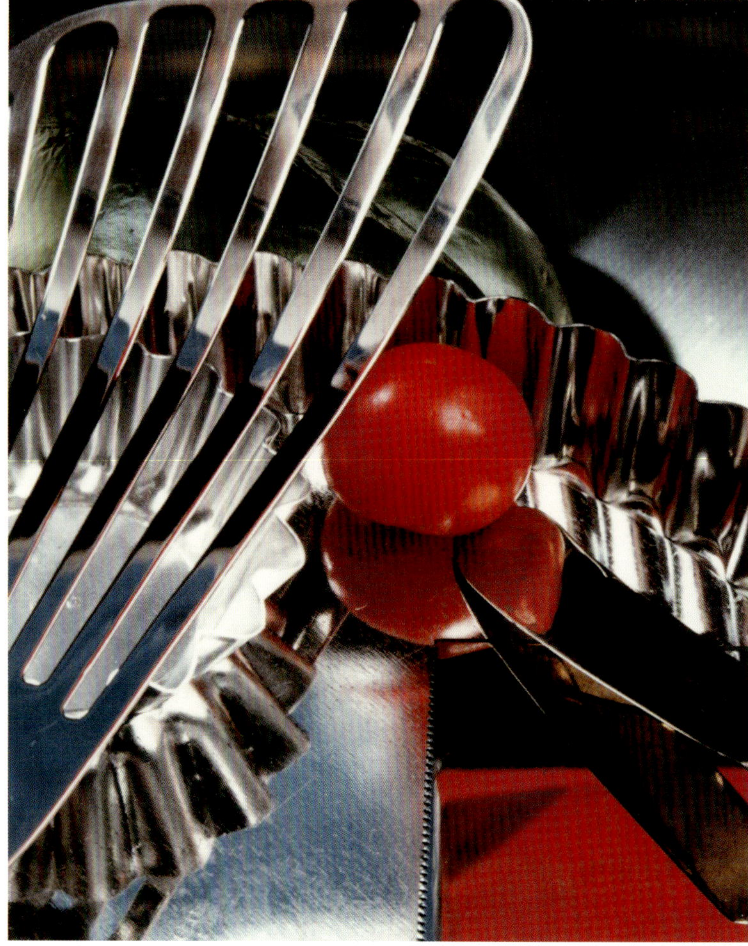

Jan Groover, *Untitled*, ca. 1978
© Musée de l'Elysée, Lausanne/Jan Groover Archives

Laboratory of Forms: Photographs by Jan Groover at the Musée de l'Elysée, Lausanne, Switzerland, September 18, 2019–January 5, 2020

Shot in Soho

P. D. James once said that London's Soho district was a "cosmopolitan village" with good food, great shopping, and sordid crime. Before its more recent polished incarnation with boutique hotels and a new Crossrail transit line, Soho was a magnet for disobedience and debauchery, yet it still remains a destination for artists of all types. *Shot in Soho* presents images by photographers such as Anders Petersen, William Klein, and Corinne Day, who profiled the infamous neighborhood. Not simply an exercise in nostalgia, the exhibition also looks at present-day Soho through images of romantic connections in a new commission by the emerging Irish photographer Daragh Soden. Together, *Shot in Soho* celebrates an ever-changing, one-square-mile enclave that contains, as James noted, "all things to all men, catering comprehensively for those needs which money can buy."

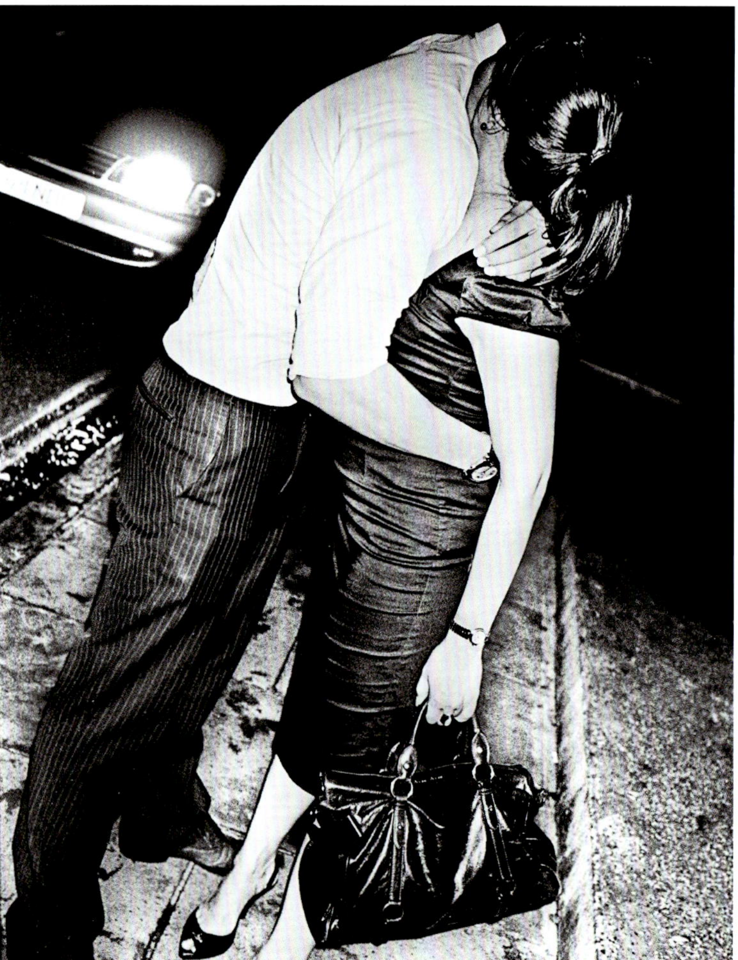

Anders Petersen, *London 150*, 2012
© the artist

Shot in Soho at the Photographers' Gallery, London, October 18, 2019–February 9, 2020

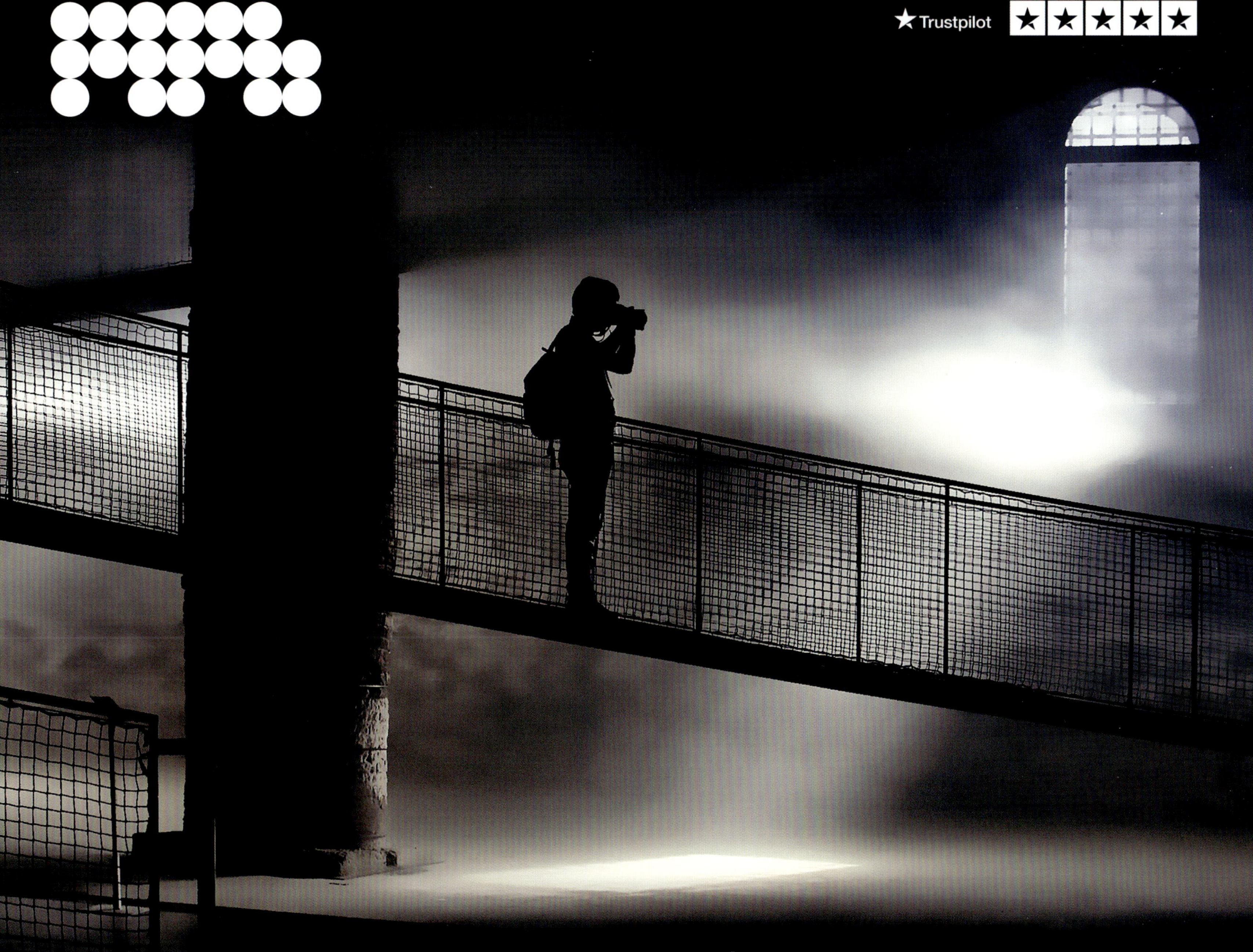

Access amazing equipment the easy way.

Trade in and upgrade your setup with MPB. Get a free instant quote and free shipping both ways.
MPB checks, grades and individually photographs every item to ensure maximum reliability,
and there's a free six month warranty on everything. Amazing gear, immediately accessible.

MPB is the quick, easy and secure way to trade in your camera gear.

Change gear.

www.mpb.com

@mpbcom

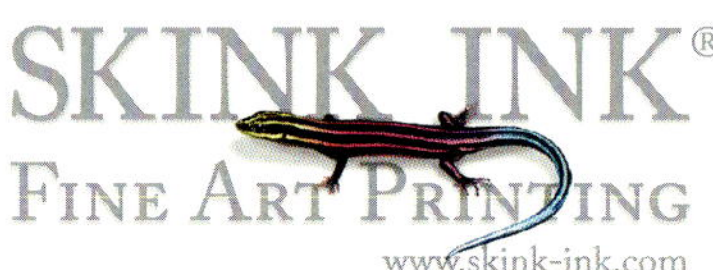

Paper much like *Vanilla* is one of the most under appreciated substances in our lives. Perhaps it's familiarity that has dulled our appreciation but as with vanilla there is no such thing as 'plain' paper.

When you print on a fine paper it elevates everything about your work. We carry over 80 unique papers in stock at all times. Cotton rags, photo rags, fibre rags. Washi papers, pearls, semi-matts and barytas. We produce editions and prints for exhibition in museums and art galleries around the world.

Our studio in Williamsburg, Brooklyn is where we realize artists' and photographers' work on the most beautiful papers available. Come browse our paper books and feel inspired.

Fine art inkjet printing for
artists, illustrators, designers
& photographers

177 N. 10th Street Rm G, Brooklyn, NY 11211
646 455 3400 | www.skink-ink.com | @skink_ink

Spotlight
Mark McKnight

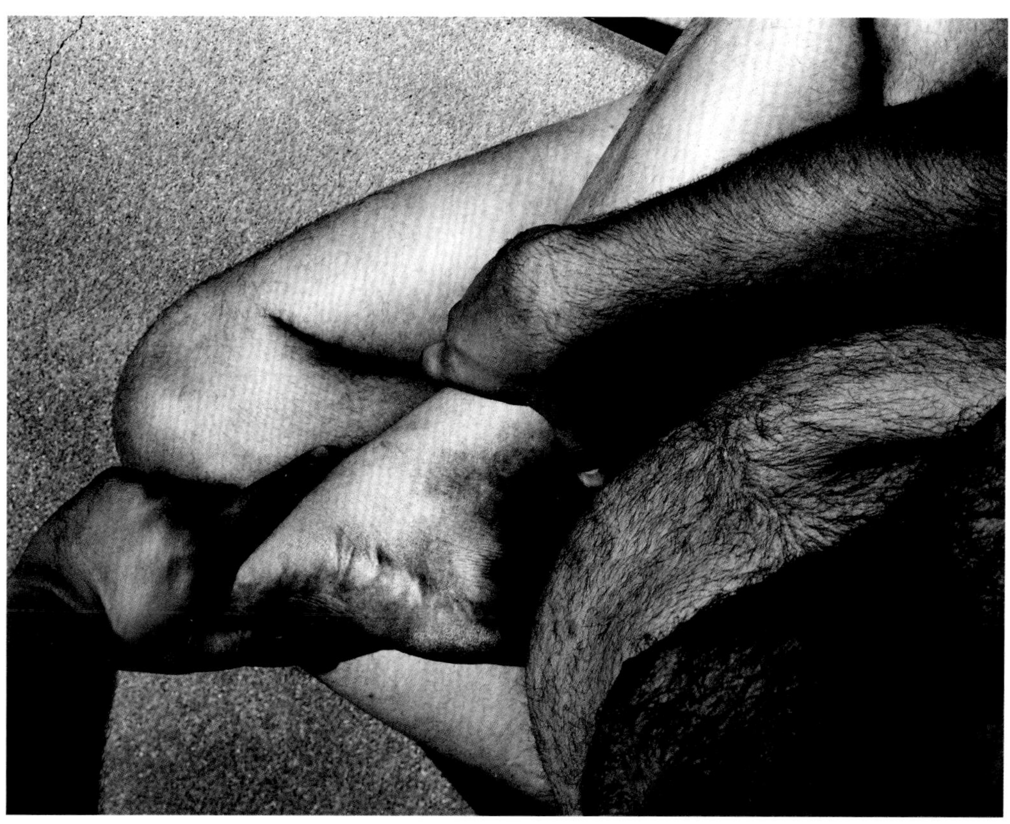

**In the male body and the physical world,
an unexpected seduction**

Garth Greenwell

"I think we're all constantly on the precipice of becoming another thing," the photographer Mark McKnight says. A logic of transformation—of metaphor—animates his defiantly analog, large-format, black-and-white photographs. A torn bag of asphalt suggests the broken flesh of an animal; a blistered wall rhymes with a man's mottled back; the play of light across tar reveals a cosmos. Bodies, landscapes, buildings are depicted in a way that makes them nearly interchangeable, equivalent to the eye and also, disquietingly, to our sympathy, so that traces of adhesive on a wall might be scars from a severed limb.

The extraordinary energy of McKnight's images comes from a harnessing of contrary, even contradictory, forces. McKnight, who was born in Los Angeles, in 1984, chooses as his subjects men he knows and frequently is attracted to,

members of his queer LA community. His photographs are redolent with intimacy, an extravagant tenderness. And yet, he photographs these men in ways that seem deliberately untender: starkly lit and in claustrophobic proximity, with every blemish displayed, frequently in postures, like that of *Ballerino* (2018), of literal abjection. It's a treatment that suggests cruelty, though the pictures are never cruel; they are, it seems to me, the opposite of cruel. Almost always, the expected focus of tenderness and sympathetic attachment—the human face—is obscured, turned away from the camera or cropped out of the frame. McKnight challenges us to find grace in what might at first seem a graceless image, to linger on the elegance of the curves of a man's flesh, to imagine, between body and shadow, a surreal pas de deux.

McKnight has resisted the idea that facelessness in his work stems from a desire for furtiveness or anonymity, insisting instead that it allows the men to be archetypal, figures of longing, time, vulnerability. But both anonymity and archetype are forms of abstraction, an abstraction that doesn't cancel out the intimacy of the work but throws it somehow—as McKnight's shadows, which he over-develops to an abyssal black, do for the surfaces that cast them—in starker relief. McKnight's photographs of male bodies at once invite us close and ward us away; they are, in that way, mimetic of a particular experience of desire, a continually frustrating seduction.

"The pictures, like all things, are too complex to fully reconcile," McKnight told me recently from his studio in LA. "And that's something I appreciate about the pictures, not something that I run

Previous page:
Bodyfold, 2019

This page, below:
Ballerino, 2018; right:
The Black Place, 2019
Courtesy the artist

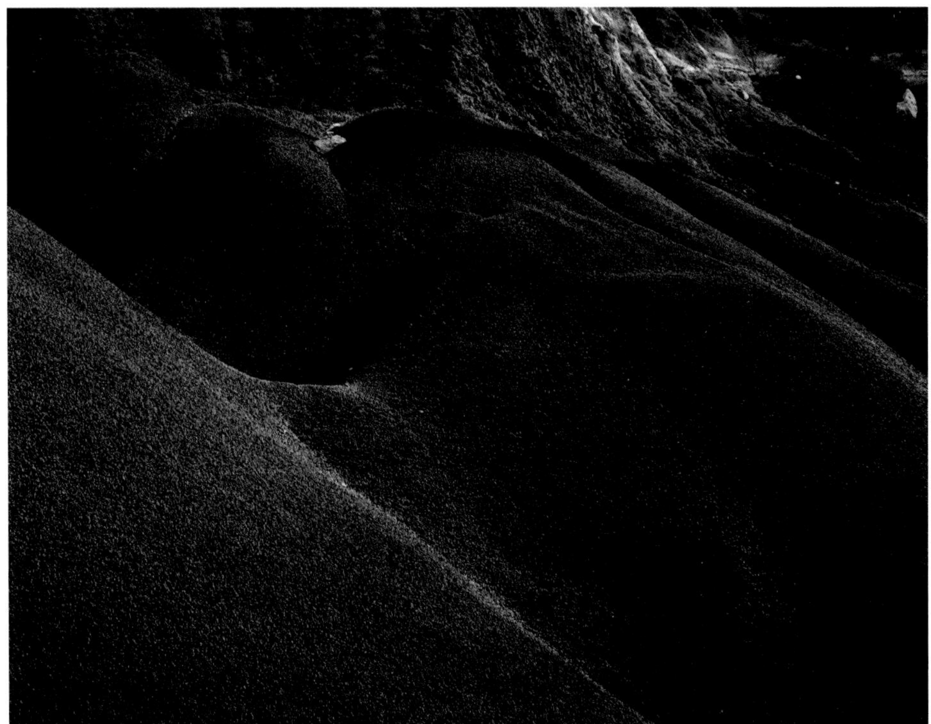

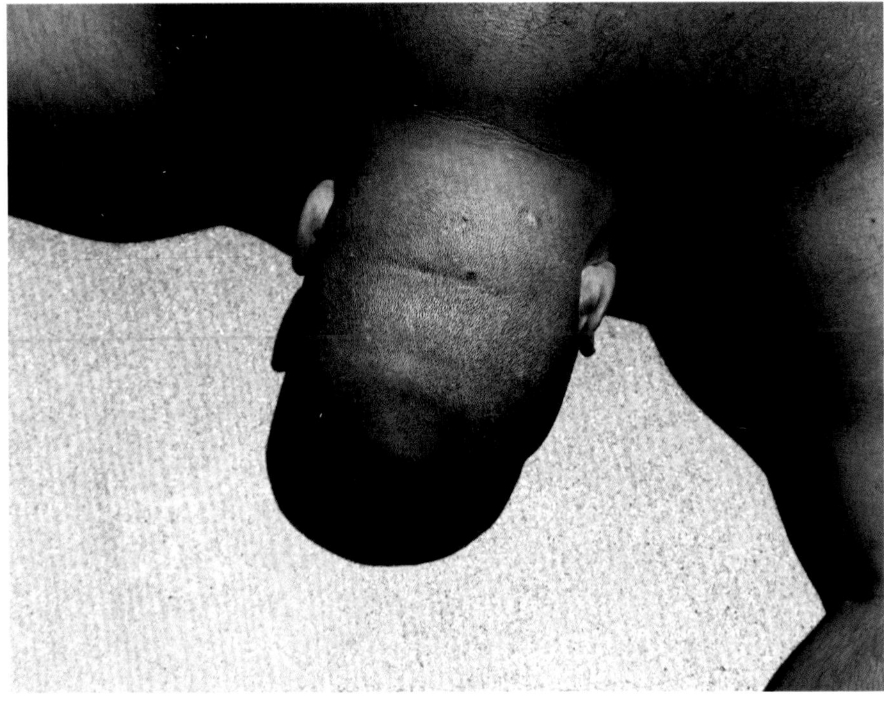

from." McKnight's willingness to abide with the irreconcilable gives these photographs their quality of inexhaustibility; it transforms them into objects of contemplation. Perhaps the contradiction in the work I can least account for, and that therefore feels most powerful to me, is the fact that although McKnight rejects so many of the usual sources of affect—facial expression, social context, identifiable narrative—his work is drenched in affect, supersaturated with emotion in a way that feels almost operatic, exuberantly queer.

Take, for example, *Bodyfold* (2019). The subject at first seems clear: a man sitting in the sunlight, his right leg folded over his left. But the details are

indeterminate: Is he sitting directly on the concrete, or perched somehow above it? Is that black triangle at the bottom of the image a shadow or a chair? He's naked, and the camera gazes into his lap—it could nearly be, but isn't quite, the subject's own gaze—but what we might have thought would be the object of desire is hidden from us, the leg pulled tight against the body to hide his cock from view. Or maybe nothing is being hidden; maybe the man is indifferent to us, maybe the posture is for his own comfort. There's a suggestion of self-sufficiency in the way he holds himself, his ankle gripped by his right hand, his toes by his left, the thumb stretched along his sole. The photograph's erotic intimacy lies in that touch, I think,

its suggestion of pleasure given by and taken in himself.

Bodyfold moves me because of its subject, a type of body—hairy, thick, nonwhite—often excluded from the canons of beauty; but it moves me more because of the intricacy of its composition, the complexity of pattern that gives the photograph its compelling density. How curious that so much of the photograph's affect lies in what might seem to be affectless geometry—but then, that geometry is the measure of the craftsman's care, the claim to value we always make when we transform something into art.

It took hours for me to become conscious of *Bodyfold*'s most heartbreaking detail: the hairline crack in the concrete in the upper-left-hand corner of the image. It's a little death's head, I think, a touch of entropy, time's signature: an organic curve that echoes the man's body and reminds us of the transience that—voracious, indiscriminate—claims everything we lavish our care upon, concrete as surely as flesh.

Garth Greenwell is the author of *What Belongs to You* (2016). A new book of fiction, *Cleanness,* is forthcoming in January 2020.

Mark McKnight is the winner of the 2019 Aperture Portfolio Prize. His solo exhibition will be on view at Aperture Gallery, New York, from November 14 to December 20, 2019.

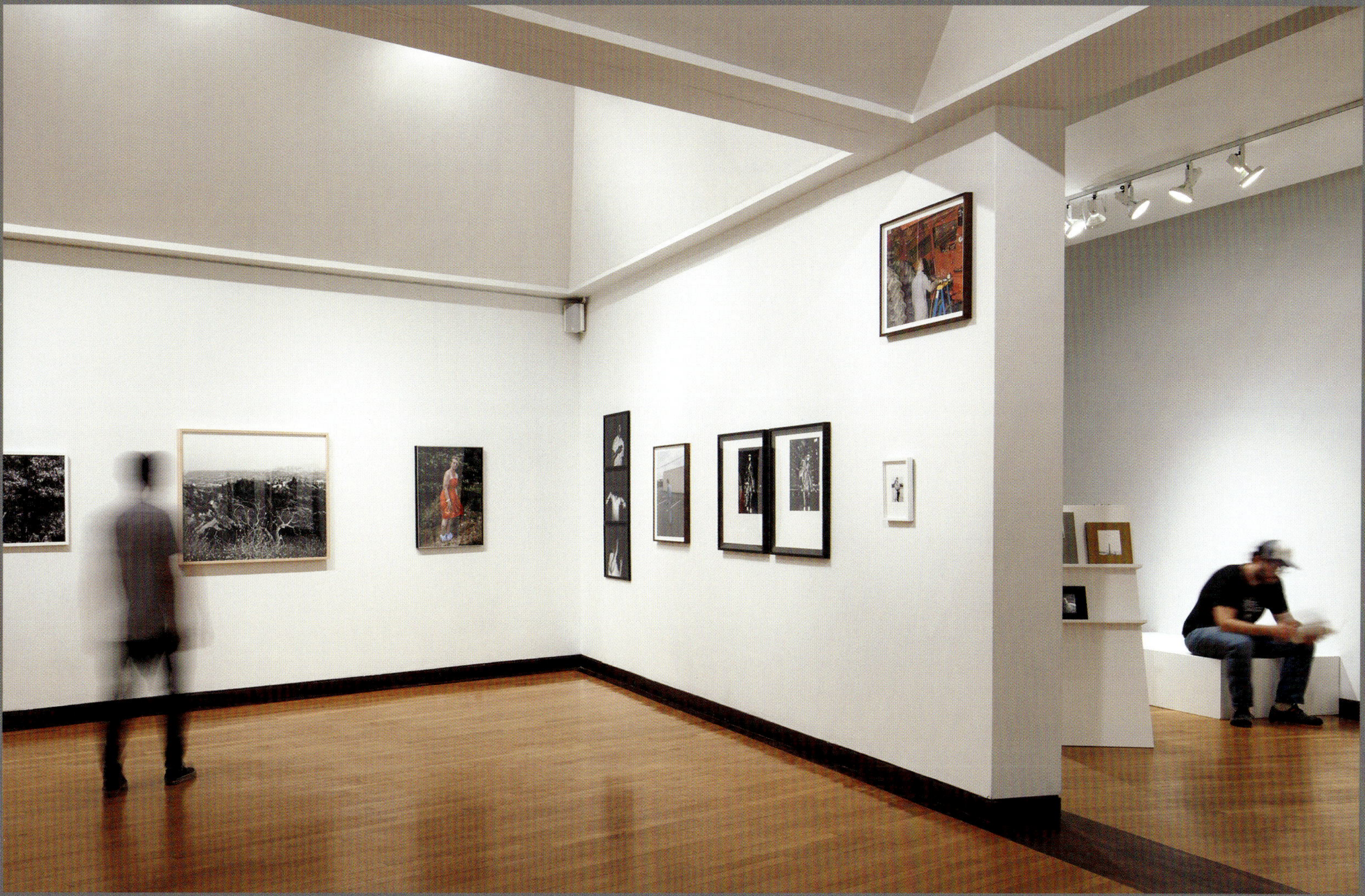

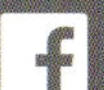

Photo: Kevin Kunstadt, MFA '17

International Limited-Residency
MFA PHOTOGRAPHY

FACULTY AND LECTURERS INCLUDE:

Robert Lyons—Director, Michael Vahrenwald, Dr. Jörg Colberg, Alice Rose George, Michael Schäfer, Mary Frey, Mark Steinmetz, Ute Mahler, Alec Soth, Dru Donovan, John Priola, Thomas Weski, Felix Hoffman, Lisa Kereszi, Irina Rozovsky, Paul Schiek, Hiroh Kikai, Andrianna Campbell, Melissa Cantanese, Ed Panar, David Campany

ALUMNI INCLUDE:

Sanne Vils Axelsen (DK), Josee Schryer (QC), Lucy Helton (UK), Dagmar Kolatschny (DE), Chikara Umihara (Japan), Saleem Ahmed (USA), Tim Carpenter (USA), Matt Genitempo (USA), Stuart Richardson (Iceland), Robin Dahlberg (USA), Emma Phillips (NZ)

UNIVERSITY OF HARTFORD
HARTFORD ART SCHOOL

hartford.edu/photomfa

200 Bloomfield Avenue | West Hartford, Connecticut 06117

hartford art school–mfa photo

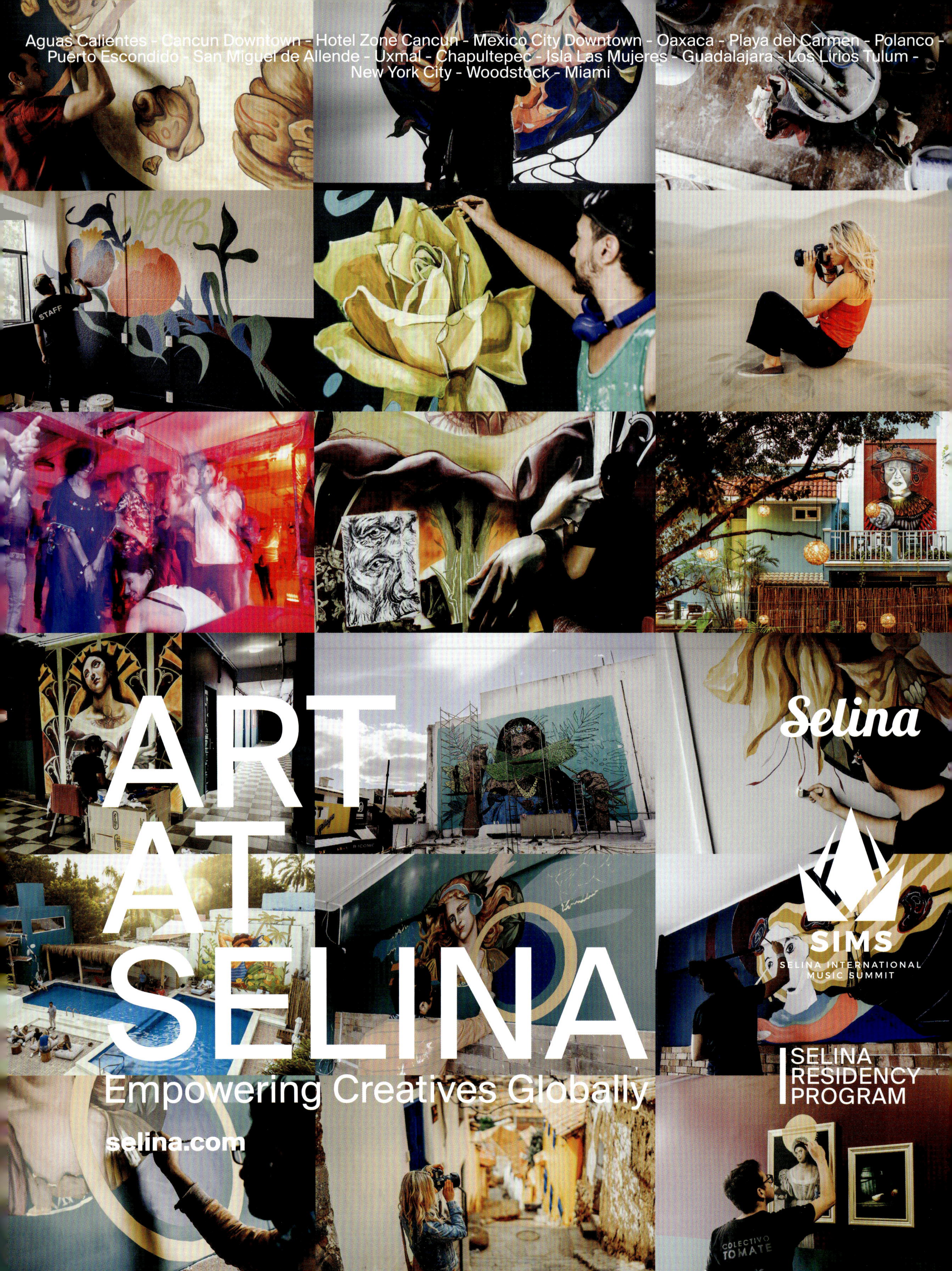

Aguas Calientes - Cancun Downtown - Hotel Zone Cancun - Mexico City Downtown - Oaxaca - Playa del Carmen - Polanco - Puerto Escondido - San Miguel de Allende - Uxmal - Chapultepec - Isla Las Mujeres - Guadalajara - Los Lirios Tulum - New York City - Woodstock - Miami
STAFF
Selina
ART AT SELINA
Empowering Creatives Globally
selina.com
SIMS
SELINA INTERNATIONAL MUSIC SUMMIT
SELINA RESIDENCY PROGRAM
COLECTIVO TOMATE

Redux
Rediscovered Books and Writings

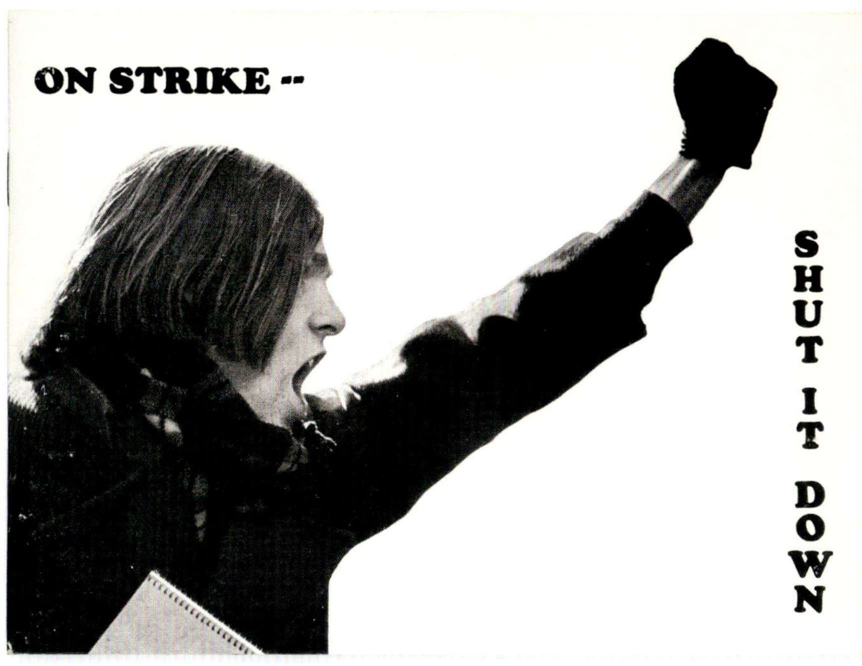

A photojournalist's dramatic account of student uprisings in Wisconsin

Brian Wallis

Fifty years ago, in February 1969, black student activists at the University of Wisconsin–Madison called a strike against racism, demanding more African American students and faculty, more relevant courses, and amnesty for black protesters. This extraordinary weeklong demonstration, which culminated in a standoff between over ten thousand students and about nineteen hundred fully armed National Guard soldiers, is succinctly documented in a small but powerful forty-page photobook titled *On Strike: Shut It Down* (1969), published within weeks of the confrontation by local photojournalist Richard Faverty, with pithy text by Joel Brenner, editor of the university's student newspaper.

The protest was part of the nationwide Black Campus Movement, which exploded in the year following the assassination of Dr. Martin Luther King Jr. in April 1968. African American students at Wisconsin–Madison first staged a conference on black revolution and issued a proclamation of thirteen demands, then initiated demonstrations that included a campus shutdown and a march on the state capitol.

When local police were unable to control the growing crowds of thousands of (mostly white) student protesters, on February 12, the governor called in the overzealous, battle-ready National Guard to confront the unarmed students.

From its militant cover, showing a student protester thrusting forward a clenched fist, to its final image, of Faverty with his cameras ducking under the outstretched bayonets of a row of guardsmen, *On Strike* uses a deft command of photojournalistic storytelling to capture the escalating drama. Faverty's initially humorous photographs depict mostly white students jeering at cops or clamoring over a statue of a seated Abraham Lincoln. Double-spread images of surprisingly violent confrontations follow, with police using clubs and tear gas on the students. Finally, when the National Guard appears, things get real. One photograph shows the students from the guardsmen's point of view, staring over the barrel of a Jeep-mounted machine gun. Another image depicts a phalanx of baby-faced guardsmen, looking unprepared, yet armed and ready to kill. In the end, violent clashes were quelled, and the university acceded to many of the black students' demands, but Wisconsin–Madison remained for years ground zero for the student-led antiwar and protest movement.

Faverty, who just last year threw away his gas mask from those days, is now a professional photographer of entertainers in Las Vegas. He recalls that he made *On Strike* strictly to document the dramatic news events he had witnessed, with no specific models in mind. He took all of the photographs, designed the layout, engaged Brenner to write the text, and paid for two thousand copies to be printed. Faverty sided with the black students' cause, but *On Strike* is strikingly nonpartisan, more reportage than propaganda. "It may seem quaint by today's standards," Faverty says, "but back then I really believed that the role of the photojournalist was to be impartial and objective. Now we know that that is impossible."

Cover of *On Strike: Shut It Down* (Madison, Wisconsin: Beckett Associates, 1969)

Brian Wallis is a writer and curator based in New York.

Curriculum
A List of Favorite Anythings
By Max Pinckers

"Every documentary body of work is made with the intention of it becoming a book in its final manifestation," says Max Pinckers. The Brussels-based photographer, who was raised in Asia and Australia, has self-published five books of photographs made in India, North Korea, Thailand, and the United States—all since 2012. Though Pinckers's work broadly falls into the category of documentary photography, he doesn't believe in objectivity or neutrality. His recent series *Margins of Excess* (2018) responds to a "post-truth" world. Considering people who have been called out as frauds—a white woman who pretended to be black, an author who fabricated a Holocaust memoir—Pinckers combines press clippings and intentionally misleading staged photographs to question the fluidity of meaning.

Francis Alÿs, *When Faith Moves Mountains*, 2002

Belgian artist Francis Alÿs addresses urgent social, political, and economic realities in simple and poetic ways. In his performance *When Faith Moves Mountains*, Alÿs staged what he calls a "social allegory" as a political response to turmoil in the streets of Lima, Peru. The artist and five hundred volunteers equipped with shovels moved a huge sand dune several inches over the course of a day. In another piece, *Sometimes Making Something Leads to Nothing* (1997), Alÿs pushed a block of ice through the streets of Mexico City until it completely melted away.

Johan Grimonprez, *dial H-I-S-T-O-R-Y*, 1997

Belgian artist Johan Grimonprez is a true master of documentary storytelling. His film *dial H-I-S-T-O-R-Y* helped me understand the subconscious power of photography and film and their ability to shape reality into a self-fulfilling prophecy. It's a montage of television footage tracing the history of airplane hijackings, in which the terrorist is in turn hijacked by the mainstream media. The narrative is interspersed with dialogue between a terrorist and a novelist who, using text excerpted from Don DeLillo's books *White Noise* and *Mao II*, play a zero-sum game.

Hito Steyerl, "Documentary Uncertainty," 2007

Among her many great texts, Hito Steyerl's essay on the documentary form has had a significant influence on me. It especially considers documentary's relationship to truth, reality, ethics, and politics: "The only thing we can say for sure about the documentary mode in our times is that we always already doubt if it is true."

Han Mu Do

Han mu do is a Korean martial art that focuses on physical, spiritual, and philosophical training. Founded by grand master Dr. He-Young Kimm, it combines multiple techniques, including kicking, punching, joint locking, throwing, ground grappling, meditation, and breathing. Practicing han mu do became a defining part of my teenage life in Singapore, giving me an understanding of a deeper mind-body-spirit relationship through chi (internal energy). I learned self-discipline, confidence, and the ability to deal with stressful situations. I advise everyone, old and young, to take up martial arts, meditation, or tai chi for good health.

James Turrell, *Meeting*, 1980–86/2016

I've always been impressed by great land art of the 1960s and '70s—such as Michael Heizer's *Double Negative* (1969) and Robert Smithson's *Asphalt Rundown* (1969)—but the masterpiece of Conceptual art in which I experience light and space in their purest form is *Meeting* by James Turrell. *Meeting* possesses a photographic quality: a frame is placed as a window onto the sky, which functions as a living image, constantly shifting, demanding our attention. In its site-specific space, at MoMA PS1, *Meeting* has a contemplative aspect; one can sit in silence, admiring the power of such a simple intervention.

Ian Cheng, *Emissaries*, 2015–17

With artificial intelligence, computer vision, machine learning, algorithms, and generative adversarial networks very much becoming part of our everyday lives, I admire artists who find new aesthetic strategies that reflect on these technologies. Ian Cheng's *Emissaries*, a trilogy of live-simulation works, does just that. It's a never-ending video game that plays itself. Based on complex computer-generated simulations, a world populated by a cast of artificially intelligent characters develops naturally. Through interactions with each other, the characters create their own narratives, endlessly, in a self-contained ecosystem.

Renzo Martens, *Episode III: Enjoy Poverty*, 2008

I saw this film, which is set in the Democratic Republic of Congo, for the first time in 2010. Renzo Martens's approach to dealing with global inequality, postcolonialism, and the exploitative image economy that mediates them is radical. I later had the privilege of having Martens as a teacher at the Royal Academy of Fine Arts (KASK), Ghent. I appreciate how he presents a critical view of both documentary filmmaking and institutional critique.

Jorge Luis Borges, *Collected Fictions*, 1998

My love for Jorge Luis Borges's writing began when I met author and translator Alberto Manguel, who as a teenager had read to a middle-aged and blind Borges. *Collected Fictions*, translated by Andrew Hurley, opened a new perspective on the world for me. Each short story delves into the strange ways reality and fiction intertwine. In Borges's true art of storytelling, we learn deeper insights into how the world works, the power of imagination, and the interconnectedness of life.

Joshua Oppenheimer, *The Act of Killing*, 2012

Having grown up in Indonesia, I have a deep affinity with the country's culture (I spoke fluent Indonesian as a child). So Joshua Oppenheimer's *The Act of Killing*, about the perpetrators of the Indonesian anti-Communist killings of more than one million people in 1965 and 1966, has stayed with me. Revealing a narrative that I was not familiar with and using a documentary strategy I had never seen before—reenactments cut with surreal, dreamlike scenes—Oppenheimer's film has become one of the most important references for a project I am currently working on, in which Kenyan Mau Mau veterans, in a series of theatrical demonstrations, claim their rights as victims instead of terrorists.

Omer Fast, *Spielberg's List*, 2003

Spielberg's List, a two-channel video installation by Israeli-born artist Omer Fast, intercuts interviews with residents of Kraków, Poland, who worked as extras on the set of Steven Spielberg's 1993 feature *Schindler's List* with excerpts from Spielberg's film, as well as footage by Fast of both the dilapidated Płaszów concentration camp and a re-creation of the camp built for the filming of *Schindler's List*. During the interviews Fast conducts, the extras seem to mix up their personal experiences from the Spielberg film with actual historical events. The video is a beautiful reminder of how memory, fiction, history, imagination, and experience are fluid and kaleidoscopic.

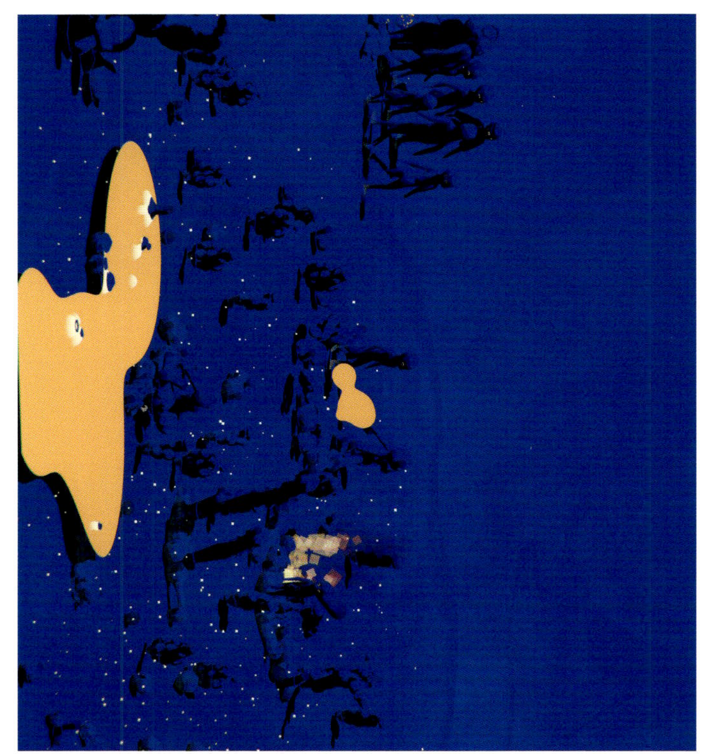

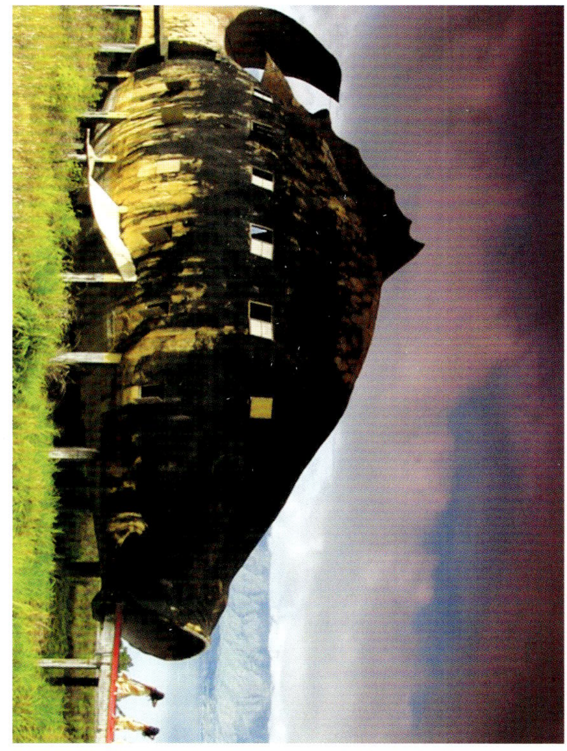

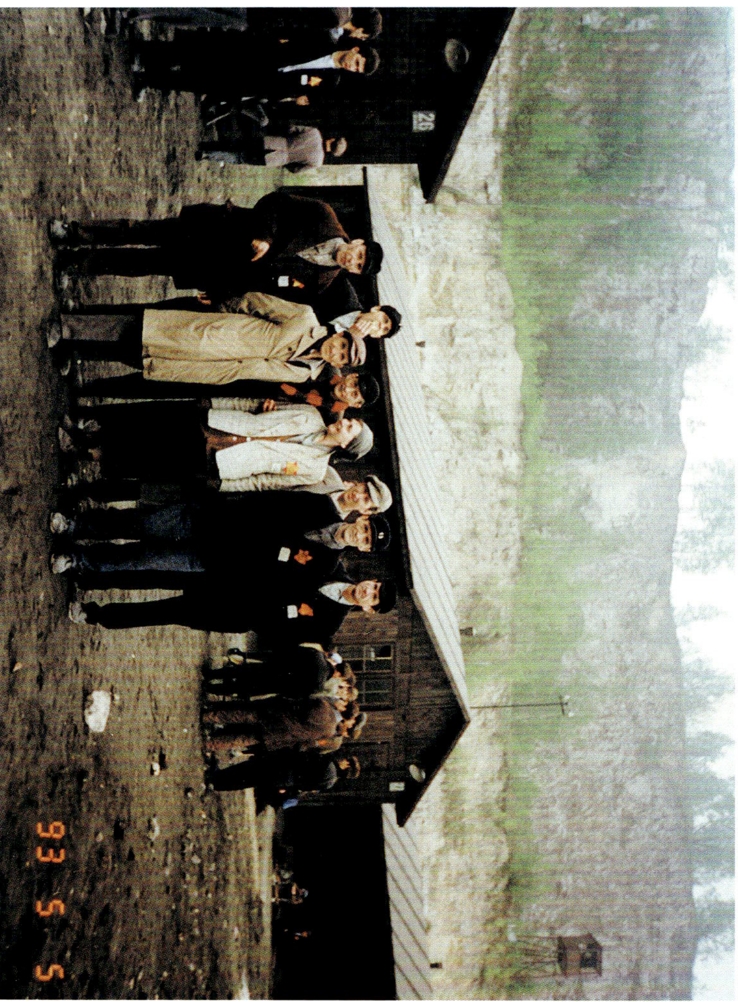

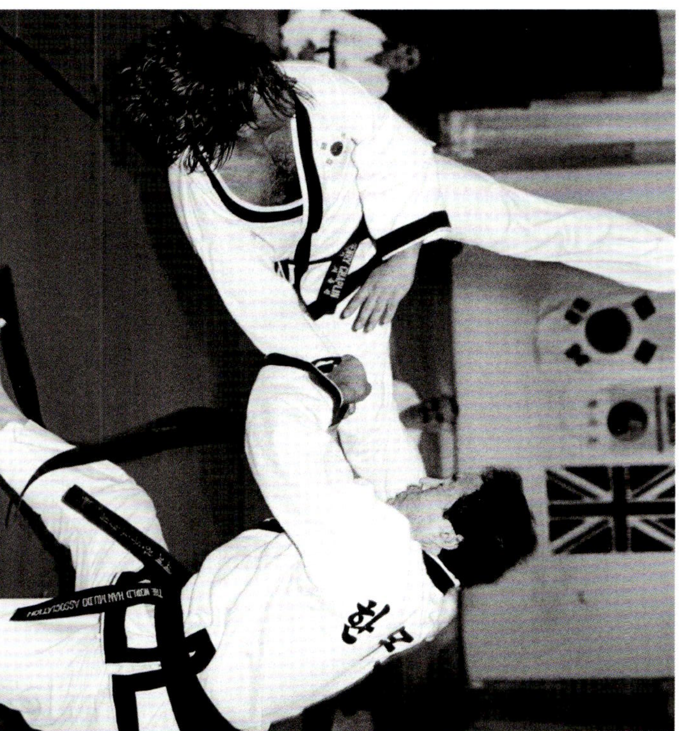

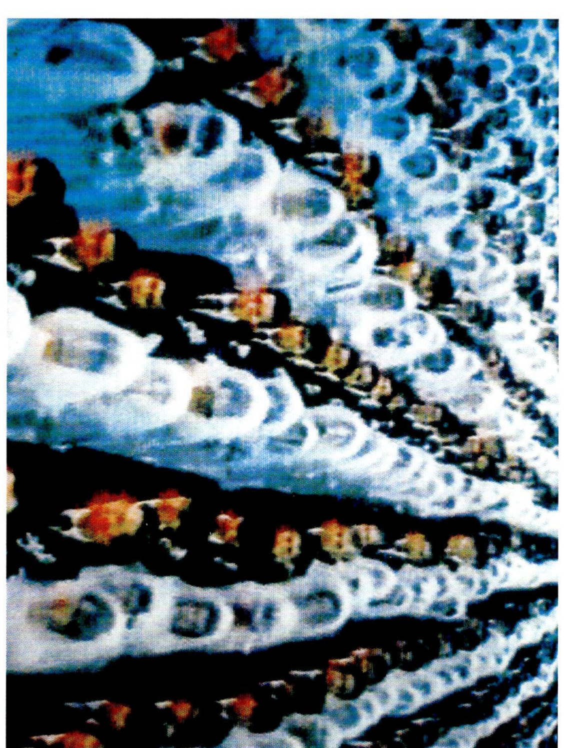

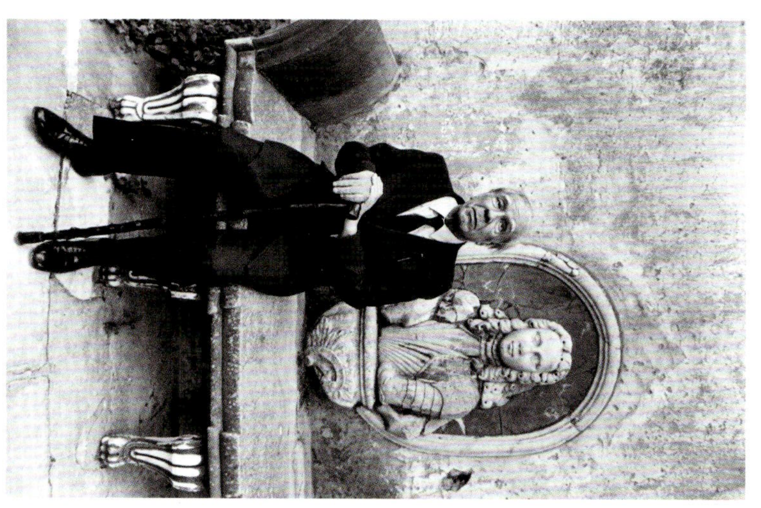

Exhibitions
More than 370 exhibitions
in 25 years

Collection
Over 24 500 pieces

Photography
Biennial
Contest aimed at promoting and
driving photography production
nationwide

FotoMexico
International Photography Festival
www.festivalfotomexico.com.mx

PICS
Mexican emerging and
contemporary photography
online platform
www.pics-ci.com.mx

Education
Photography production
seminar & National encounter of
photography investigation

Publications
Luna Córnea magazine, essays on
photography & other books

CENTRO
DE LA IMAGEN
Plaza de la Ciudadela 2, Centro Histórico,
Mexico City

www.centrodelaimagen.cultura.gob.mx

f /centrodelaimagen.mx
⊙ @cimagen
🐦 @cimagen

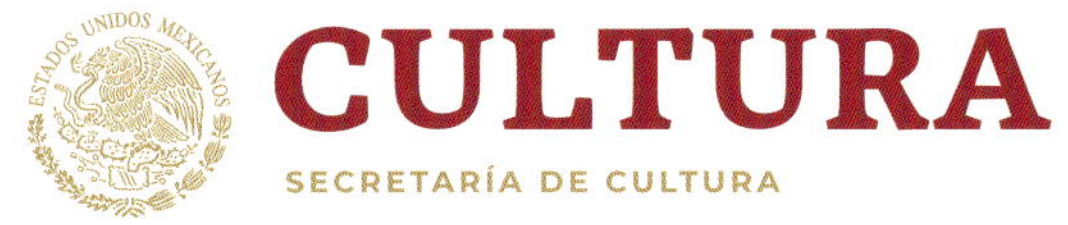

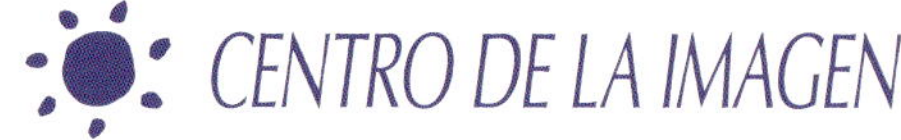

PHOTOGRAPHS
October 8 | New York | Live & Online

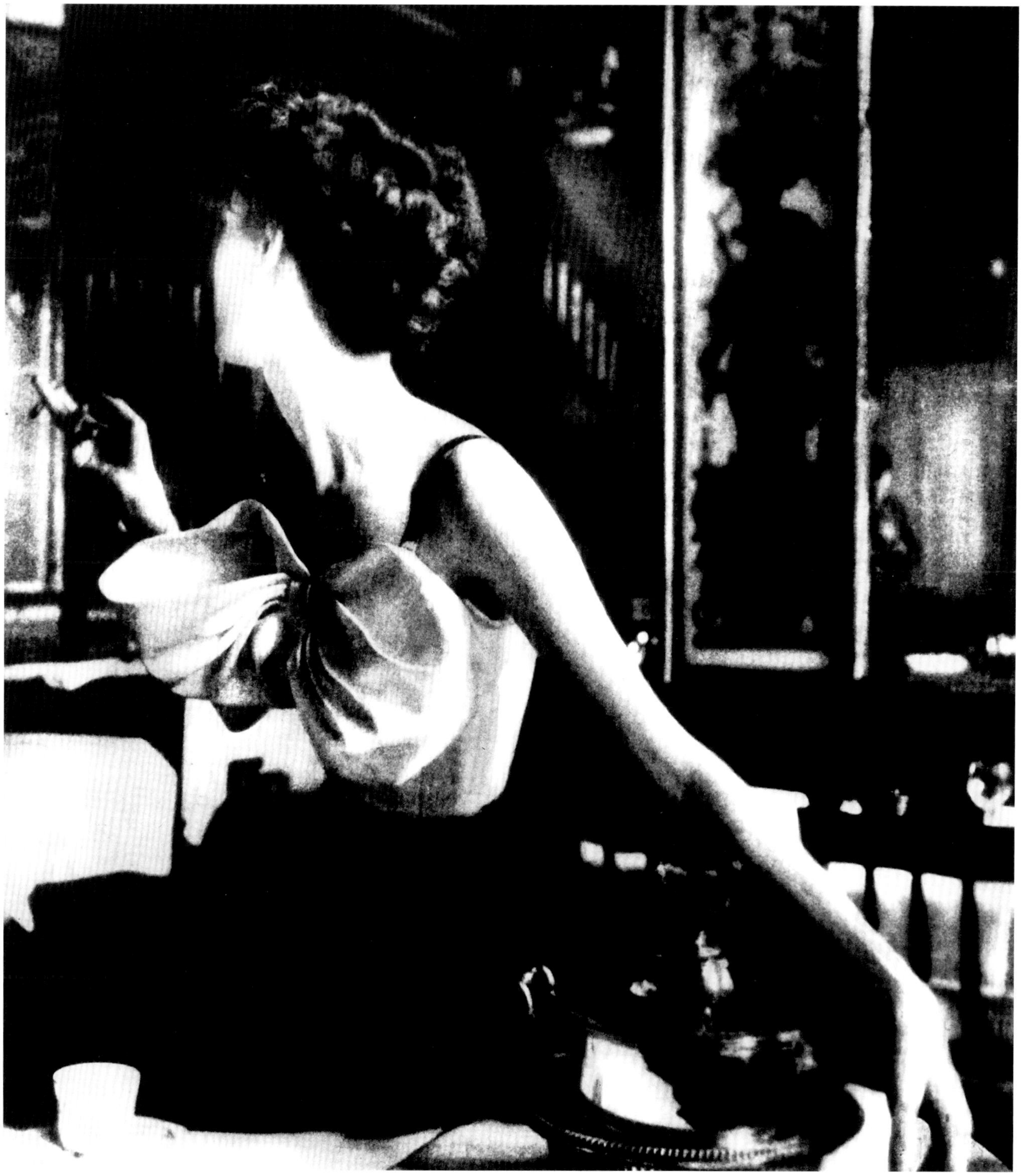

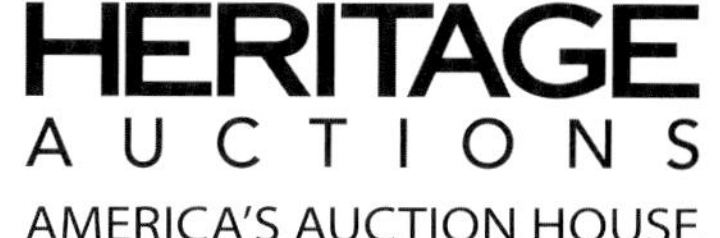

Lillian Bassman (American, 1917-2012)
Across the Restaurant: Barbara Mullen in a dress by Jacques Fath at Le Grand Véfour, Paris, Harper's Bazaar, 1949
Gelatin silver print, printed later
33.5 x 29 inches
Estimate $25,000-35,000

VIEW | TRACK | BID
HA.com/5416

Inquiries:
Nigel Russell
212.486.3659 | NigelR@HA.com

DALLAS | NEW YORK | BEVERLY HILLS | SAN FRANCISCO | CHICAGO | PALM BEACH
LONDON | PARIS | GENEVA | AMSTERDAM | HONG KONG

Always Accepting Quality Consignments in 40+ Categories
1 Million+ Online Bidder-Members

HERITAGE
AUCTIONS
AMERICA'S AUCTION HOUSE

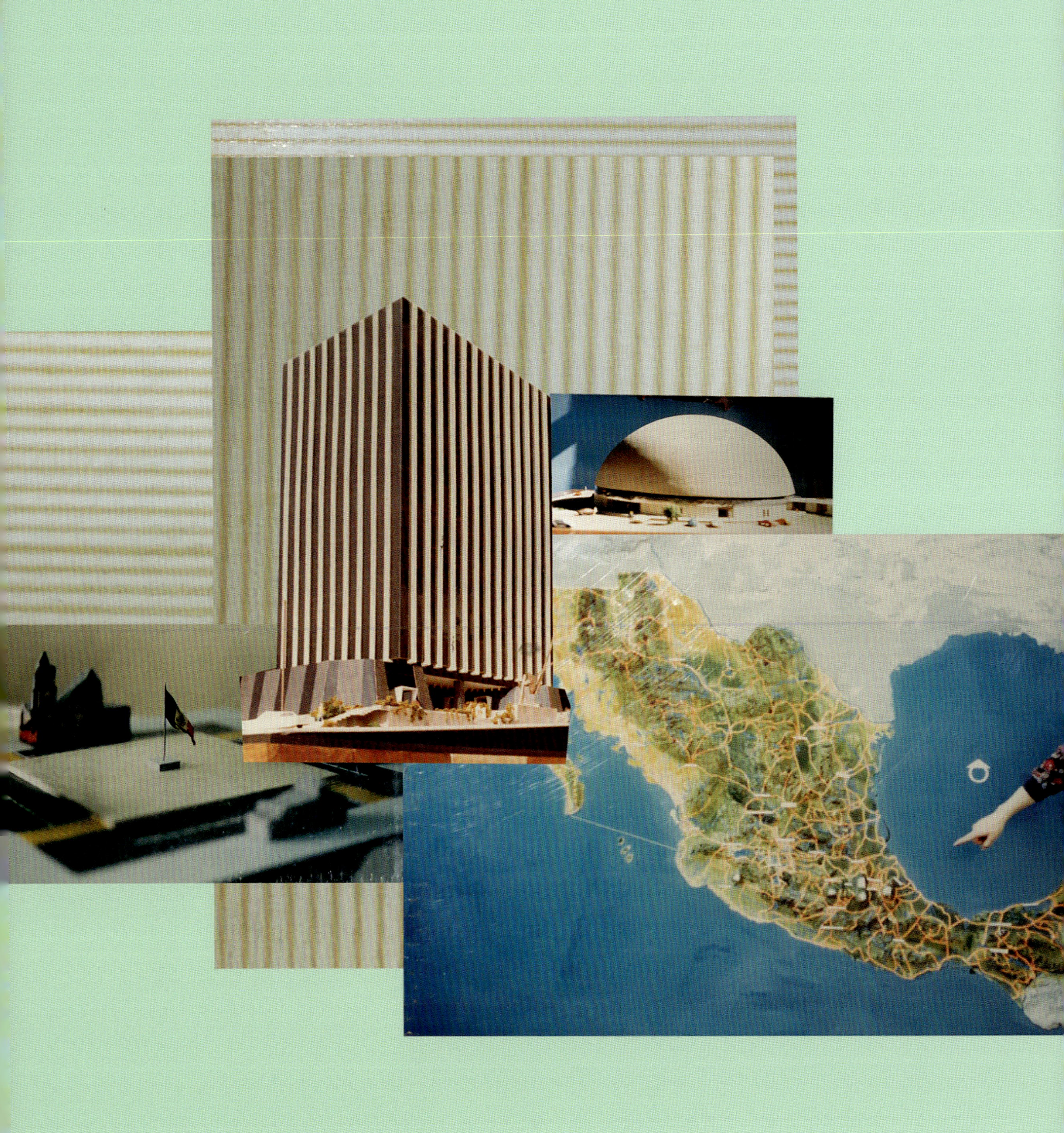

Mexico City

"Mexico City, as we all know, is a small town of fourteen million," Roberto Bolaño wrote in *The Savage Detectives*, set in the 1970s and one of the great novels about the sprawling capital. As in Bolaño's day, the city continues to host a thriving and cosmopolitan cultural scene. And photographers remind us that the city's history reaches back much earlier than its founding in 1325. Pablo López Luz considers the geography here in geological time by tracing the uses of rock that remains from the eruption of volcanoes around two millennia ago. The flow of stone "provides a means for meditation on the ancient origins of Mexico City and its amazing persistence," writer Álvaro Enrigue observes. "An almost-seven-hundred-year-old town that has gone through innumerable invasions, earthquakes, bombings, and floods, yet always returns as a stronger and more brilliant version of itself."

For this issue—produced in partnership with the Centro de la Imagen in Mexico City, and following our previous city-focused editions, including those on São Paulo, Tokyo, and Los Angeles— we offer an array of stories and portfolios that reflect the vitality and imagery of Mexico City and its artists, home to a photographic culture as diverse and varied as the city itself. Graciela Iturbide, once an assistant to the modern maestro Manuel Álvarez Bravo, is Mexico's grande dame of image making. She has traveled the country widely, driven by empathy and an insatiable curiosity. "My camera was a pretext for getting to know Mexico's traditions and culture," she remarks in an expansive interview with publisher Ramón Reverté.

The texture of the metropolis—its streets, buildings, infrastructure—often figures as a subject. "Mexico City street life displays both petty freedoms and ad hoc systems," Museo Jumex curator Kit Hammonds writes in his assessment of the city's experimental 1990s art scene, when Francis Alÿs made psychogeographic interventions at street level and Melanie Smith went macro, creating dizzying bird's-eye views of the capital's interminable growth. More recently, public spaces have served as a stage for Miguel Calderón's pictures of urban idiosyncrasies, from a culture of falcon handlers to a man occupying the space beneath an iconic fountain.

All cities must negotiate holding on to the past while modernizing. Melba Arellano studies the interiors in the city's commercial center, portraying, as Mario Ballesteros writes, "the physical and metaphysical time lags that are an everyday occurrence in Mexico City." Sonia Madrigal's taxonomy of individuals crossing a concrete barrier on the Chalco–Ixtapaluca expressway resonates with current controversies and cruelties around borders, while Mexico City–based photographers Maya Goded and Mayra Martell devote their work to telling the stories of *los desaparecidos*—the thousands of women who have disappeared over the last decade under the cloud of drug-cartel violence in and around Ciudad Juárez.

In Mexico City, history is very much present, as artists reconsider the past to tell narratives from the personal to the social. Iñaki Bonillas, a self-described "attic photographer," reworks the archive of his grandfather, who moonlighted as a conceptual artist while working as an aluminum salesman. Yvonne Venegas reedits her father's work as a wedding photographer in Tijuana to look for moments of beauty and vulnerability that fall outside the official script of matrimonial bliss. A police-magazine archive belonging to Carlos Monsiváis, one of the great chroniclers of Mexico City, offers a picture of defiance and gender fluidity in the twentieth century. Today, Jesús Léon captures the continuity of underground scenes in his visceral account of club and queer culture. A "savage detective" for contemporary times, Léon investigates and records life in all its ecstasy and debauchery, in his own "small town."
—**The Editors**

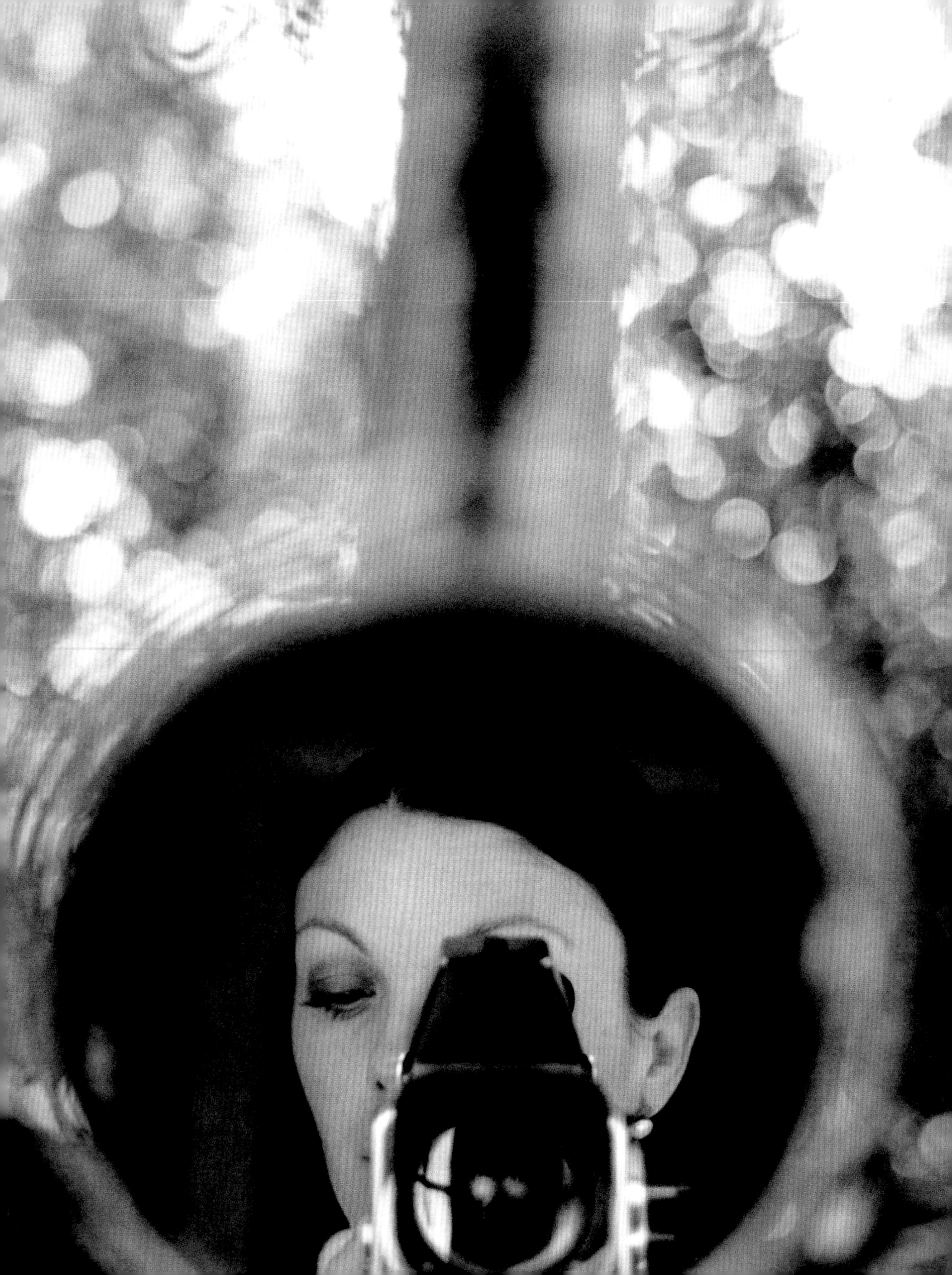

Graciela Iturbide
Dreams & Visions

A Conversation with Ramón Reverté

For more than fifty years, Graciela Iturbide, recognized today as the greatest living photographer in Latin America, has envisioned the diversity of life in her native Mexico. Her lyrical, black-and-white images of street scenes in Mexico City, of Seri women in the Sonoran Desert, of political rallies in Juchitán, and of details inside Frida Kahlo's bathroom are revered throughout the world. At the age of twenty-seven, aspiring to be a filmmaker, she enrolled in a university class with the maestro of modern Mexican photography, Manuel Álvarez Bravo. The experience was formative. "More than being my teacher of photography," she recalls, "Don Manuel taught me about life."

Earlier this year, the editor and publisher Ramón Reverté visited Iturbide at her home in the Mexico City neighborhood of Coyoacán. One wall of her living room is lined with soaring shelves full of beloved photography books. In her studio located across the street—built by her son Mauricio Rocha, a noted architect—she keeps altars of objects and books that belonged to Álvarez Bravo and Josef Koudelka. At the time of Reverté's visit, Iturbide had recently opened two major solo exhibitions, one at the Museum of Fine Arts, Boston, and another at the Palacio de Cultura Citibanamex, in Mexico City's historic center, which drew hundreds of thousands of visitors.

Here, Iturbide speaks intimately about her beginnings, her passion for photography and books, her long-standing interest in Mexico's Indigenous cultures, and her favorite photographers, including Álvarez Bravo, who has been, as she says, "her guru." On one occasion, Iturbide told Álvarez Bravo that she was traveling to Paris to visit museums. "But why," he replied, "if you can see it all in books!" Iturbide, a relentless reader, took his advice, but only partly: she has never stopped traveling.

My camera was a pretext for getting to know Mexico's traditions and culture.

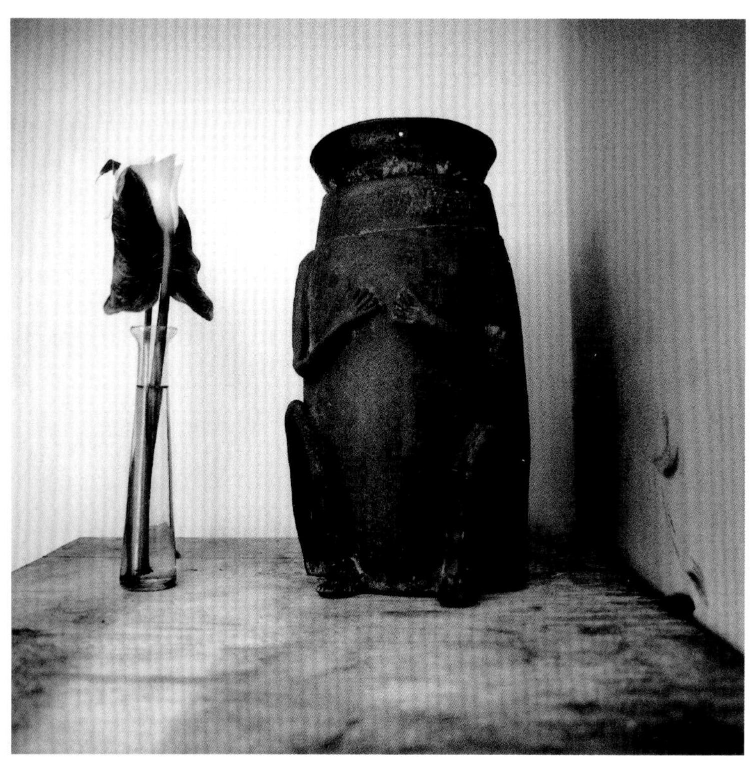

Ramón Reverté: I'd like to ask about the beginning of your career—I'm sure you've probably gotten the same question a thousand times—how did you come to photography? And I'm curious whether from an early age you enjoyed painting and photography, or is it an interest that was ignited as a result of your meeting Manuel Álvarez Bravo?

Graciela Iturbide: In my family, there wasn't an affinity for any of those things. I wanted to be a writer from a young age. My father, who was very conservative, wouldn't let me attend university because women were supposed to stay at home. I married very young. I quickly had three children. I wanted to study philosophy and literature, but I couldn't because, with three children, I had no time.

At an early age, I had a camera, and I took photographs because my father was an amateur photographer. I loved to go into his closet and steal his photographs, which led to various punishments, but my father should have been proud I was stealing his photographs.

In 1969, when I was already married and twenty-seven years old, I heard on the radio that there was a university where you could study film, and I enrolled. It was very easy to get admitted; everyone got in because it was when the film school was just getting started. That's where I met Manuel Álvarez Bravo, who was giving photography classes. I had the book he had published during the 1968 Olympics in Mexico and brought it to him so he could sign it. I asked if I could take his classes, and he said yes. No one went to his classes because everyone wanted to be film directors. After two days, he said, "Listen, I'd like you to be my *achichincle*," and I said, "Of course." An *achichincle* in Mexico is the person who assists the construction worker and does a bit of everything.

That's how my life changed. We spoke a lot about painting. We listened to a lot of music. It was my salvation in life because he had a very different way of thinking than my family. On one occasion, he told me, "You know what, Graciela, divorces help because one can start anew." It was like he was opening me to life. Within a year, I was divorced, without any struggle, without any issue.

RR: **Tell me about your parents. Did you go to exhibitions when you were little?**

GI: Not so much to exhibitions, but we went to concerts, to the opera, to musical things. Sometimes my father would take us to the Cervantino Festival. I was very young then and was somewhat interested in cultural things. My parents' parents had haciendas. With the revolution, and then under President Lázaro Cárdenas, they lost everything. My father had to work from a young age to support his family. At the age of sixteen, he started working in Oaxaca with the archaeologist Alfonso Caso, strangely enough, as his assistant. He never had a formal profession. My mother played piano recitals when she was young, and she loved classical music. She also drew. She was more sensitive to those kinds of things. But I wouldn't say it was a cultured family. It was a bourgeois family.

RR: **When you decided to study film, was it because you liked film, or because you saw some kind of escape? Was it a conscious decision?**

GI: Yes, because I wanted to. I told myself, In film, there is a script, and I want to study literature, so I might as well study film and see what I can do from there. I did it out of my need to study something because I had never been allowed to. It was an urgent need within myself.

RR: **So photography wasn't an interest of yours at that time?**

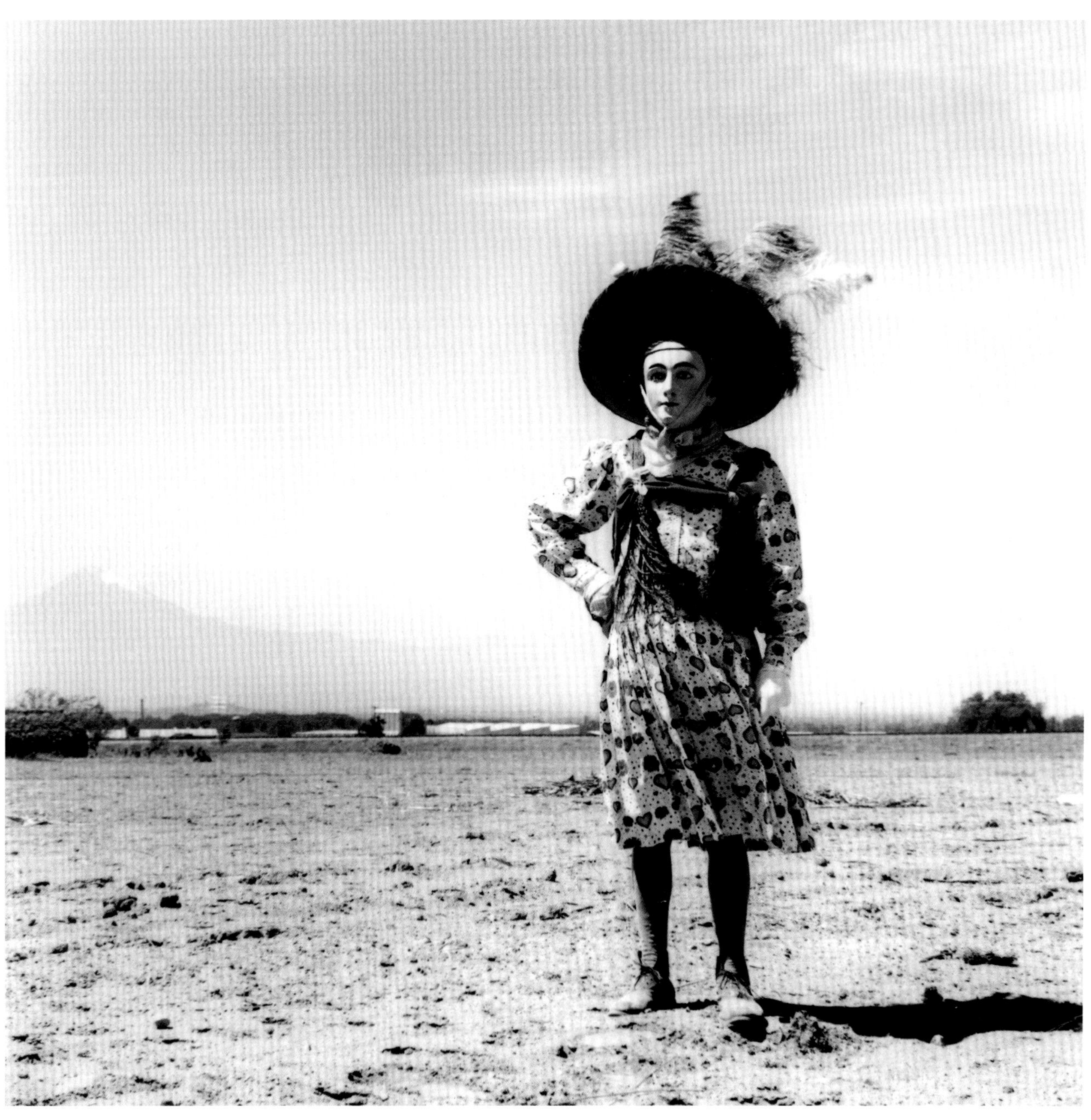

Carnaval (Carnival),
Tlaxcala, 1974

GI: I took photographs as a child because my father gave me a camera when I was eleven years old. But I took photographs of things like churches, from the bottom up, stranger things than my cousins and siblings photographed. I always saw my father taking photographs, and he did a bit of film, but just as a hobby.

RR: **So it's really Don Manuel who introduced you to the world of photography?**

GI: More than being my teacher of photography, Don Manuel taught me about life. I was already developing my own film because I had taken some photography classes before taking lessons with Manuel. So one time I asked him, "Maestro, how do you properly develop a roll of black-and-white film?" And he responded, "You know, Graciela, go to the photography store, buy yourself a roll of film, read the instructions, and that's how you do it." He never told me whether my photographs were good or bad. Never. But he spoke to me a lot about painting. He spoke to me about literature. We listened to opera in the afternoons.

He made me see life in a different way than I had lived it as a child. When I lived with the father of my children, who was a more liberal man than others I had known, it also helped a bit in my development. In my time, it was unlikely for husbands to say, "Yes, yes, of course, go study." It wasn't very easy.

RR: **How long were you working with Don Manuel?**

GI: I worked with Don Manuel for about two years. But I stayed near him all my life, that's why I live here. When I separated from my partner, I came to live here [the Coyoacán neighborhood of Mexico City] because Álvarez Bravo told me, "They're selling a little plot of land over there, Graciela. Come here to Coyoacán."

RR: **Photography wasn't an easy path to making a living.**

GI: I've had money, I've had no money, but when I didn't have money, there were rolls of film in my refrigerator. I've always been taking pictures. At the very beginning, and when I got divorced, the only work I had was for hire for magazines like *Mundo médico* (Medical world) and *Médico moderno* (Modern doctor) to go photograph operations.

RR: **And what did you photograph?**

GI: Births. Once I won an award for a cover that I shot. They paid me monthly. I didn't have to be there the whole time, only when they commissioned things. It's the only work I've ever had for hire, and I loved it.

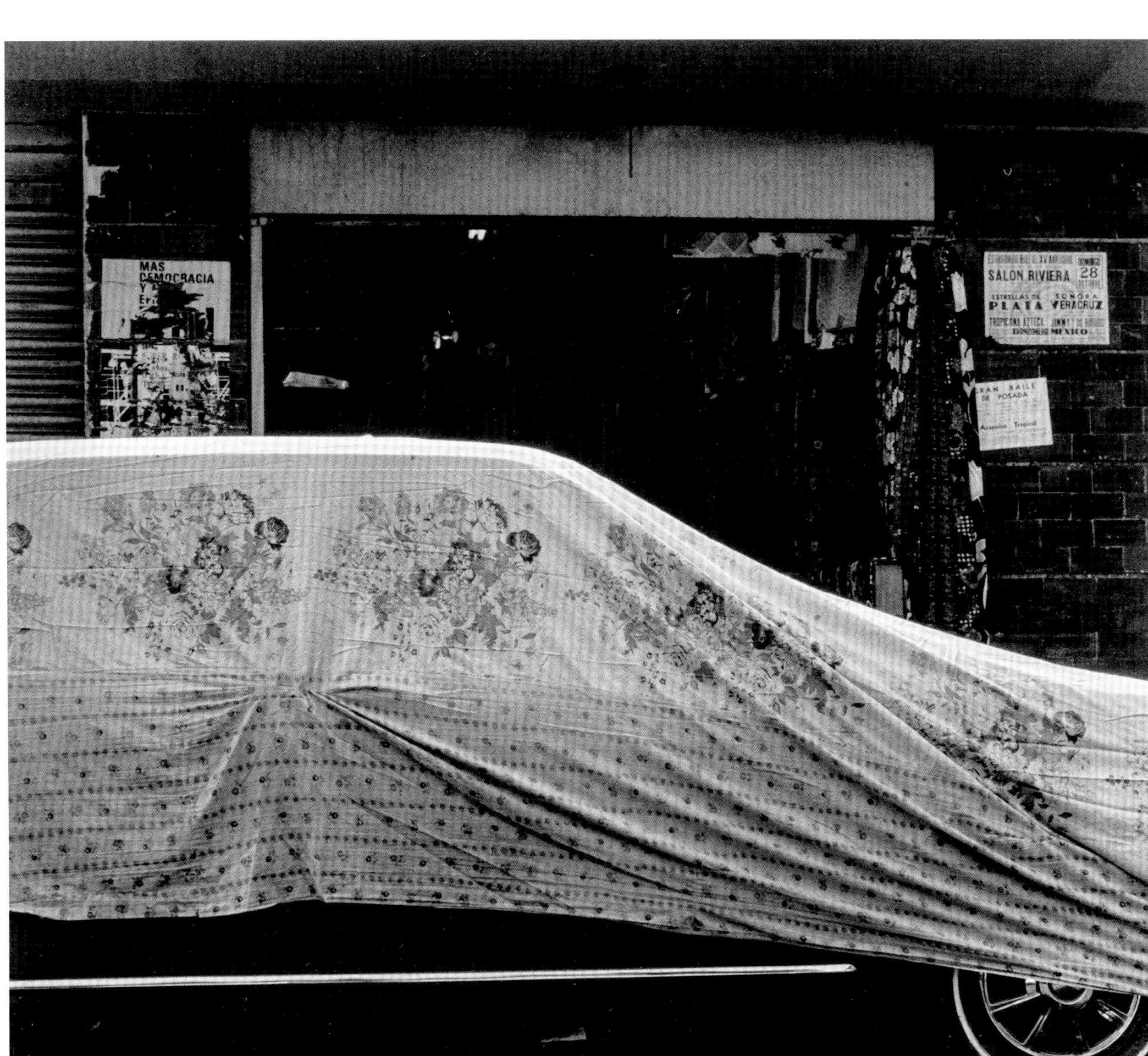

This page:
Carro (Car), 1972

Opposite:
Mano urbano (Urban hand),
Mexico City, 1973

RR: **What was your first contact with the photography world? Was it at the INI [National Institute of Indigenous Peoples] that you first began?**

GI: I only did a project with the ethnographic archive at the INI. They made various films and published seven books about this archive under the direction of Pablo Ortíz Monasterio. It was my job to go to the desert with the Seri, and I was fascinated.

RR: **The first exhibition you had was in Mexico, and then it traveled to New York.**

GI: My first exhibition was at the Orozco Gallery with Paulina Lavista and Colette Álvarez Urbajtel. And then it traveled to New York, with a photographer named Larry Siegel, who had been my teacher here in Mexico before I went to study with Álvarez Bravo. He was the director of the gallery in New York.

RR: **So that exhibition had nothing to do with Don Manuel?**

GI: Yes, that exhibition came about thanks to Manuel because Larry spoke with him and Manuel decided that it should be three women: Paulina Lavista, Colette, and me. After that, I started to have solo exhibitions.

RR: **How did you manage to maintain a family at such a complicated time, in addition to being a woman on your own, in that era in Mexico, with three children?**

GI: At the beginning, I had the help of my husband, then I worked for *Médico moderno*, and then I worked taking photographs of people who asked me to take photographs.

RR: **Portraits?**

GI: Lots of portraits, even weddings. I managed. I made money, but I never stopped taking my own photographs. I loved going to the country to be with Álvarez Bravo.

RR: **You continually saw Manuel Álvarez Bravo?**

GI: Always. Until the end. I always went to see him to speak with him, to listen to music. The thing is that I didn't want to be his assistant anymore because I didn't want him to influence me. I had to cut the umbilical cord.

RR: **Even though Don Manuel's influence is present in your work, in the most positive sense, you had a personality all your own in your photography from the very beginning. What is it**

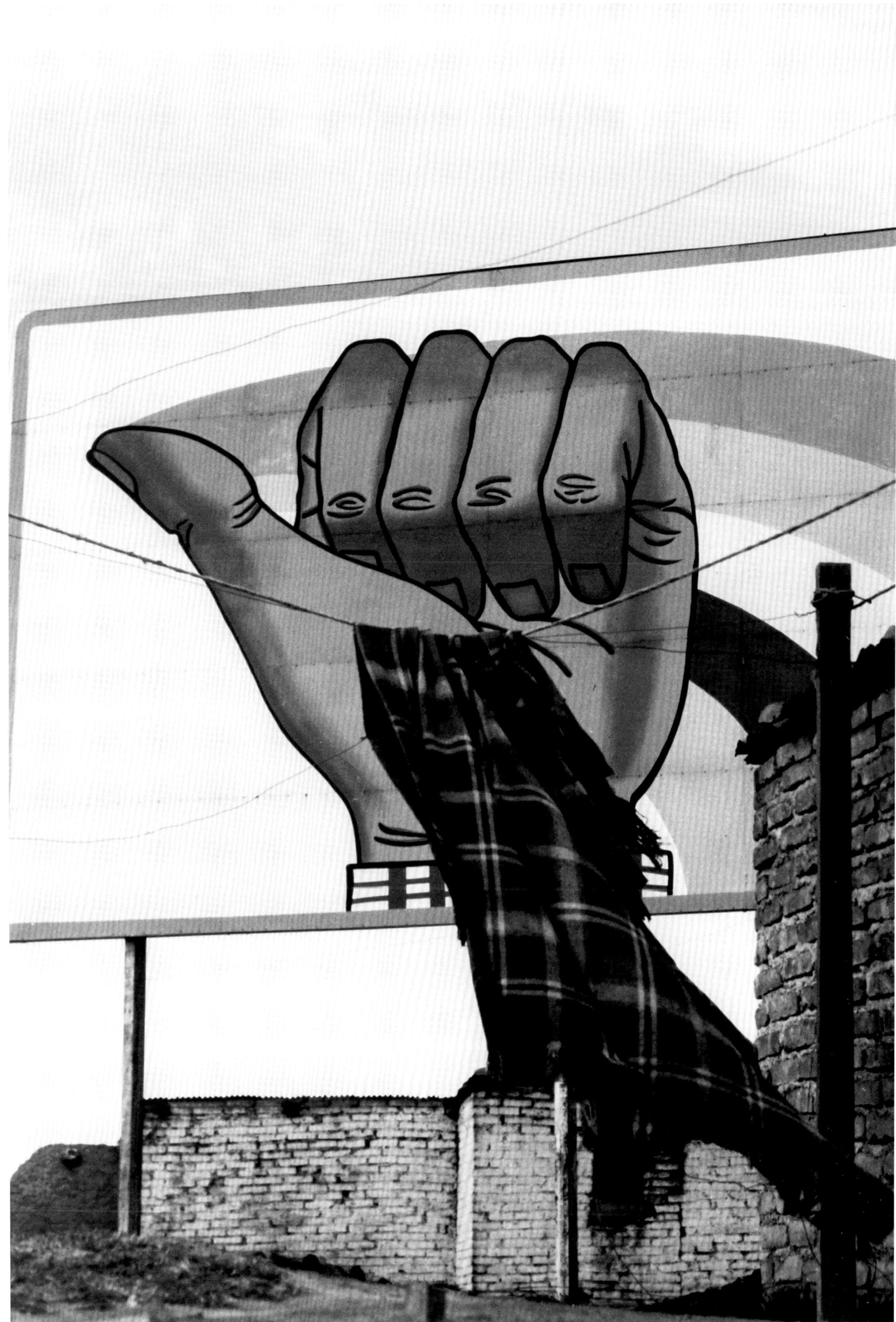

e c s e

that truly moves you to take photographs? If you go somewhere now, what motivates you? What is it you want to photograph immediately?

GI: It's never clear to me what I want to photograph. I always go out walking, even when I'm asked to go photograph something in particular. Surprise is what gets me to pull the trigger on the camera. If I say, "Ay! What a wonder!"—then I press the trigger.

RR: **Do you take lots of photographs?**

GI: A normal amount. I'm not like the people who came from Magnum. When I took them to Manuel's house, they saw a dog on the rooftop and started to take a ton of photographs. Manuel always said to me, "*Chaca chaca chaca chaca*, why so much junk, Graciela? For what?" I learned a different way of taking photographs from Álvarez Bravo, because he always took one or two shots. If, by chance, he took two, it was already too many. In my case, if I come across something and I like it, I could even take three or four photographs, but I'm not a compulsive photographer. Sometimes I'd take more than one shot in case the negative gets scratched. I always took photographs calmly and enthusiastically and with surprise.

RR: **If I were to go with you to photograph for two days in Oaxaca, what would the process be like?**

GI: I went to these villages with my camera so that people would know that I was a photographer, and I lived with them, which created solidarity. If I go to a festival where photography is allowed, then I take photographs because it's allowed. If I see that it isn't allowed, that people don't want me to take photographs, I don't. I don't have a telephoto lens, nor a tripod, nor flash. It's how I've always worked, with a handheld camera but always with people's complicity. Sometimes, people ask me to take their photographs, like with *Magnolia* [the iconic photograph from the 1979–89 series *Juchitán de las Mujeres*]. I was at a cantina, and she was there, and she saw me with my camera and said, "Ay, ay, my love, take my photo." I went upstairs with him, or with her, to the room, he got dressed, he made himself up, and I went on taking photographs as he wished, exactly as he wished.

RR: **It's obvious that you share empathy with people.**

GI: Yes, it's beautiful when people ask you to take their photograph. When I go to Juchitán or when I am with the Seri, for me they are not "the other" because they also come to visit me at my house, the same with the Mayo [the people of Sinaloa] as with the Juchiteco. These are people of my country, just like me.

And yes, I have a capacity to feel empathy. I try not to hurt people. That's why I just have a normal lens that allows me to come close to people, and somehow they accept me even if I don't ask permission. In some way, with the camera, I am asking. There is an implicit permission.

RR: **And have you always worked in 35mm?**

GI: I started out with a 35mm camera, and then I had a Hasselblad. I work in two formats, in 6 by 6 and in 35mm. It depends above all if I'm photographing landscapes or objects, which is when I prefer to use a large-format camera.

RR: **Do you prefer photographing the world of Indigenous people or the urban world?**

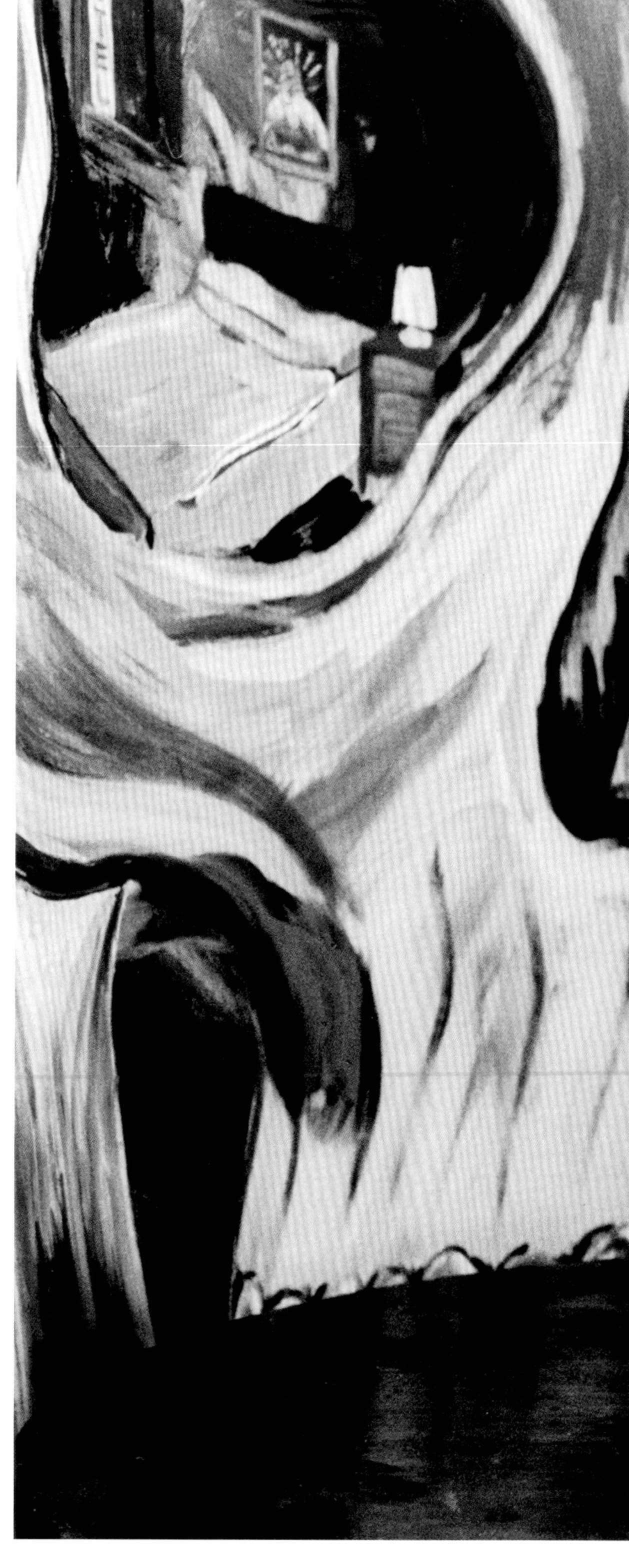

GI: My camera was a pretext for getting to know Mexico's traditions and culture. I also love taking photographs in other parts of the world: India, Panama, Italy. But, of course, my first photographs were in Mexico because it was a way to get to know my culture, which I didn't have access to as a child because I lived in another world. That's why I tell you that I owe everything to Álvarez Bravo. He opened my eyes to my country's culture.

RR: **In Mexico City, in addition to what you photographed in the beginning and the series *El baño de Frida* (Frida's Bathroom, 2005), what other things have you photographed?**

GI: My first job was in the historic center. It fascinated me. I love the Zócalo. I love the Templo Mayor. I love everything that goes on in the center of Mexico City. I have photographs from there—of the

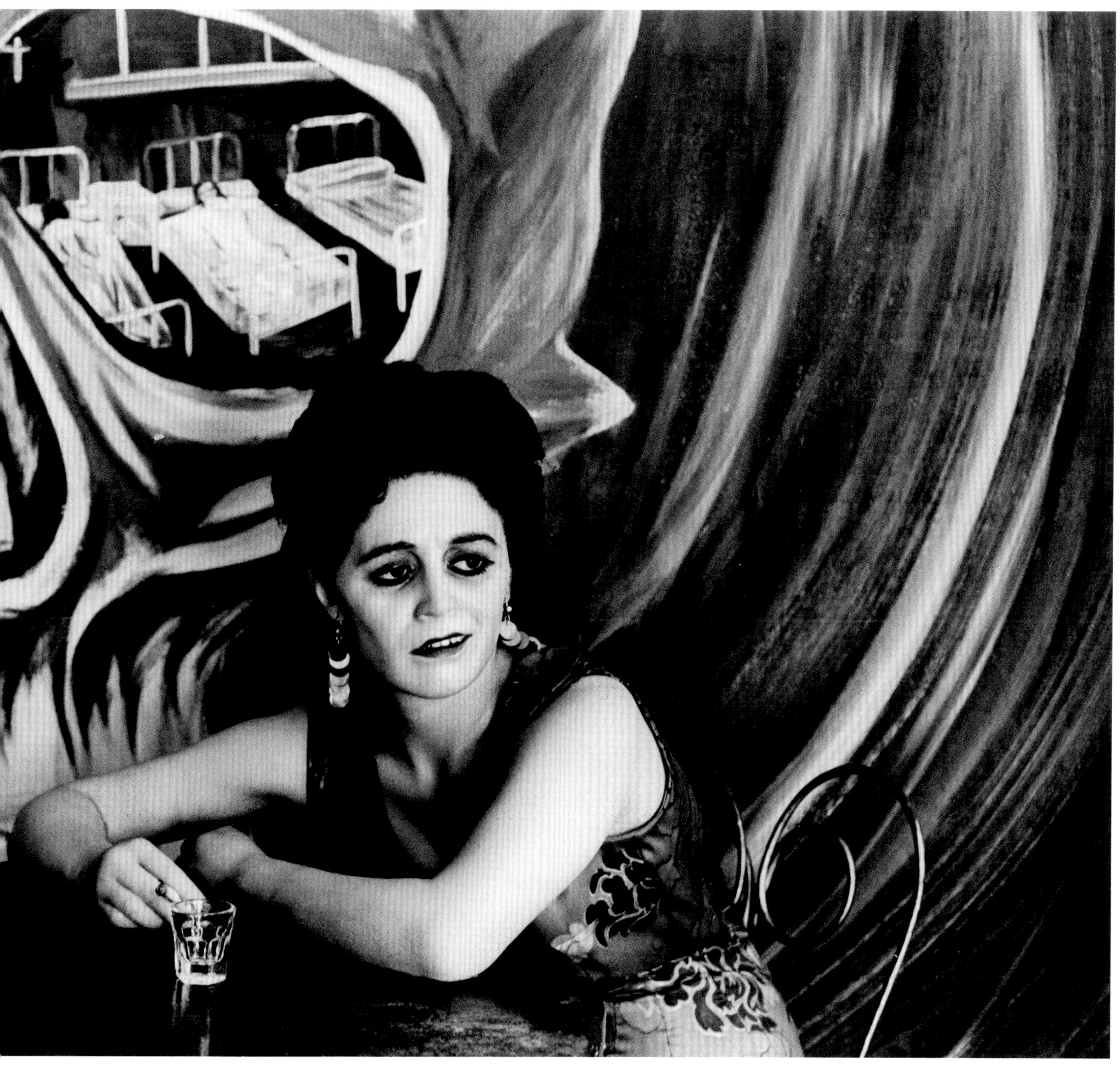

vendors with their serpents selling medicine, the pachuco, the woman of wax, the man with the frames who walks along the street, the circus—that I hadn't published until the recent exhibition at the Palacio de Iturbide [Palacio de Cultura Citibanamex in Mexico City].

RR: Have you photographed Coyoacán, the neighborhood where you live?

GI: Now that I live here, no. Before, I would say yes. Now I give the people who live here a bit of respect, because they know I am a photographer. But when I didn't live here, I would come with Álvarez Bravo to photograph the Barrio del Niño Jesús.

RR: Was Álvarez Bravo already living in Coyoacán? How did you work with him?

GI: Álvarez Bravo lived in Coyoacán since the day I met him until he died. Sometimes I would go with him to the *centro* because he liked taking photographs of the shopwindows, the mannequins, all of that. But I couldn't take photographs with him because one day he said to me: "As it says in the Gospels, Graciela, *copiaos los unos a los otros*—copy one another," which is to say, "Don't even think about copying me." He didn't have to say it because I've never taken a photograph that someone else has taken, never; but it was lovely of him because he said it in a very elegant way.

On the weekends, we would go to the countryside to photograph landscapes. When I was photographing the killing of the goats in the Mixtec community in Oaxaca, if I had gone without my camera, I wouldn't have been able to tolerate it; the camera protects you. Imagination is something very important in photography. Someone said, and I think it has to do with Dante, that "the imagination is the well where fantasy rains down." I was photographing the little goats, but I was also seeing the Bible—I'm not Catholic but there are things in the Bible that I love. I was being reminded of the sacrifice of Isaac. With that reading, I could interpret what I was photographing in my own way, with imagination. Without my camera, I could never have watched a little goat wail.

RR: **Are you aware when you take a good photograph, or is it only after developing them that you say, Ah, how beautiful?**

GI: Sometimes I'm aware, but I operate with surprise. When I don't like something, I can't take a photograph simply because it's a good document. It has to be something that touches my heart in order for me to push the camera trigger. Besides, you're always encountering things, it's not difficult. You go here and you come across something wonderful, you go there and you find something wonderful. For me, it has a lot to do with the imagination. And with fantasy.

It's interesting that it has to do with fantasy because the photographer is supposedly keeping a record and interpreting the world that she is seeing. Once when I was photographing Juchitán, someone said to me, "That isn't Juchitán," and I said, "No, of course this isn't Juchitán, it is *my* Juchitán."

RR: **Is there work of yours that you like more than others, with which you are more content?**

GI: No. You know, I don't have a distance from, nor judgment about my work in Juchitán. I can tell you one of the places where I've been most happy is Juchitán because of the friendships that I had with people. I don't have the ability to judge my work. It's very difficult for me. Only when I have my contacts, and I see them, I once again begin to feel the excitement I'm telling you about. Henri Cartier-Bresson says that the decisive moment is when you take a photograph, but for me there are two decisive moments: one is when you take the photograph and the other is when you discover what it is that you actually photographed. I didn't remember having photographed *Mujer Angel, Desierto de Sonora* (Angel Woman, Sonoran Desert, 1979) until I saw the contact sheets.

RR: **So sometimes you do get surprised by a photograph you hadn't thought was going to be very good?**

GI: Exactly. That's why I say that there are two moments for me— not just the moment that Cartier-Bresson describes, but also the decisive moment of having the eye to see what it is you've done. And to know to select the image, you have to feel some sort of surprise. One's intelligence, eye, and heart must be present in equal measure.

RR: **Something that surprises me when I speak with you is that you know so many photographers. You know William Eggleston, you know Josef Koudelka quite well, you knew Christer Strömholm, you know Japanese photographers like Eikoh Hosoe. How do you manage to live in a seemingly closed-off world, in your house, which is wonderful, in the middle of Coyoacán, and meet so many photographers in different parts of the world?**

GI: When I travel I have the opportunity to meet people. I met Eikoh Hosoe when we were both working on a project for *A Day in the Life of America* (1986). The only one I wanted to meet in my life was Josef Koudelka, and I met him circumstantially in Cartier-Bresson's house. And I met Cartier-Bresson with Álvarez Bravo. When we were in Paris, we went to see him, and we became very good friends. I met Strömholm in Sweden.

RR: **Of the photographers you know, whom do you like the most?**

GI: Koudelka, with whom I also have a very close relationship. Every time I travel to Paris, I go to visit him at his studio. I really like Francesca Woodman, a woman who committed suicide very young, who made a great deal of self-portraits. I love Robert Frank. I loved Diane Arbus. When I started I wanted to be like Diane Arbus. I would say, Now, that came out as beautiful as a Diane Arbus photograph.

RR: **And William Eggleston?**

GI: He's a friend of mine. I'm going to tell you something. In the beginning, I didn't understand his work. When I saw his first books, I wondered, What is going on with these photographs? It was only later that he began to fascinate me.

RR: **And William Klein, by whom you have a number of books— does his work interest you?**

GI: I met him in Paris with Cartier-Bresson, but I never ended up having a close relationship with him like I have with other photographers. I bought Klein's book on New York when I was just beginning to be a photographer, and it's one of my most prized books. I was enchanted by his way of photographing a city.

RR: **Your library is impressive. Do you spend much time looking at photography books?**

GI: Every night, I take a photography book, I look at it, I look at it again, I take another, and then I turn to literature, but I look at my photography books a lot, a lot. I love them. I always discover things I hadn't seen before.

RR: **From Latin America, who are your models in photography?**

GI: Miguel Rio Branco. Of the first Latin American photographers I met, there was Raúl Corrales and [Alberto] Korda in Cuba. The ultra-famous photograph of Che [Guevara], that oddly enough Korda himself did not choose—it had to be chosen by an Italian from his contact sheets. In 2017, I took part in the Colloquium of Latin American Photography and got to meet all of the photographers from Latin America.

RR: **Do you identify in any way, for example, with Paz Errázuriz?**

GI: She is my friend. I love her work. But do I identify myself with it? I don't, because our work is utterly different.

RR: **Right, they are different, but sometimes you touch on similar subjects.**

GI: Perhaps, but I identify with Koudelka, though my work has nothing to do with his. Look, if I've fallen in love with the work of any photographer, it's Koudelka.

RR: **Have you met Claudia Andujar?**

GI: Yes. I met her in Brazil.

RR: **Why do you think there are so many talented photographers in Latin America who are female?**

GI: I've always been asked if I've suffered in my work because I am a female photographer. Never. I want to tell you about a photographer

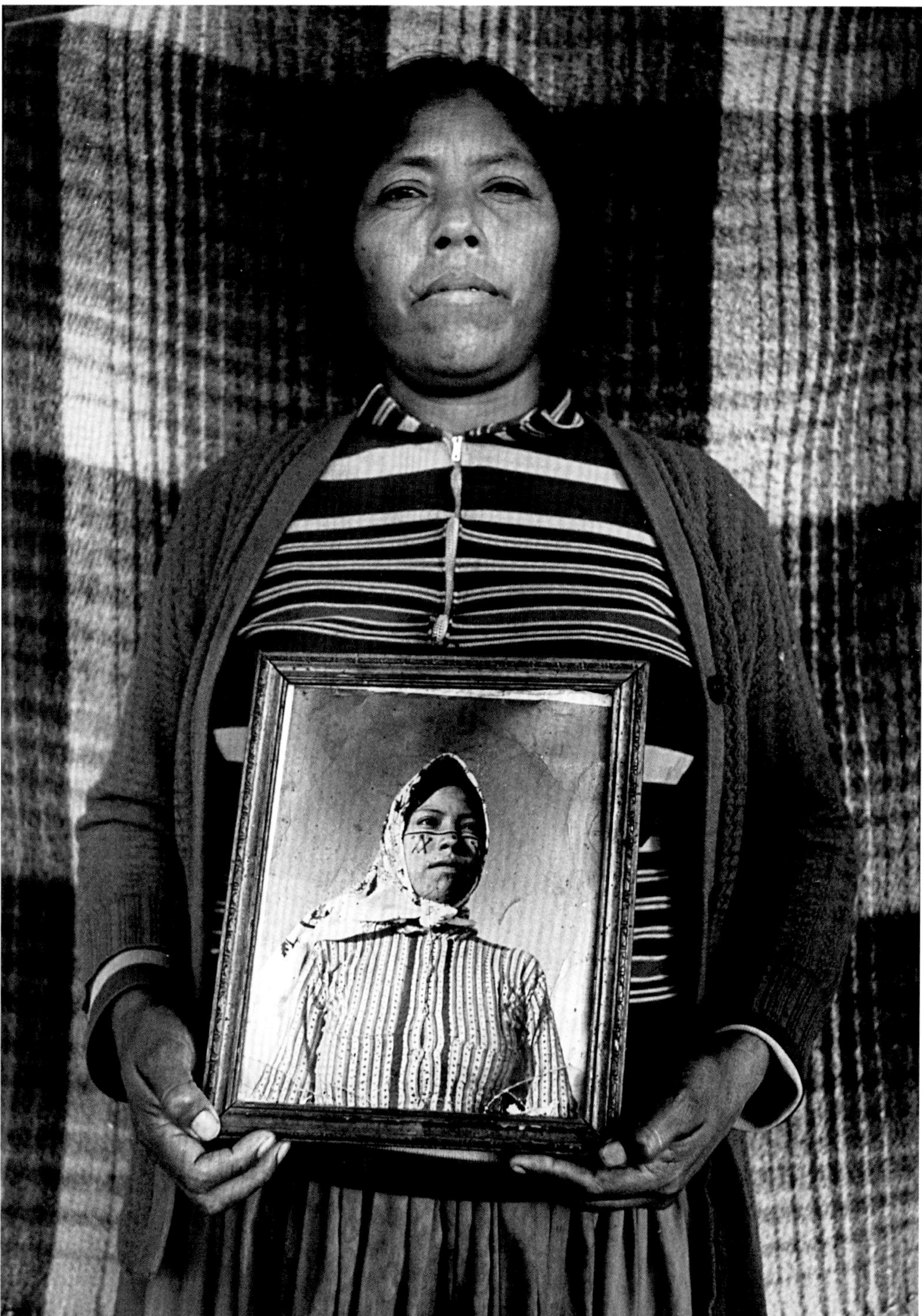

called Maruch Santíz. She is an Indigenous woman from San Juan Chamula. She photographed a series of rituals that have to do with everything her grandfather told her. Maruch continues to wear traditional clothing, but they don't like her in Chiapas—her husband left her because she became famous, her parents too, and yet she persistently continues taking photographs.

RR: **But in your case, becoming a photographer didn't impact you.**

GI: Well, studying film was an issue for my family. And becoming a photographer was an issue in my family. And getting a divorce was an issue in my family. It wasn't that easy, now it's easy, but it wasn't so easy before. Mexico is very conservative.

RR: **And from Mexico? Are there photographers who interest you?**

GI: Nacho López fascinates me. I love Rodrigo Moya. In Mexico, there are very good photographers, as much in journalism as in Conceptual art. It is a country that's flourishing—that's why I give you the example of Maruch, an Indigenous woman from Chiapas who takes a small course and becomes a tremendous photographer.

RR: **Do you have color photographs?**

GI: I have thousands of color slides, thousands, but I took them for work that I did for hire. I took a number of color photographs, but I see the world in black and white. When I'm photographing with my camera in black and white, I'm seeing in black and white. When I'm photographing in color, I have to see if yellow goes with purple or not.

RR: **So you identify with black and white.**

GI: Black and white is more abstract; there are more shadows. In my case, like Cartier-Bresson and Koudelka, if I took two or three color photographs, that's a lot. As Octavio Paz said, apropos of Álvarez

For me there are two decisive moments: one is when you take the photograph and the other is when you discover what it is that you actually photographed.

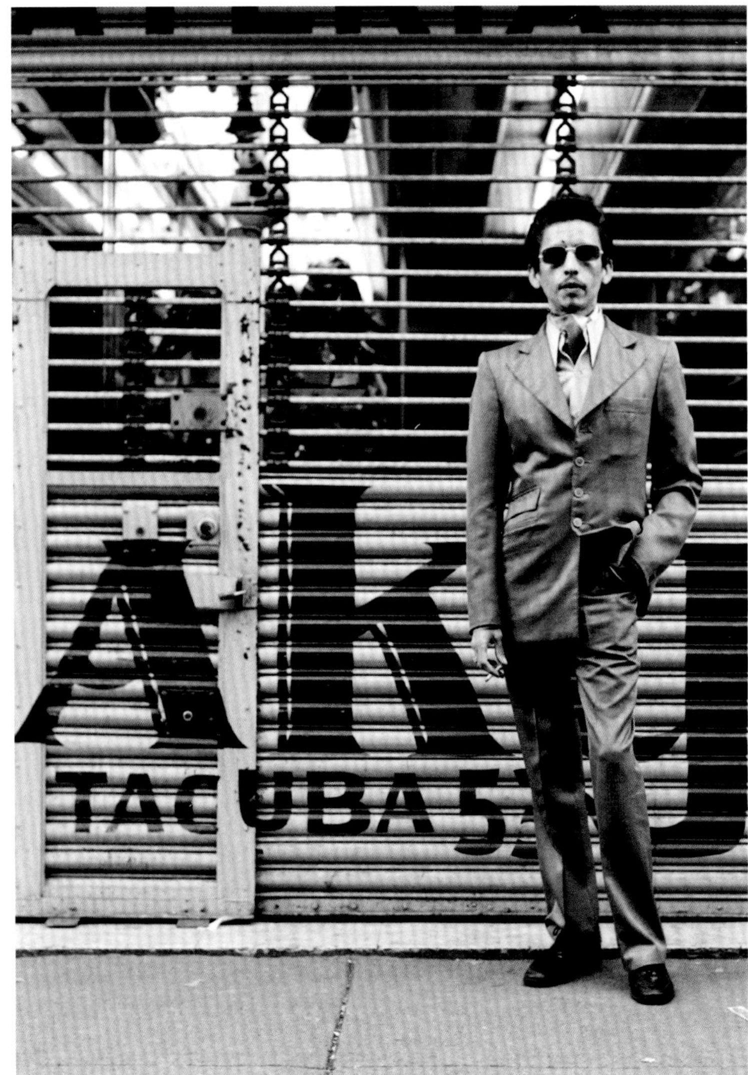

Bravo's photographs, "Reality is more real in black and white." And mind you, Álvarez Bravo also had color photographs.

RR: But his language is in black and white.

GI: You said what I should have said: my language is in black and white. And in film as well. What little film I've done has been in black and white. And the films I most love to watch are in black and white.

RR: What have you done in film?

GI: Right now, I'm editing a work about the life of the painter José Luis Cuevas. I started it when I was studying film in 1971. I recently found the unfinished material. I salvaged it by accident. But if I had gone into film, I would have been a black-and-white filmmaker.

RR: Do you think film has influenced your work?

GI: Yes. My cinematic background and, above all, Italian neorealism. All those filmmakers in black and white. And also [Federico] Fellini, [Ingmar] Bergman.

RR: And Andrei Tarkovsky, about whom you've spoken to me once before.

GI: Tarkovsky! Of course! For me, if you ask me whom I'm jealous of in life within the artistic realm, it would be Tarkovsky and Piero della Francesca. *Nostalghia* (1983) begins with the Madonna in labor who opens, and birds come out. It can't be! How wonderful!

Painting has also had a tremendous influence. As Álvarez Bravo used to say to me, "Graciela, you have to look at lots of paintings." He didn't tell me you have to look at lots of photography. Once I told him, "I'm going to Paris, maestro." "And for what?" he asked me. "To see museums." "But why if you can see it all in books!" I loved that he said that to me. When you see lots of things that are of interest to many different disciplines, it emerges a bit in your work.

RR: In the end, everything is visual education.

GI: Everything.

RR: Is there something pending that you're looking forward to photographing?

GI: I'm very interested in stones. And then I'd like to continue with air, water, and wind. I went to Japan, and I said to myself, I'm going to photograph stones, and, of course, they didn't end up interesting me. You have to become surprised and then become surprised again with the photographs in order to edit them afterward. It's difficult. Sometimes, like Álvarez Bravo used to say— I always talk about Álvarez Bravo, forgive me, but he's like my guru—"Graciela, it's just that the little shrews have already come," the muses, right? So, I think it's true, that all of a sudden there's something that inspires you, and you begin to work. I'm the kind who photographs what I find. What comes my way. What falls from the sky.

Ramón Reverté is the editor in chief and creative director of Editorial RM, a publishing house based in Mexico and Spain.

Translated from the Spanish by Elianna Kan.

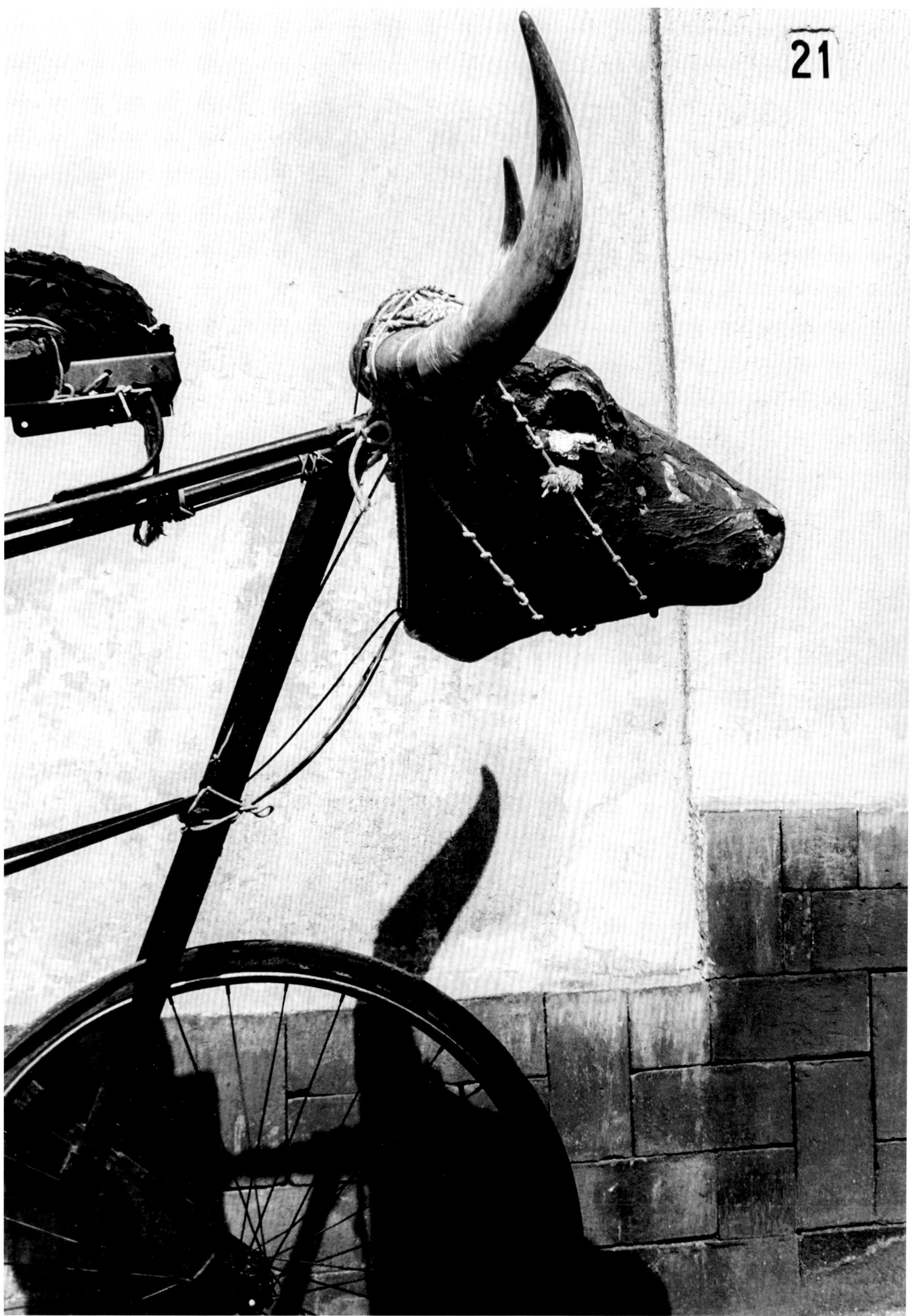

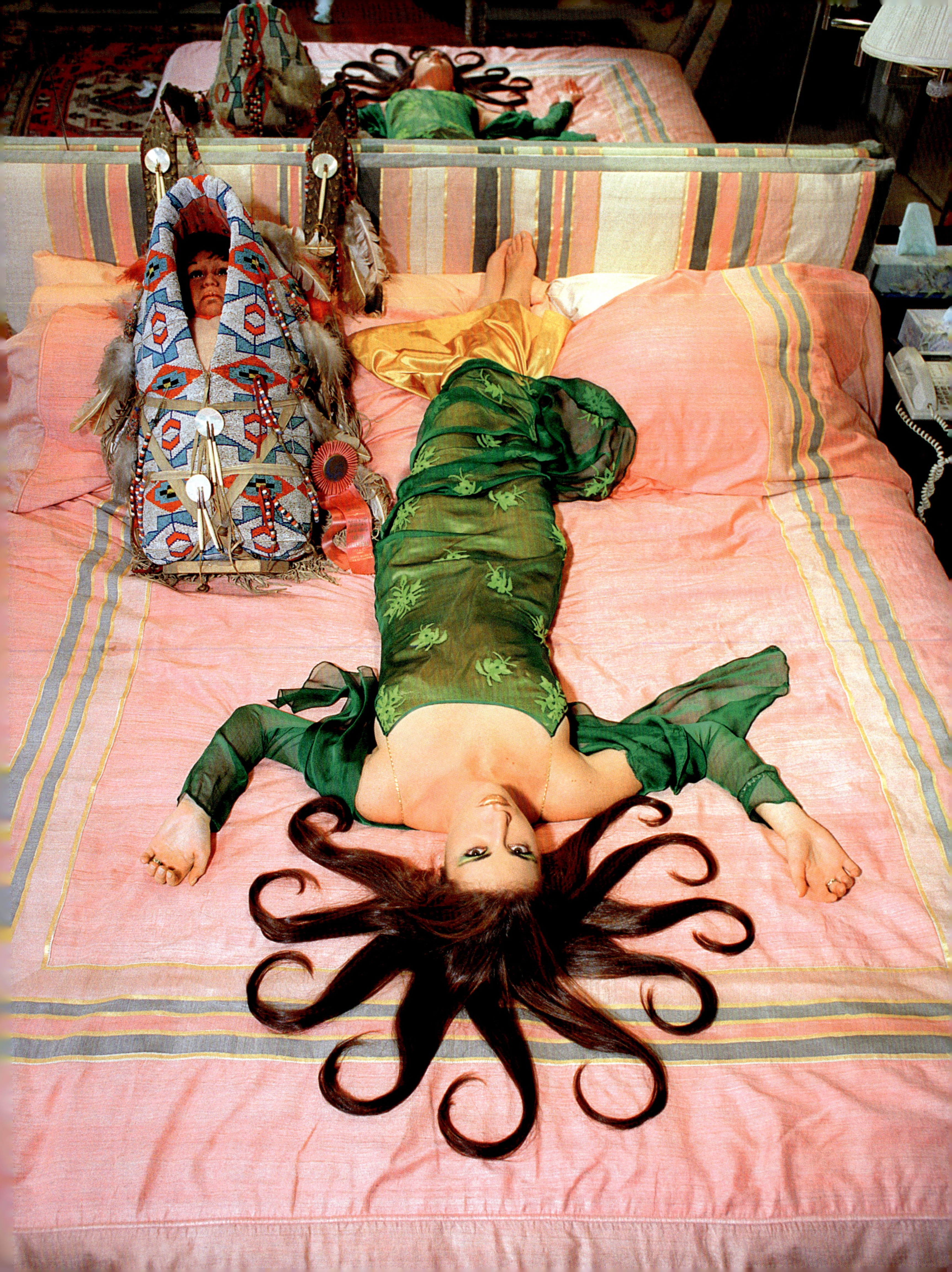

Spiral City

In the 1990s, a group of inventive young artists remade Mexico's capital as a backdrop for experiments in photography, film, and performance.
Kit Hammonds

While Mexico City has been intermittently a progressive and modern city with a cosmopolitan culture, it has been equally notorious for state-, military-, and narcotic-related violence and corruption, along with sharp class distinctions. On September 19, 1985, one of the country's most devastating earthquakes occurred in the city. Hundreds of buildings fell, and thousands of lives were lost. Whole neighborhoods in the center lay abandoned, and distrust in the government was rampant, a condition that was exacerbated in the years that followed, as in 1994, when Mexico entered into the North American Free Trade Agreement with the United States and Canada, widely considered at the time to be serving only the elite. Against this backdrop, however, something of a renaissance took place in the 1990s, with sudden attention being paid to the city by contemporary artists. In the wake of another devastating earthquake in 2017, occurring thirty-two years to the day after the 1985 tragedy, it's instructive to look back at a formative period of Mexico City's role in today's globalized art market and at the work of artists who impacted the continuing image of the metropolis as precarious and creative in equal measure.

Among the markers of this shift was the arrival of European artists—including Francis Alÿs, Santiago Sierra, and Melanie Smith—who chose Mexico as a place where they could work outside

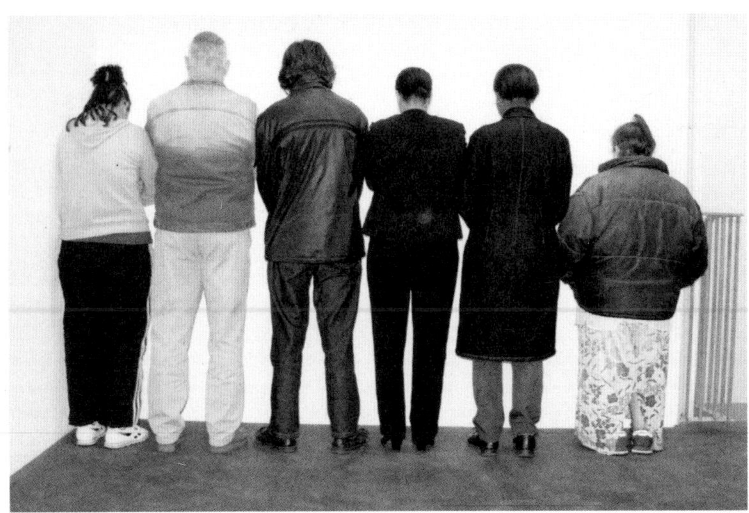

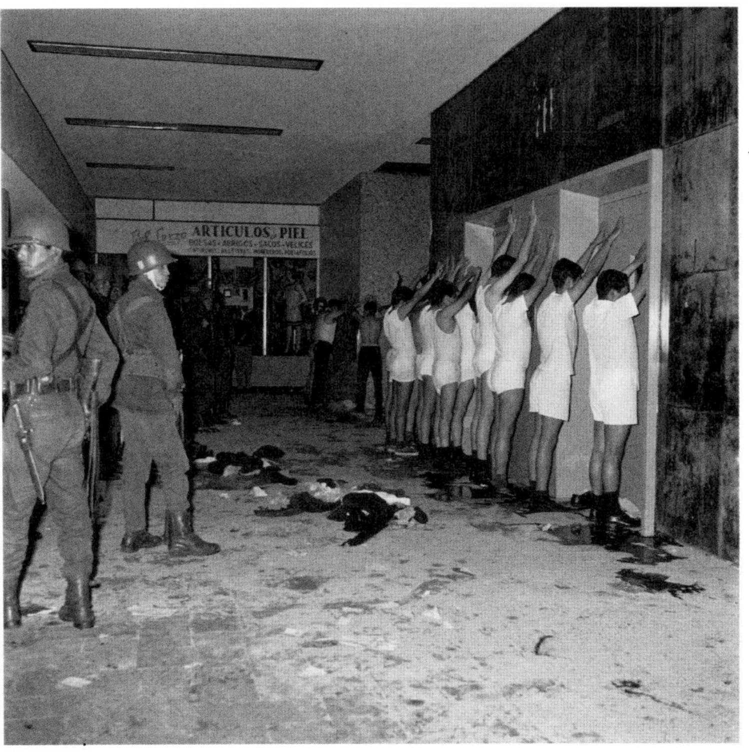

the confines of the established art circuit. Alongside a number of Mexican artists—Miguel Calderón, Silvia Gruner, Yoshua Okón, and Gabriel Orozco, to name but a few—these contemporaries frequently used the social milieu as a studio in which to enact performances, interventions, and works of assemblage from and amidst the prolific detritus that could be found in the streets and markets. Hostile bureaucracy butting up against the anarchic informality of street life became the physical backdrop and sounding board for their practices. For many, the Zócolo, Mexico City's edgy and dilapidated historic center, particularly around the Calle Licenciado Verdad, provided both constant stimulus and affordable rent and, in turn, became a place where artist-run galleries emerged, as documented in Daniel Montero's 2014 exploration of a pivotal moment in contemporary art—and the emergence of a critical debate on Mexico's increasingly significant position in a global market—*El cubo de Rubik, arte mexicano en los años 90* (The Rubik's Cube: Mexican art in the '90s). Others colonized the Condesa area, opening exhibition spaces such as La Panaderia in the then run-down neighborhood that has since been gentrified.

Mexico City street life displays both petty freedoms and ad hoc systems. For these transplanted artists, one might consider it a mise-en-scène, but something of a partial one, alongside the stereotyped images of the megalopolis. Trained as an architect, Belgian artist Francis Alÿs arrived as part of a humanitarian project to aid reconstruction following the 1985 earthquake. In his earlier artwork, Alÿs had developed distinctive, poetic, and personal investigations of a city's flows and ambiences more than its physical environments. This approach lent itself to an artistic practice that coalesced in Mexico, where he chose to remain. Alÿs's walking excursions through the dilapidated city center saw him tapping into its own sometimes languid, sometimes staccato rhythms. Activities such as pushing a block of ice through the streets until it melted into nothingness or wearing a magnetic pair of shoes that attracted nails, bottle tops, and other discarded shrapnel of the comings and goings of the city's inhabitants were among his strategies. Often derived from observation of everyday activities, they presented an appropriation of psychogeographical methods in a "third-world" context. In his meanderings, Alÿs was especially drawn to the contrast of modern and premodern found in the urban fabric, which he described as paradoxically existing in the Zócolo, around which many of these works were made. As he has described it: "Does it matter even if or up to which point this modernity has really been lived here…? What matters today is just the memory of it, fictitious or real…. All the ingredients of modernity may be there, but the city often continues to function on the basis of a pre-modern parallel economy."

Whether Alÿs was reenacting and reframing the overlooked quotidian aspects of people's routines and labors or commissioning premodern laborers to copy his own paintings, his images and actions accrued their potency from the city itself. Alÿs's works also avoided a singular definition: photographic documentation of his performances was presented in the gallery, alongside video and drawings, while reproduced images on postcards, with short didactic texts adopting the style of Conceptual art, were intended to be distributed beyond its confines. As philosopher Jacques Rancière writes, the aesthetic revolution of modern times "shifts the focus from great names and events to the life of the anonymous; it finds symptoms of an epoch, a society, or a civilization in the minute details of ordinary life." Alÿs and his contemporaries created their own exceptional moments that circulated within the ordinary.

The Spanish artist Santiago Sierra took a more antagonistic approach to the city's movements of traffic and people. Simply documented in black-and-white photographs and video, his piece *Obstruction of a Freeway with a Truck's Trailer, Anillo Perférico*

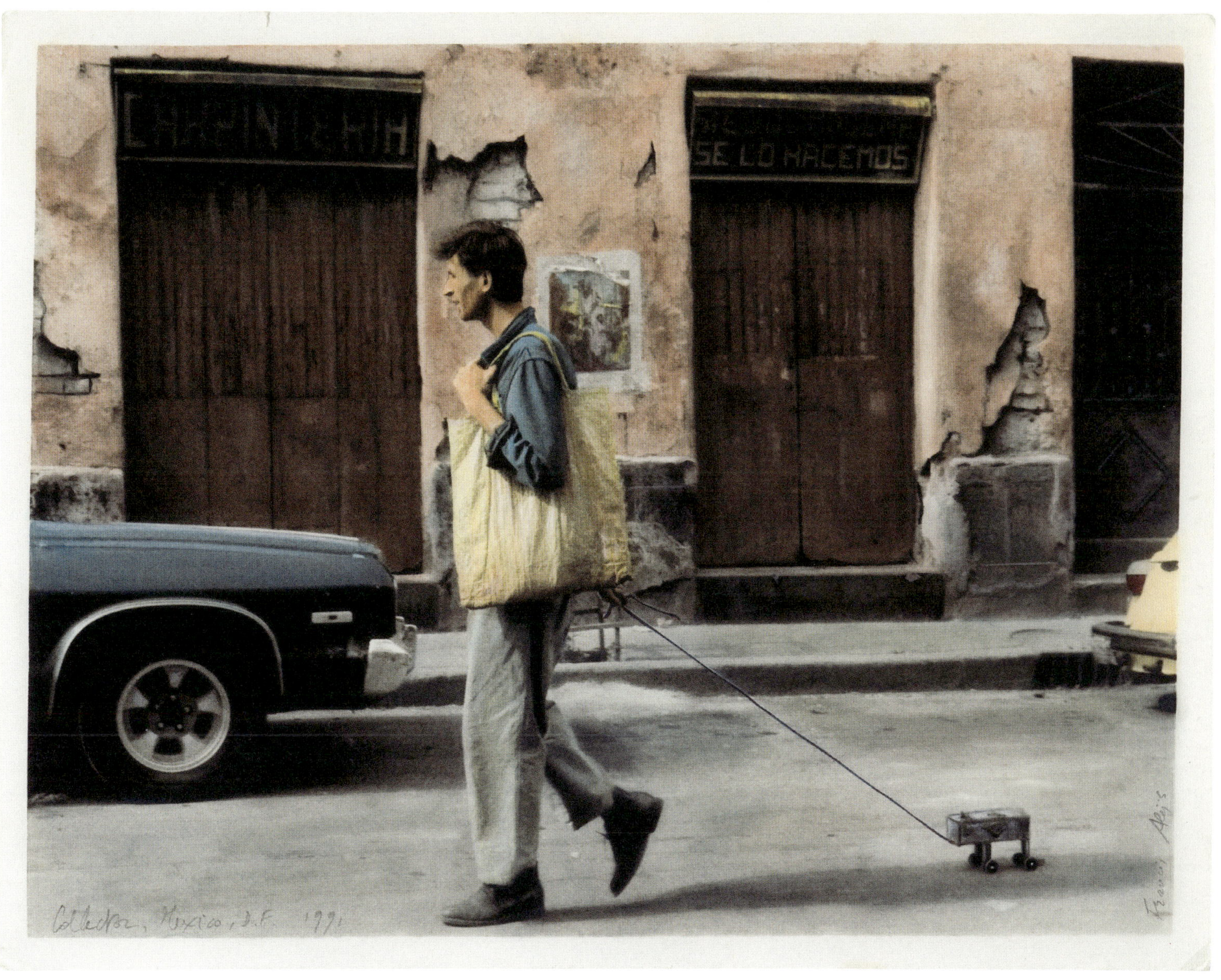

**Francis Alÿs, *Collector,
Mexico, D.F.*, 1991**
© the artist and courtesy
the artist and David Zwirner,
New York

Alÿs's images and actions accrued their potency from the city itself.

Sur, Mexico City, Mexico. November 1998 (1998) appears to depict an unusual, quasi-criminal action. Sierra refers to the work in terms that blur sociopolitical and Minimalist aesthetics, stating that it "consisted of positioning a white prism perpendicular to the road, generating a traffic jam." As the artist also noted, "the driver didn't mind" being asked to perform a five-minute rupture on the at times dystopic Fordian roadways that are more often than not at a standstill anyway. The work reenacts a significant experience of the city many would recognize; delivery trailers reversing to jam the traffic on a Mexico City freeway exit are not, in fact, uncommon. Nor is its location arbitrary. The work is observed from a footbridge loaded with its own history of violence and protest, while toward the rear stands Gonzalo Fonseca's 1968 *Torre de los vientos* (Tower of the winds), a sculpture that forms part of the Ruta de la Amistad (Route of friendship), a seventeen-kilometer-long sculpture park designed to be viewed by drivers on their way to the Olympic stadiums for the 1968 games.

More broadly, Sierra's actions emphasized capitalist imbalances and dehumanizations as part of a broader question of institutional power versus the individual. In a series of works realized both in Mexico and elsewhere, Sierra imposed his art directly on people's bodies, replicating the conditions of exploitation for remuneration that are often found in Latin America. The lines of bodies that appear in his photographic documents—whether of addicts being paid the price of a heroin fix to be tattooed or of the unemployed to simply stand against a wall—echo photographs of the student

Smith's film moves at a biological rather than geological speed as it pans over mainly informal and unplanned dwellings.

oppression by police during the protests at the time of the 1968 Olympics. In particular, one piece of reportage stands out as an antecedent: Manuel Gutiérrez Paredes's photograph of the police searching detained protesters. Cemented in the Mexican cultural imagination, this lineup of subjugated students arrested at the Tlatelolco demonstrations, where forty-four people were killed, lingers more than the constructed media images that the games were meant to project. As the president of the Organizing Committee of the games stated: "Of least importance was the Olympic competition; the records fade away, but the image of a country does not." Undoubtedly, such brutal authoritarianism would be the lasting image, even if it was a distinctly modern one, compared with the rural depictions that persisted prior to the 1960s. It is not merely the physical but also the psychic resonance that is embedded in reportage of events like this, or of the subsequent traumas, captured by photographers such as Enrique Metinides, of violent robberies, plane crashes, and disasters. While veracious in many respects, these pictures amplified imagery of violence and "low" culture over other more positive aspects of life in Mexico City.

Sierra's and Alÿs's photographic works are often deliberate snapshots not intended to be part of the photographic canon per se, but rather a use of the camera as an apparatus of vérité and documentation. Sierra's images, perhaps more than others, are consciously engaged in creating a particular idiom. The choice of black and white at a time when color film was already the norm lent a deliberately staged air to the records of his actions. Both Sierra's and Alÿs's form of photography sits between journalism, documentary, and the street photography of Weegee and his ilk. Certainly it is informed by these traditions in its framing and intention, just as it is informed by post-Minimalist and Conceptual art imported from the United States and Europe.

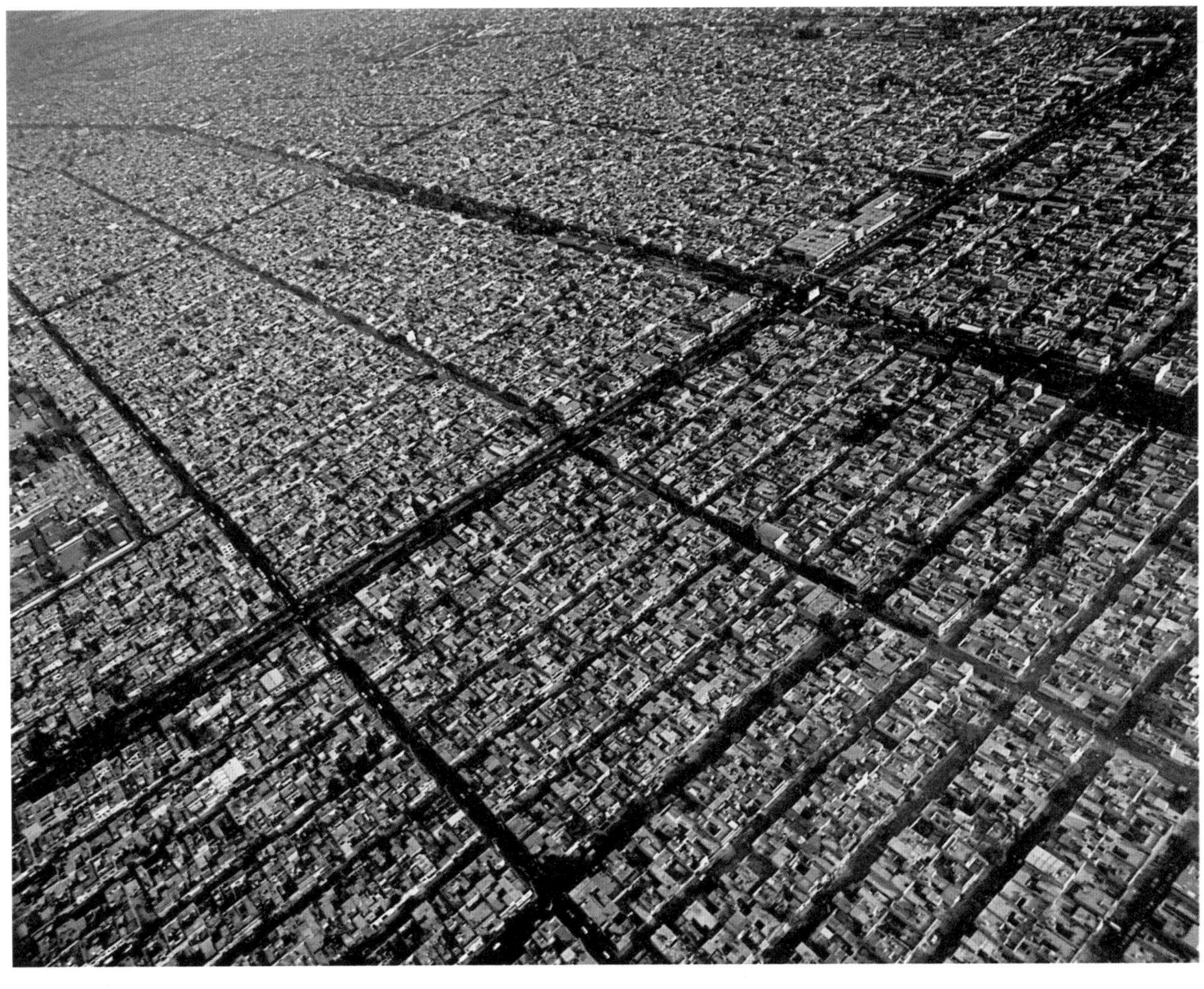

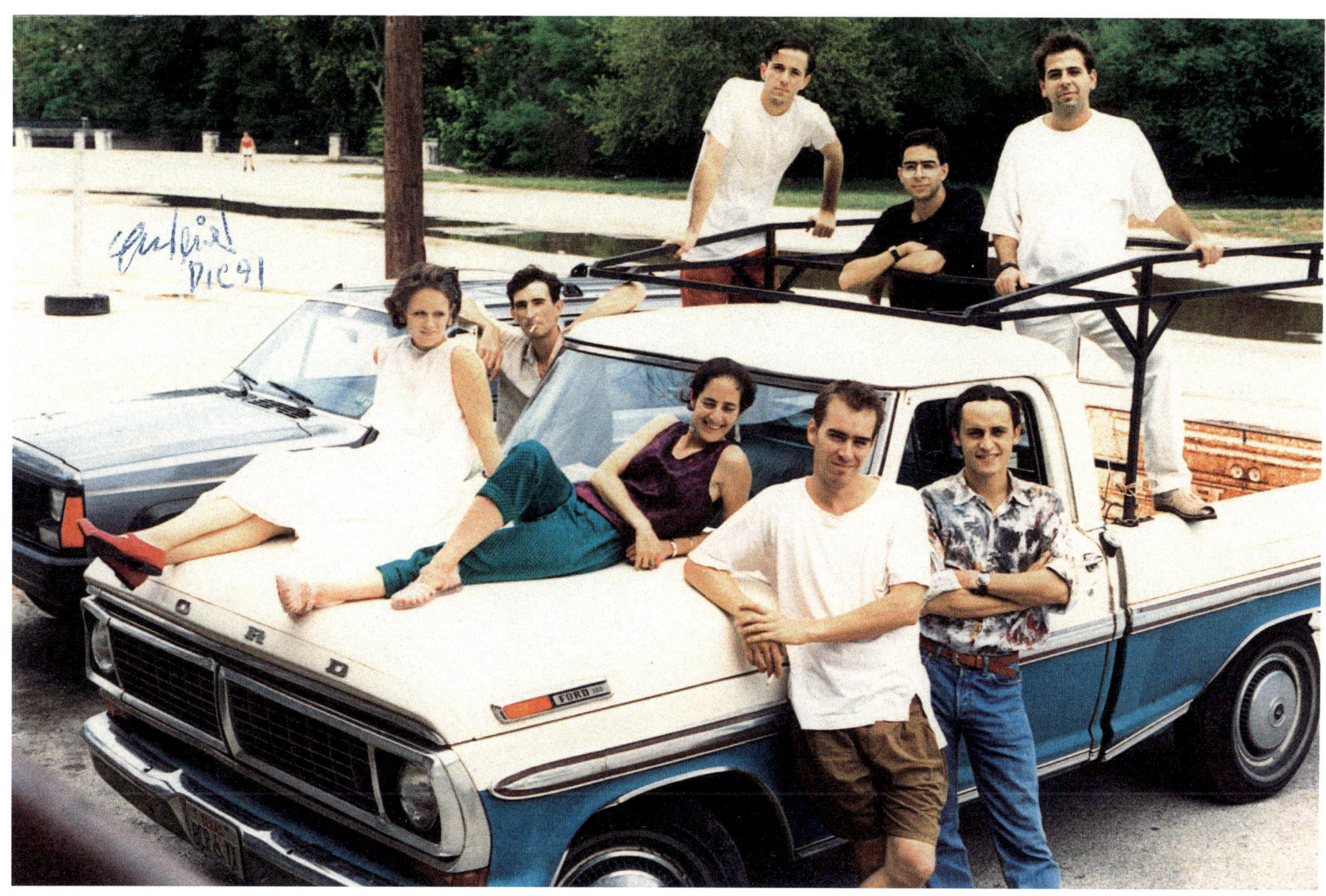

Photographer unknown,
Artists from the exhibition
D.F., curated by Alejandro
Díaz, at BlueStar
Contemporary Space,
San Antonio, Texas, 1991.
Bottom row, left to right:
**Melanie Smith, Francis
Alÿs, Silvia Gruner, Thomas
Glassford, Gabriel Orozco**
Courtesy David Zwirner,
New York

In 2002, Melanie Smith, a British-born artist (who contributed to the 1990s art scene in Mexico City with the weekly Mel's Café she ran in her studio then), created *Spiral City*, a project including a movie and still photography of Mexico City that pay homage to *Spiral Jetty* (1970), Robert Smithson's landmark earthwork tucked behind a remote promontory of Utah's Great Salt Lake and his film of the same name. Smithson's film is not only an image of *Spiral Jetty* and its landscape; it also explores cultural ideas and phenomena that are just as influential in constructing the mythology of a place, such as science fiction and natural-history museums. These intercut references add a modern mythical dimension to his documentation. Smith applied Smithson's methodology to Mexico City, itself constructed on a drying lake bed. In *Spiral City*, the seemingly boundless grid of Mexico City's housing, all low-rise and barren, whether in low-income or middle-class neighborhoods, has the same sense of accretion as Smith's inspiration. Her film moves at a biological rather than geological speed as it pans over mainly informal and unplanned dwellings. Seen in this way, the city resembles Mike Davis's description of it, in his book *Planet of Slums* (2005): "The giant amoeba of Mexico City, already having consumed Toluca, is extending pseudopods that will eventually incorporate much of central Mexico, including the cities of Cuernavaca, Puebla, Cuautla, Pachuca, and Queretaro, into a single megalopolis."

This is not to suggest that these practices were the only approaches of relevance in the 1990s and into the early 2000s. Gabriel Orozco was producing sculptural interventions in dilapidated interiors, vacated lots, and other liminal urban sites in both Mexico and New York, where he was simultaneously based. Many of these assemblages of discarded materials appear animate, suggestive of mythical figures as much as of playful forms, drawing on two distinct histories of modern and premodern to forge his own hybrid aesthetics. Silvia Gruner was using her own body as a tool to explore relations with traditions and identities, which also reflect the dualistic time frame in which Mexico seemed to exist.

Mexico City has always been full of extreme contrasts. Another facet, one that few artists have engaged, is that of the enclosures of the wealthy industrial classes, the thirty-eight families who control the majority of economic and political power in the country. Daniela Rossell's portraits of society women in their homes, grouped together under the series *Ricas y famosas* (Rich and famous, 1994–2001) and *Third World Blondes* (2000–2002), are the exception, although they also play with certain stereotypes. How these images were produced and circulated are as significant as what they portray, revealing the codes of viewing embedded in both local and international contexts even more acutely than artists who work in Mexico City's public spaces.

Rossell's portraits are remarkable on many levels. Among the first thing one notices about their main subjects is their propensity to be blond, a social marker among Mexican wealthy classes that differentiates them from their housekeepers and maids, many of whom appear in the photographs in subservience to their employers. The homes of these women have been referred to as gilded cages, and the overadornment of their interiors is akin to those of the bodies that inhabit them, often with fantastical implications—for instance, one woman is seen dressed as a mermaid with Medusa-like hair, with the bed as her sea, and a Native American doll lying beside her.

Rossell's work was produced in full cooperation with her subjects; Rossell, who is from the same class herself, was able to gain access to these extravagant homes through family and social ties. We can see these photographs as representations of people as they choose to present themselves. In this light, perhaps it is too easy to judge the excessive taste and apply the same criteria to the person within the image. Somewhat inevitably, once unveiled to the world at large, these isolated creatures and their exotic artificial universes were critically addressed in the media and by art-world cognoscenti for the brash way in which they displayed and performed wealth. Once it became clear that they had become the subject of ridicule, many of those pictured withdrew their consent. Given the nature of family businesses and the nature of business itself in Mexico, often intertwining legitimate and not-so-legitimate practices, Rossell found it impossible to continue with the project, and found herself under genuine threat.

The images in *Ricas y famosas* are, in fact, neither celebratory nor parodic, but rather a means of addressing attitudes toward women, particularly in the media. It should not be overlooked that the series' title is itself taken from a long-running telenovela and suggestive of the vacuous stereotypes it portrays. Arguably, Rossell's lens reveals not just the absurdities of wealth but also the public mores and judgments of the upper class—demonstrating a self-awareness that is noticeably lacking in the art of her European colleagues working in Mexico during the same era, who often placed acts within a deprived social sphere without truly being part of it.

Kit Hammonds is a curator at Museo Jumex in Mexico City.

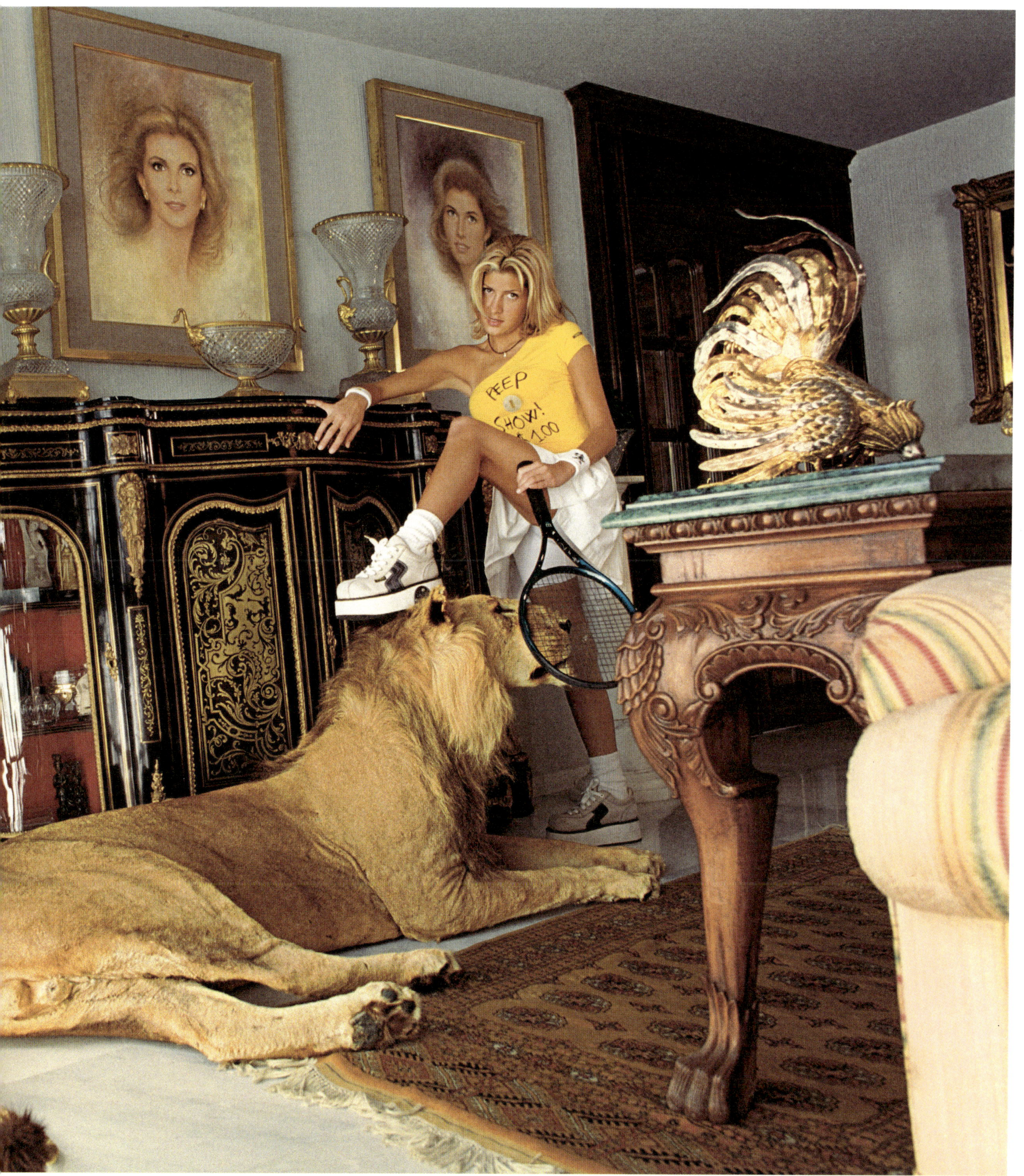

Daniela Rossell, *Untitled,*
1999, from the series
Ricas y famosas
Courtesy Estate of Candy
Jernigan and Greene Naftali,
New York

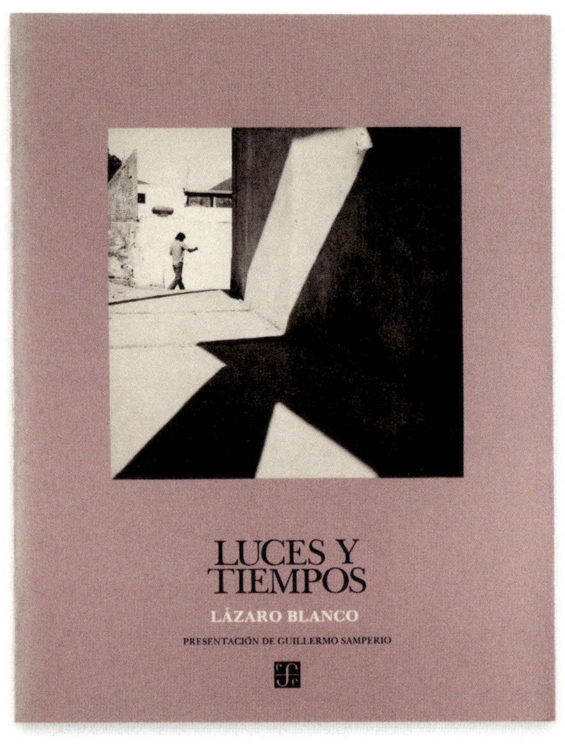

LUCES Y
TIEMPOS
LÁZARO BLANCO
PRESENTACIÓN DE GUILLERMO SAMPERIO

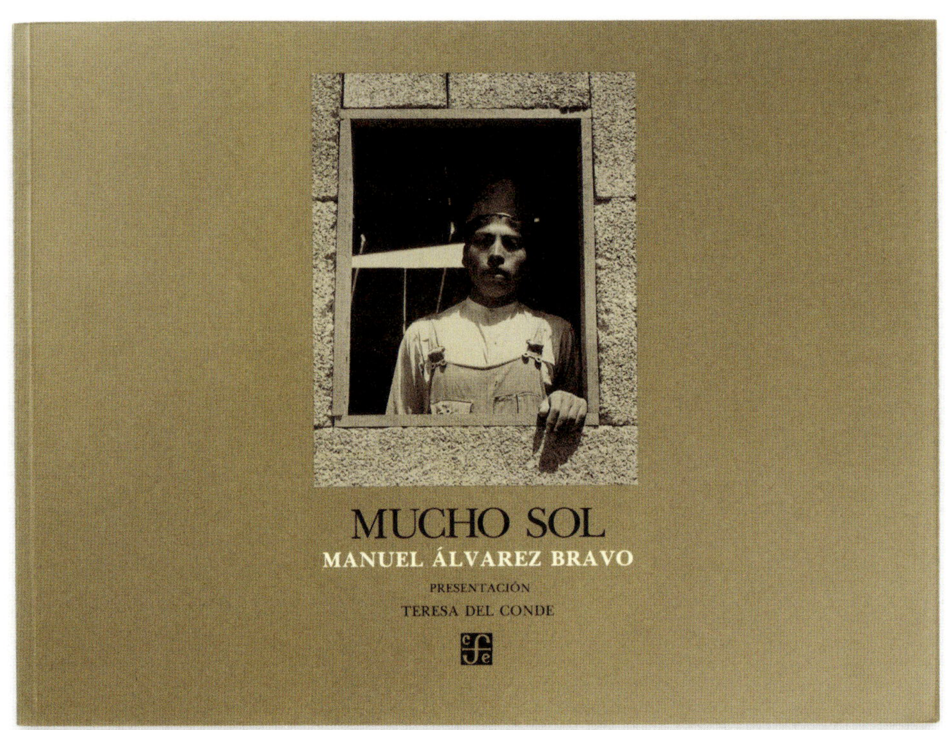

MUCHO SOL
MANUEL ÁLVAREZ BRAVO
PRESENTACIÓN
TERESA DEL CONDE

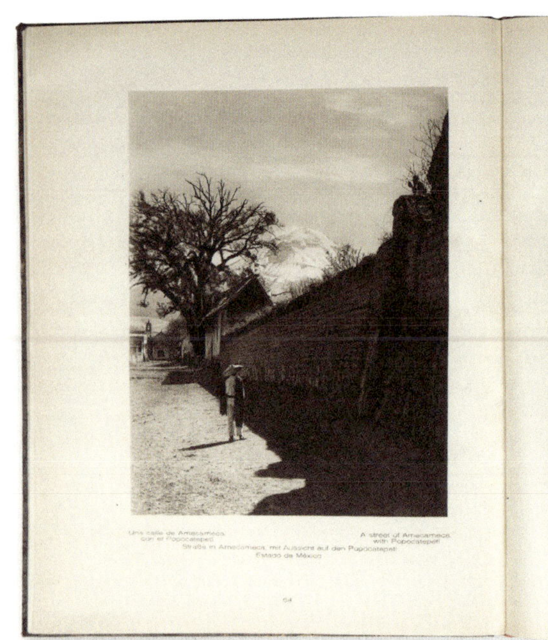

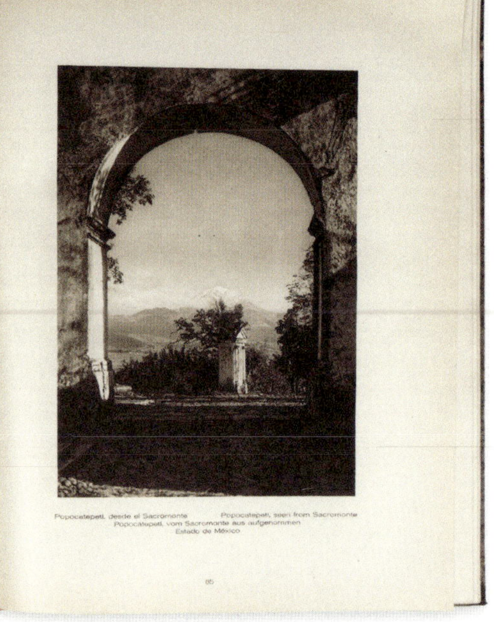

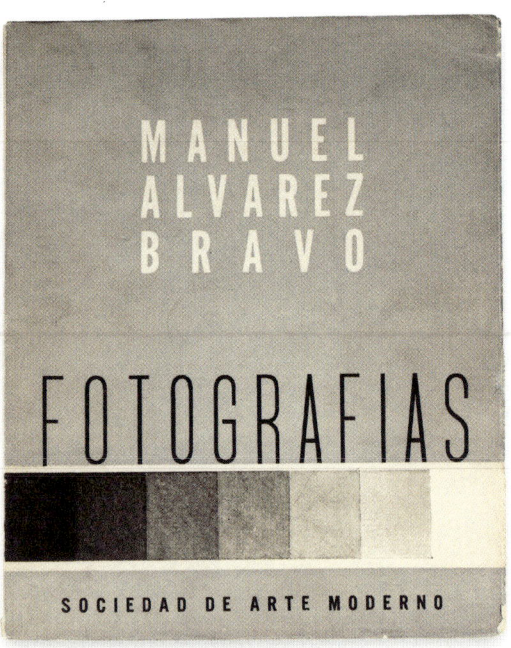

MANUEL
ALVAREZ
BRAVO

FOTOGRAFIAS

SOCIEDAD DE ARTE MODERNO

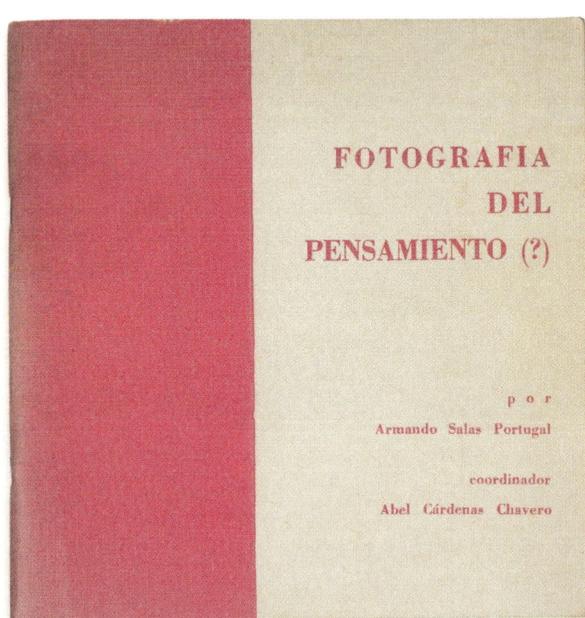

FOTOGRAFIA
DEL
PENSAMIENTO (?)

por
Armando Salas Portugal

coordinador
Abel Cárdenas Chavero

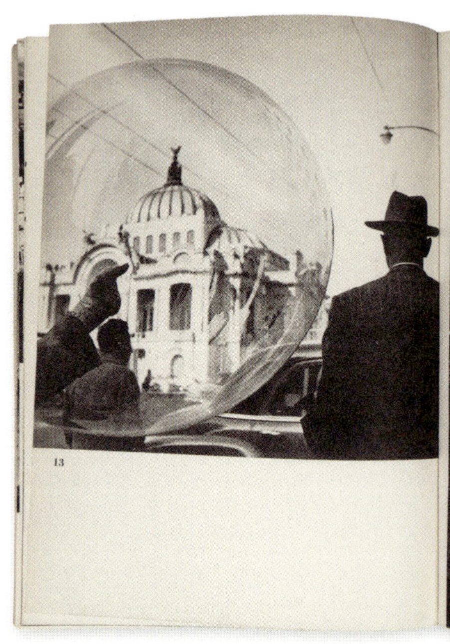

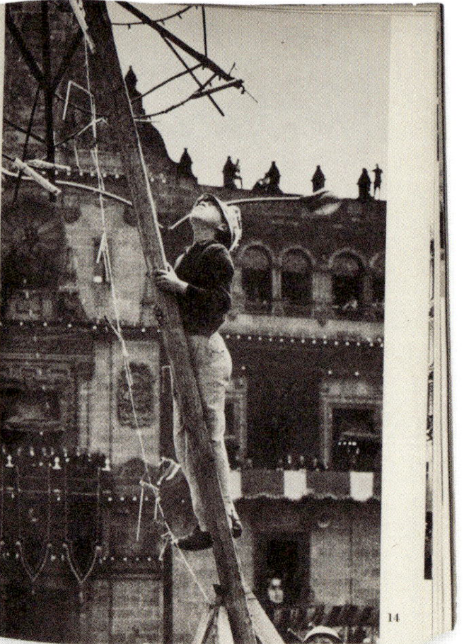

Mexico and the Photobook

Mexico's relationship to photobooks is nearly as old as the country itself. Agustín Víctor Casasola's never-completed *Álbum histórico gráfico* (Historical graphic album) sought to capture Mexico's revolution in the early twentieth century. Since then, photobooks have continued to evolve alongside Mexico's diverse and multicultural society. Perhaps the best embodiment of this spirit is Pablo Ortíz Monasterio, a photographer, editor, curator, and prolific collector. Ortíz Monasterio edited *Río de Luz* (River of light), a government-funded book series featuring monographs by Latin American photographers such as Pedro Meyer and Mariana Yampolsky. In 1994, along with his peers in the photography community, Ortíz Monasterio founded the Centro de la Imagen in Mexico City, where he has served as chief curator and editor of *Luna Córnea*, a magazine that promotes critical dialogue around photography.

Horacio Fernández, a photography historian, is a publishing legend in his own right. Fernández curated the lauded *Fotografía Pública: Photography in Print 1919–1939* (1999) at Spain's Museo Reina Sofía and edited *The Latin American Photobook* (Aperture, 2011). For this issue, Ortíz Monasterio and Fernández met in June following the opening of the show *Fotos en libros, libros en fotos* (Photos in books, books in photos), a collection of photobooks and photographs from the Centro de la Imagen's collection, gathered over the last forty years by the Consejo Mexicano de Fotografía. At Ortíz Monasterio's home in Coyoacán, they spoke about the long legacy of photobooks in Mexico, from Manuel Álvarez Bravo's early work and Lourdes Grobet's portrayal of *lucha libre* to Alejandro Cartagena's inventive self-publishing.

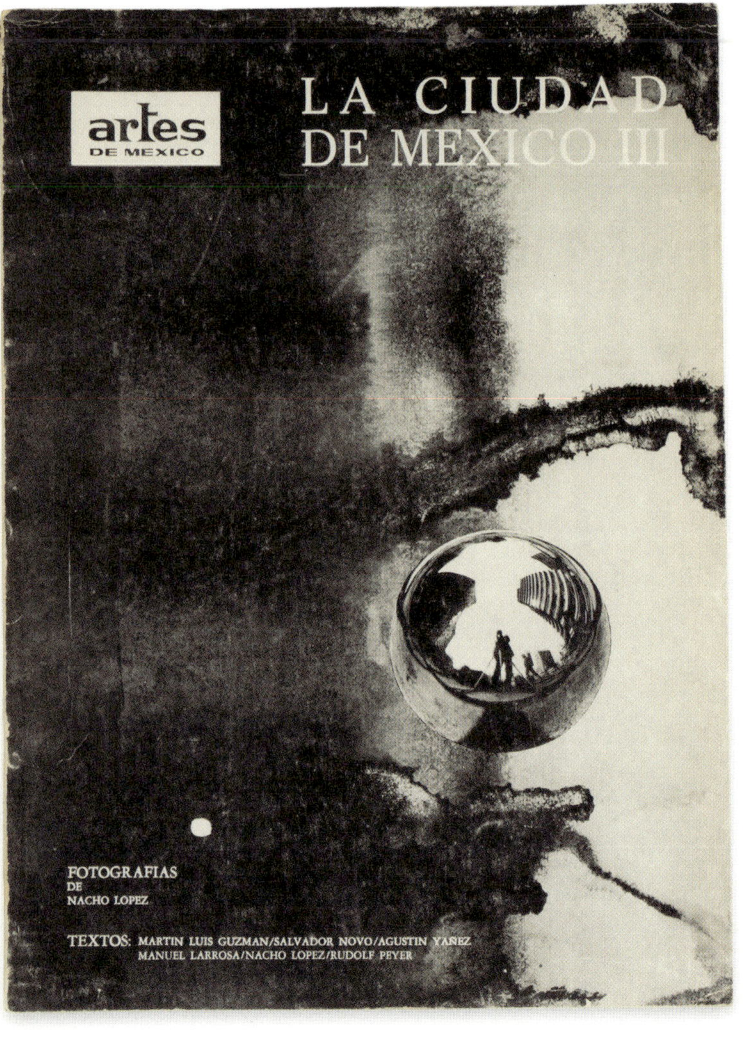

Pablo Ortíz Monasterio: In Mexico, there have been books that contain pictures glued on their pages since the nineteenth century. The government of Porfirio Díaz published special issues in order to commemorate the country's independence. But the first important photography book was *Álbum histórico gráfico* (Historical graphic album, 1921) by Agustín Víctor Casasola, a masterpiece that was meant to become an encyclopedia with many volumes, of which only one was published.

Horacio Fernández: Casasola was an editor, owner, and manager of the archive and its projects. In *Álbum histórico gráfico*, he narrates the Mexican Revolution through the images of a number of photographers, including Manuel Ramos and Hugo Brehme. Brehme was also the author of *México pintoresco* (Picturesque Mexico), a work that, when reedited in 1923, became part of the Orbis Terrarum series, which defined the image of Mexico abroad. There are other important books from those years, such as *Chimeneas* (Chimneys, 1937), a work both literary and photographic, with images by Agustín Jiménez, a fascinating photographer who later dedicated himself to cinema.

POM: There is another great book of his, *Molino verde* (Green windmill, 1932). It practically contains no text, but it is the work that best depicts urban modernity through Mexican nightlife, a delight among all photographs portraying this *monster* [Mexico City].

HF: An Art Deco cover in full color opens to a cabaret full of girls wearing no clothes and clients hiding their faces.

POM: But Jiménez transforms it and turns vulgarity into modernity by means of different inks that illuminate the bodies, highlighted through contrasts, fragmentations, and vertiginous perspectives. Censorship haunted the book. We only know of three copies of it. *Molino verde* is the holy grail.

HF: There is also another important aspect of Mexican photography: magazines. From the 1920s onward in Mexico, images filled pages and pages of popular magazines publishing the *nota roja* [visually explicit reports on violent crimes], pornography, sports, tourism, and other affairs. The quality and visual richness of these magazines alone shaped a history of Mexican photography.

POM: The first monograph with ambitions to become a photobook was published in 1945, dedicated to a leading figure: *Manuel Álvarez Bravo: Fotografías*. It is a cocktail—a very Mexican one—in which rabid modernity saw no conflict with tradition. It included more than one hundred pieces, including gelatin-silver copies. Nowadays it's very valuable.

HF: The book changed Álvarez Bravo's career. He was working in cinema back then. As a result, he was regarded as a leading photographer of his generation and was able to pursue a successful career.

POM: Later on, an outstanding work in 1968 was *Fotografía del pensamiento* (Photograph of the mind) by Armando Salas Portugal, a photobook based on the experiment of putting couples together around a photographic plate and asking them to concentrate on the unexposed film while listening to music. Afterward, the film was developed in a darkroom.

HF: It meant doing something almost magical: portraying people based on their musical sensations. An excellent example of abstract and experimental photography. In his images, human presence is irrelevant. What he cares about are layers, colors, textures.

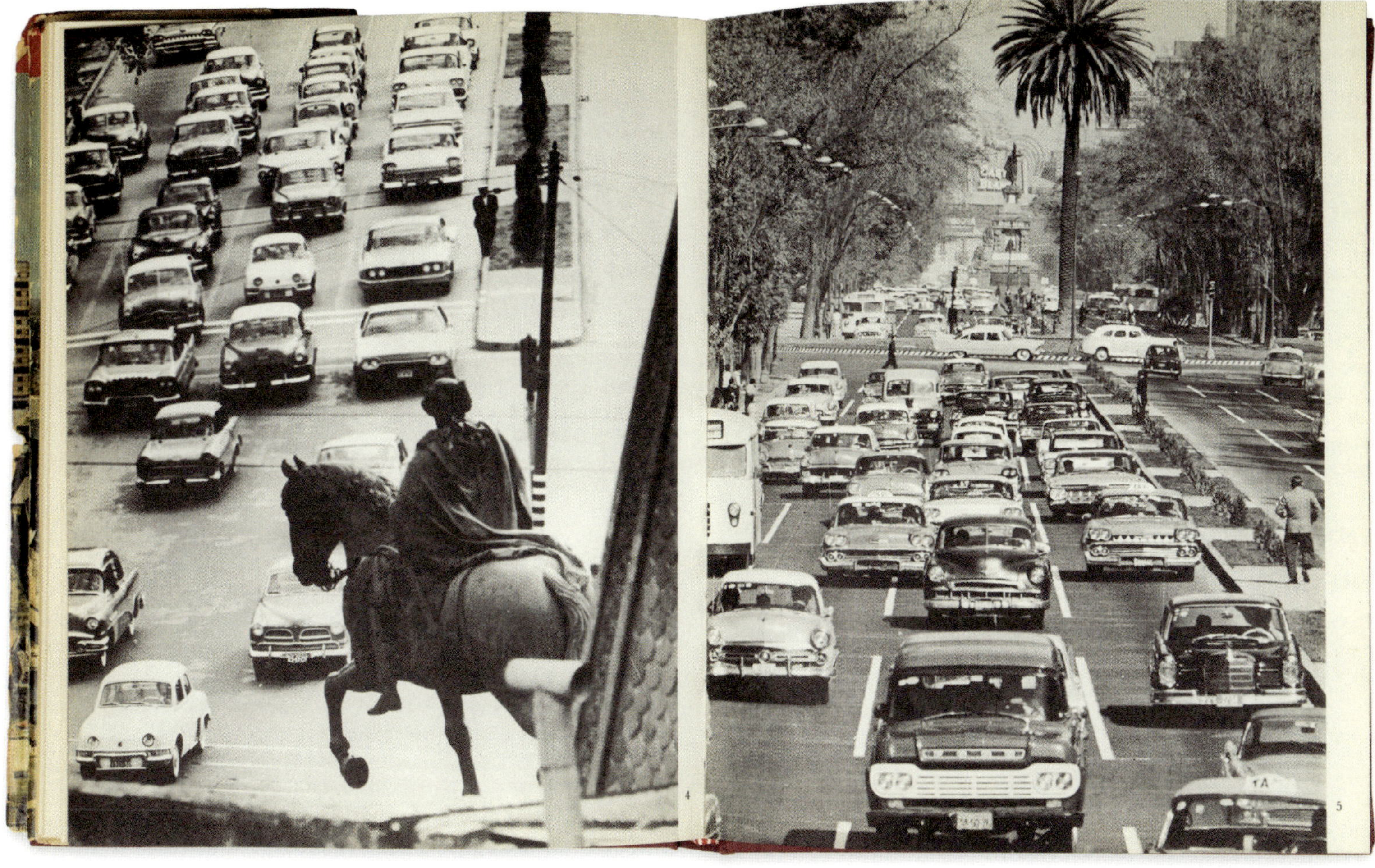

POM: **Other books from this period document the pulse of the streets by looking at people. With "La Ciudad de México III" in 1964, Nacho López filled a complete issue of *Artes de México* magazine with images of people hanging out at bars, stadiums, police detention centers, et cetera. This is when graphic designer Vicente Rojo appeared as a leading figure in the production of photographic books, including, among others, *Nueva grandeza mexicana* (New Mexican grandeur, 1967), with photographs by Héctor García. This was printed by the publishing house Era, where Rojo was a partner and art director, taking care of typography, page layout, image sequence, and coherence. At that time, publishing houses were private enterprises. Apart from Era, the publishing house Siglo XXI produced *América, un viaje a través de la injusticia* (America: A journey through injustice, 1970) by Enrique Bostelmann and *Para verte mejor, América Latina* (The better to see you, Latin America, 1972) by Paolo Gasparini.**

HF: In the 1970s, photography was in jeopardy. Latin America went through military dictatorships, imperialist abuses, guerilla movements. It was a political era, present in photobooks like those by Gasparini and Bostelmann, who traveled across Latin American countries intending to visualize the contradictions between real and potential politics and economy. Bostelmann was more of a humanist: he sought empathy with the underprivileged. Gasparini, in turn, took sides with the revolution, with a masterful use of propaganda. Yet he was hypercritical of the art of the moment: depoliticized abstract art. Pictures express opinions, criticize, reveal. These books are exceptional among propaganda photobooks, not only in the Mexican or Latin American scenes. They are key books, acknowledged in exhibitions and publications.

POM: **There are also links between writers and photographers, as is the case of *Nueva grandeza mexicana*, with text written by** Salvador Novo. Álvarez Bravo, a very well-educated man and a voracious reader, should be emphasized here too. The titles of his images are of a poetic nature. Octavio Paz wrote poems based on them.

HF: The books on Mexico City created by López and García—the latter including another splendid text by Carlos Monsiváis in its second edition—are two of the best urban books of all time. They follow the path pioneered by William Klein in his books on New York and Rome, which inspired photobooks all over the world. For Mexicans, the key lies in the people and the streets, not in architecture or landmarks. García's book begins with images of colonial and touristic Mexico that are transformed into pictures of stimulating street life, and ends with futuristic and incredible photographs. In López's book, the colonial city only serves as a viewpoint to observe the modern one. His work is a monument to Mexico City.

POM: **From the 1980s onward, Mexican editorial life became more active and complex.**

HF: In this period, Mexico became the cultural capital of Latin America in terms of editing and photography. Dictatorships brought exiles like Roberto Bolaño to the city. Era, Joaquín Mortiz, and the Economic Culture Fund, the main Spanish-language publishing houses, turned their attention to photography. The Economic Culture Fund created a specific photography collection called Río de Luz (River of light), consisting of author monographs that are, in turn, photobooks, since they present excellent editing and design work.

POM: **Río de Luz was financed with public funds. Twenty issues were published focusing on Latin America. We thought there could have been a photographic explosion comparable to a literary boom. The editorial committee was formed by Luis**

Cardoza y Aragón, Graciela Iturbide, Rojo, Álvarez Bravo, Victor Flores Olea, Felipe Garrido, and me.

HF: Río de Luz dares to be Latin American and does so with diversity. There are more formal works, some that are rather political or journalistic, others that are anthropological essays, short thematic anthologies, and even a study on the history of Mexican photography with a beautiful title.

POM: *Sobre la superficie bruñida de un espejo* (On the polished surface of a mirror, 1989), with an essay by Olivier Debroise and Rosa Casanova.

HF: Río de Luz is a unique editorial project. It is also worth mentioning the Latin American Photography Colloquiums that were held in Mexico during the late 1970s and early '80s, where important exchanges resulted in the publishing of other photobooks created by major Latin American authors.

POM: Another project I have also been in charge of since the Centro de la Imagen was created is the *Luna Córnea* magazine. Back then, we thought, Okay, there are very good photographers; there is an audience; there is interest; there are exhibitions; but criticism is scarce, therefore, photographic culture is poor. We decided to embark on a visual and written magazine in which politics, literature, social sciences would fit. The intention was to develop independent criticism.

HF: Mexico is not that different from other countries in this respect. Back then, photography had a minuscule presence in museums, at universities, in collecting. *Luna Córnea* was launched at the Centro de la Imagen—with your support—where it proudly continues to be produced, now under the direction of Alfonso Morales Carrillo.

Urban chaos has no solution, but the photographer loves it so deeply that the reader falls in love with it too.

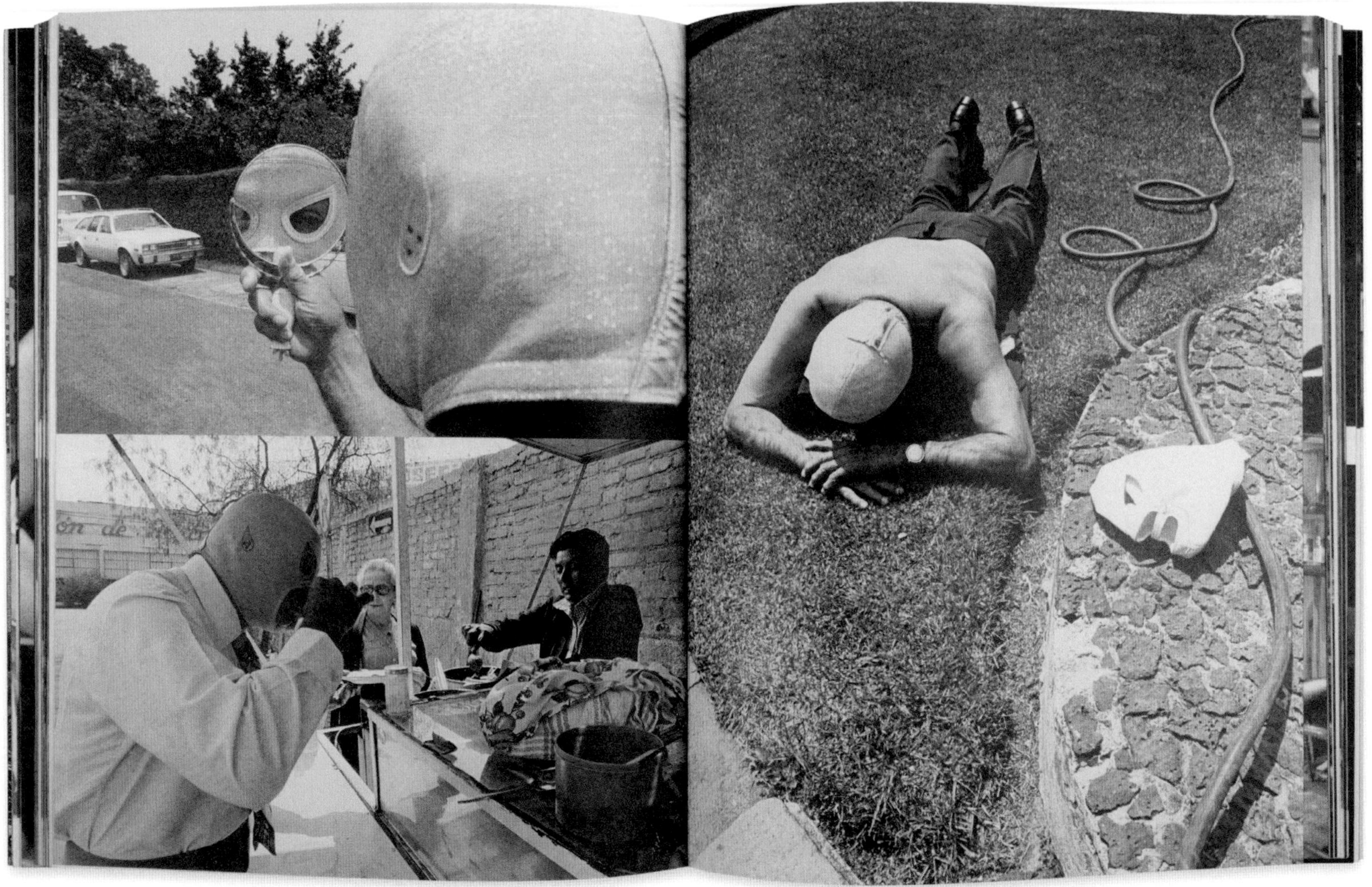

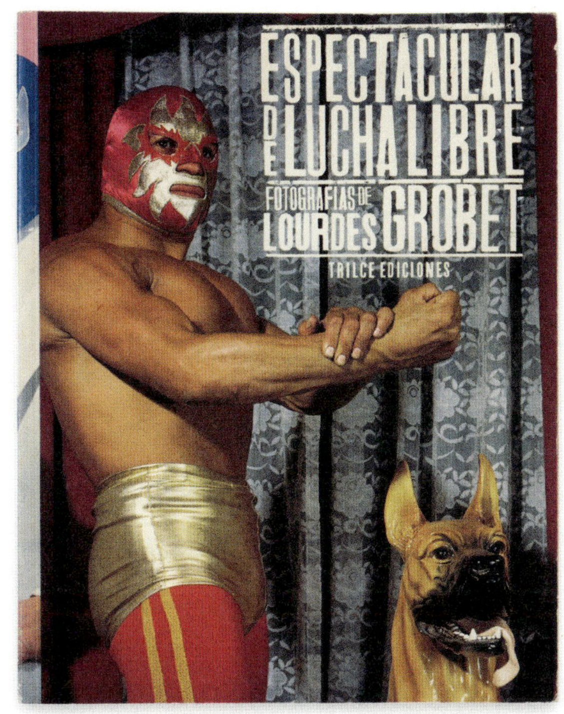

ESPECTACULAR
DE LUCHA LIBRE
FOTOGRAFIAS DE
LOURDES GROBET
TRILCE EDICIONES

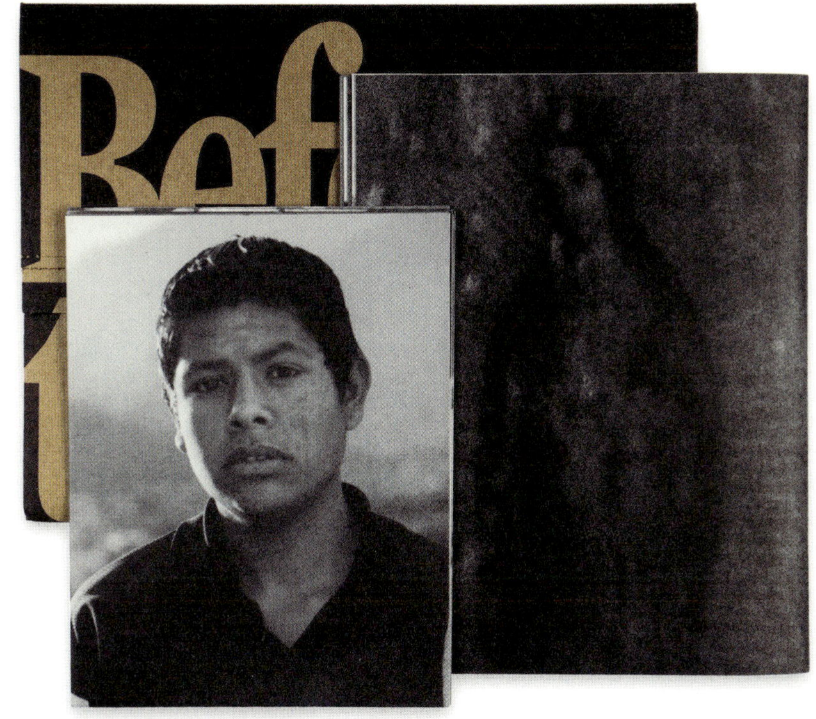

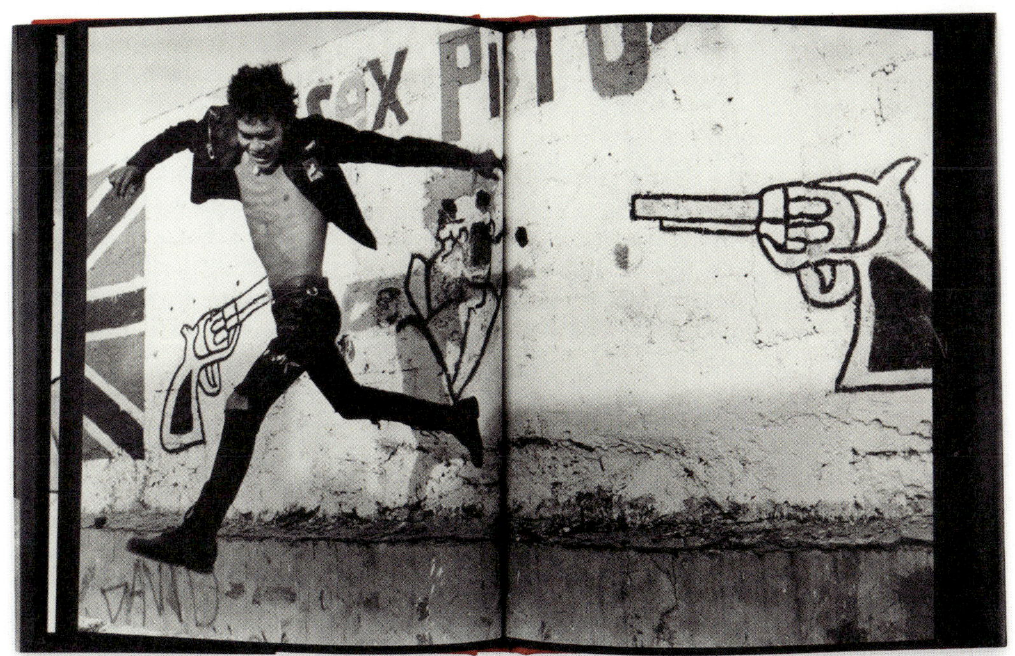

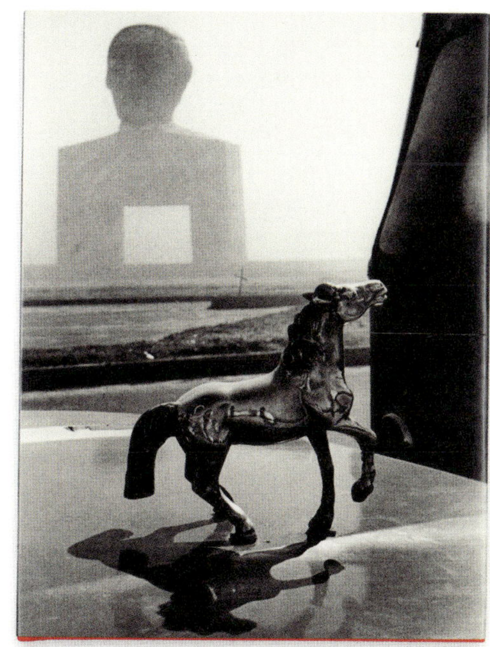

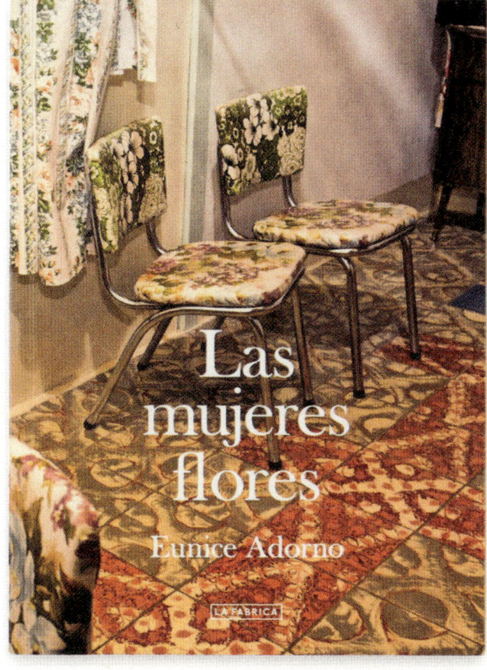

Las
mujeres
flores
Eunice Adorno
LA FÁBRICA

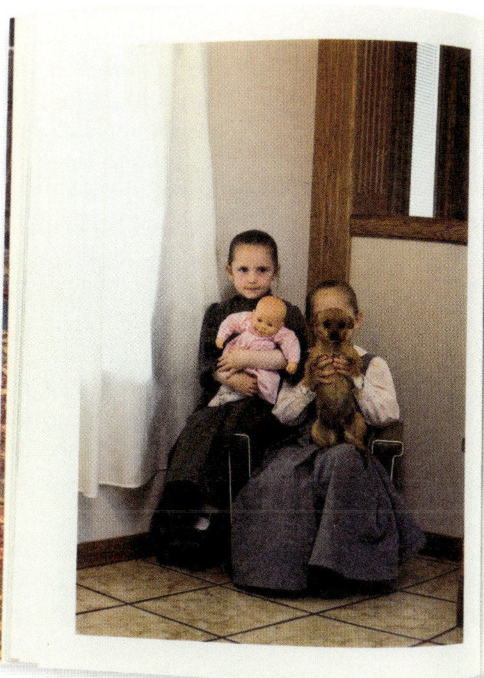

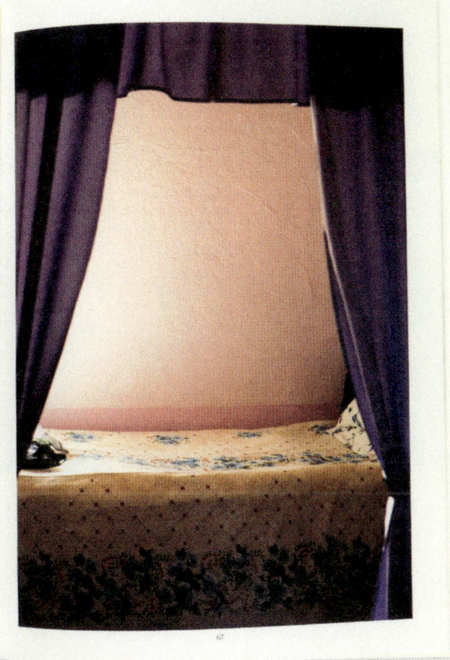

Cartagena's books could be previews of photobooks in the future, which—among other things—will have no homeland.

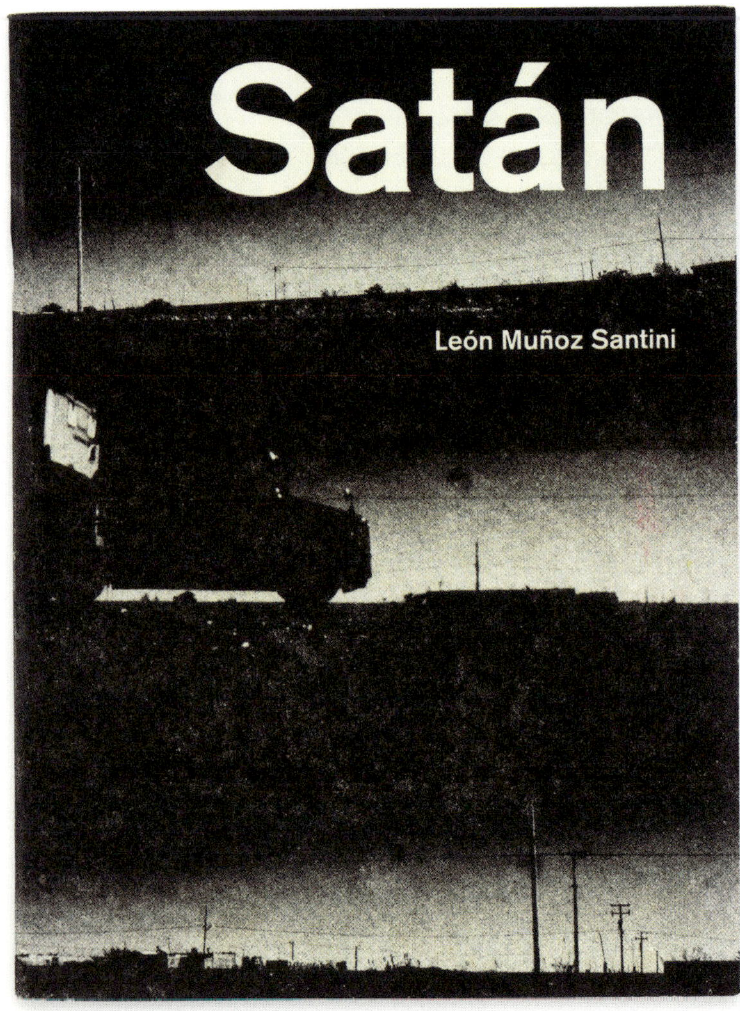

POM: *Río de Luz* and *Luna Córnea* are collective projects benefiting from public support, albeit operating independently.

HF: From the 1990s, your book *La última ciudad* (The last city, 1996) is worth highlighting.

POM: *La última ciudad*, using spectacular photogravure, continued the tradition of López and García: documenting monstruous Mexico City. I do not intend to describe it, but rather to picture what it is like to throw yourself out into streets where you find implausible situations—both joyful and painful— of a city full of contrasts and with astonishing energy.

HF: *La última ciudad* has as much of López as it does of Daido Moriyama: it is appropriating both Mexican and international photography. Urban chaos has no solution, but the photographer loves it so deeply that the reader falls in love with it too. *La última ciudad* is *Blade Runner*, an apocalyptical city, a timeless one, full of rhythms—a silent music that moves it all, with unclassifiable characters found on corners, empty plots or highways that are very different from the friendly settings of Alfonso Cuarón's film *Roma* (2018), which could well have among its sources *Jueves de Corpus* (Corpus Christi, 1971), a small photobook printed by the publishing house Diógenes, which also produced photobooks as brilliant as *Avándaro* (1971), by Graciela Iturbide, or *Chile o muerte* (Chile or death, 1974).

POM: There's also *Espectacular de lucha libre* (Wrestling spectacular, 2005) by Lourdes Grobet, who has documented Mexican wrestling for decades. In addition to the photographer, this book also features Morales Carrillo, who is not only an editor but a writer and wrestling enthusiast, as well as Juan Carlos Mena and Deborah Holtz, editors and designers from the publishing house Trilce. It has been a bestseller, with several reissues that circulate not only among photographic book fanatics, but also among the public interested in the world of fighting.

HF: Masked wrestlers are the Mexican superheroes. Grobet is their chronicler: costumes of urban heroes and villains presented in choreographies that are in reality theater; dances as funny and colorful as the design of the photobook itself; a set of anecdotes and observations that go beyond what they describe. A monument to pop culture.

POM: This is followed by another book by Turner, a publisher based both in Spain and Mexico. In *Ricas y famosas* (Rich and famous, 2002), Daniela Rossell presents the Mexican oligarchy most closely linked to political corruption. Rossell is the granddaughter of a former governor from the PRI [Institutional Revolutionary Party], and her friends—the protagonists of this photobook—descend from politicians who became rich along the way. For the first time in Mexico, there was a public document of these people—the very rich and ostentatious— made in a playful manner. When it was published, political magazines and weeklies showed it on front pages. Some people were offended. It was explosive.

HF: In Mexican photography, the presence of women photographers is important. Rossell is part of a powerful group: Tina Modotti, Mariana Yampolsky, Lourdes Grobet, Graciela Iturbide, Maya Goded, Yvonne Venegas, and Eunice Adorno.

POM: There is something new in the picture: a conceptual book, *Miguel Calderón* (2007), published by Turner and created by Calderón, who did not take any of the photographs shown.

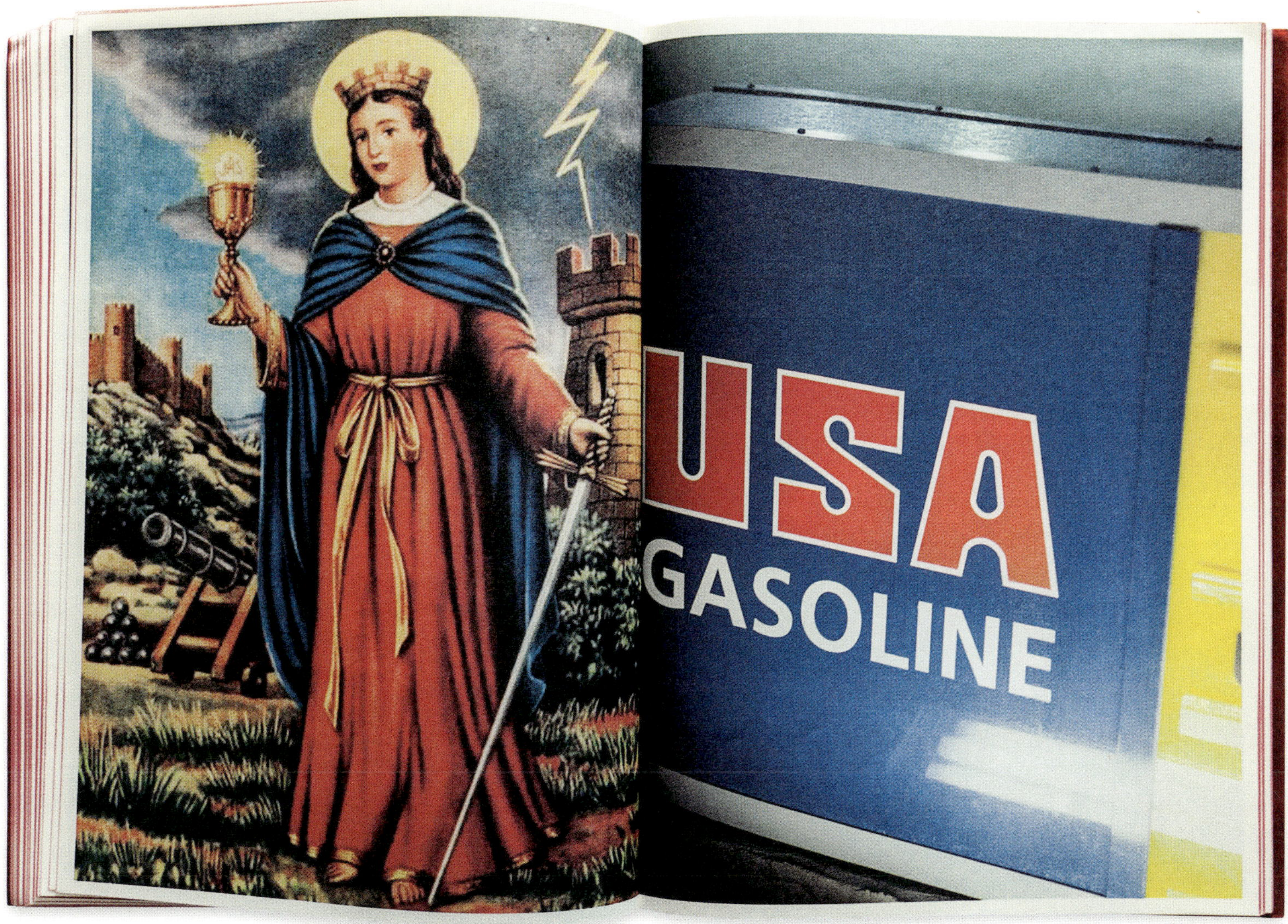

From his grandfather, he inherited a box full of photographs with one single protagonist: the grandfather himself hanging out with girls in Acapulco. The book immediately became a success—and not only in Mexico.

HF: Calderón ventures into the archive, but in a satirical way. He mocks himself, his family, his medium, and archival photography. It is a strange and beautiful photobook that apparently criticizes a person, but, in reality, advocates for individual freedom and carpe diem. In these books we've discussed, there is a complex vision of Mexico back in the day: a dynamic popular culture, decadent oligarchy, chaotic life among urban disorder with no prospects for change or future hope.

POM: **In the recent scene, it is worth noting the role of Ramón Reverté as art director and editor at RM, a publishing house that produces historical and contemporary works in Mexico and Barcelona, creating bridges that have enriched Mexican photography. Another independent project is the publisher Inframundo, started by photographer Ana Casas Broda, which has produced around twenty books in the past years.**

HF: There is also a new and decisive phenomenon in the latest photobooks: self-publishing.

POM: **Alejandro Cartagena is an artist based in Nuevo León, and, from there, he has developed a particular aesthetic. He has several books to his credit, which have become increasingly radical. I love the ones about Santa Barbara. Subsequently he has made several that are innovative, not only** in terms of photographic language, but also in how he presents photographs in the photobook format.

HF: Cartagena's books could be previews of photobooks in the future, which—among other things—will have no homeland. Mexico is no longer Mexico: it goes beyond the Rio Grande. It is the United States, and much more than that. Nowadays, photobooks are printed and read anywhere, both on paper and online. The books on Santa Barbara represent something dreamed of: a Disney-like ideal that is actually occupied by a diverse multicultural and multiracial society, a kaleidoscope that is undoubtedly an image of the future.

POM: **I believe his most powerful book is *Before the War* (2015), about a town where the narco is deeply rooted. It includes a poster with "the good" on one side and "the bad" on the other, as well as intriguing booklets—all printed on cheap paper. A powerful vision. Another relevant character is León Muñoz Santini, who owns the publishing house Gato Negro. He prints small editions of political and conceptual content, close to fanzines. An example is *Satán* (2017), a photobook of images, three per page, taken during a tour around all of the streets of Ciudad Juárez, shooting one image after the other from a car. Five hundred pages of house facades with no human presence. Gato Negro's project is one of the most interesting editorial undertakings at the moment.**

This conversation was moderated in Mexico City by Andrea Celda Laurent-Atthalin.

Translated from the Spanish by Enrique Pérez Rosiles.

Pablo López Luz

Álvaro Enrigue

The first time I saw an image by Pablo López Luz, I thought that his work dealt with the problem of abstraction in photography. To register the mineral-infused waves of the volcanic-rock walls of Mexico City, in his series *Piedra Volcánica* (2018–19), seemed, at first impression, like a meditation on layers of texture and tone. It was not until I saw his pictures with fragments of the city's detritus—the bumper of a parked car, bird shit, a piece of a lamppost, regular trash—that I understood the artist's approach to be exactly the opposite: to make an index of Mexico City's skin.

Skin is the most obvious and most mysterious of our organs: it's a liminal fortress, our concrete connection to the world, the moving map that defines a self, the codex in which whatever beauty we may have interacts with marks of past pains. The Mexican author Margo Glantz has written that the fundamental document with which the generation of the conquistadors claimed the land of the Americas as property was their skin: the scars of past combats were the only inscriptions left of a confusing moment of which nobody else could give testimony.

Piedra Volcánica gives an organizing principle to López Luz's work and is characterized by the presence of walls rising from the original chaos of untamed volcanic basalt rock. The flow of the stone locked between the sidewalk's cement and the wall provides a means for a meditation on the ancient origins of Mexico City and its amazing persistence: an almost-seven-hundred-year-old town that has gone through innumerable invasions, earthquakes, bombings, and floods, yet always returns as a stronger and more brilliant version of itself. The unpolished basalt functions as the register of a past whose grammar we stopped processing long ago, but which keeps boiling in the collective unconscious, as our cultural peculiarity, as an open question about how the world would look if the Aztecs had won the war.

After years of working throughout Latin America, in 2018, López Luz returned to Mexico City—his hometown, and mine—where, the same year, Museo Experimental El Eco commissioned him to make a series of pictures loosely related to the museum's building, designed by the neo-Mexicanist architect Mathias Goeritz. López Luz started the project by documenting the volcanic-stone surfaces of pre-Hispanic and colonial temples, but soon the material of those constructions became the true subject of his research. Expanding on that formalist quest, he began to photograph the lava valleys left by the Paricutín and Xitle volcanoes, as well as the basaltic modernist architecture of neighborhoods such as El Pedregal or Ciudad Universitaria.

There is something uncanny about the photographer rediscovering an intimacy with Mexico City after a long absence by studying the persistence of basalt as a construction material in the metropolis's skin. I grew up on top of the same lava mantle: knees and elbows endlessly scratched by stone walls so treacherous that a soccer ball can be ripped if bounced in the wrong place. The danger of those rocks is not limited to their rough edges: in Mexico City you always have to roll over a stone with your shoe before picking it up because scorpions tend to nest there. But that volcanic skin, like the city itself, is tough and hospitable at the same time: there is that chill in the shadow cast by a basalt wall, its smell when it rains, the beautiful ways in which the bravest of seeds extend their roots and embrace the rock to flourish, letting us remember that no matter how hard the stone waves are, our skin is still the mark of our persistent individuality.

Álvaro Enrigue is a Mexican writer based in New York and a professor at Hofstra University. His latest novel, *Now I surrender and that's all*, is forthcoming.

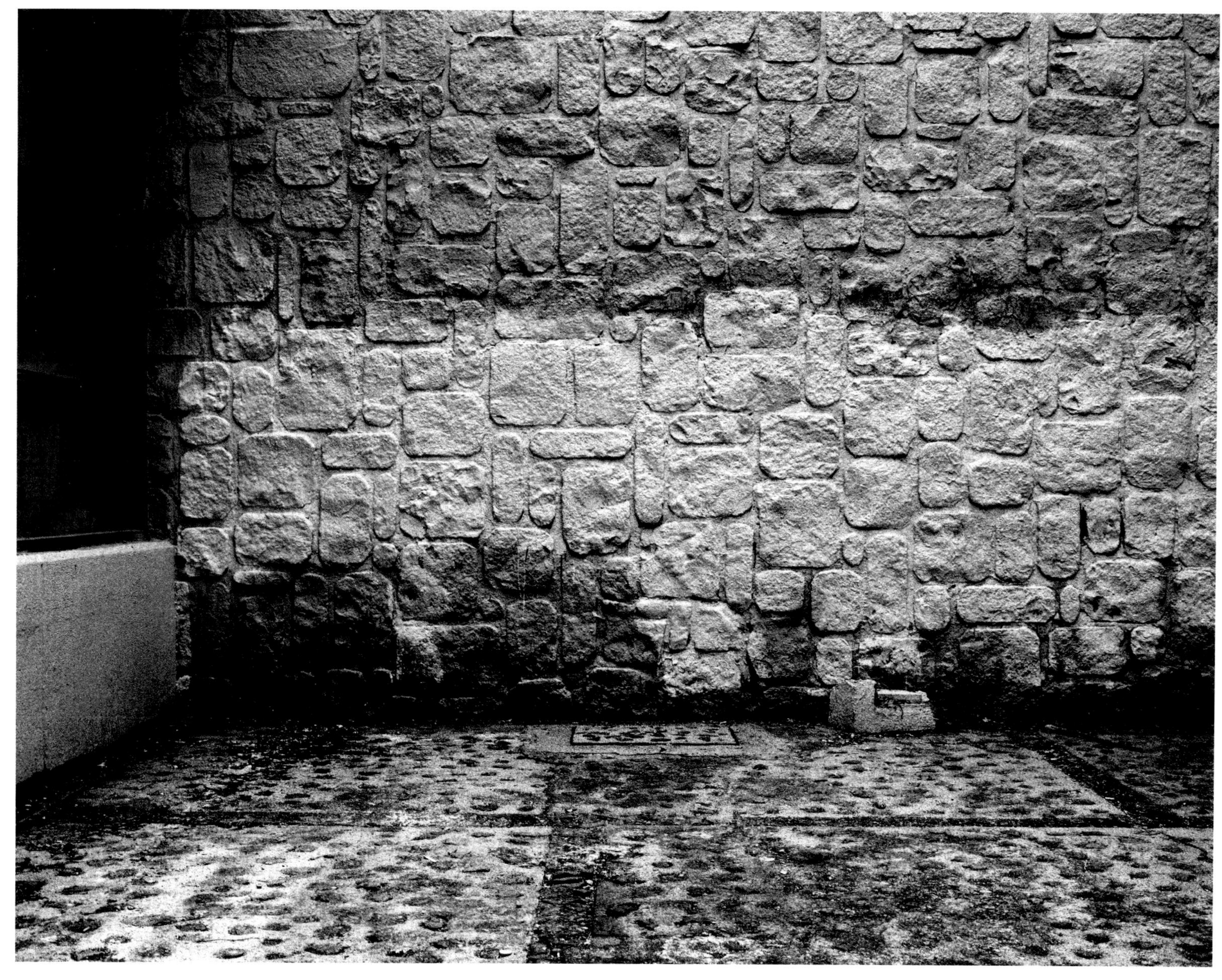

C.U. XV, Ciudad de México, 2018

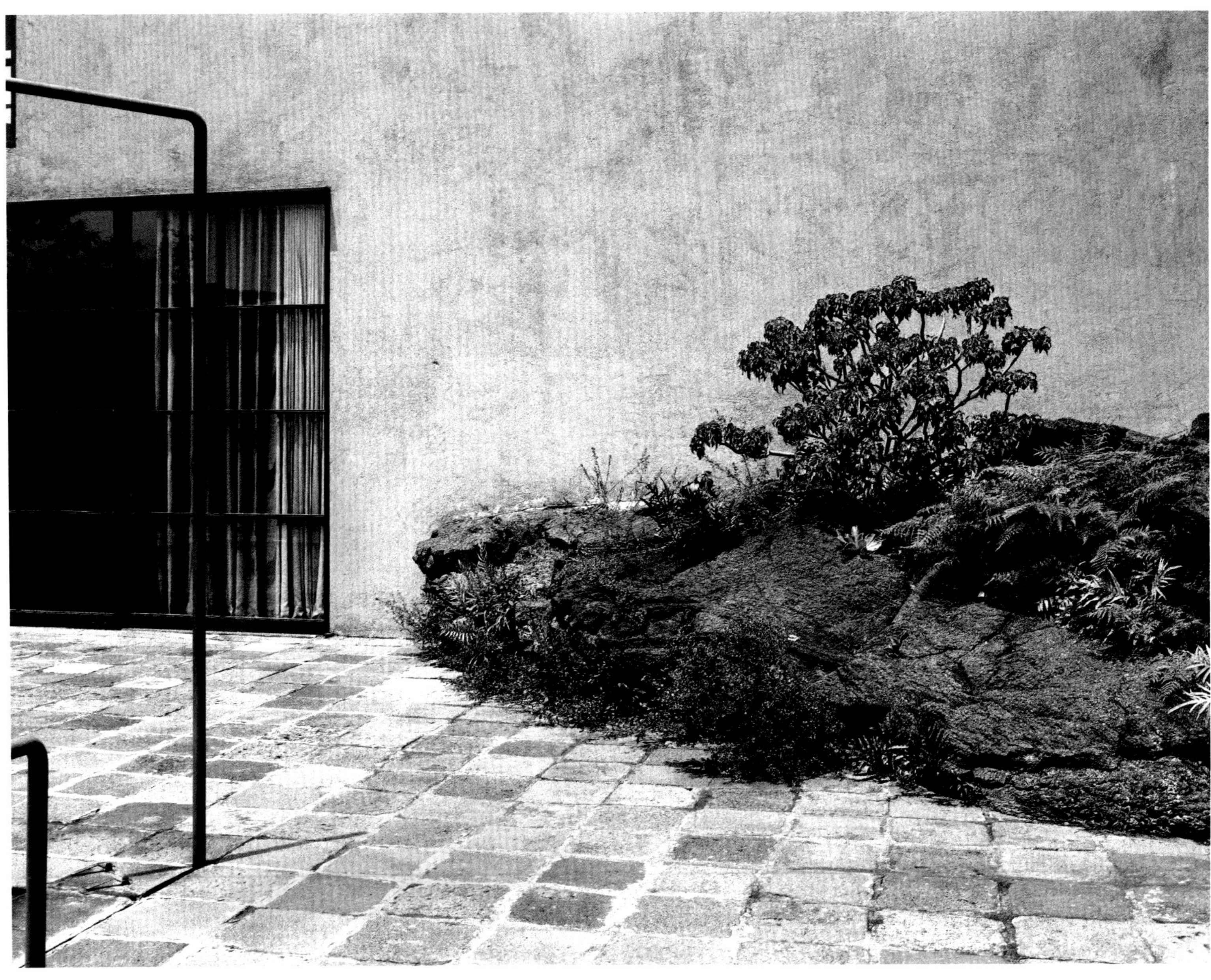

*Casa Pedregal II, Ciudad
de México, 2018*

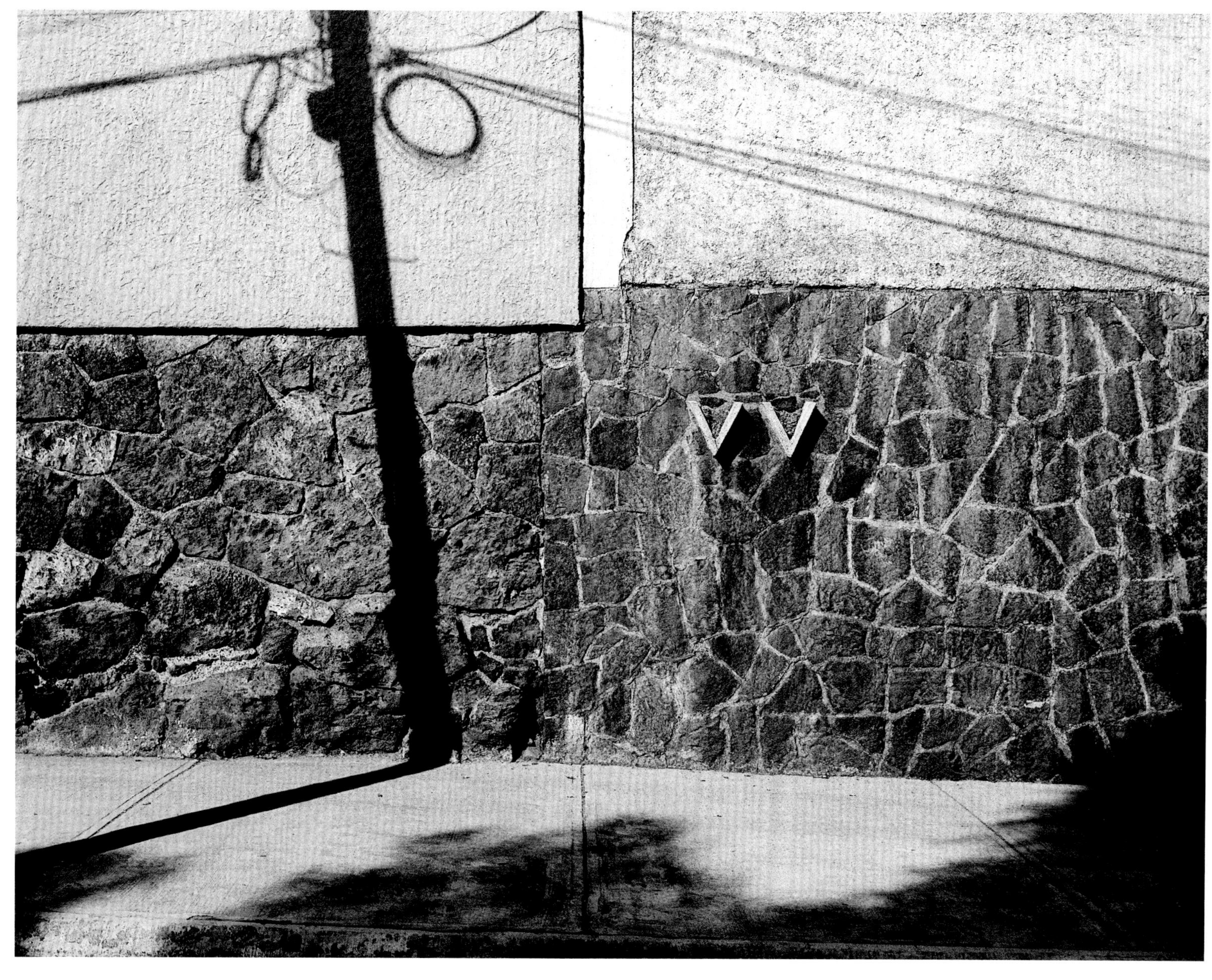

*Jardines del Pedregal
XXXIII, Ciudad de México,*
2018

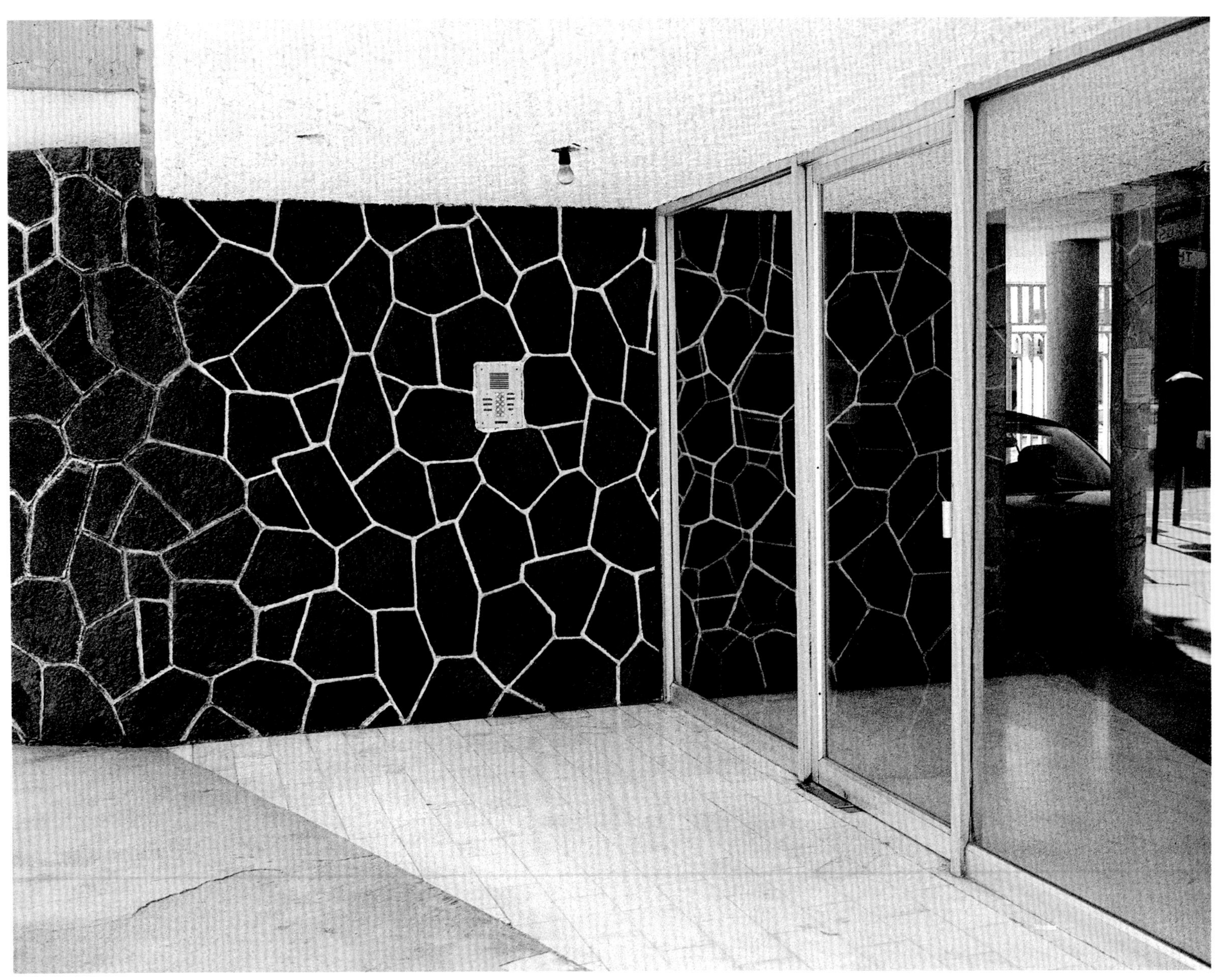

Colonia Anáhuac I, Ciudad
de México, 2019

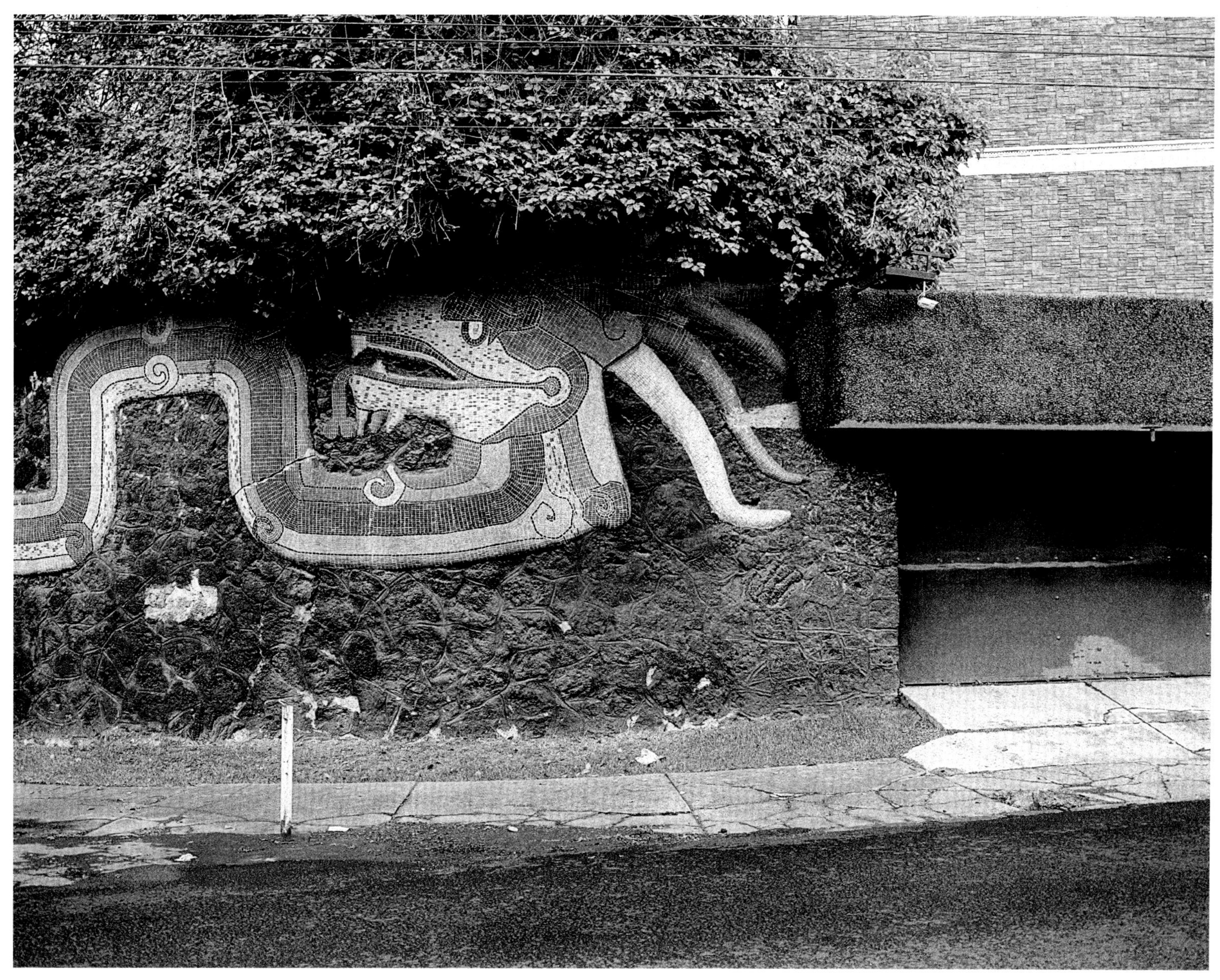

*Jardines del Pedregal
XXVI, Ciudad de México,*
2018

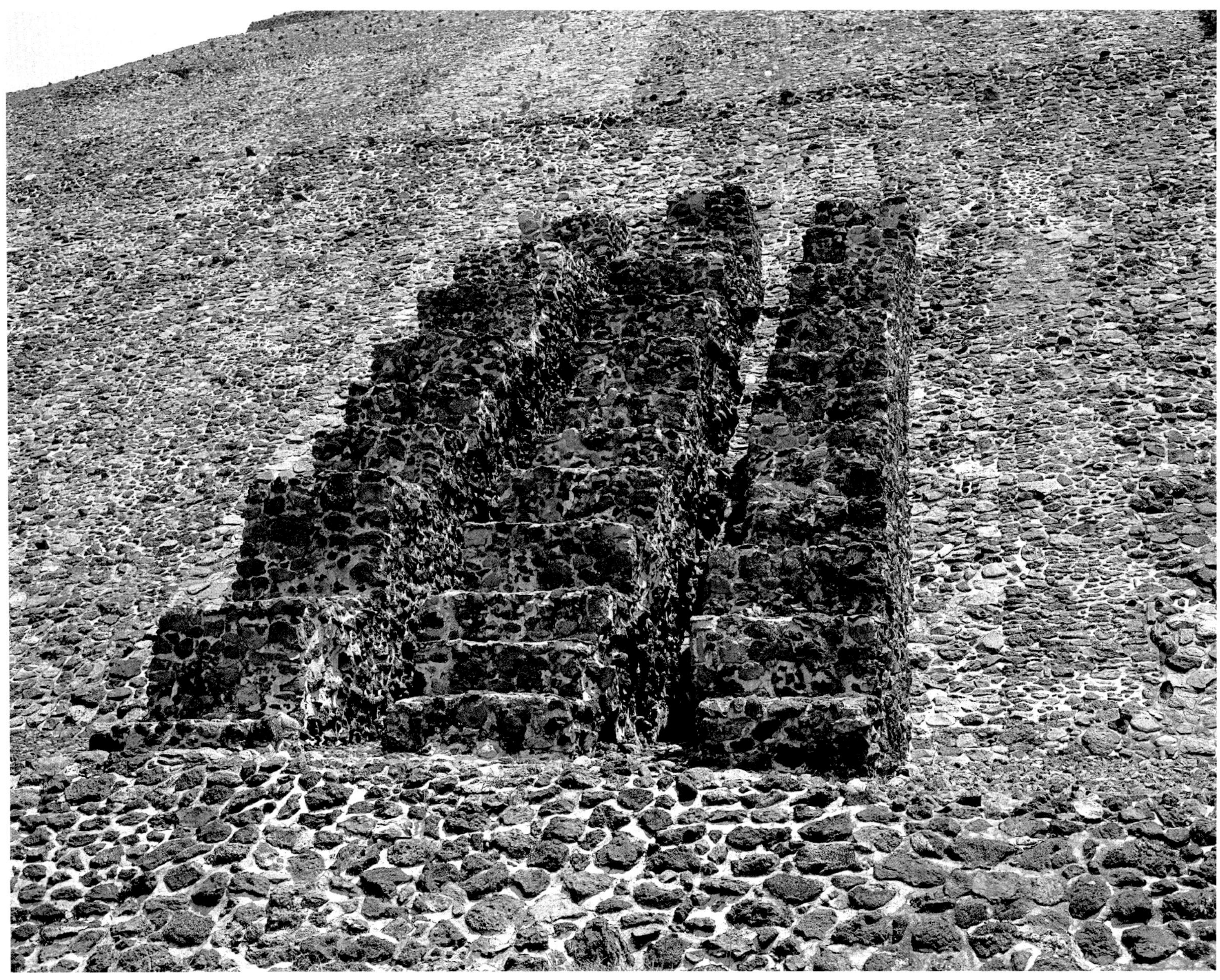

*Teotihuacán II, Estado de
México, 2018*

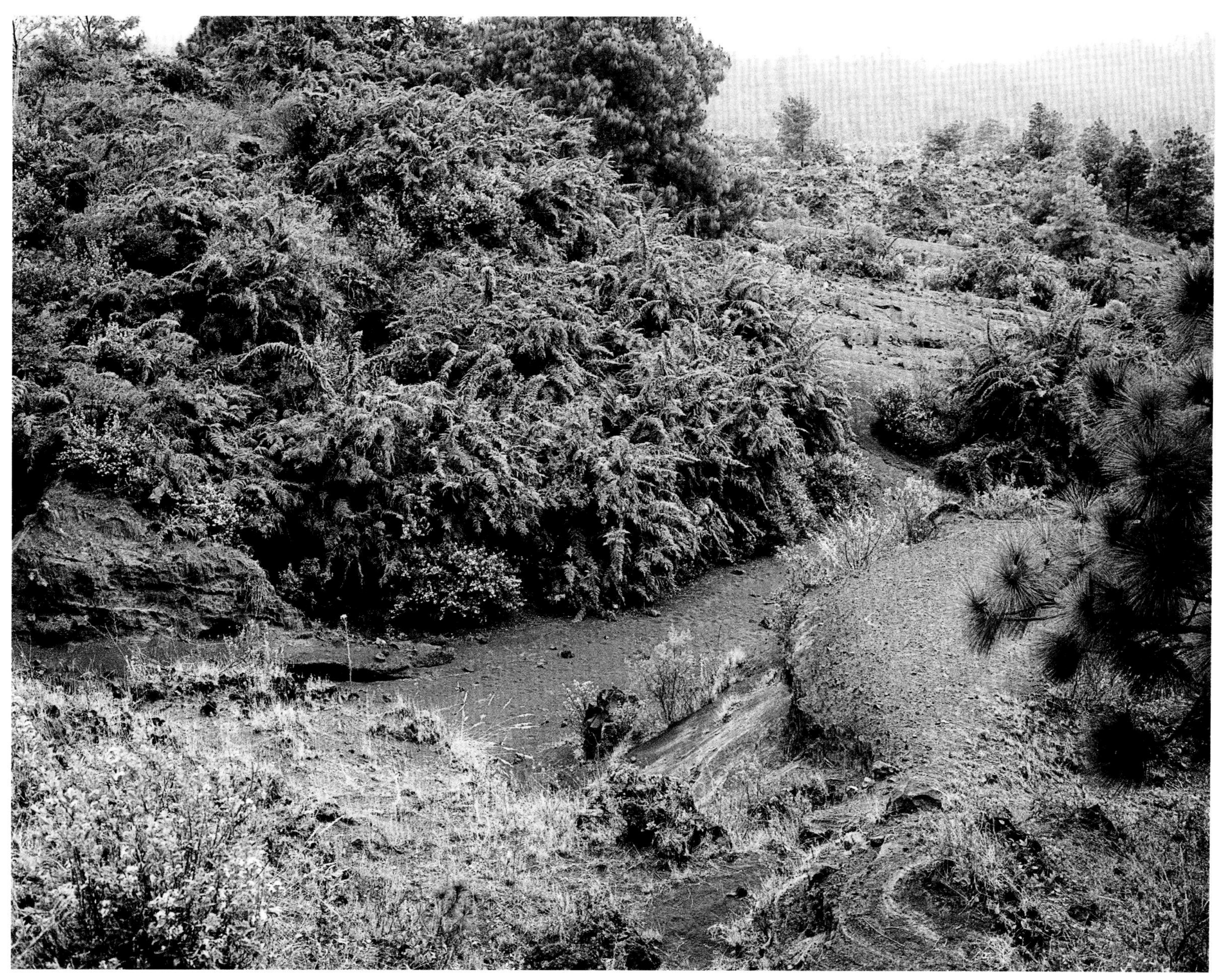

Volcán Paricutín II,
Michoacán, **2018**

**All photographs from
the series** *Piedra*
Volcánica, **2018–19**
Courtesy the artist

Miguel Calderón

María Virginia Jaua

I remember a few days after the earthquake of September 19, 2017, I went to see Miguel Calderón at a space a friend had lent him. We tried to watch a few fragments of the video he had been working on about the life of Camaleón, its main character, a strange man who works by night as the bouncer at a bar and, by day, as a falconer. But I struggled to concentrate. I had arrived from Spain to Mexico just a few days prior and found myself in a state of shock on seeing the damage Mexico City had suffered. I remember photographing the cracks in the walls of the house Calderón was using as a studio in the neighborhood of Condesa.

Calderón was born in 1971, in Mexico City, and produces work—antiformal, and a bit anarchic—that is distinctive within the Mexican art world of the last few decades. He often displays tremendous freedom when it comes to his choice of medium, working across installation, video, photography, painting, music, and writing. At first glance, Calderón seems to be an artist who avoids dealing with major themes such as politics, the economy, ecology, or colonialism. But upon close viewing, larger concerns emerge: one's search for meaning in life, the relationships between power and work, the energy of living beings, and also the underlying power of things.

In a recent video and photographic project titled *El placer después* (Pleasure afterward), Calderón uncovers the well-kept secret of a man—somewhere between watchman and indigent—who has lived for many years, without anyone noticing, in a space underneath the Fountain of Cibeles in the neighborhood of Roma, which, along with Condesa, was among the most damaged in the earthquake. The fountain, a replica of one in Madrid, was a gift to Mexico City by exiled Spanish Republicans to thank their hosts for their hospitality during the Spanish Civil War. In one image, the man's face peeks out, his arm propping up his head in the position of *The Thinker*. (Other pictures reveal the subterranean space beneath the public monument.) Calderón struck up a friendship with this person who, until the recent earthquake, tended to the maintenance of the fountain dedicated to the goddess Cybele, cleaning her and ensuring her upkeep. He also re-created a scene he had witnessed in which two drunk tourists from the United States crashed their car and went swimming in the fountain.

Whether because of luck, or serendipity, or connection, or empathy, Calderón unlocks and discovers hidden worlds, strange beings, and unusual situations throughout the city. Policemen on motorcycles attempt and fail at complex balancing exercises in their effort to create a perfect human triangle. A man swallows a young woman's hand, reminding us of François Rabelais's Pantagruel or Francisco Goya's painting *Saturn Devouring His Son*. A body falls through a hole in the asphalt. A finger is disguised as a Swiss Army knife. All are examples of the aplomb, accident, and sense of humor with which the artist constructs certain images. Sometimes his work borders on writing, not only because of its characters and situations but also because of the method he uses to re-create images he saw, or thought he saw.

Calderón's knack for penetrating obscure worlds and rituals is also evident in his series of photographs depicting birds. In these images, we enter a universe of people who dedicate themselves to breeding and taking care of falcons, eagles, hawks, and other birds of prey. This age-old practice comes from the East, likely China. Calderón's interest in birds goes back to his childhood when, by chance, he saw a falcon for the first time in a pet shop. He was so seduced and obsessed by the sight of this animal that, in order to obtain it, he bet his first creation—a one-of-a-kind bicycle he had built. Calderón managed to win the falcon and keep the bicycle. The intense relationship he forged with the animal proved essential in his period of adolescent discovery.

In contrast to the artist's more absurdist images that might make us laugh, the photographs with birds feel more serious. Birds are believed to be the closest relatives of the dinosaurs, and yet humankind has managed to train them. This symbiotic process, in some ways, means reining in and appropriating their animal strength. The animal becomes so merged with the human that the mutual submission arising between them is a kind of devotion to a freedom that, deep down, is known to be unobtainable. For Calderón, this existential concern manifests itself in a triangle of experiences and free associations—bird, bicycle, art—all representative, in their own way, of the aspiration to break free and transcend.

María Virginia Jaua is a writer and editor based between Mexico City and Madrid.

Translated from the Spanish by Elianna Kan.

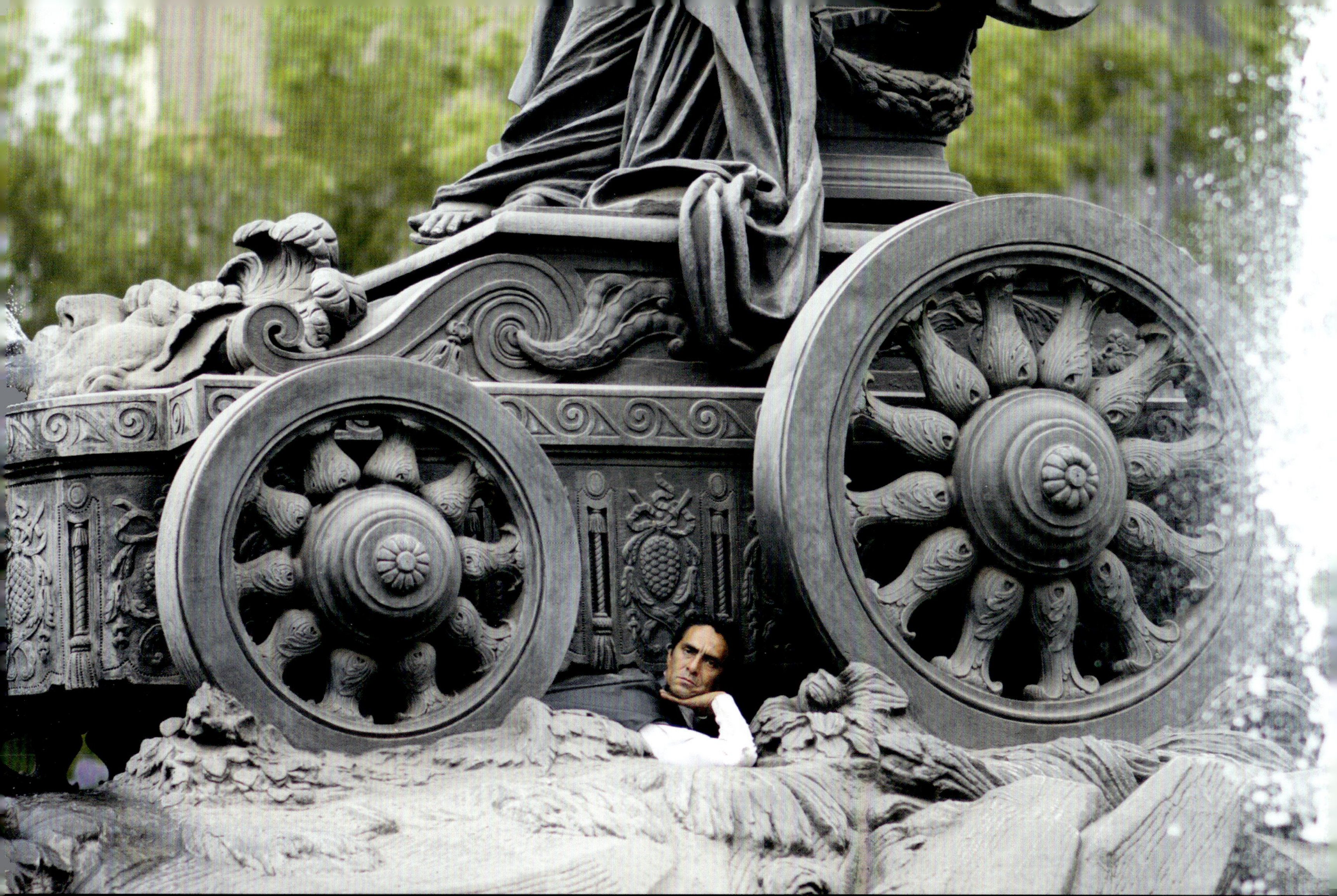

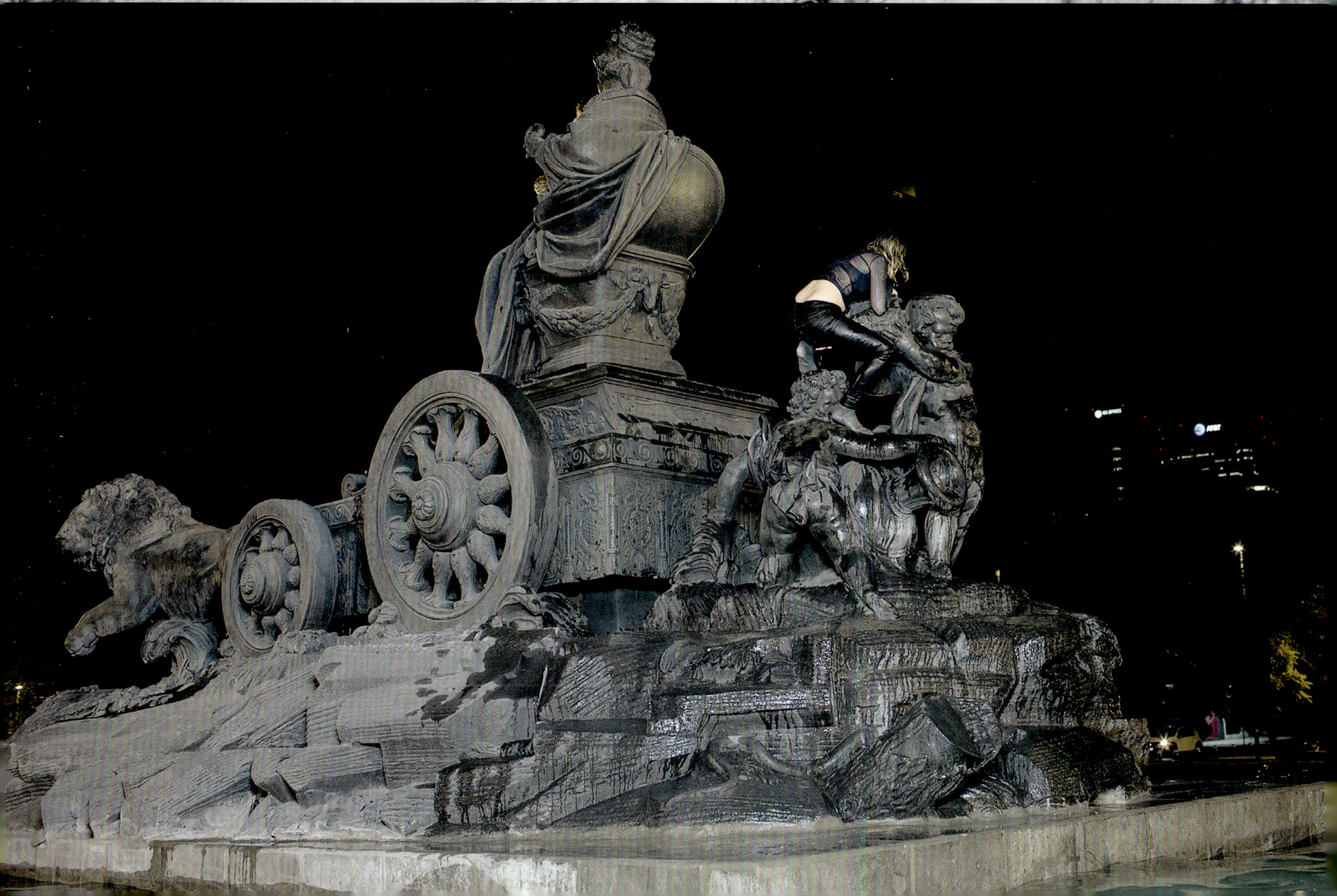

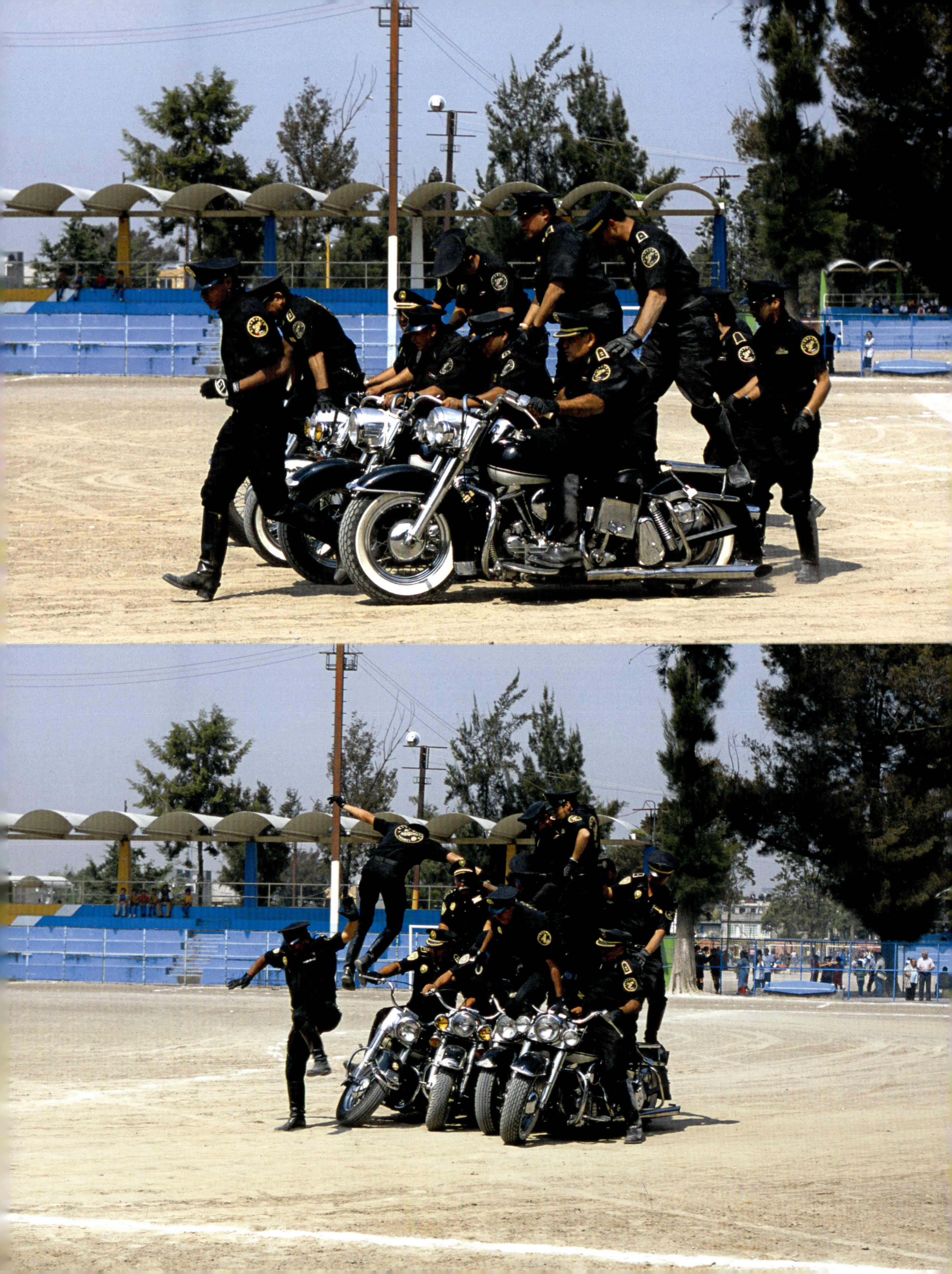

Page 61, top:
Cibeles 2, 2018;
bottom: *Cibeles 3*, 2018

Opposite, top:
Perfect Triangle 5, 2010;
bottom: *Perfect Triangle 2*,
2010

This page:
Untitled, 2012

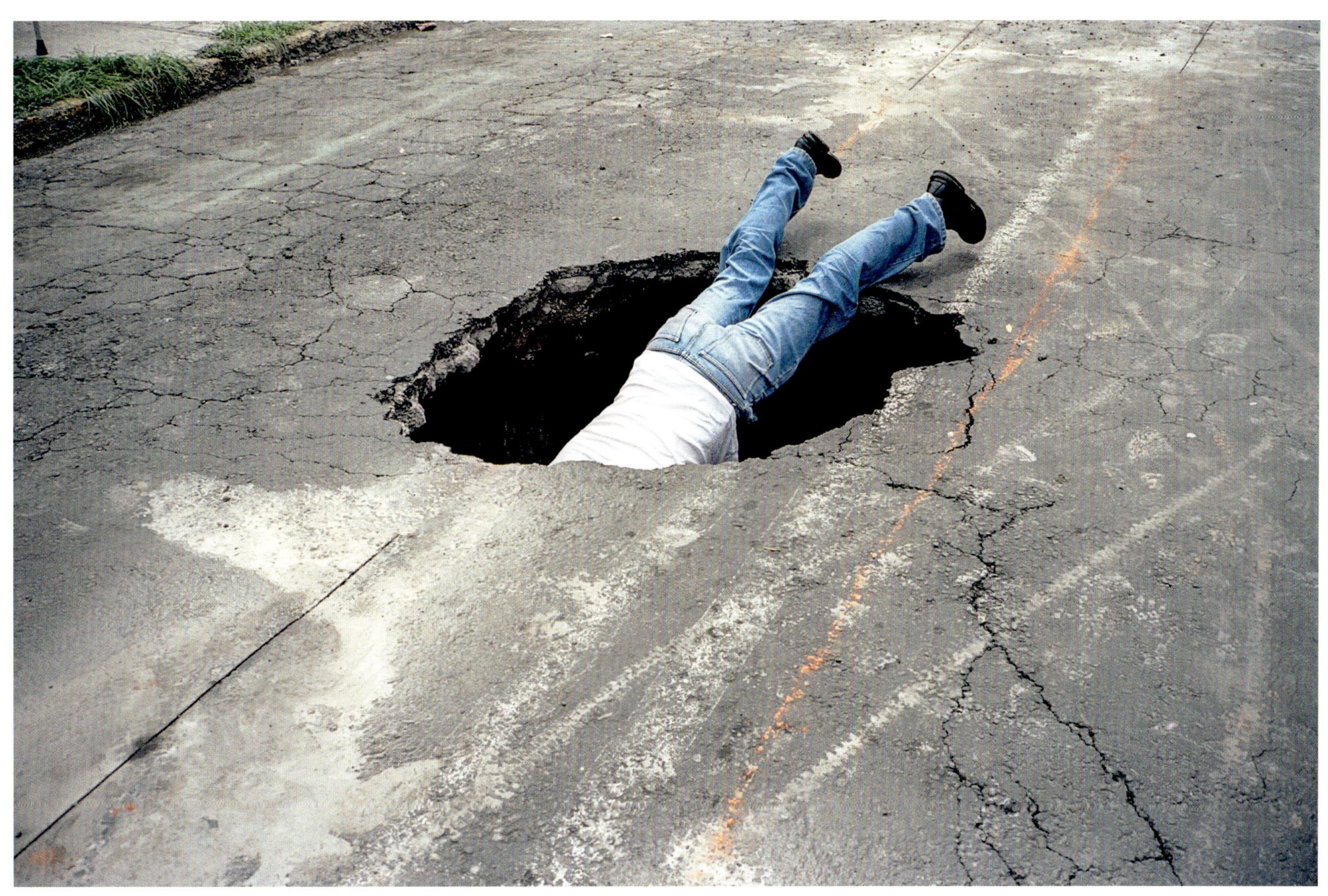

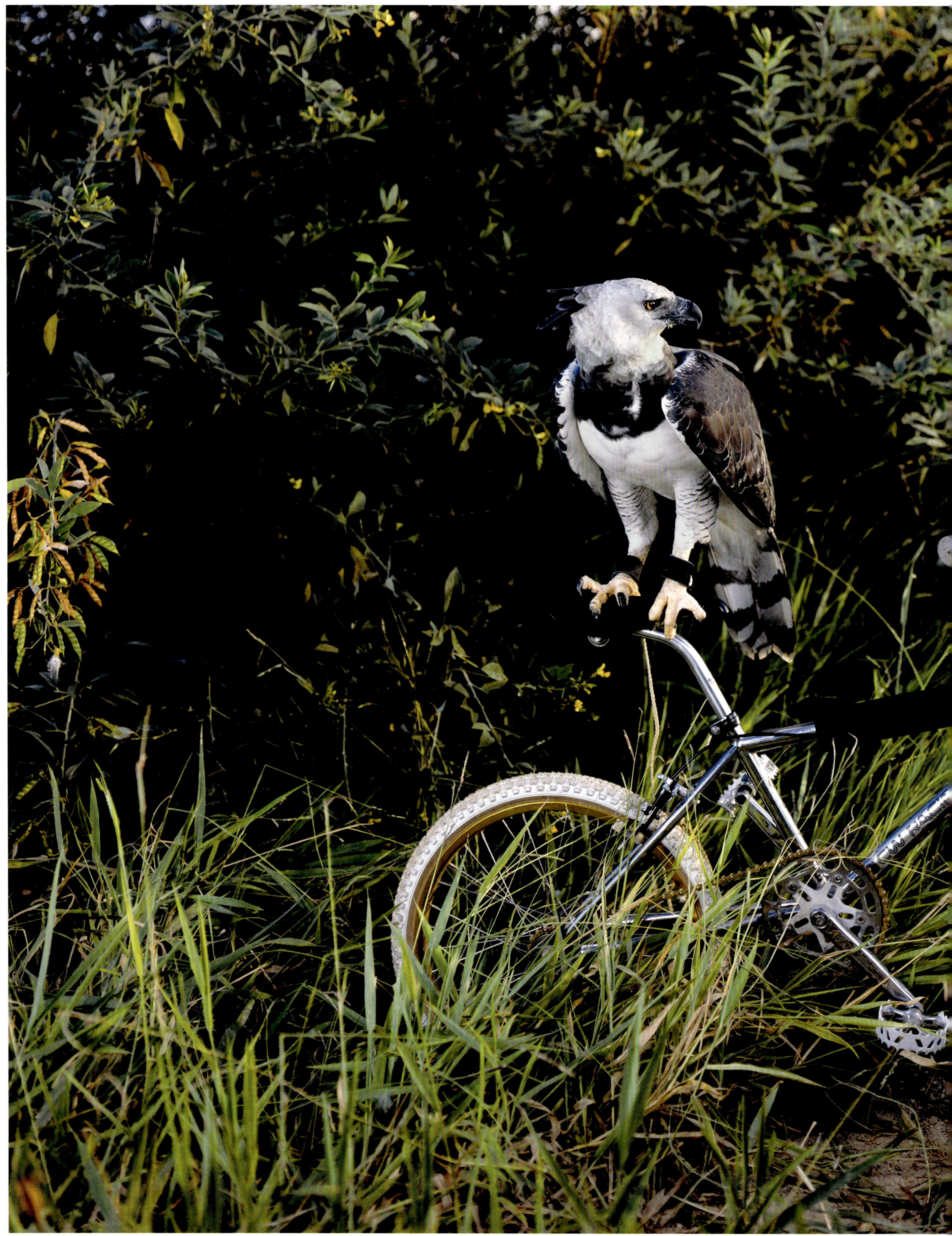

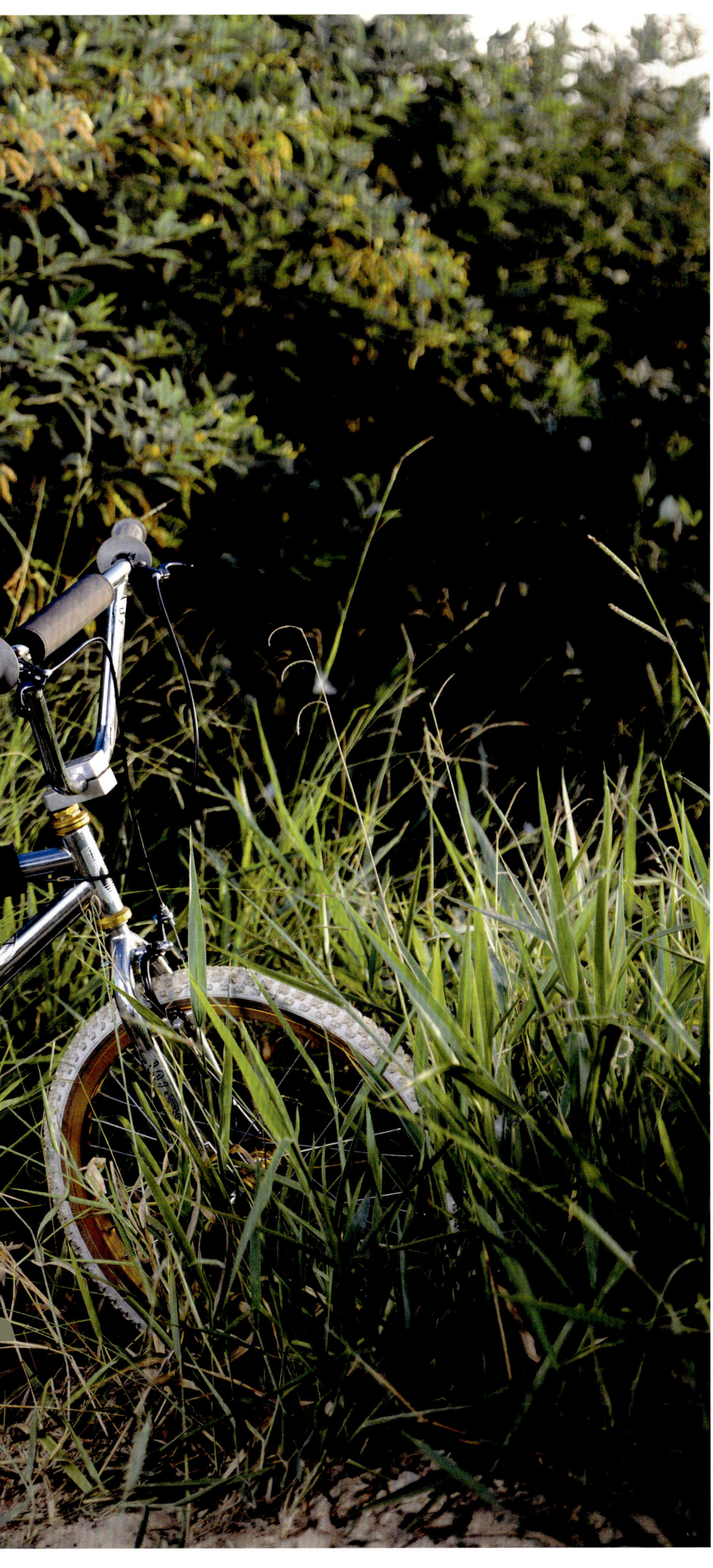

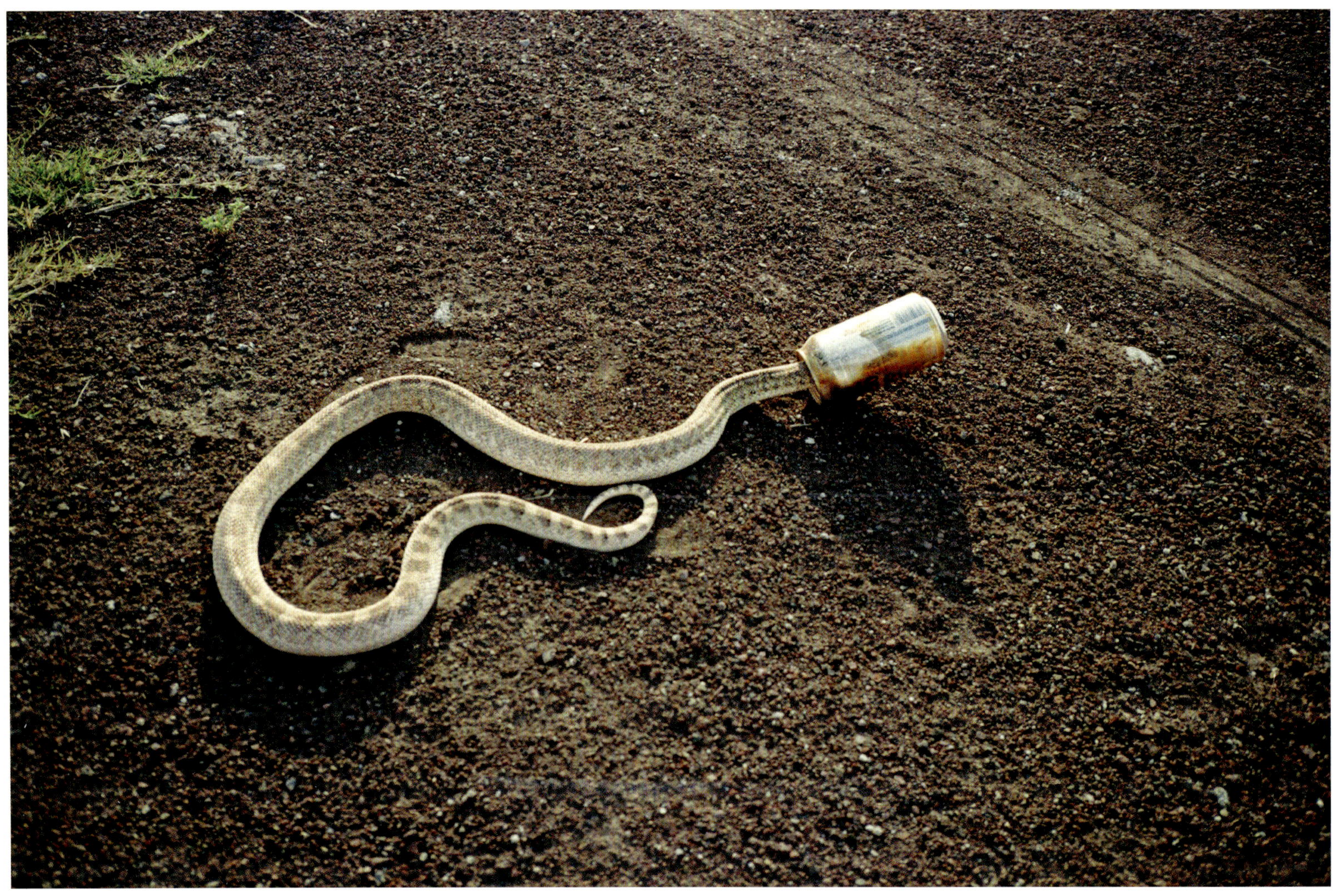

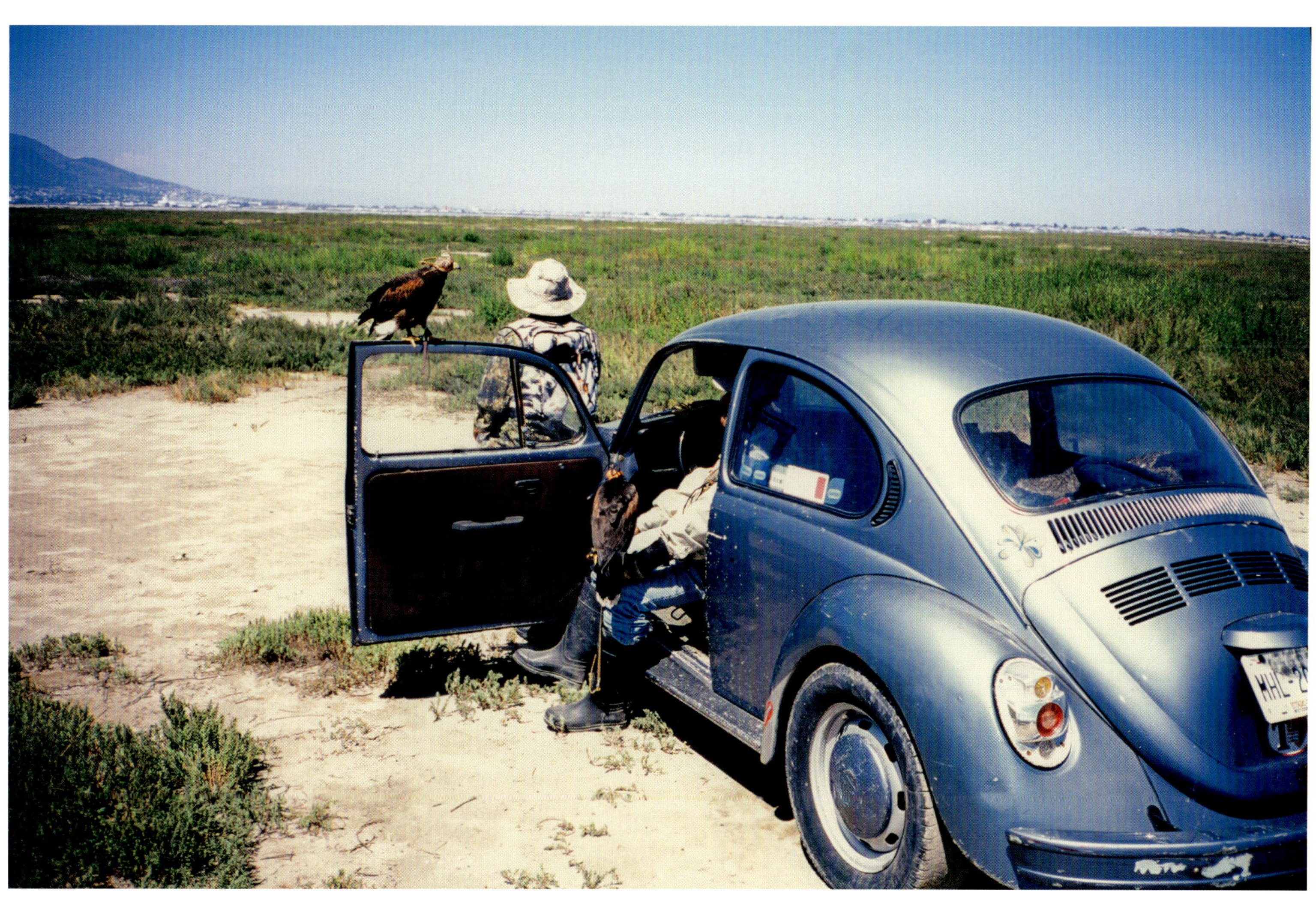

Color Scheme White, 2012
All photographs courtesy
the artist and Kurimanzutto,
Mexico City/New York

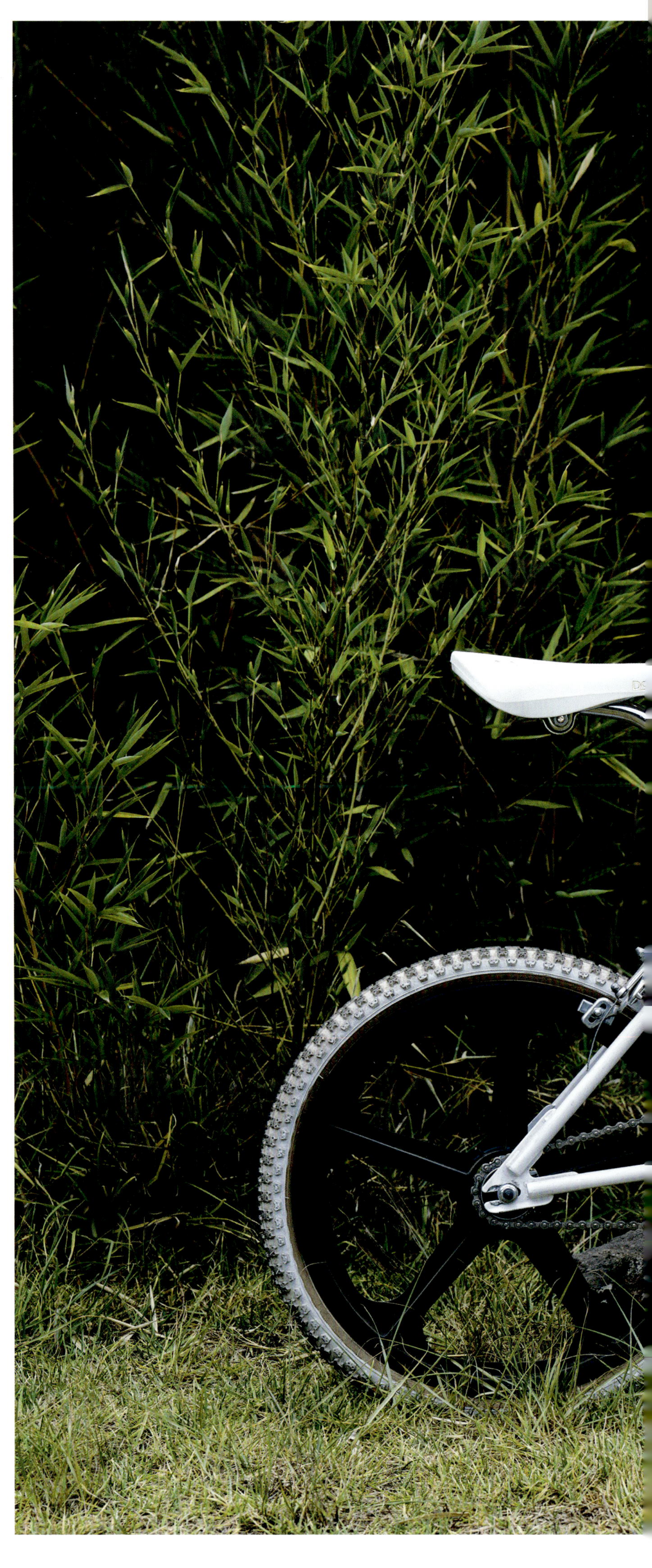

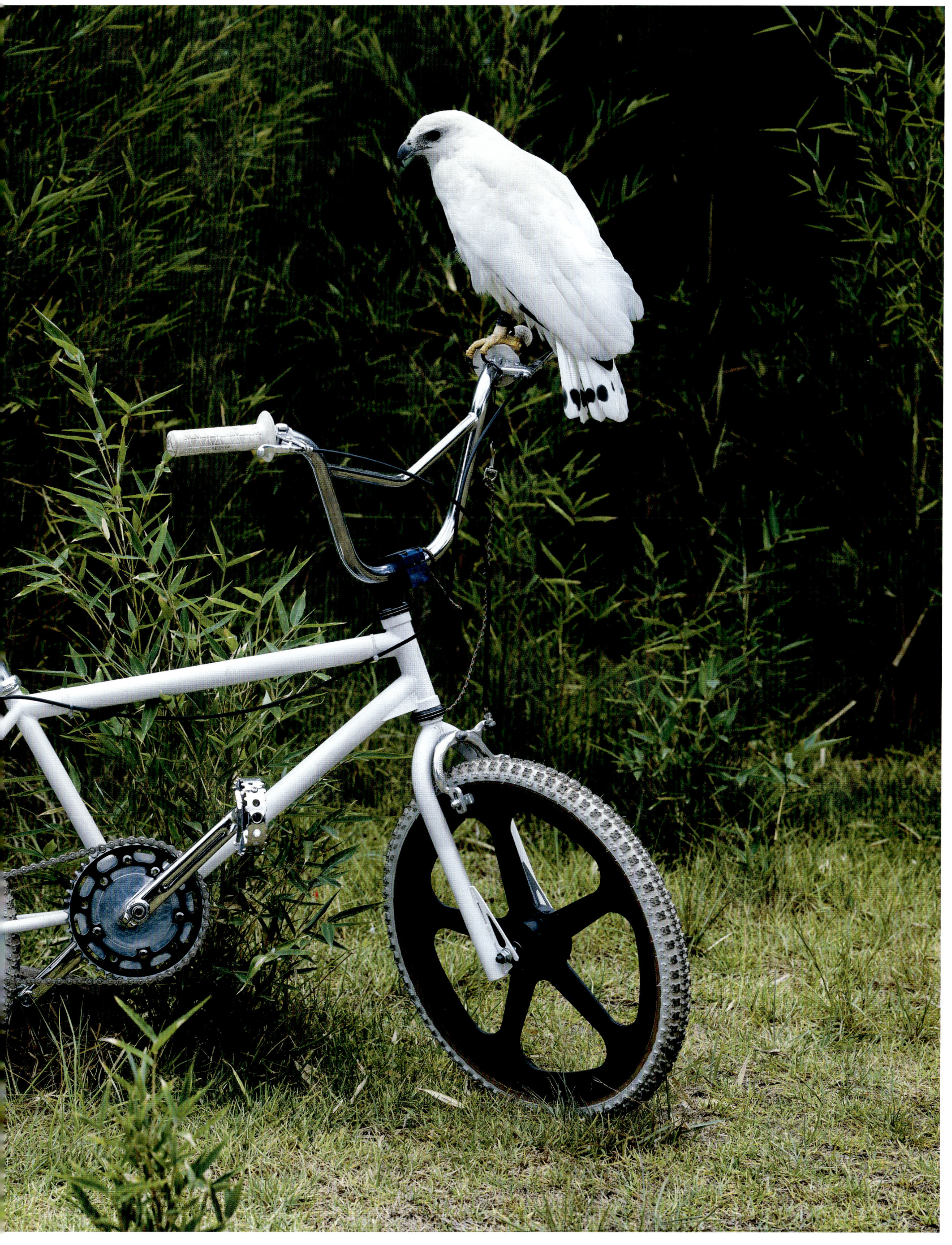

Gabriel Orozco

María Minera

Walter Benjamin described Eugène Atget as a photographer who "always passed by the 'great sights and so-called landmarks'" but instead was attentive to "a long row of boot lasts … or tables after people have finished eating and left, the dishes not yet cleared away." We could go on: nor would he overlook a flowery carpet hanging from a window to dry under the sun, or a bakery display with piled-up bread forming peculiar geometric patterns. That is, Atget was the rare kind of photographer who was interested not in human beings, but rather in the traces they left in the world.

An artist like Gabriel Orozco fits comfortably into this category. Instead of following in the steps of Mexican photographers dedicated, above all, to trying to penetrate "the country's soul"—as French Surrealist André Breton would say—by means of its people, Orozco focuses on the footprints of those people, or of others abroad, as he is a tireless traveler. Manuel Álvarez Bravo, in *Los agachados* (The crouched ones, 1934), portrays a group of laborers wearing ragged and dusty clothes, sitting on benches chained to the bar of an old diner. The men have their backs to the camera and the shadow produced by the metal curtain of the place cuts off their faces, making them appear crouched (with the double meaning of *agachado* because it refers also to people who allow themselves to be subdued).

Orozco, in turn, creates an image, *Sillas de espera* (Waiting chairs, 1998), that could almost be the same image, except in his work everyone is gone. On a visit to India, he captured a row of four empty plastic chairs, each one positioned under a dark circle on the wall—marks left by the sweaty heads of individuals who have waited sitting on those chairs throughout the years, now almost replaced by their own ghosts who sit patiently in that deserted space. In his approach, Orozco resembles Atget, preferring to show an unpopulated world, where there are only vestiges of human life.

The significant difference is that, for Orozco, all these traces function, above all, as sculptural matter. The photographic image is secondary. What primarily interests him is what is happening not as a photographic instant, but as a form. To him, that shot of a waiting room in India is only indirectly photographic. One could call it *collateral*, in that it accompanies a sculptural event.

Since the beginning of his career, back in the 1980s, Orozco saw himself as an artist whose working materials were not inside an atelier but rather out on the street. The type of sculpture that seemed possible to him was not made with a chisel, but discovered in the configurations taking place randomly in the world, without the artist's intervention—or, at most, subtle intervention. Like that mattress left on a sidewalk (*Futon Homeless*, 1992), which the artist perceives as a sculpture not because of its being a mass—which it is—but rather for the way it is rolled up on itself to the point of completely challenging the idea of a mattress as an object used to sleep on, and turning it into some sort of involuntary Henry Moore sculpture left to its fate on a New York street. Yet, Orozco does not take the mattress into an exhibition space—first of all, because he would need a moving truck. Rather, he takes a photograph that, while being a sign of something we can perceive happening in the real world, is also a signaling: literally, a way of pointing out that peculiar organization of matter in space, which is nothing but sculptural.

And, as a matter of fact, he sometimes decides to alter what is happening in order to precisely highlight the condition of an object. Another example, *Tortillas y ladrillos* (Tortillas and bricks, 1990): next to a gas cylinder, the artist finds a series of piled-up bricks. This composition could have been enough to him; these volumes of clay have sculptural traits on their own but, at the same time, lack specificity: they are nothing but towers of ordinary bricks, like the ones you would see anywhere. The artist

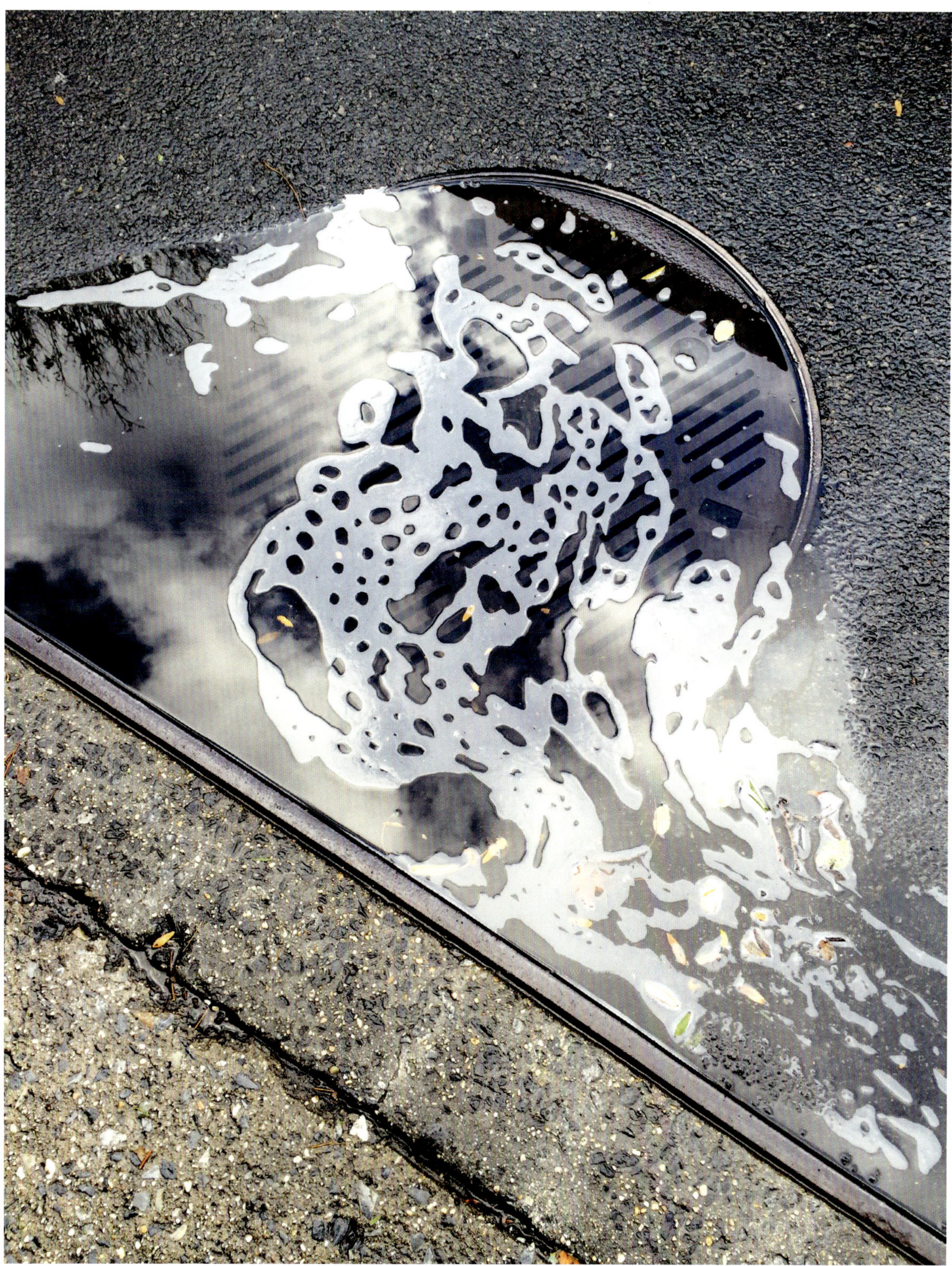

Top:
Sillas de espera
(Waiting chairs), 1998

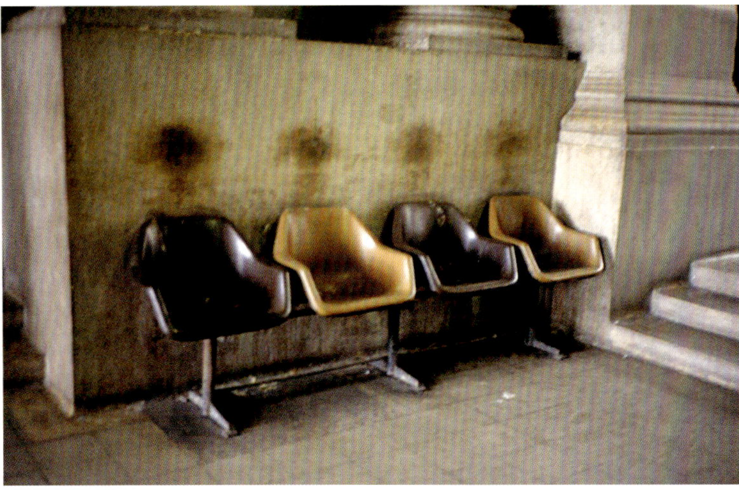

Right:
Tortillas y ladrillos
(Tortillas and bricks),
1990

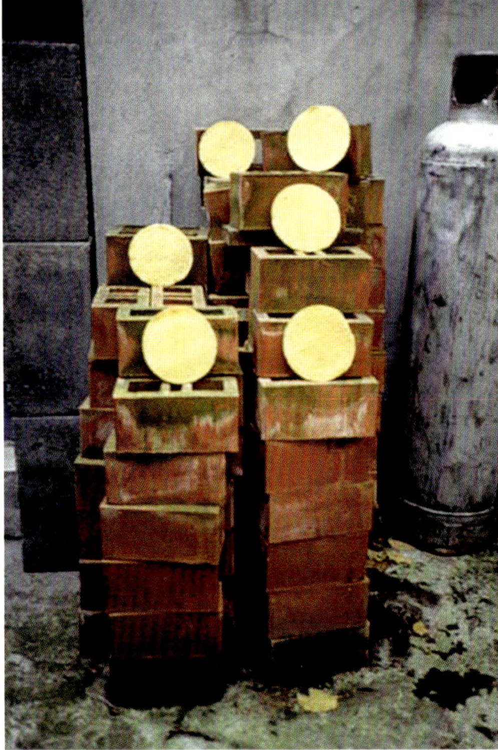

then proceeds to place a tortilla on top of each pile. A minimal gesture, but one that gives the scene that strangeness, bringing together, at the same time—as Benjamin would say—the absence of intention and the most absolute intentionality.

But is photography then not the work itself but a mere record? "It is the work indeed," says Orozco. "As, in some cases, it is the only way I have to present something, an idea, an experience. I do not use an image as a 'patronizing' document intending to show something important to the others.... That doesn't interest me. My intention is that the image presents itself as a chair, a tree, a fact: it is there." The thing is: that which "is there" is indeed there, but in an unsustainable present outside the photographic image. That is to say, it does not operate in the same way as does a statue in the park, which will be there every time you return. Orozco's statues are only there when he sees them. Afterward, they disappear, like that egg (*Sunny Side Up*, 2015) that has just been poured on a plate, which most probably ended up fried and in someone's stomach. However, for a few seconds, that sunny-side up could boast of being a colorful, viscous planet. Here we are seeing an image act as a transportable doppelgänger of a momentary sculpture.

It is the photographic image that allows us to put ourselves in the sculptor's place and see what he saw, from where he saw it. The gravity-defying knife in *Knife on Glass* (2000) is there, floating in the air, but only if one looks at it from a very precise angle. Look a few centimeters beyond, and the trick of the glass that holds it is revealed. In that sense, photography can be seen as a second act that, while closely participating in the creation of the form, does not stop being an ulterior reflection that adds, through its unique point of view, a new condition of possibility to the work. To Orozco, not only does photography capture, but it also sculpts.

Orozco's work is about identifying the sculptural quality of certain spontaneous formations in space, and also about creating structures that express their sculptural value only when being captured. Nowhere does this become clearer than in *Piñanona en el muro* (*Piñanona* in the wall, 2013), an image in which the sculpture is made half of leaves, half of shadow, something that could by no means translate into sculptural volumes due to the elusive nature of the shadow. One begins to understand what Orozco has said about photography: that rather than a window, it is "like a 'space' that tries to capture situations." This is how his images are to be seen: as receptacles of transient and fragile, nonetheless forceful, material incidents.

María Minera is an art writer based in Mexico City.

Translated from the Spanish by Enrique Pérez Rosiles.

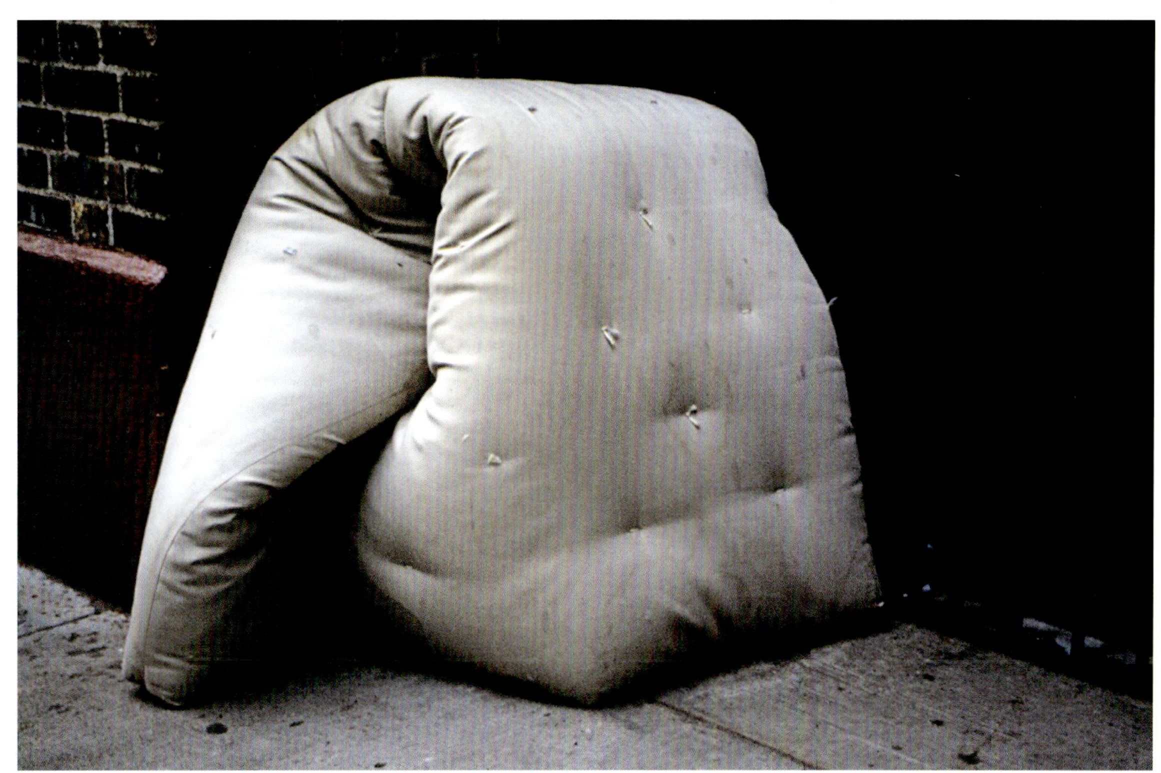

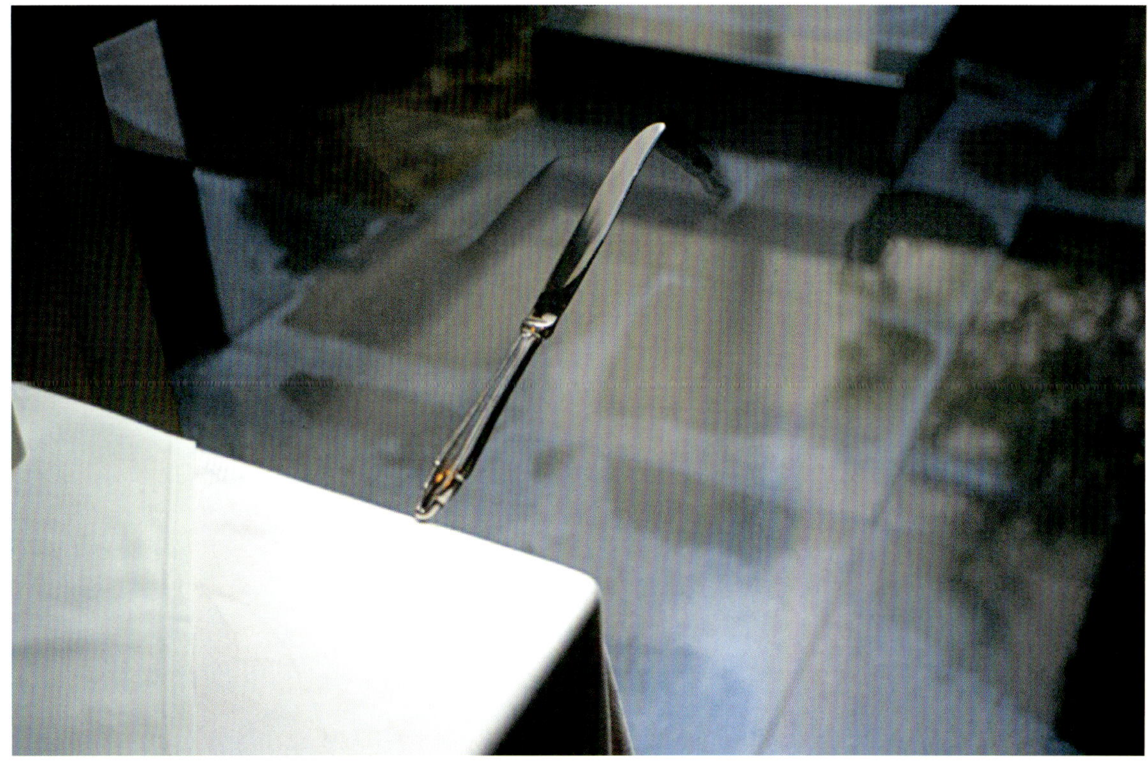

Futon Homeless, 1992;
Knife on Glass, 2000

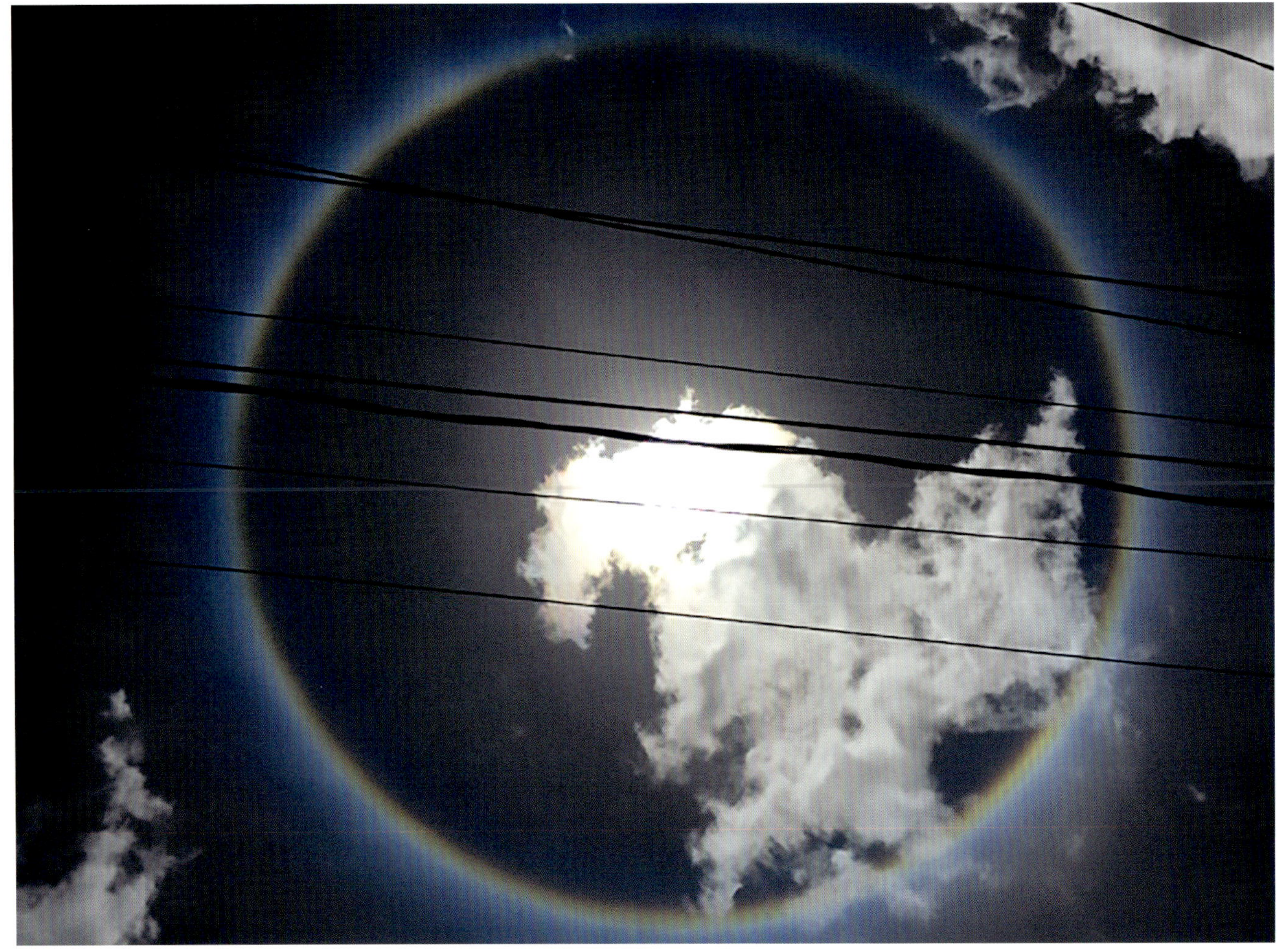

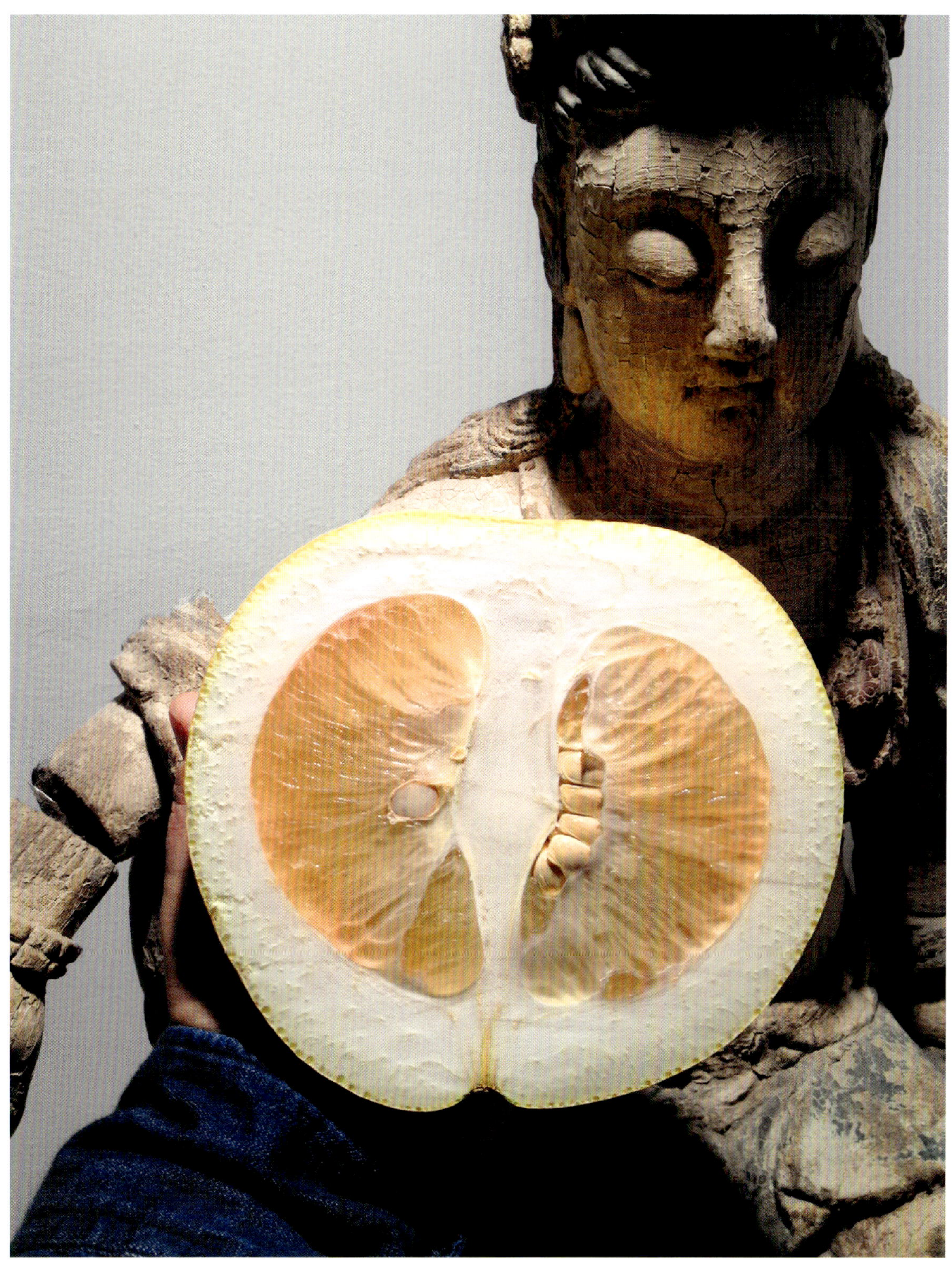

Pollo pescuezo, 2016

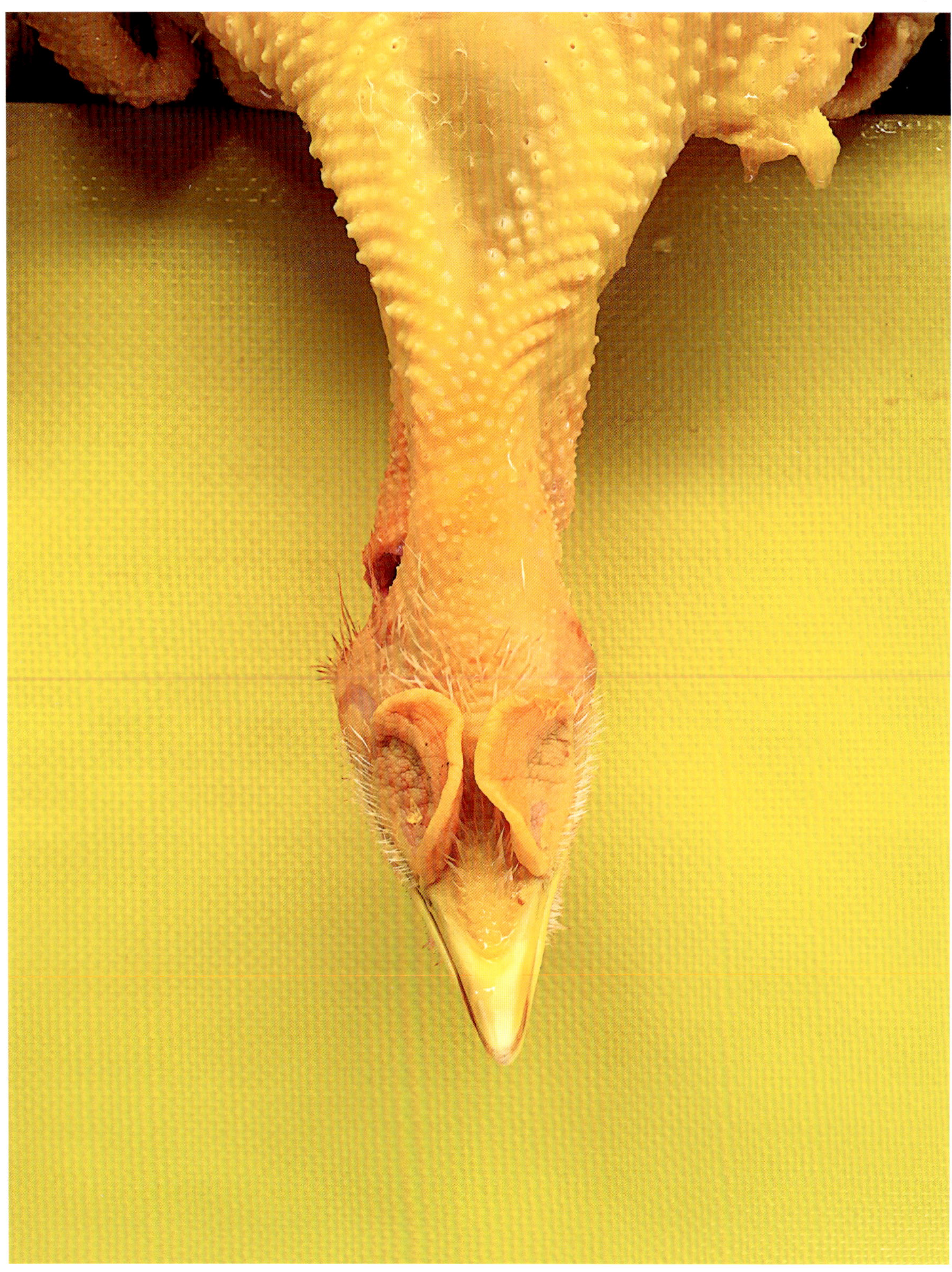

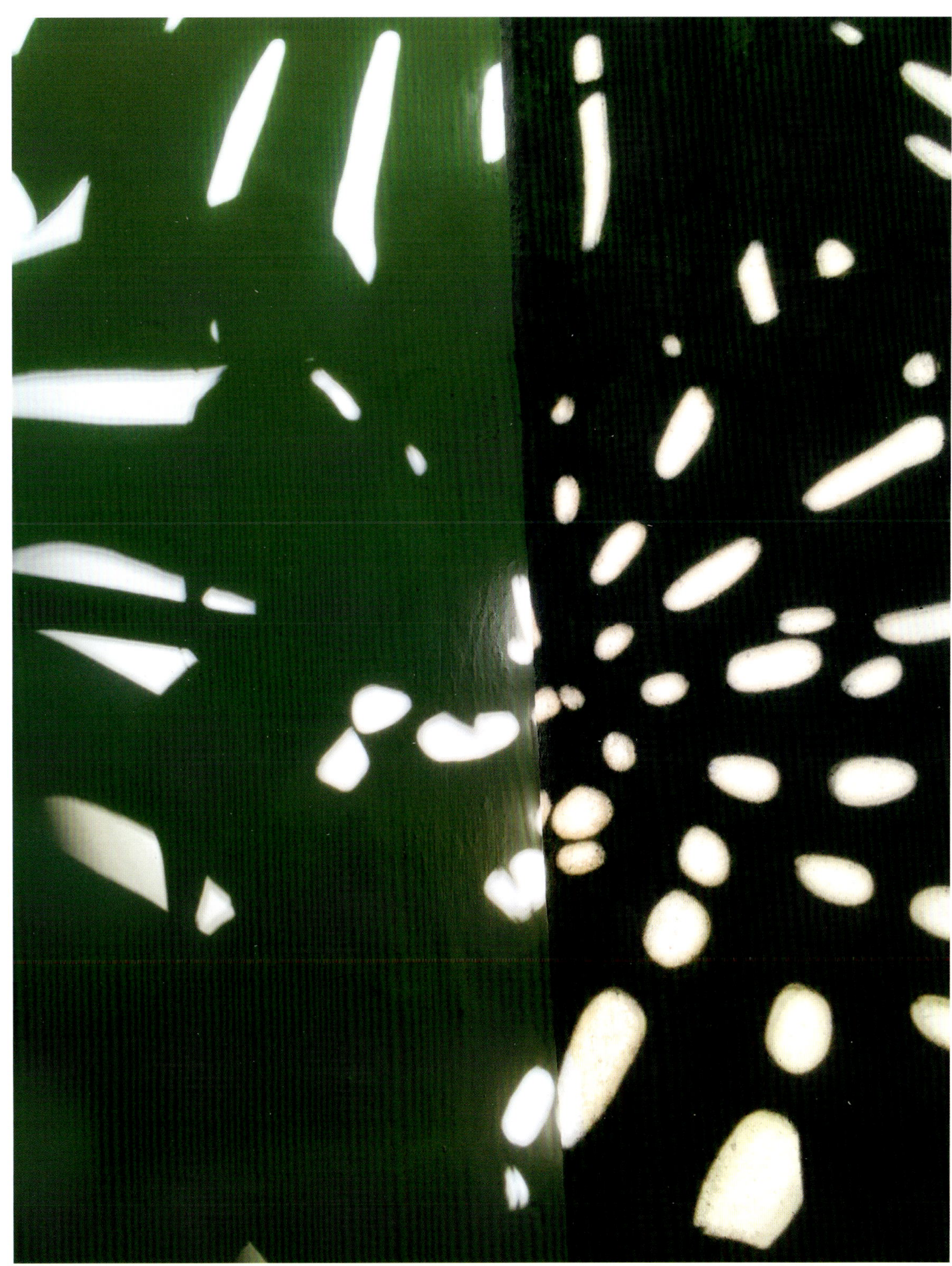

Piñanona en el muro, 2013
Courtesy the artist; Marian
Goodman Gallery, New York;
and Kurimanzutto, Mexico
City/New York

Lake Verea

Alejandro Hernández Gálvez

Black square. Not the one Kazimir Malevich painted in the second decade of the past century, but the one British physician Robert Fludd included in his 1617 treatise, *Utriusque cosmi maioris scilicet et minoris metaphysica, physica atque technica historia* (Metaphysical, physical, and technical history of both the macrocosm and the microcosm). In the book's fourth chapter, a square, not totally black due to the printing technique, has the inscription *"Et sic in infinitum"* (And so on until infinity) on each of its four sides. Fludd describes this illustration as showing, "in the form of an utterly black smoke," the raw material of the universe "without dimension or form, without color or perception, neither still nor in movement." This black square exceeds the limits of representation. Perhaps like Malevich's, it presents the point, first, where the representation turns into itself and, second, where it exceeds its limits into infinity.

The images of Francisca Rivero-Lake Cortina and Carla Verea Hernández, made by four hands and four eyes since 2005, explore what a photograph can do. Working together as Lake Verea (both were born in Mexico City in the 1970s), they expand the concept of singular photographic processes and procedures: from the way of making the image—sharing identical cameras with different lenses so that they can't be completely sure who took each shot—to how they are exposed in a space and how they produce their prints, the two deploy pictures in series and position them in narratives, always in the plural. Their 2008 series *Portrait of Mr. Luis Barragán Morfin, Architect, from His 1957 Cadillac Coupe de Ville* shows the contradictions of a mechanical ruin—outworn luxury, imaginary speed, the modernity of a now-antiquated car—that only by reference, in the semi-dark garage of Barragán's house, reveal much about its owner and driver.

In *Dark Rooms, Barragán in Penumbra* (2012–13), Lake Verea continue explorations of spaces in the house that Barragán designed in 1948 and inhabited for close to forty years. (The house was listed, in 2004, as a UNESCO World Heritage site.) Engaging in a dialogue with Barragán, an architect whose work has so often been associated with light and color, to the point where that reference has become practically meaningless, Lake Verea photographed the rooms at night, with no other illumination than moonlight entering through the windows. Some of these images may seem totally dark, at first sight, until we understand that we can see the colors of blackness and the delineations of forms as if we were drawing them out from the raw material of the almost-black picture.

Lake Verea explain their work as a kind of archaeology, another discipline that tries to draw light from darkness, whether defining time periods or ascertaining underground depths. Many of their findings are not graspable at a simple glance. It seems evident that each photograph—whether printed in a book or a magazine, or exhibited in a gallery—goes both deep into itself and beyond its margins. It could be written on their four sides, as on Fludd's black square, *"Et sic in infinitum"* … and so on until infinity.

Alejandro Hernández Gálvez is an architect, a writer, and the editor of the Mexican architectural magazine *Arquine*.

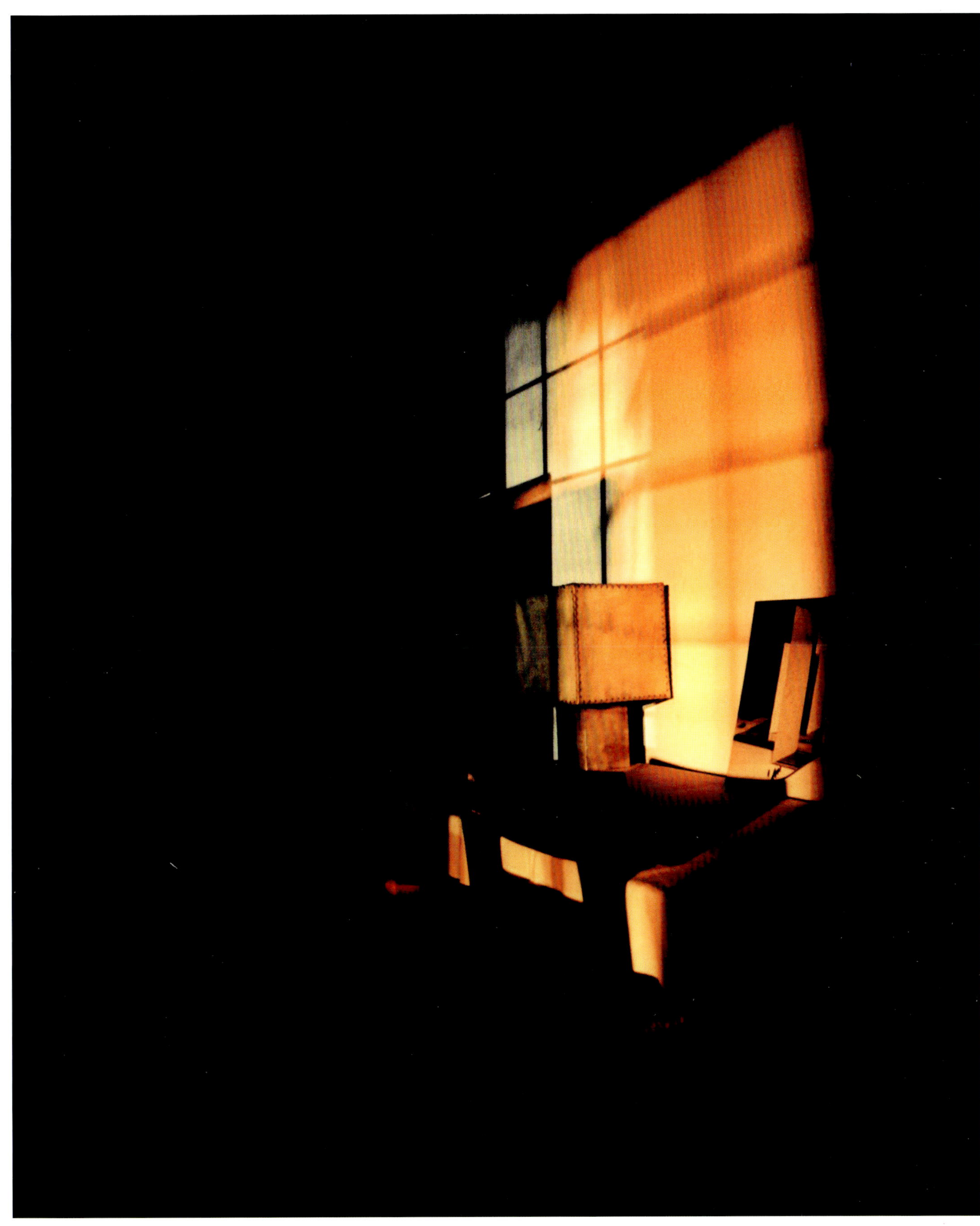

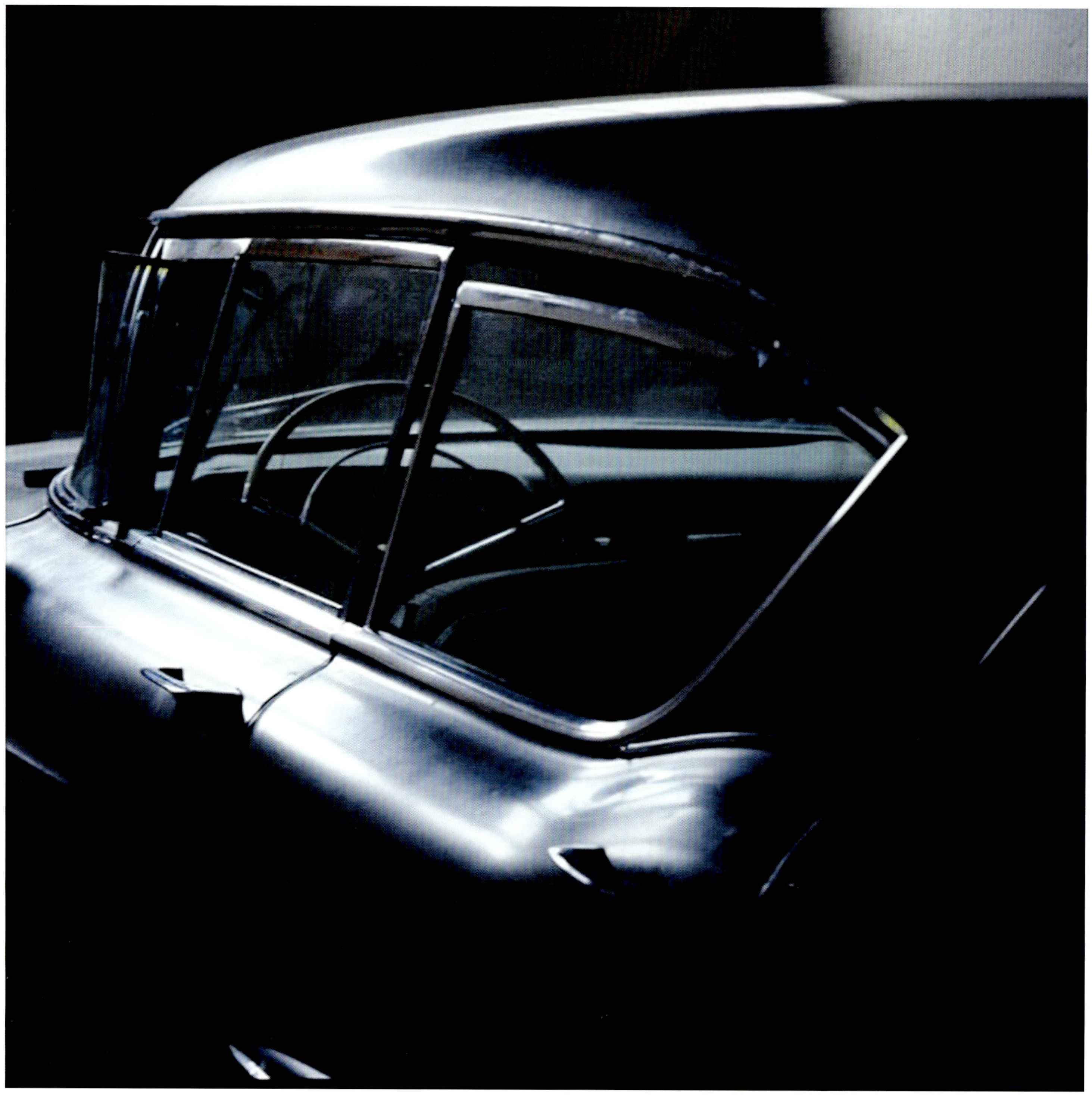

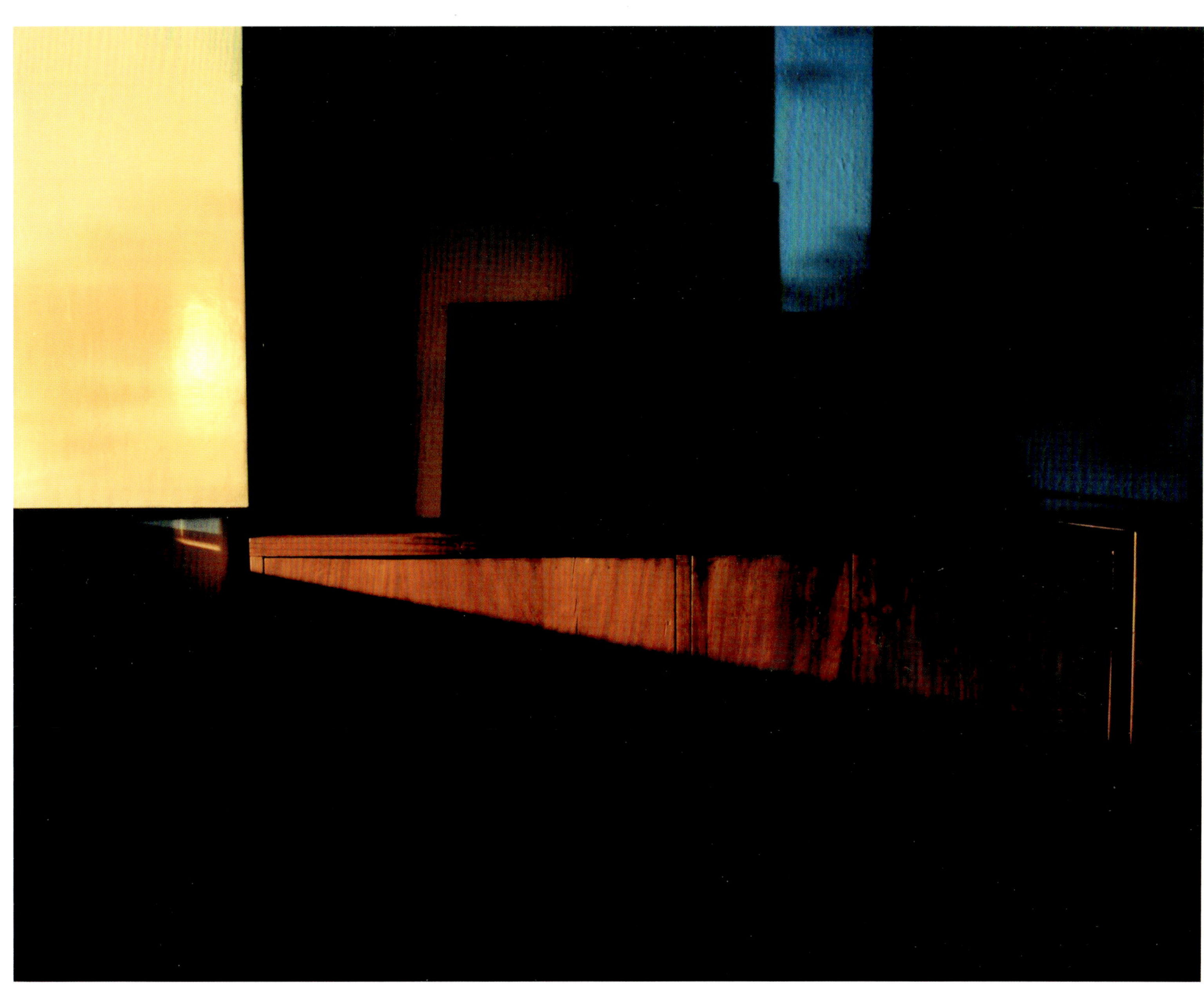

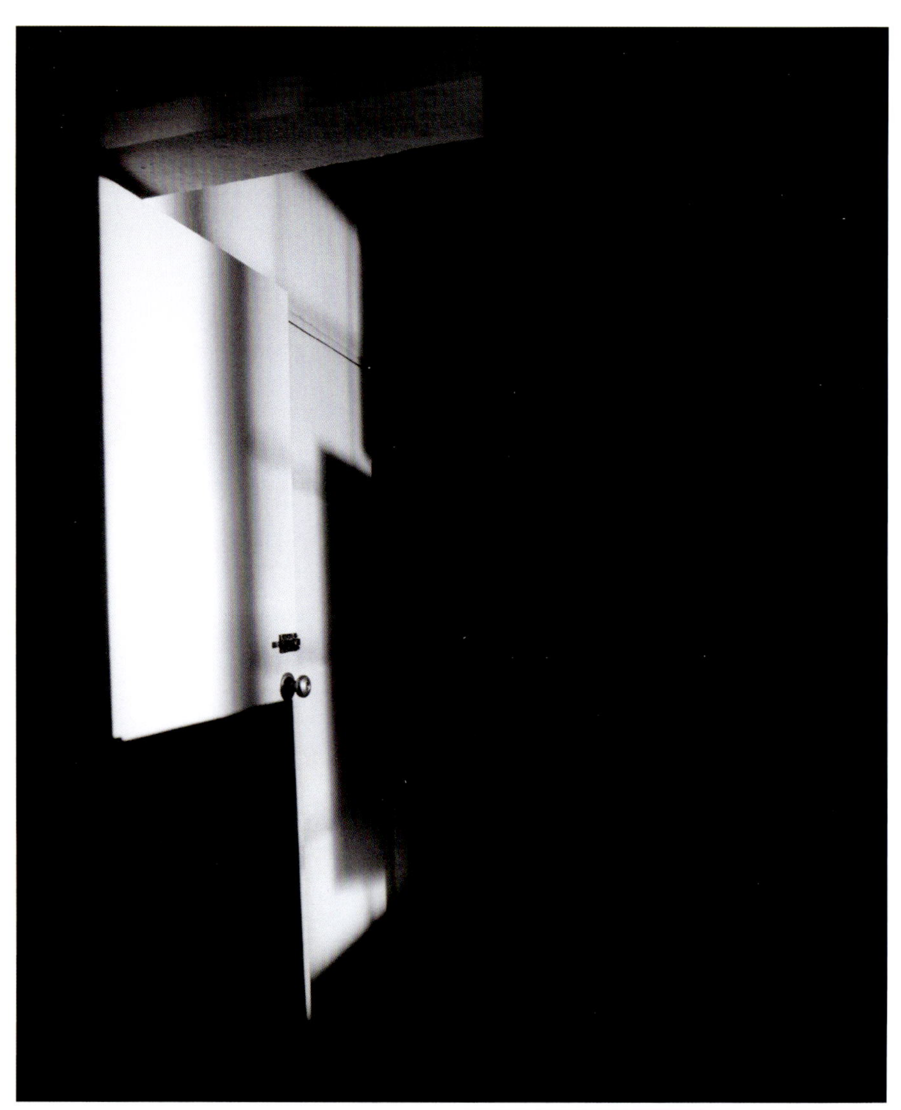

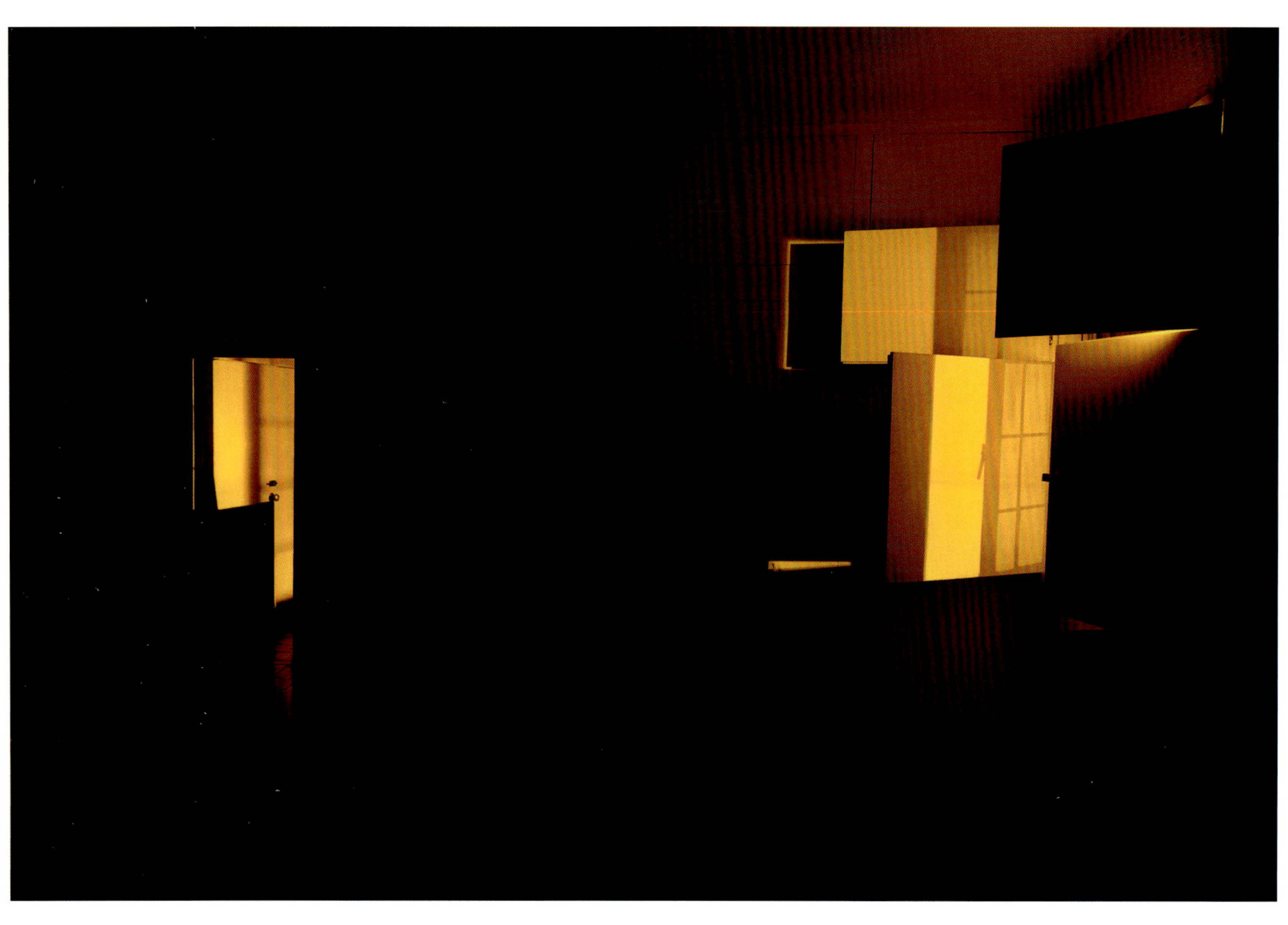

Page 80:
From the series *Portrait of Mr. Luis Barragán Morfin, Architect, from His 1957 Cadillac Coupe de Ville*, 2008

All other photographs from the series *Dark Rooms, Barragán in Penumbra*, 2012–13
Courtesy the artists

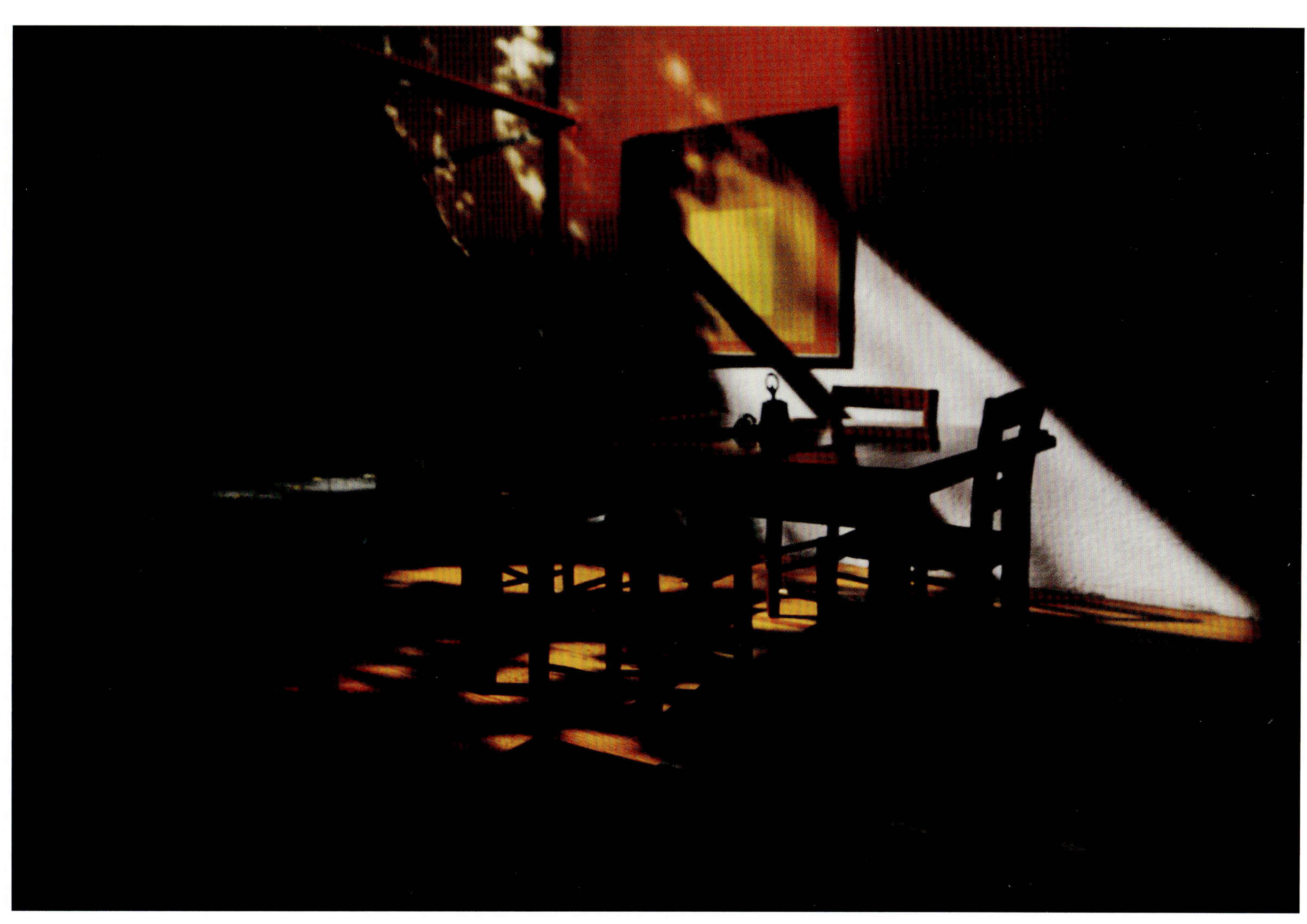

Melba Arellano

Mario Ballesteros

There are cities that embrace change with a particular enthusiasm: quick to wipe out traces of anything that feels even remotely out-of-date, constantly refurbishing, rebuilding, and reinventing themselves. Other cities seem burdened by history or nostalgia, permanently stuck in the frame of the past. Mexico City can't make up its mind. We are quick to adopt the new but never let go of the old.

Whatever lands in Mexico City never leaves: bebop and boleros, perms and plastic stretchy hair bands, pachucos and cholas, Formica counters and leatherette stools, German street organs and candied apples, gold teeth and Sunday picnics, peach-colored wallpaper and bright-blue eye shadow, hand lettering and feathered crowns, shiny polyester slacks and zebra prints, plastic flowers and fiberglass chairs, printed holograms and cock fights, Datsuns and Galaxies, Hi-NRG dance crews and imitation-Warriors gangbangers, religious processions and massive mosh pits, medieval social hierarchies and racial stratification, baroque brought back on Churrigueresque steroids, shawarma turned tacos al pastor, goths versus emos, a fervor for ancient stone idols or flesh-and-bone pop idols that never die.

Cities either change or die out. Mexico City only saturates and superimposes itself onto an atemporal mess. Photography typically attempts to capture a specific moment in time. Melba Arellano, on the other hand, manages to portray the physical and metaphysical time lags that are an everyday occurrence in Mexico City.

Without resorting to visual clichés, Arellano, who was born in Mexico City in 1977, scours the traditional barrios of the town's center—many of which have been hit by an onslaught of gentrification and real estate speculation in the past decade—tracking down leftover or marginal examples of normalcy from previous lives. A man sitting at the exact same desk since 1977. A woman sporting a hairdo that was all the rage in 1983. A particularly pale spot on a weary carpet where someone collapsed and died in the 1950s. A skirt first worn in 1994. The day before the crash of the peso. Arellano zooms in on these details, at once banal and transcendental, that completely escape most people's perception in the bustle of day-to-day interactions.

Arellano's candid portraits of people, shop fronts, and unassuming intimate interiors are existential pauses that shine light on an odd persistence, on the pointless resiliency of cultural plethora and human accident. These snapshots become instantly timeless by registering bits and pieces of the present, the past, and the unforeseen future contained in those very same fragments. Adopting slightly theatrical and slightly uncomfortable poses in front of slightly makeshift backdrops that celebrate idiosyncrasy and popular taste, her characters seem perfectly dressed up and made up to play their part in this everyday theater that repeats itself over and over and over again, and that we like to think of as real life.

Mario Ballesteros is editor in chief of *Travesías*, a Mexican travel and culture magazine.

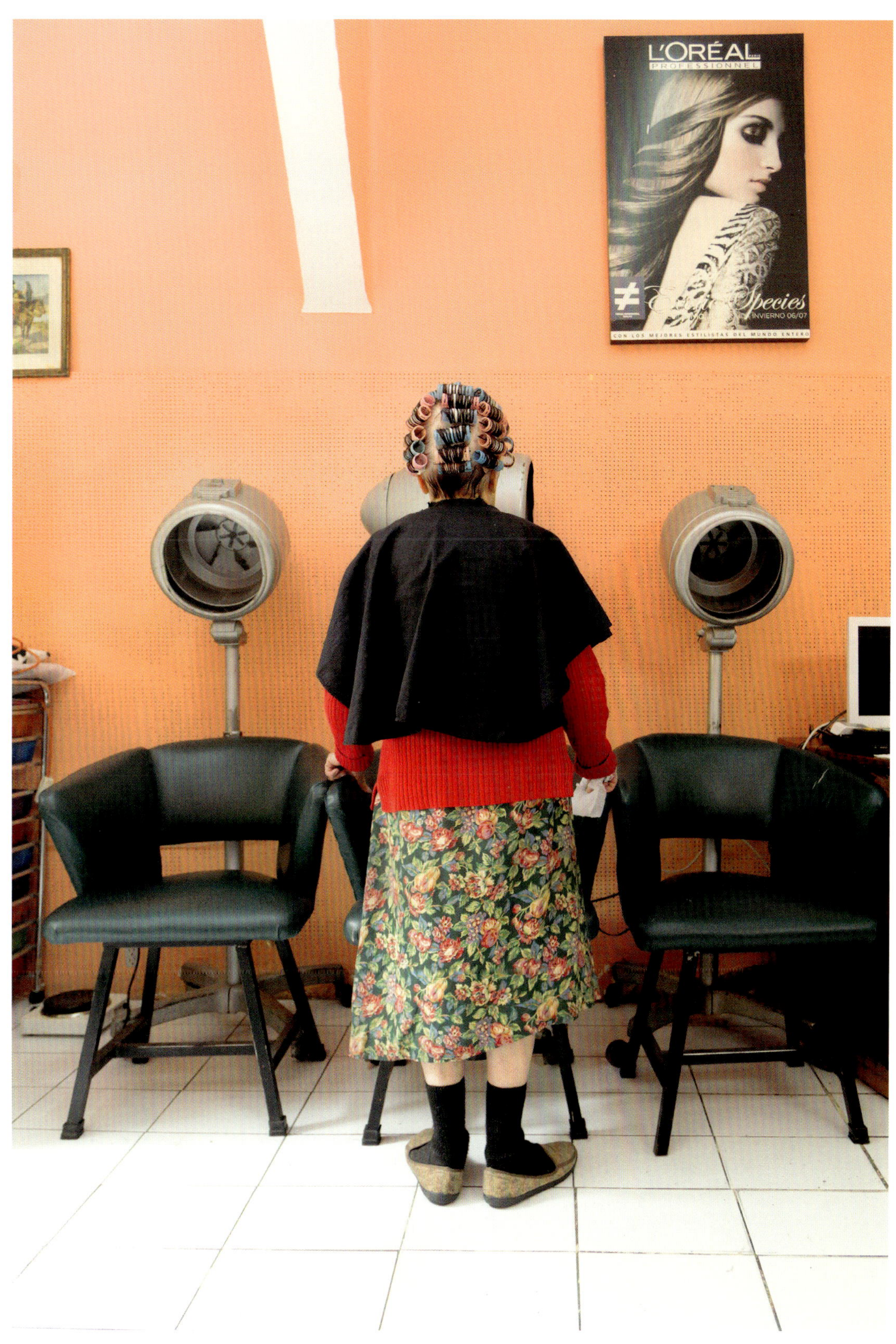

L'ORÉAL
PROFESSIONNEL
Species
INVIERNO 06/07
CON LOS MEJORES ESTILISTAS DEL MUNDO ENTERO

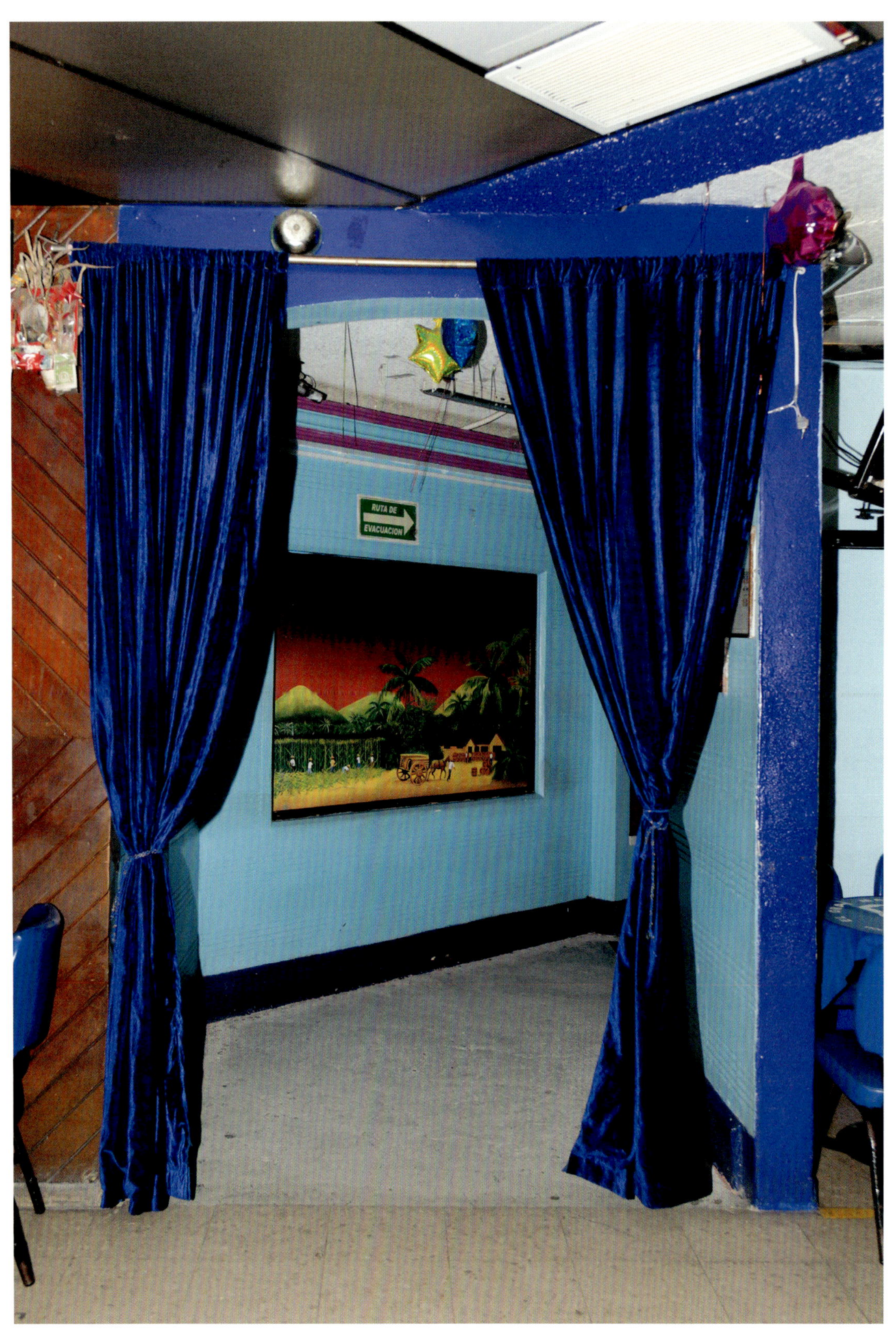
RUTA DE
EVACUACION

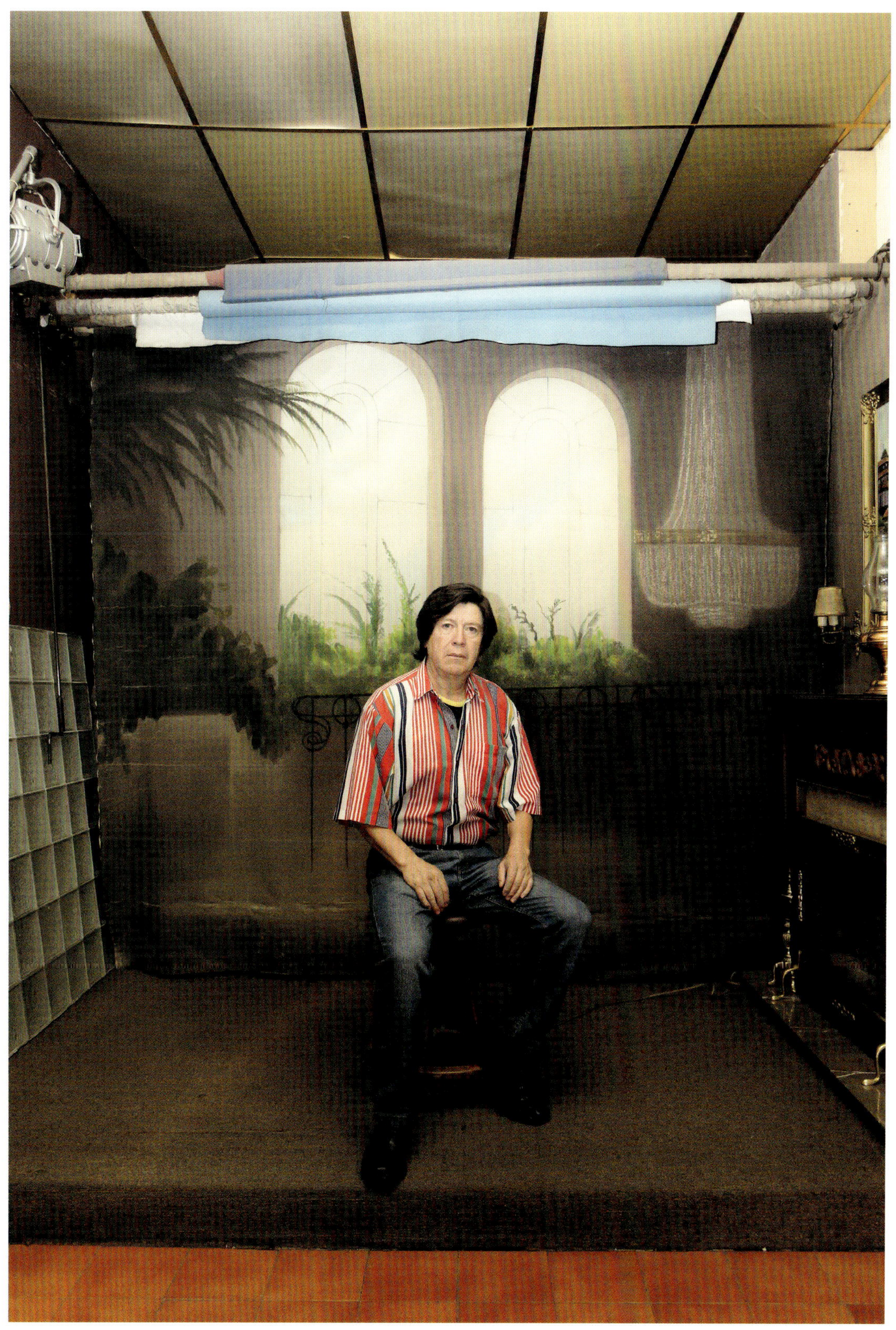

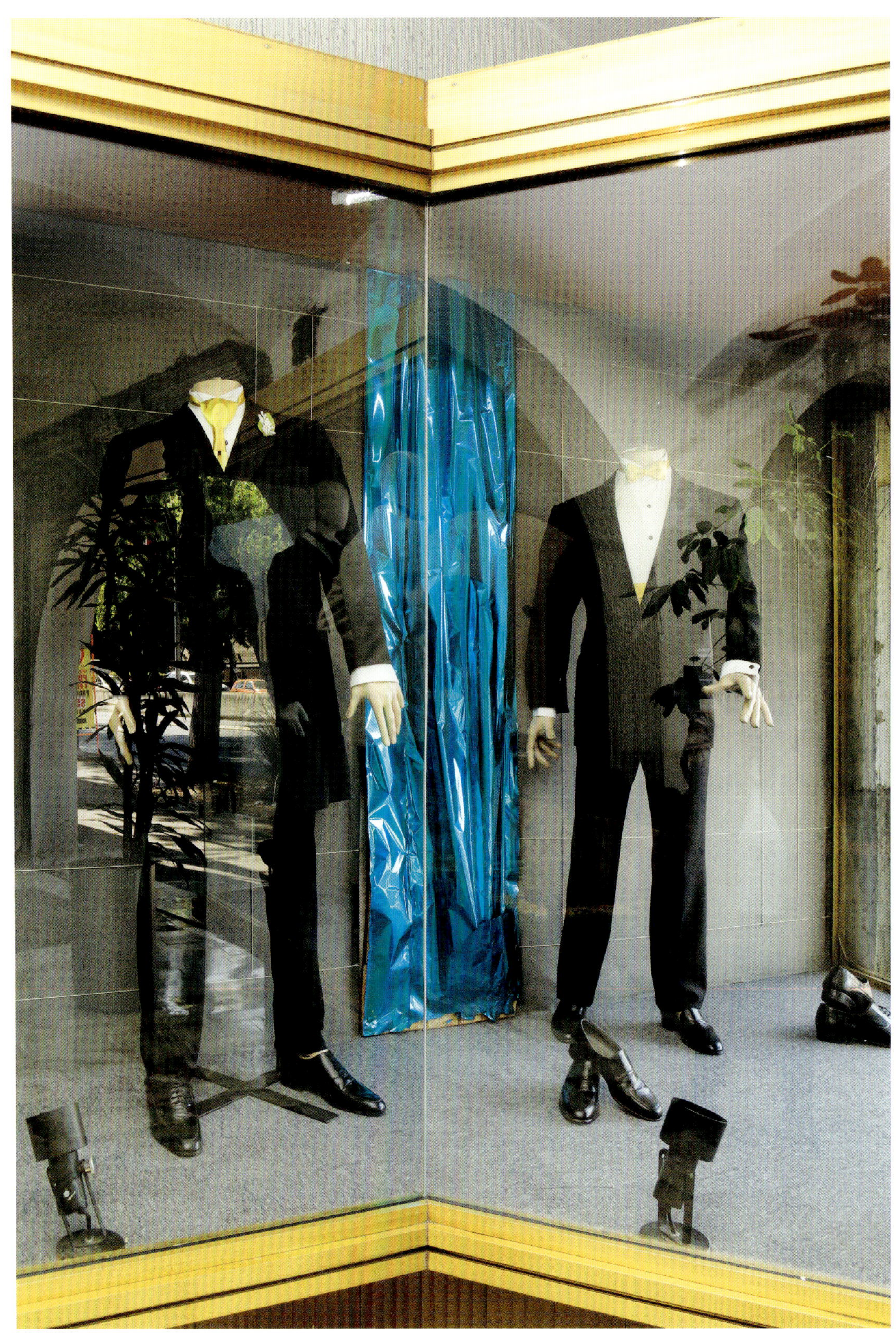

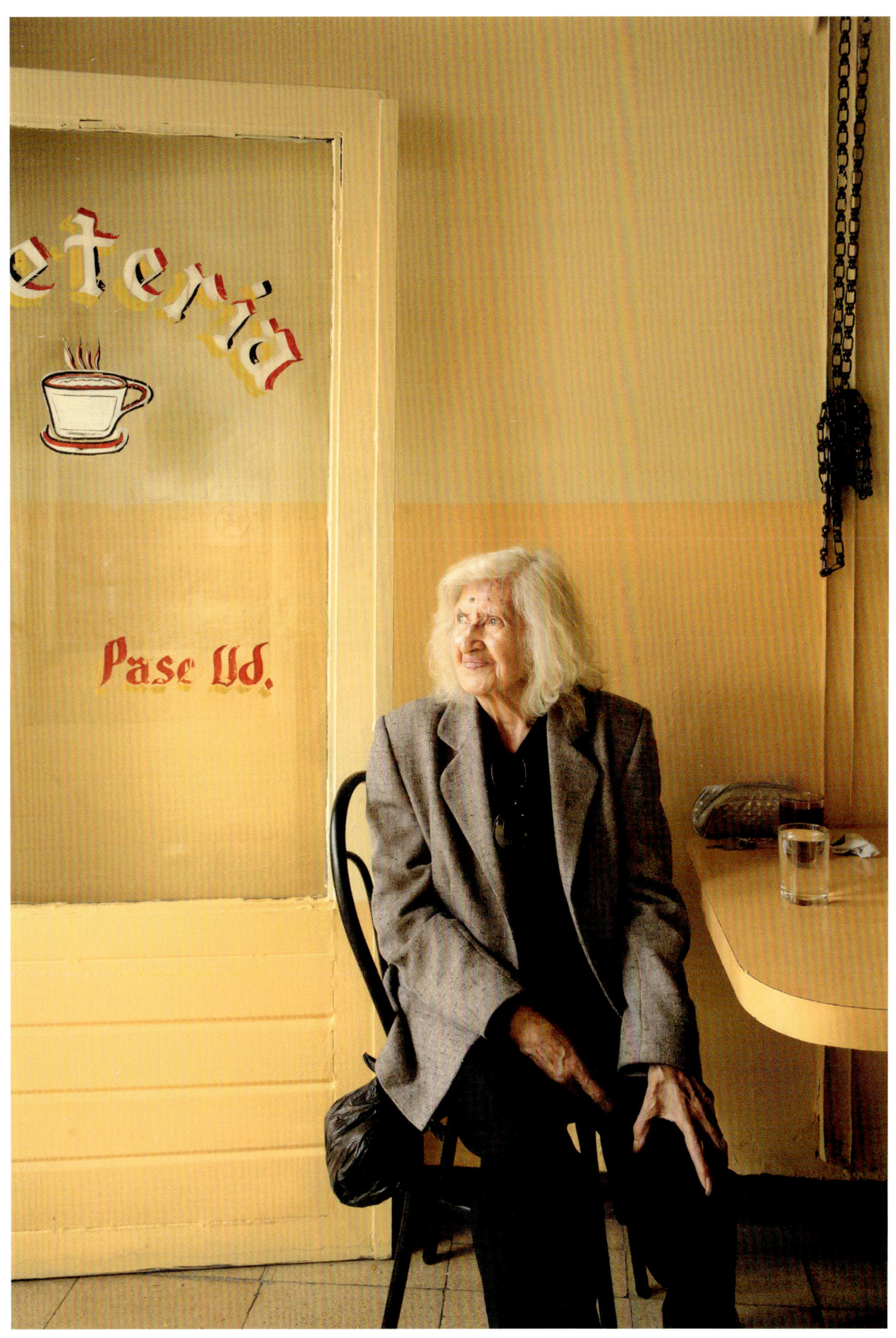
etería
Pase Ud.

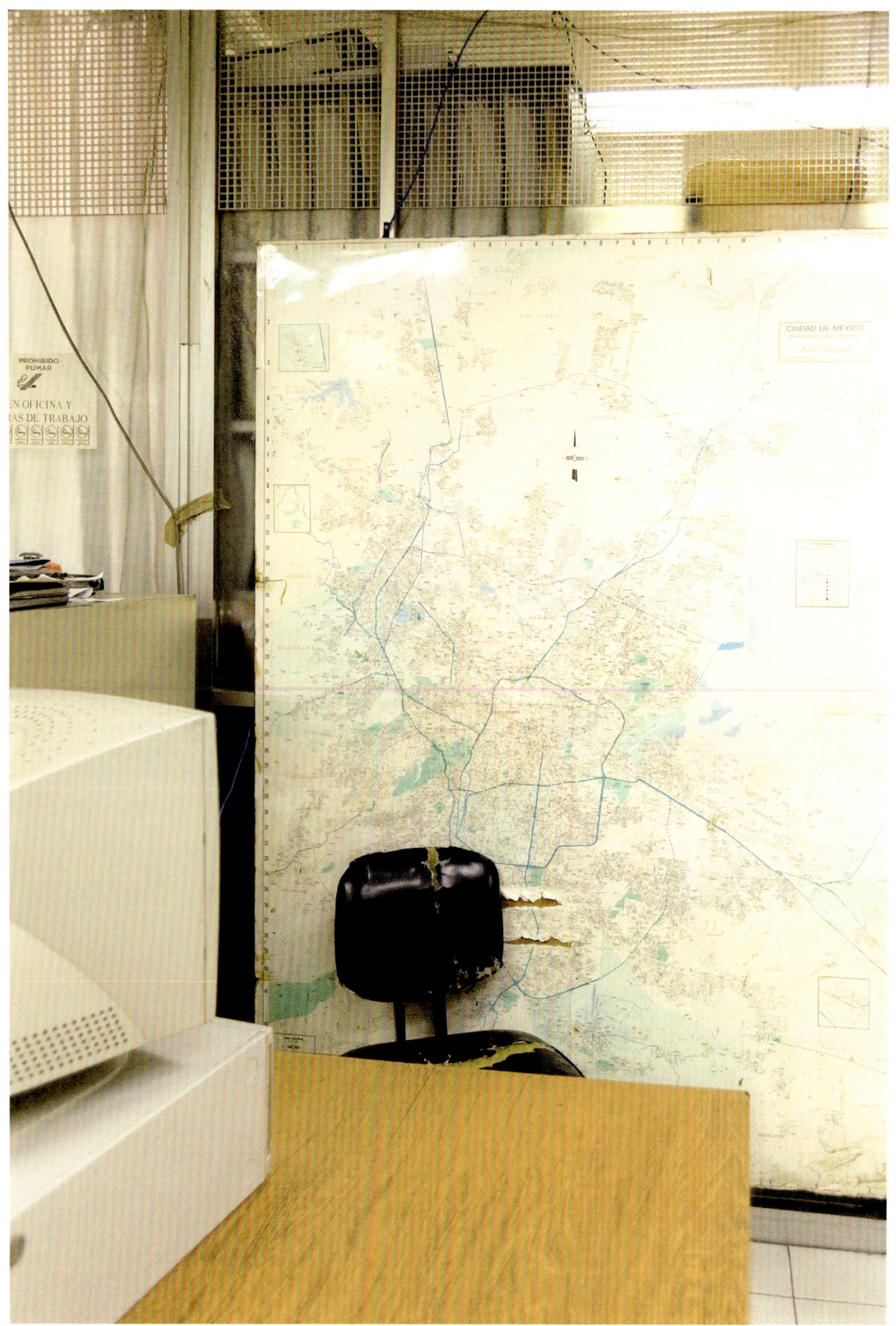
PROHIBIDO
FUMAR
EN OFICINA Y
RAS DE TRABAJO
CIUDAD DE MEXICO

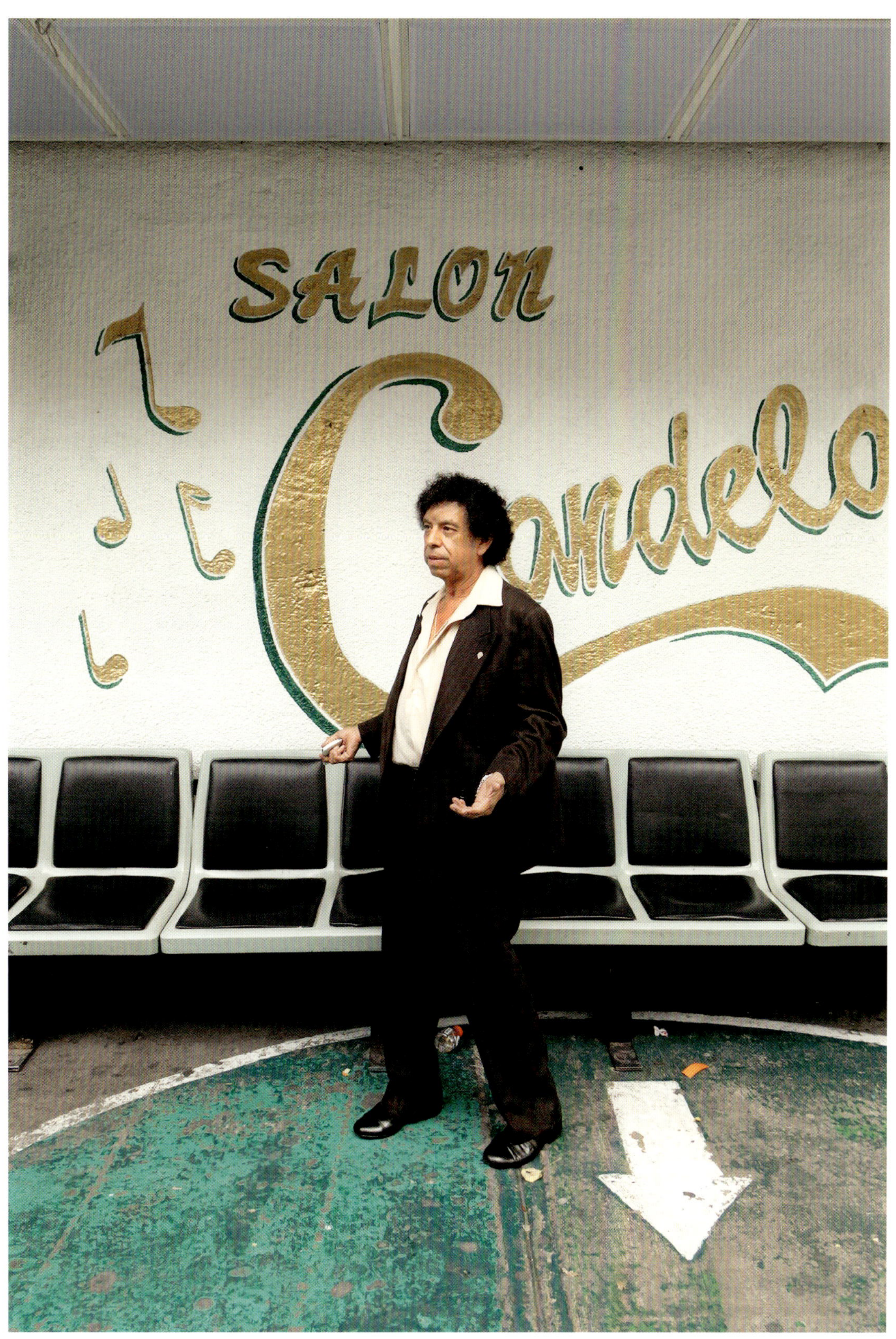

All photographs from
the series *The Persistence
of the Margin*, Mexico City,
2015–ongoing
Courtesy the artist

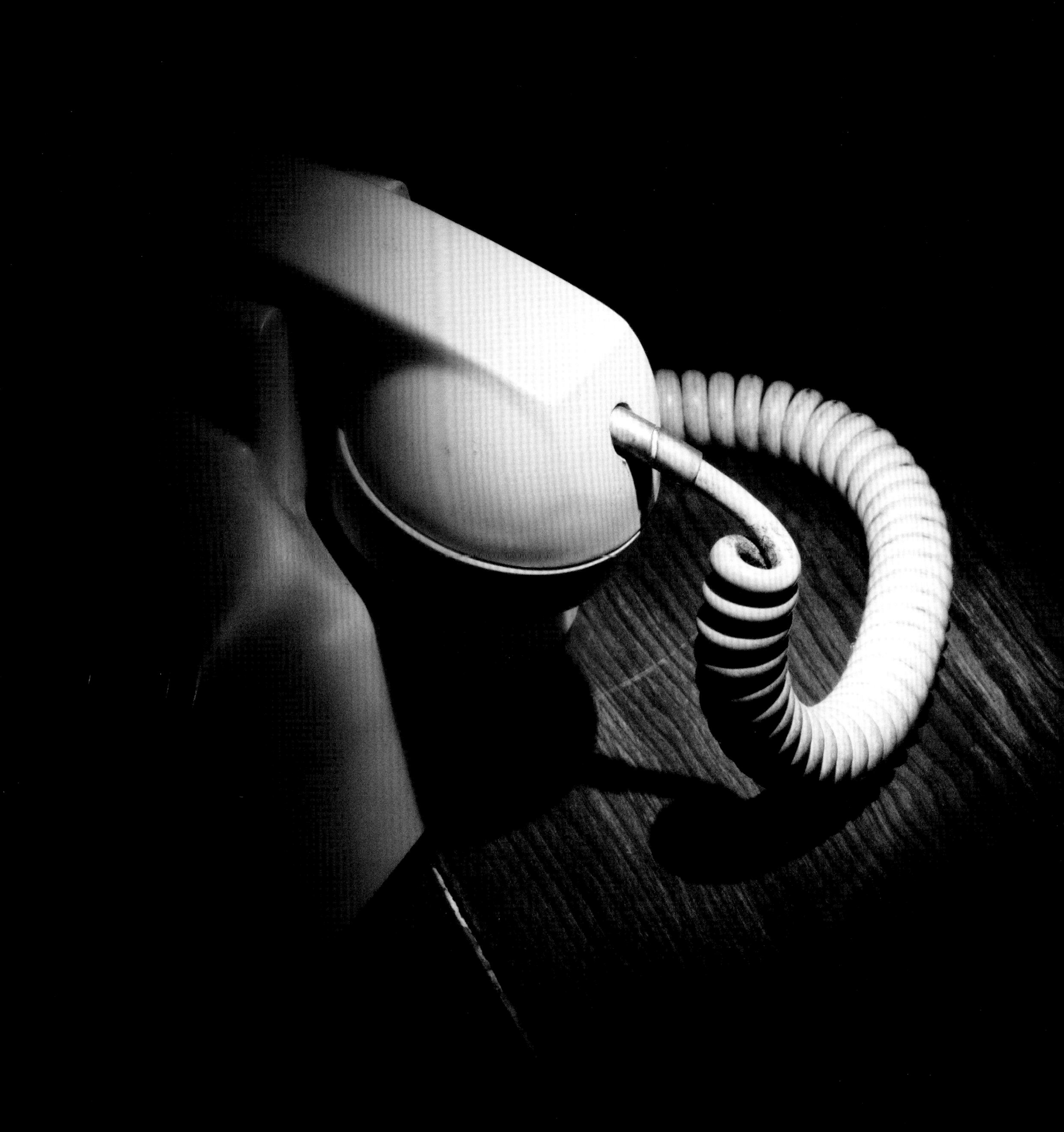

The Shadow and the Flash

Iñaki Bonillas in Conversation with Iván Ruiz

In 2003, Iñaki Bonillas inherited a collection from his Basque grandfather, José Rodríguez Plaza, who had arrived in Mexico as an exile from Spain decades earlier. J. R. Plaza had an expansive imagination. He photographed himself dressed up as various characters from American Westerns and made business cards for jobs he never held. The J. R. Plaza archive would become an enduring long-term project for Bonillas, one of Mexico's most insightful artists when it comes to transforming the field of photography. His rigorous, decidedly experimental methodology encompasses photography, video, installation, site-specific interventions, and artist's books.

Bonillas, who in his youth worked as an "assistant to the assistant" in the photographer Carlos Somonte's studio, has long been interested what he calls the "extra-photographic aspects of the medium." In his deeply researched exhibition projects, from interventions inside Casa Luis Barragán to collaborations with bookbinders, he pushes beyond the two-dimensional to plumb private and collective memory. His work integrates photography in a creative process wherein reality, fiction, and the fluctuating worlds of word and image all coexist.

All of this was on display last year in *Ya no, todavía no* (No longer, not yet), his first solo exhibition at Kurimanzutto, in Mexico City, which drew upon the techniques and skills of analog photography and what the filmmaker Robert Bresson has referred to as "the intelligence of the hands." "I am a curious, restless person," Bonillas told Iván Ruiz when they spoke recently at Bonillas's studio in the Roma neighborhood of Mexico City. "I constantly feel the impulse to extend my research to other territories."

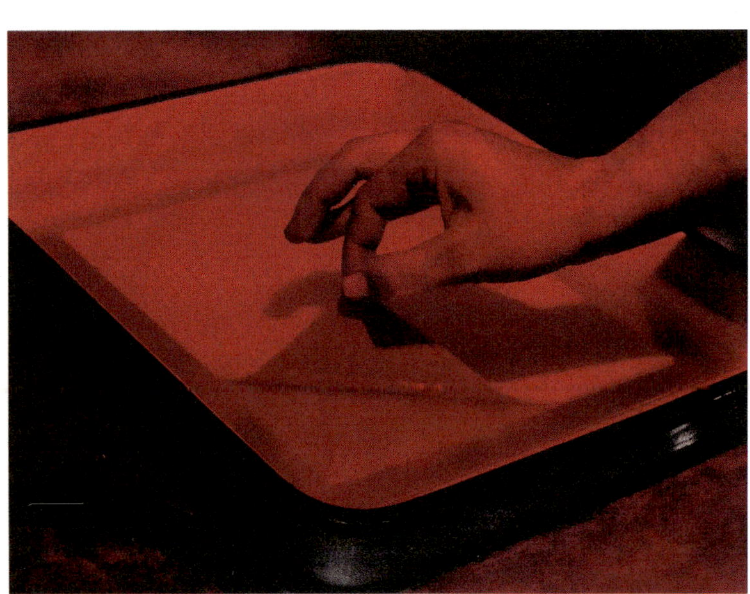

I'm like a kind of attic photographer, someone who's more attuned to the residue of what someone has forgotten in the darkroom.

Iván Ruiz: **Iñaki, you started your ascent in the world of photography very early. How do you situate yourself in relation to your precociousness?**

Iñaki Bonillas: I don't know exactly why, but one day, when I was very young, I expressed to my mother that I had a certain interest in photography. This would have been in the early '90s, when I was still in high school, and at that time, any kind of extracurricular activity was quite welcome in my home. My mother was a single mother, so having the kid occupied in the afternoons was a positive thing. We looked into possible photography courses to which I could apply. I studied at the Nacho López Photography School very briefly—I never finished the course, but my interest in photography remained.

At the same time, in my high school, there was an older student who was already a precocious artist in his own right. He put his library, made up primarily of art history books, but with a specific focus on the so-called Conceptual art period, at my disposal. Those were some of the first art history books to inspire me.

IR: **What specifically sparked your curiosity about what we now call analog photography?**

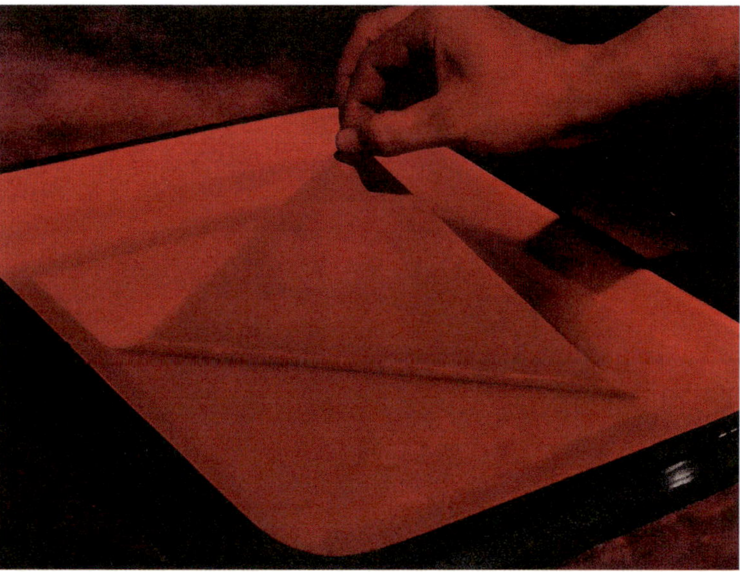

IB: From the moment I began studying photography, I had to study traditional analog methods. That being said, the digital era was already approaching. So, in a way, I began studying something that was already obsolete from the outset, something on the verge of dying out, or of transforming into something else. I started working with a medium that was already the memory of itself. Certainly, the work of artists like Jan Dibbets, Sol LeWitt, John Hilliard, Hanne Darboven, and John Baldessari, who incorporated photography into their practices, resonated with me. I also sensed that the majority of my colleagues who studied fine arts were always complaining that the colleges in those days, at least in Mexico, were very focused on traditions that were deeply rooted in the technical, and there wasn't necessarily any intellectual development. So I thought I could skip that stage and not follow the path of all my academic colleagues.

IR: **Another important part of your initial training was assisting photographers, one of whom was Carlos Somonte.**

IB: Not only was Carlos Somonte a very well-known photographer, but he was also my uncle. I barely knew him when I was young, but my mother noticed that I was taking my studies in photography seriously and urged me to contact my uncle to see if I could take things a step further.

I was still in school, and every day after class, I would head straight to his studio, and that's where I spent all my afternoons. I was actually the assistant to the assistant, because I was still too young to have that much responsibility. But that's where something important occurred for me. In a way, being the assistant to the assistant, you become responsible for all things peripheral to photography: you are the one who installs the lights, who prepares the cyclorama, the one who takes the film rolls to the lab, the one who comes back to the lab an hour later to see if the shots came out underexposed or overexposed. In short, you are the one who is in charge of preparing everything that's needed in order to take a photograph, but you do not take the photograph yourself. This limit allowed me to begin to work in the margins of the notion of the photographic, and to become more interested in the extra-photographic aspects of the medium.

IR: **In this country, at least since the founding of the Consejo Mexicano de Fotografía in the '70s, there have been clearly defined boundaries between the practices of photojournalism, documentary, and artistic photography, but not so much the area of conceptual photography. Would you define yourself as a conceptual photographer?**

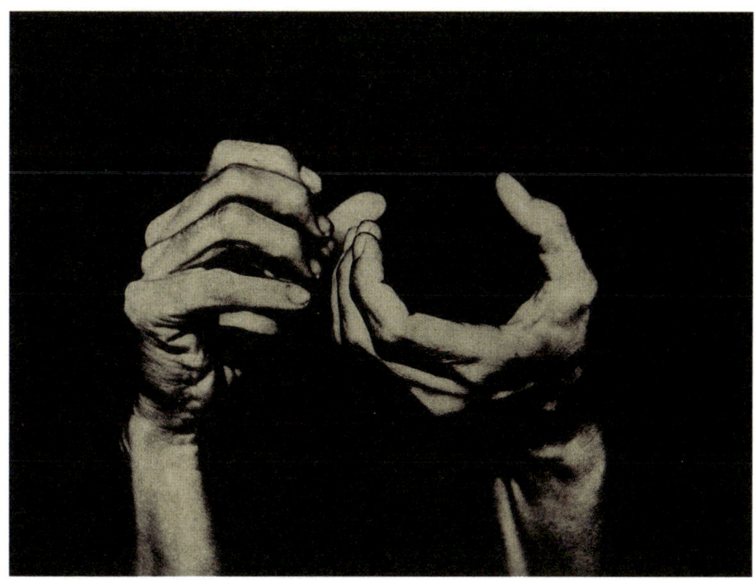 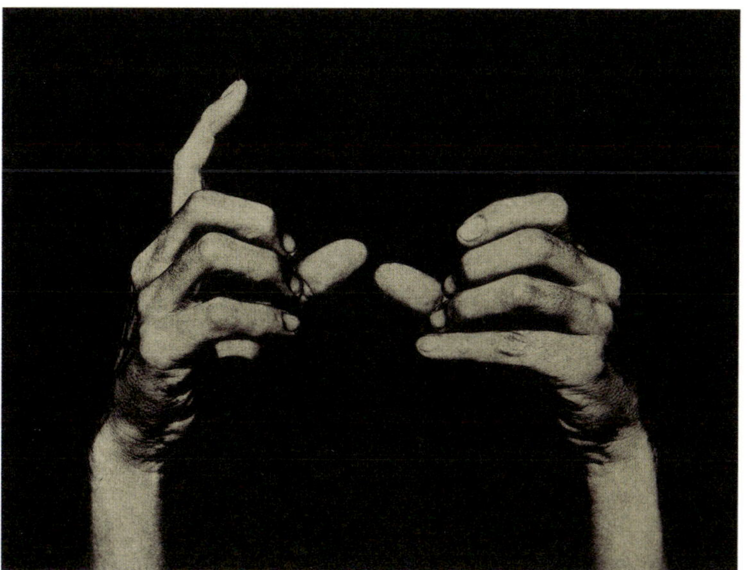

IB: Much of my work has been tied to the photographic archive— a familial photographic archive that I tend to consult. All this has made me think that in reality I'm more like a kind of attic photographer, someone who's more attuned to the residue of what someone has forgotten in the darkroom, of what someone has abandoned, of the things that are in disuse, or obsolete— that is, materials that have gone unnoticed, or have been left in a space lacking in the conditions necessary for their preservation, and that end up undergoing alterations, perhaps because of a moth, humidity, a fire. And this is the territory in which I feel I move best, the territory of the antiquarian, of the restorer. In my work there is always this kind of secret conversation with a dead or anonymous person, with someone who underlined a book, for example, and left a series of annotations, or simply with solitary and forgotten images that have served as inspiration for me.

IR: **Why do you think your work draws attention in the world of photography?**

IB: I have the sense that as time has gone by, photography as a field has become more expanded and expandable, and in a certain sense that has been good for me, because now my work fits more naturally in the world of photography. László Moholy-Nagy mentions that the most surprising possibilities can be discovered in the photographic material in itself, and I couldn't be more in agreement with him. It is increasingly common for artists to work with images that were not necessarily originally produced by them, as I have almost always done, and these are no longer considered appropriations, but works in their own right. I get the feeling that before the distrust in these practices was generalized, but little by little that has changed. So, I imagine for all these reasons, my work has been shown, cited, and represented in this sphere of the art world called photography.

IR: **Let's go back to your background, to your intellectual biography and the texts that made an impression on you, which have a lot to do with conceptual photography and also with the relationship between photography and the visual arts in general.**

IB: Well, in 2003, I inherited this collection from my family, an archive that I named J. R. Plaza, which was how my maternal grandfather used to abbreviate his own name. In working with this archive, I discovered a whole series of images where my grandfather appears dressed as a cowboy, seeming to imitate characters from American Westerns or in the style of the Marlboro Man. My

This page:
Adiós fotografía (Bye bye photography), Mexico City, 2018

Overleaf:
Una tarjeta para J. R. Plaza (A business card for J. R. Plaza), Mexico City, 2007
Courtesy the artist and ProjecteSD, Barcelona

J. R. Plaza
Encargado Mostrador

Ferr. Los Dos Leones
Rib. San Cosme No. 116   Tel:35805

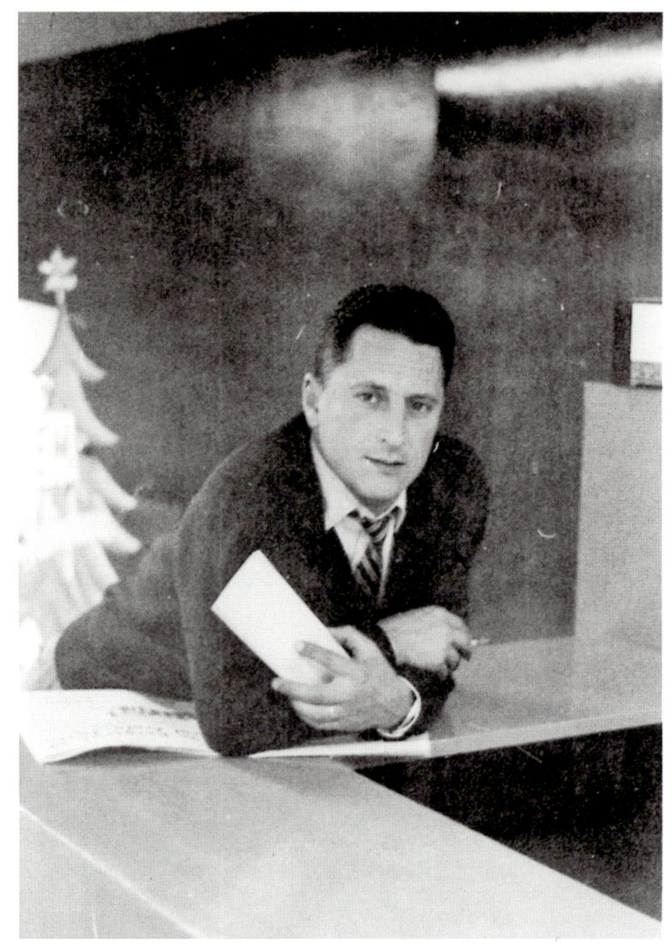

J. R. Plaza
Modelo

Dinamarca No. 25,16
Tel: 46-09-64

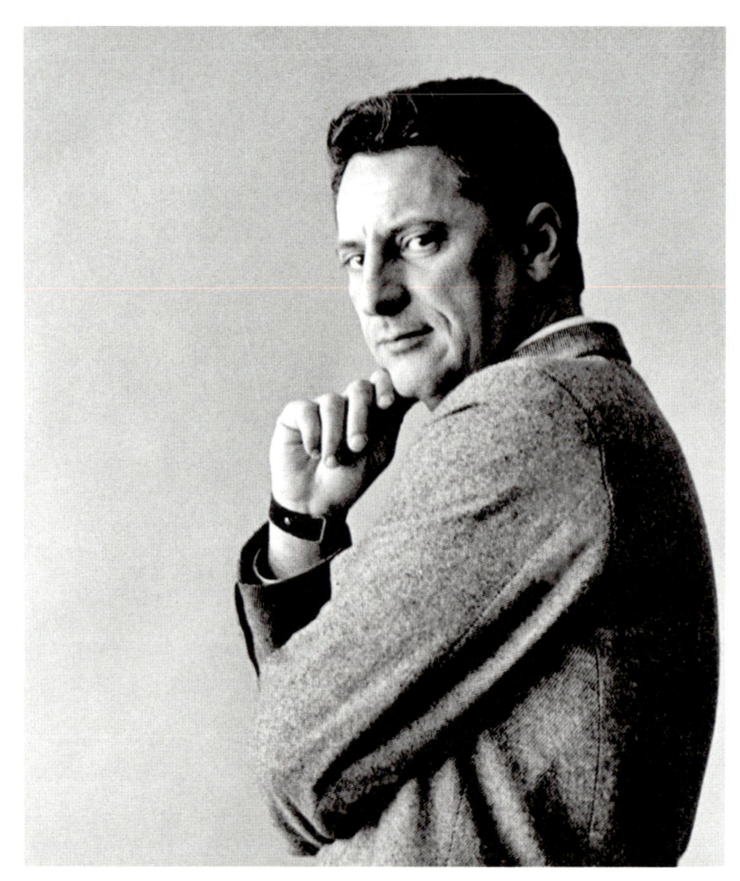

J. R. Plaza
Armador

Dinamrca No. 25,16
Tel :46-09-64

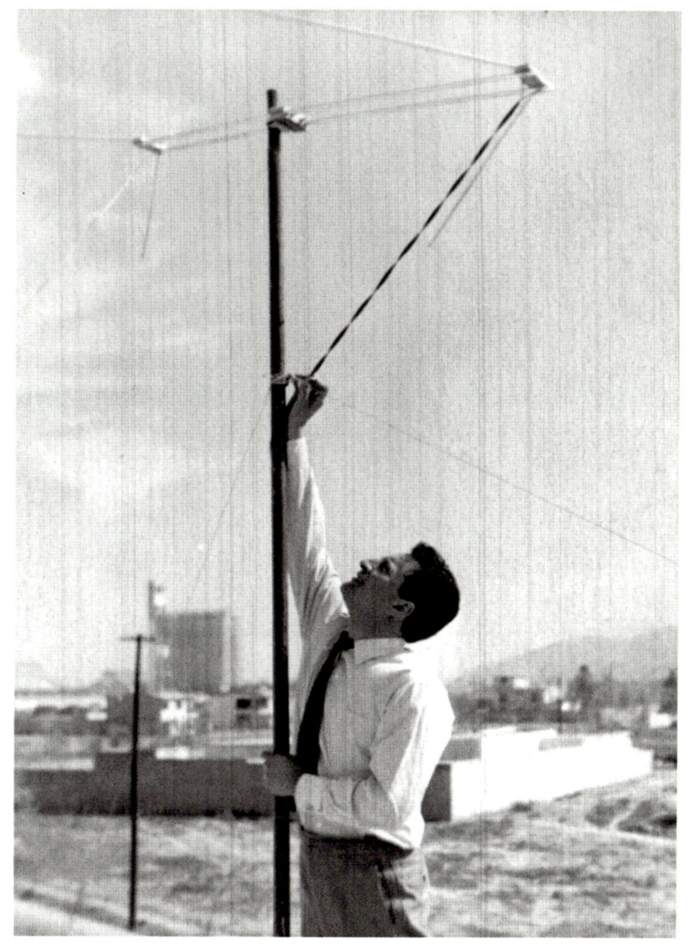

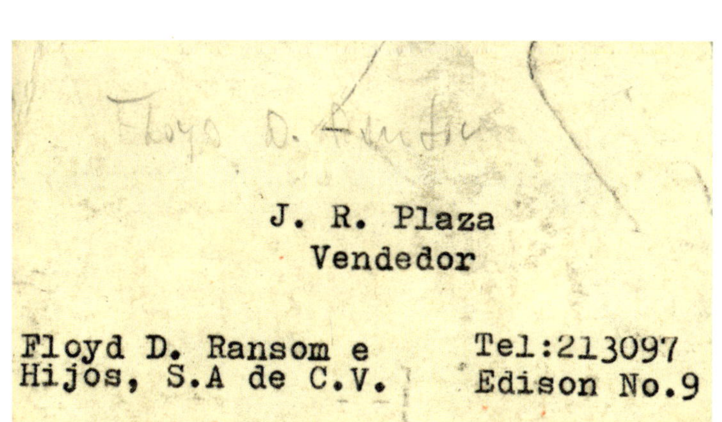

J. R. Plaza
Vendedor

Floyd D. Ransom e   Tel:213097
Hijos, S.A de C.V.   Edison No.9

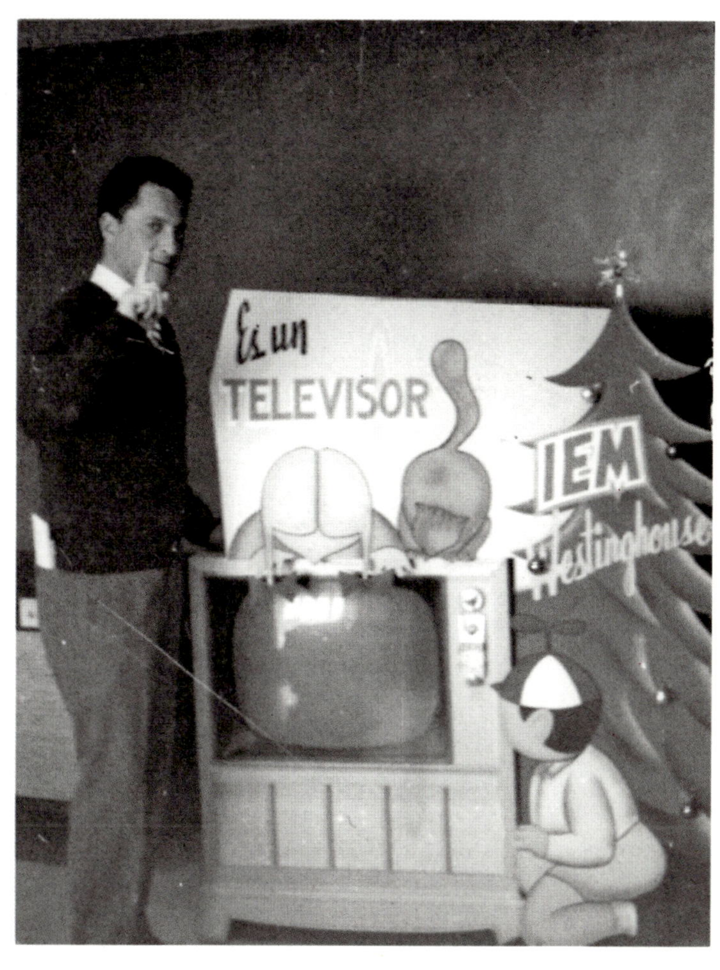

I spend a lot of time looking for traces of images that are hidden somewhere.

grandmother gave me a small diary my grandfather kept in Wyoming during a three-month stay; I imagine he thought that going to spend a summer in Wyoming as a young man would allow him to fulfill his dream of becoming sort of a John Wayne, but instead of that, what one reads in the diary is a series of misfortunes, everything turning out badly. And it would seem that my grandfather had returned to Mexico City after the fact and had continued with his search for his identity, but now from the comfort of a photo studio, and so he created these sets much in the style of Cindy Sherman, where he would come up with an outfit, a costume, and ask his friends to pose, duplicating images from cowboy films. All this material gave rise to a work entitled *The Shadow and the Flash*, 2007, whose namesake is a short story written by Jack London about two childhood rivals who as adults compete to discover the secret of invisibility, or the way to disappear, as perhaps my grandfather had tried to do: in the whiteness of the pages of his diary first, and in the darkness of the photographic negatives afterward.

Subsequently, I also inherited from my grandfather a card wallet, in which he had accumulated all of the cards from the various jobs he had held over the course of his life. He was mainly an aluminum seller for a Canadian company called Alcan. And in some of the empty slots left in this card holder that he had fashioned for himself, he had typed up cards with the names of jobs he would have liked to have had and that, in reality, he never had—like wood cutter, front-desk manager, model, mechanic. When I saw this card wallet, it occurred to me that there was one card my grandfather forgot to add: the card for self-portraitist, which was actually what he had dedicated his entire life to, an impossible job—who would hire you as a self-portraitist? In order to certify that he had, in fact, been a self-portraitist, I searched for a self-portrait for each of these fictitious cards and also played a bit with their opposites—a shepherd who sleeps

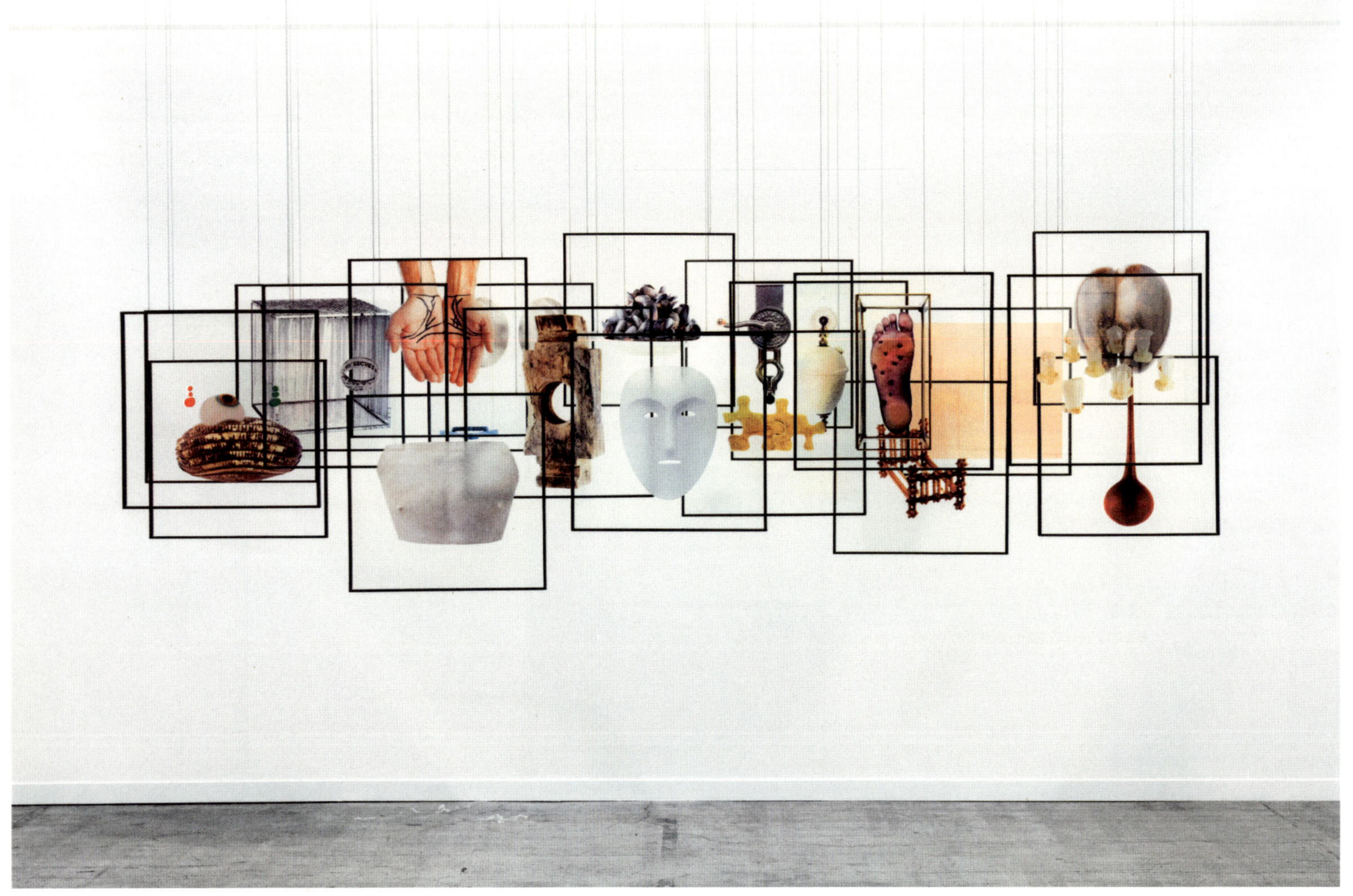

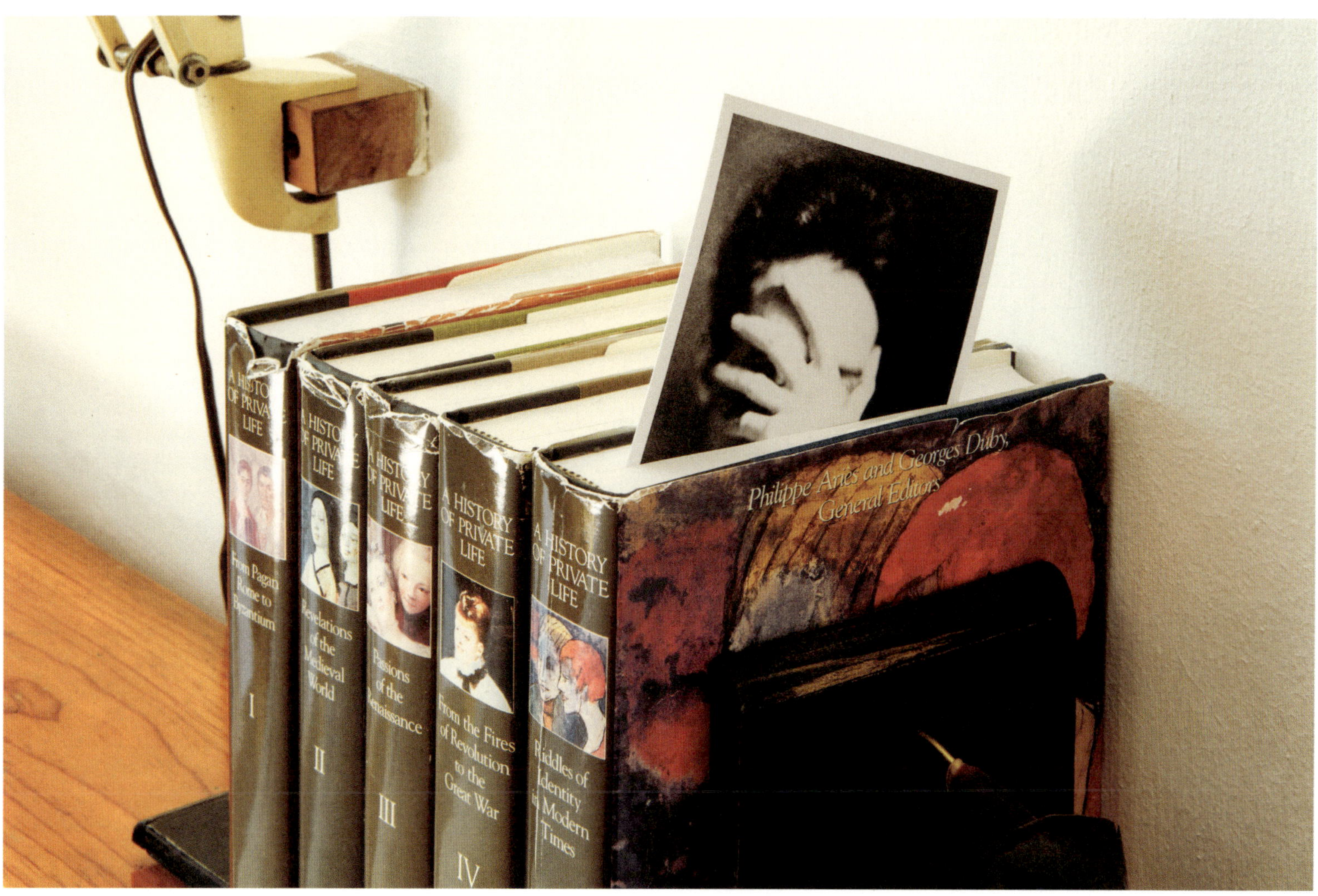

on the grass and a representative who flies and travels all the time, and so on.

All this is to say that often in my work texts come first, and then I imagine the sort of images that should come along. So, it is not uncommon that a book, or a reading, is reflected in the photographic archive—and sometimes the opposite.

IR: **I think of you not only as this photographer who's behind the scenes, but also as this figure who is undercover in order to enact a detective-like search.**

IB: Yes, I spend a lot of time looking for traces of images that are hidden somewhere. That is what I did at Casa Luis Barragán, with the project *Secretos* (Secrets, 2016), where the figure of the detective was very present. Back in 2003, I believe, I was part of a group exhibition at Casa Barragán. At that time, I decided to occupy a tiny abandoned nail in a wall with a photograph that represented solitude, quietness, and it went completely unnoticed, unseen. And that was the idea—to occupy a space with silence. So it surprised me to receive, after fourteen or fifteen years, an invitation from Estancia FEMSA to develop an investigation throughout the entire house.

For this second exploration—and hence the title—I thought about the so-called secrets that nuns in convents used to hide inside books, a practice that is not at all alien to the books we see in Casa Barragán: if one has the opportunity simply to view them from above, one can see they're filled with all kinds of tiny papers, annotations, archived inside the books. But there is also a much more direct relationship with photography, which is that this house is, in my opinion, one of the most photogenic houses of the twentieth century; it is, in a way, a house made to be constantly photographed. But in order to maintain this visual appeal, this pristine quality, every element must be perpetually in its place,

nothing out of order, and for this to happen there must be a negative of the house, a kind of second house inside the main one to accommodate things that would spoil the photograph and distort the discourse that Luis Barragán so carefully developed over the course of many years of practice within it. And for this reason, I decided to intervene only in the hidden spaces throughout the house—inside wardrobes, closets, spaces behind doors.

There are nearly ninety doors in Casa Barragán, and one can't help but ask oneself what is behind each of these doors. At one point when I was exploring the house, I was surprised to find, upon moving pieces of furniture that had been standing there for some forty, fifty years on the colored carpets of this house, that the imprints, the marks, were so deep, the traces so pronounced. I thought, Surely, if we are to refer to the most exact floorplans of the house, these marks should be part of that drawing, because they are like hidden proto-photographs in the floor. So, what I did was photograph them and put the pictures inside the most appropriate place in the house: the file chest of drawers of the architect's studio.

IR: **I'm very interested in speaking more about the work you did with your grandfather's archive. How many years from when you first inherited the archive did it take? What did it mean for you to inherit this archive, and what were the ways in which you reinvented your own practice?**

IB: In 2002, I think, I started working with Galerie Greta Meert in Brussels, and the next year we planned an exhibition. I decided to move to Belgium for a year, and I decided—please don't ask me why—to bring these thirty family albums, which I had recently … maybe not inherited, strictly speaking, but perhaps taken responsibility for.

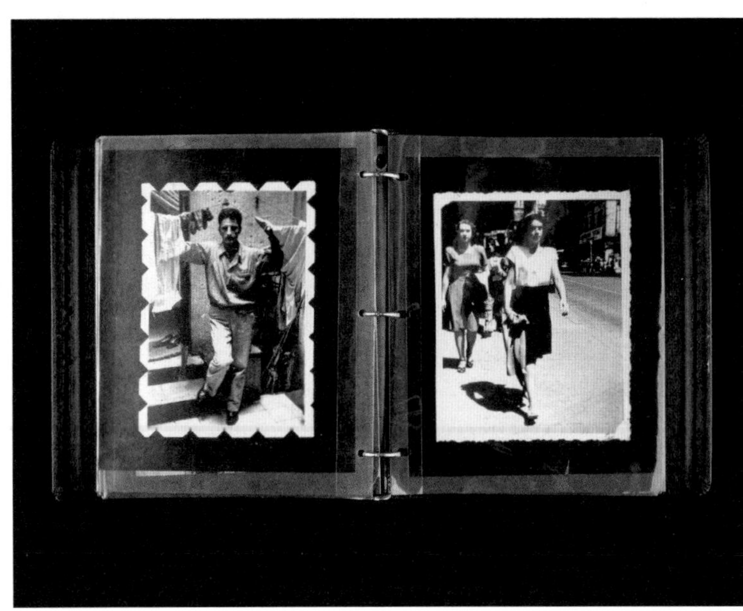

I had no idea that I would spend the next twenty years occupied with this material.

Initially, of course, I had no idea that I would spend the next twenty years occupied with this material or that the work I was doing was considered in any way related to archival practices. I just had to take something with me, and I took these albums, but I was so unclear about what to do with them that in the exhibition where I first included them, they went completely unnoticed. What I did, much to the gallery owners' headache, was reorganize the entire gallery library. What was most within reach of the viewer were the thirty family albums with which I'd traveled from Mexico to Brussels, and then next were all of the dossiers of the artists represented by the gallery—another kind of family archive. Then, on the next step, which was a little further out of arm's reach, I put all of the monographs of the artists represented by the gallery; then further up, all the catalogs of group exhibitions in which any of the artists of the gallery had participated; and then toward the top, where one could only reach with the help of a ladder, all the books that had no relation to the gallery's artists. You could say this was my first intervention, if there was one: the simple fact of having transported the archive from one library—my grandfather also had these family albums interspersed with the books on his bookshelves— to another.

The next project I presented was called *Pequeña historia de la fotografía* (Little history of photography, 2003), an homage to the essay of the same title by Walter Benjamin. And all I did was open this material to the light of day. What happens when you go through the pages of these albums, or any other image collection, is that you remember some images but then forget various others. My interest was to see what this material was made of, and to bring it to light without leaving anything forgotten. Using 4-by-5 slide film, I photographed each of the double spreads in the thirty albums and organized the slides in thirty light boxes—one box per album— and I put these light boxes on display on a giant table that ran the length of the space of the Antwerp Museum of Modern Art, where they were shown.

So, my work with the archive reflects the progression from the surface to the depth of the photographs that comprise it, a journey from the plural to the singular, one that first has more to do with the history of photography and then with the person who constructed this archive, my grandfather, who has almost become a fictional character. I often encounter viewers of my work who say, "There's no way your grandfather could have done all this, it's obvious you invented all." So I think this has been the trajectory, more or less—going from putting the archive as it is on display and ending with what could be a kind of death of the archive, where what I do is photograph the marks that have been left behind by the photographs on the plastic protecting them. My grandfather was a compulsive smoker, and the amount of nicotine and dust that accumulated between the photographs and the plastic covers is infinite.

I could continue working eternally with this legacy, because for me it is a double of the world, with infinite possibilities, but I am a curious, restless person, and I constantly feel the impulse to extend my research to other territories.

IR: **I'd like to go back to the first question, which had to do with precociousness. As opposed to other countries, in Mexico the market for photography is lacking a professional circuit; there are only a few galleries specializing in photography. You were represented early on by a gallery, and now you are newly represented by Kurimanzutto, a gallery with an international reputation—and locations in both Mexico City and New York— that has a rather significant circulation and impact. What exactly is your position as a young artist who entered the market fairly quickly and who is now globally positioned?**

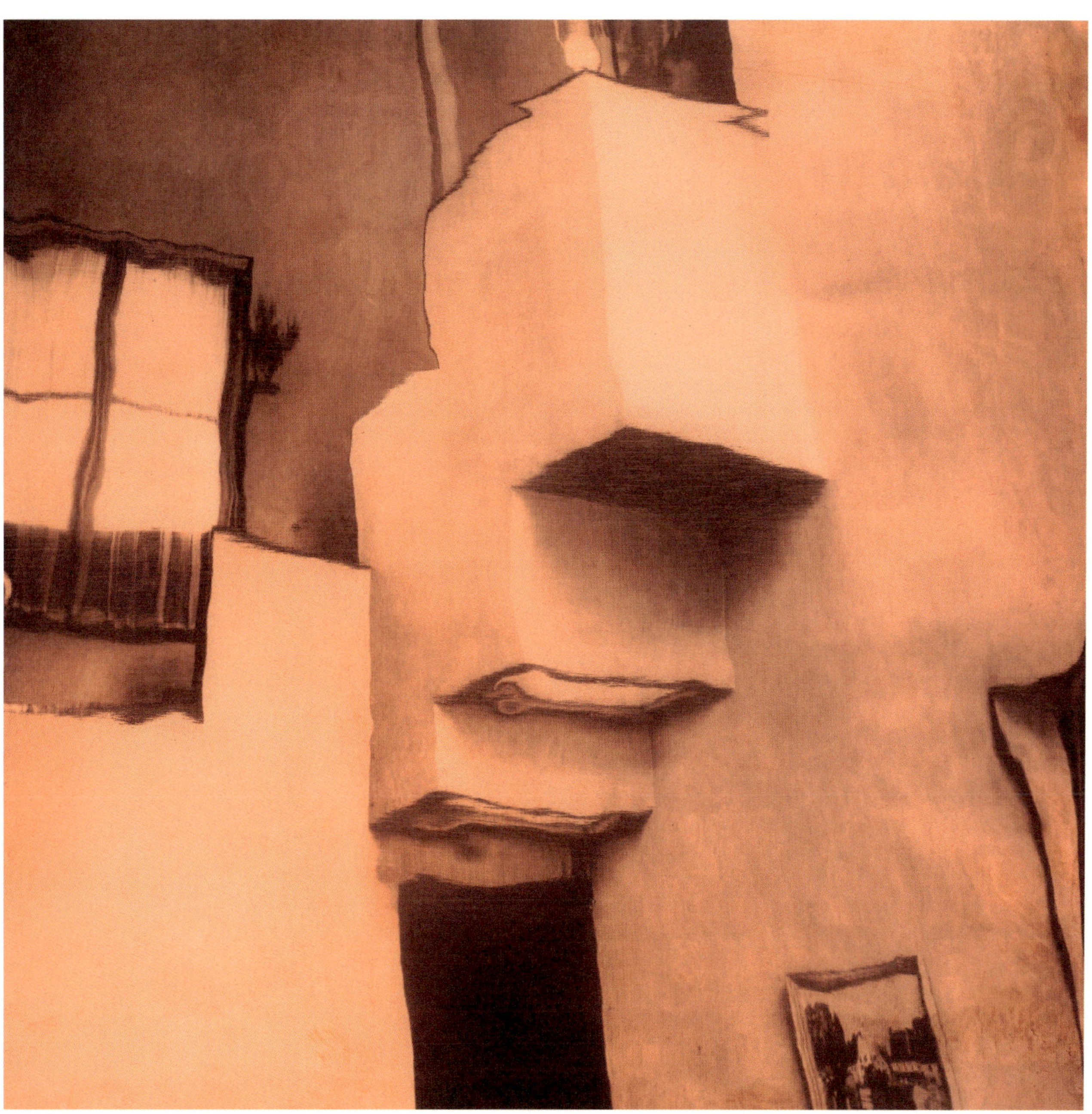

Diurnos (Diurnals),
Mexico City, 2018
Unless otherwise noted,
all images courtesy the
artist and Kurimanzutto,
Mexico City/New York

IB: There is an overpopulation of artists, and we can't all exhibit at the same time in the same institutional venues. The space of a gallery and the particular ramifications that go along with it, like art fairs, have been convenient for developing my investigations— in the first place, because they tend to come with great support. The gallerists that I work with have confidence in what I do and embrace my projects, and this allows me to develop my investigations with the pause and rhythm that my work requires. Some of my projects take years of work, from the readings I have to do to the process of trial and error I go through in order to define a work formally. So it is deeply gratifying, the freedom with which one can work in these types of art spaces. For me, fundamentally, there is little difference between presenting work in a fair, in a gallery, or in a museum, because what I do involves the same kind of research and studio, or archival, work.

IR: Perhaps to conclude, could you talk about your recent exhibition at Kurimanzutto, *Ya no, todavía no* (No longer, not yet, 2018)?

IB: It was a big show, where I presented more than twenty works, some photographic, some video works. It was called *Ya no, todavía no* because it had to do with techniques, processes, materials that are no longer as present and useful as they were, but not yet completely gone. So I tried to produce the whole show with the aid of these kinds of skills and approaches. One of the works, for example, is *Luz de seguridad* (Safelight, 2018), a sequence of photographic images of the process of lifting a piece of photographic paper from the developing tank. They were produced in a darkroom, something about to disappear, and then painted by hand—a technique even more obsolete—so as to give the impression of the typical red light used in the same darkroom. And I also did an homage to Daido Moriyama, a work with a title borrowed from him, *Adiós fotografía* (Bye bye photography, 2018). Here I asked an actress to portray, with her hands only, a photographer in action. What we see is nothing but the gestures of the hands while taking a picture and the voids that form around those hands where a camera no longer is used—yet it is somehow still there.

Iván Ruiz is a researcher of contemporary art and the director at the Institute of Aesthetic Research at the Universidad Nacional Autónoma de México in Mexico City.

Translated from the Spanish by Elianna Kan.

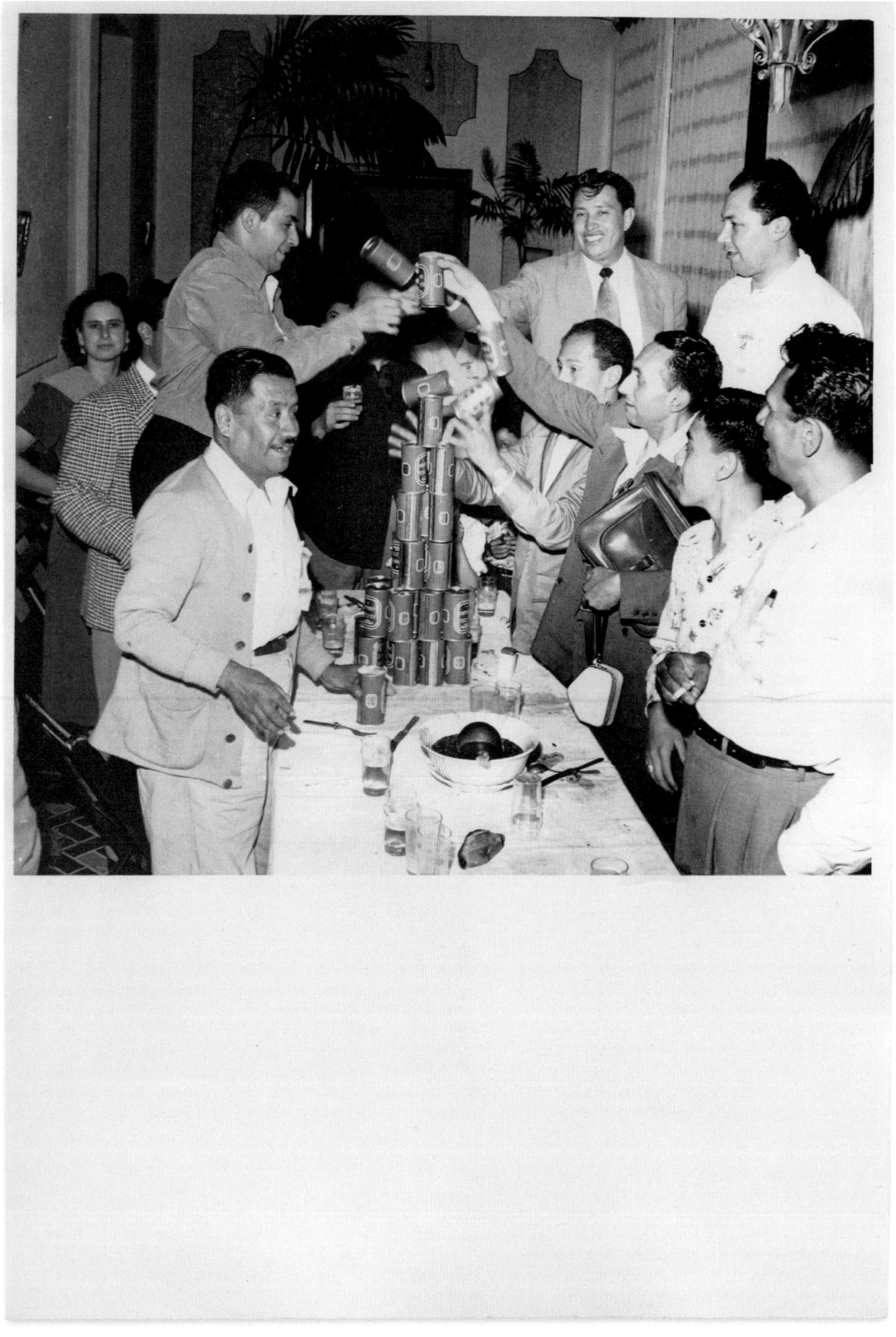

Members Only

The historic Club Fotográfico de México, with its workshops and salons, was the social media platform of its day.

Sarah Hermanson Meister

Photographer unknown, *Viaje a Oaxaca (Oaxaca trip)*, September 1952

In the early twentieth century, Alfred Stieglitz decried the insular production of amateur photo clubs in the United States, so the vitality of an international network of similar organizations over fifty years later might come as a surprise. And yet, in the years following World War II, one finds an extraordinary range of original creative production—perhaps nowhere more so than in metropolises across Latin America. In 2021, the Museum of Modern Art will open an exhibition featuring work from São Paulo's Foto Cine Clube Bandeirante (FCCB), Brazil's preeminent amateur photo club, founded in 1939. To situate these achievements, it is useful to consider contemporary activity in Paris, Tokyo, Buenos Aires, Mexico City, the German city of Saarbrücken, and elsewhere, as photo clubs in these cities regularly exchanged the work of their members through international juried salons and grappled with questions of "art" and "quality" in their clubhouses and on the pages of the monthly journals that many of these clubs produced. Impressive in their range, scale, and quality, the works that circulated in these clubs

The status of the amateur in photography has enlivened the medium ever since George Eastman introduced his Kodak No. 1 in 1889.

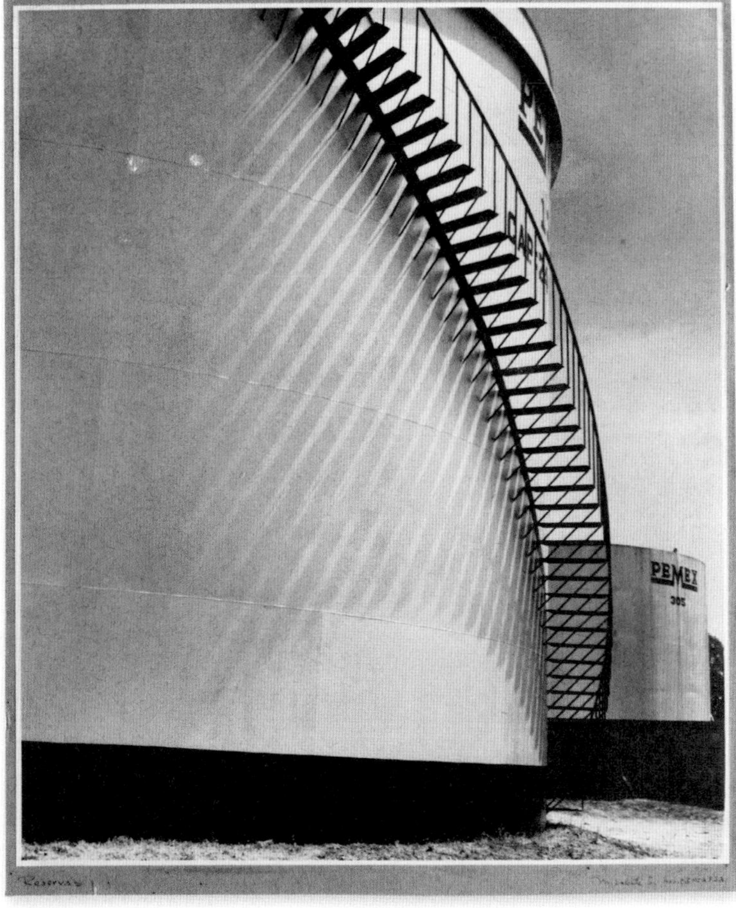

present compelling opportunities to examine the status of the amateur and the shifting concepts of aesthetics and taste.

Little has been written in Spanish or English about the Club Fotográfico de México (CFM), the FCCB's closest cousin in Mexico, one notable exception being José Antonio Rodríguez's *Ruth D. Lechuga: Una Memoria Mexicana* (2002). The CFM, founded in 1949, is still active today, albeit in a form that might be unrecognizable to its founders: at its peak, there were over two hundred members, most of them amateurs who pursued photography in their leisure time, and for whom the convivial social atmosphere nurtured at the club's headquarters and on their frequent excursions was a significant aspect of the CFM's appeal. By the late 1960s, there was a pronounced decline in membership due to political and economic factors, as well as generational disagreements between members. Of the many splinter groups, the earliest was (probably) La Ventana, founded in 1956, and the most significant was the Consejo Mexicano de Fotografía, founded in 1977, and responsible for organizing two major colloquiums on Latin American photography in 1977 and 1980.

Today there are fourteen CFM members who meet in the apartment/studio of the current president, having given up the Mexico City clubhouse at 75 Londres in Colonia Juárez, in 2015, after sixty-three years. They are a young group (average age thirty) of both professional and amateur photographers and artists who are committed to reflecting on their own practices and on expanded approaches to photography in the world today.

Such a broad-minded ethos would have been anathema in the early years of the CFM, when members essentially declared their allegiance to Pictorialism, advocating in a 1952 publication for a range of subject matter that even Stieglitz's most ardent acolytes would have found limiting. On the list of acceptable subjects: "lyrical and romantic fields and seas; pretty flowers [or] happy old people with singular, exotic features." And on the prohibited list: "destruction, crime, garbage, filth, wretched poverty," which was to say, anything that may have caught the attention of "the so-called documentary photographers, who specialize in photographing what is the most abominable, unpleasant and outrageous, [and who] use these photographs to disgrace both society and the government." Given this, one might be forgiven for expecting the work of the club's members to be dreadfully predictable. On the pages of the monthly *Boletín* published by the CFM, there is plenty of evidence that these timeless, syrupy-sweet categories were perfectly aligned with the complacent artistry of certain members. Yet it is also true that not everyone was interested in following these commands. A single box of photographs that remains in the CFM archives contains more than a few images that embraced contemporary industry and urban life.

The coexistence of members who delighted in soft-focus timelessness and those with a more engaged, experimental agenda was a hallmark of both the CFM and the FCCB, although by the early 1950s the conservative leadership of the FCCB (responsible for the content of their monthly *Boletim*) was more likely to ignore rather than attack those who strayed from their Pictorialist principles. The most notable example of this was their failure to address Geraldo de Barros's one-person exhibition at the Museu de Arte de São Paulo (MASP), in January 1951. The radical invention seen in de Barros's presentation, *Fotoformas*, challenged the very definition of a photograph, with shaped prints, forms scratched into the negatives, and freestanding displays; probably many members of the FCCB simply didn't know what to make of it. Pietro Maria Bardi, MASP's founding director, wrote a text in the accompanying brochure that may have compounded the issue: "Geraldo unwillingly photographs the real, I would say that he does not comprehend it, and, without avoiding it, he seeks to discover in it a useful purity drawn from his meditations: lines filtered so that only parts are revealed, and lights reduced into

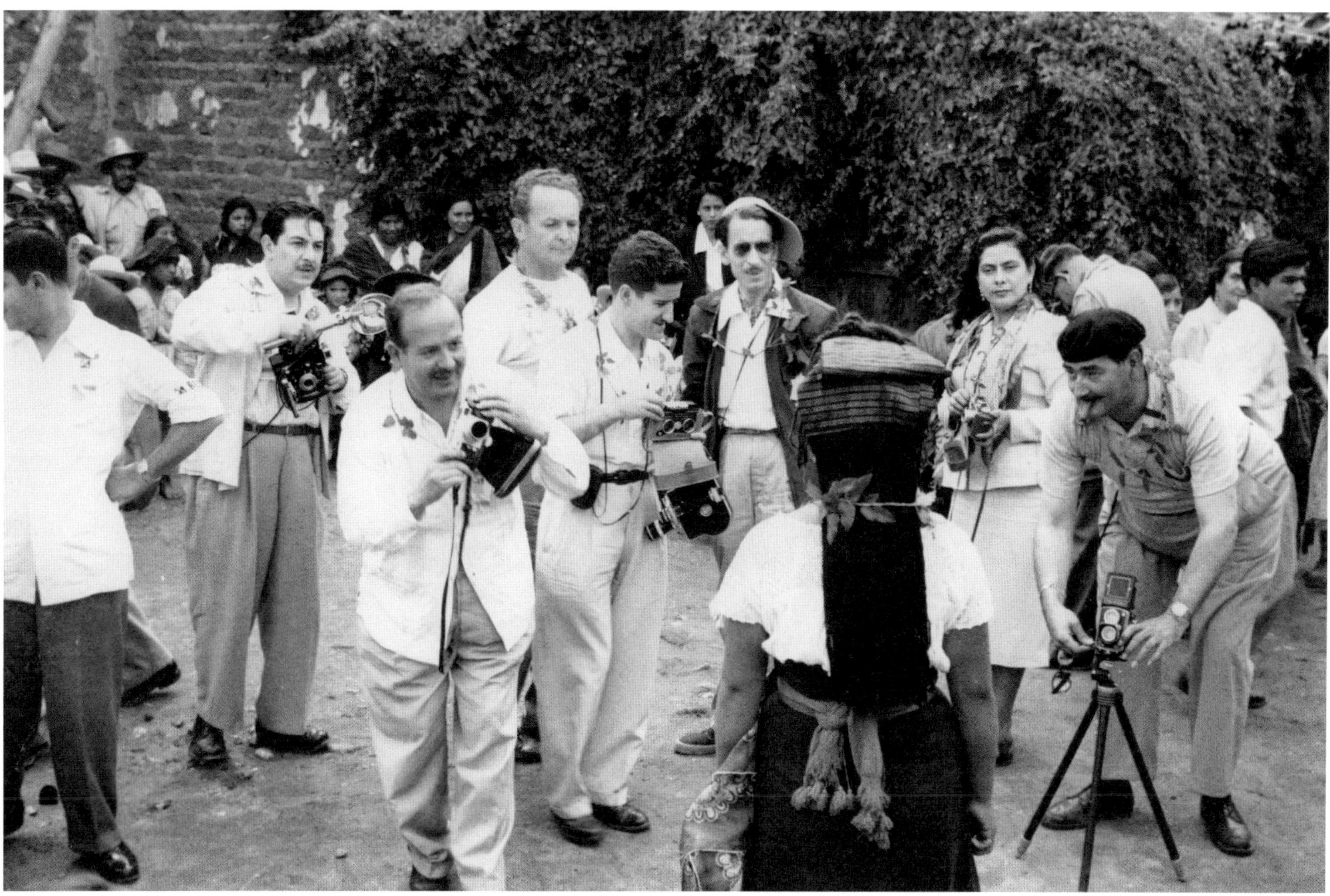

sketches from which it is impossible to reconstruct their origins." (Bardi was Italian and had moved to Brazil with his wife, the architect Lina Bo Bardi, in 1946, which may explain some of the strangeness of his phrasing, preserved in this translation by Tiê Higashi.) By contrast, Thomaz Farkas's one-person show at the Museu de Arte Moderna de São Paulo (MAM-SP), which opened in July 1949, pushed the boundaries of traditional practices with its exhibition design, if not with the photographs themselves, and was the subject of a rapturous review.

Perhaps the fundamental difference between the FCCB and the CFM is that before too long the leadership of the FCCB embraced this "modern" impulse (or at least the look of it), whereas the CFM's staunch refusal to reexamine its aesthetic values meant that it was increasingly inhospitable to distinct approaches among its members. It was similarly out of touch with contemporary trends that were familiar to most North American and European audiences through programming such as Edward Steichen's presentations at the Museum of Modern Art, New York, including *The Family of Man* in 1955, and exhibitions of the work of German photographer Otto Steinert and his Subjective Photography movement, which also traveled to the MAM-SP, in 1955.

One means of mapping this trajectory is to consider the mentions of Mexican photography and photographers in the FCCB *Boletim*, the first of which is a note in the May 1952 issue that the CFM's magazine was available in the FCCB library. By 1957, it was La Ventana, a CFM splinter group, that was honored with an exhibition in the FCCB headquarters (and a three-page illustrated article in the *Boletim*). In a mention of the First Latin American Exhibition of Photography (which opened in Mexico City in June 1959 and traveled to the FCCB and other venues in Argentina, Chile, and Uruguay), credit for the collaborative initiative is given to La Ventana and the FCCB, not the CFM.

The status of the amateur in photography has complicated and enlivened the medium ever since George Eastman introduced his Kodak No. 1 in 1889: Pictorialism is inextricably linked to photography's widespread popularity, even as a reaction against it. After World War II, preserving the distinction between fine-art photography and popular practices may have seemed less important than thinking about the medium as a way of bringing people together, culminating, perhaps, in *The Family of Man*. This impulse to connect was also expressed through the vast international network of photo clubs and salons to which the FCCB and the CFM belonged, where artists and amateurs danced, drank, and critiqued photographs together. This physical network held much in common with social-media platforms today where artists virtually socialize with millions of people whose only camera is found in their pockets.

Sarah Hermanson Meister is Curator in the Department of Photography at the Museum of Modern Art, New York, and the author, most recently, of *Dorothea Lange: Migrant Mother* (2019) and *Frances Benjamin Johnston: The Hampton Album* (2019).

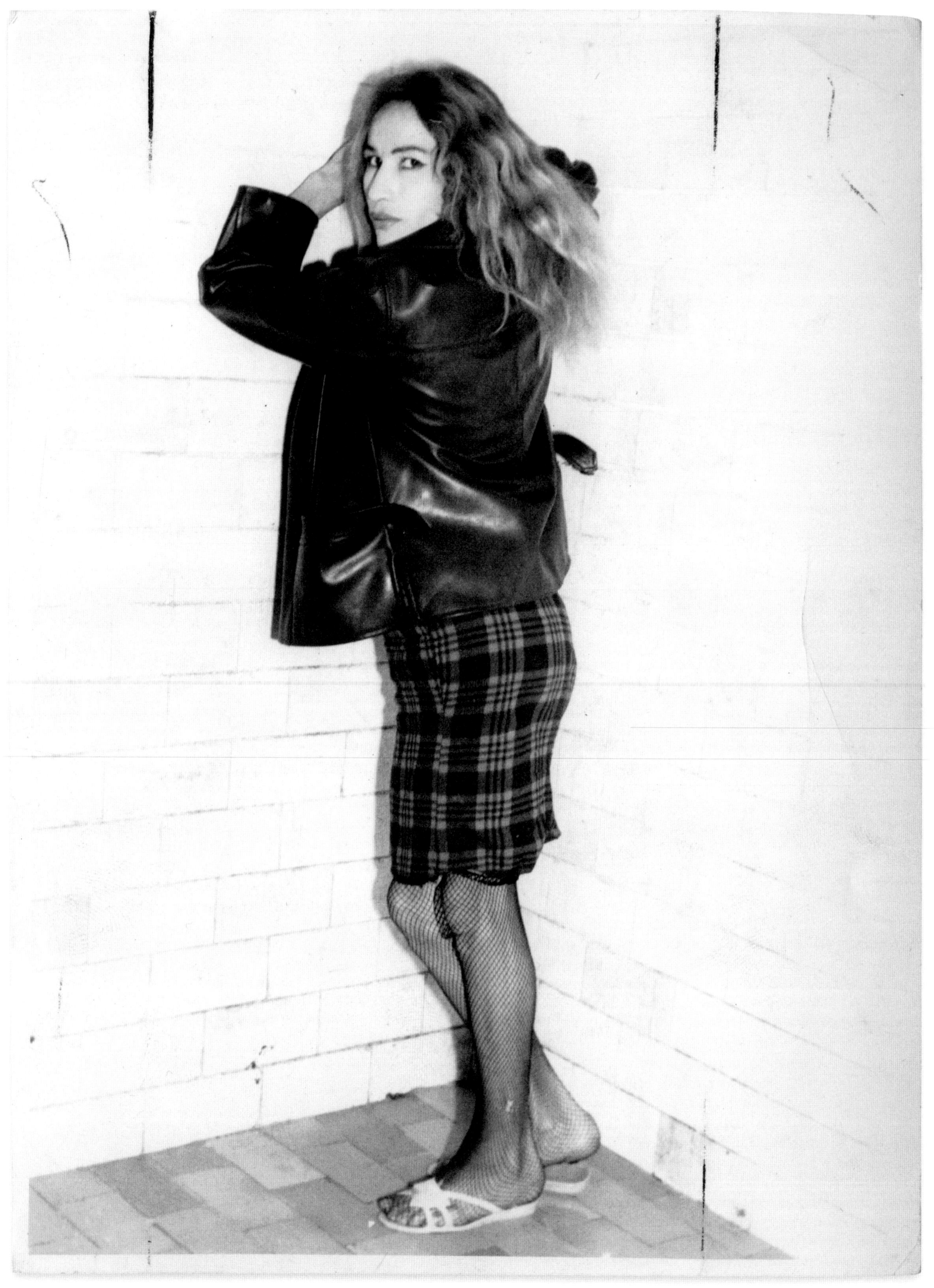

How a midcentury archive of portraits, originally published in a Mexico City police magazine, blurred the boundaries of gender.

Posing Defiance

Alfonso Morales Carrillo

In Mexico, the journalism industry began to take shape toward the end of the nineteenth century and the beginning of the twentieth century. Even so, it was not until the 1930s that the first editorial offering was made available to the general public to better meet their tastes and economic means. As a result of this shift, Mexican print journalism became an active part of the country's social life and an established source of employment. At the cutting edge of this expansion were illustrated publications, especially comic books and magazines, featuring topics ranging from general interest to specialized titles covering performance, sports, and crime.

At the time, neither the national population's high rate of illiteracy nor their lack of education, for the most part, hindered the ability of daily and weekly publications to position themselves as vehicles for information and entertainment, as well as popularizers of mythologies that reinforced dominant ideologies and nourished the collective imagination. The presence of street kiosks where these ephemeral papers were sold multiplied in urban landscapes. Their racks displayed a wide range of magazines that accounted for the vastness and diversity of the world, events in the nation and its capital, supposed changes in the political landscape of an ultimately one-party system, and news—no matter how surprising, terrible, or strange—put the reader's credulity to the test.

Estela (Raúl Montes Beltrán), Mexico City's Judicial Police headquarters, 1967

In spite of the derogatory gaze cast upon them, the subjects of Devars's photographs reclaim their capacity for self-representation.

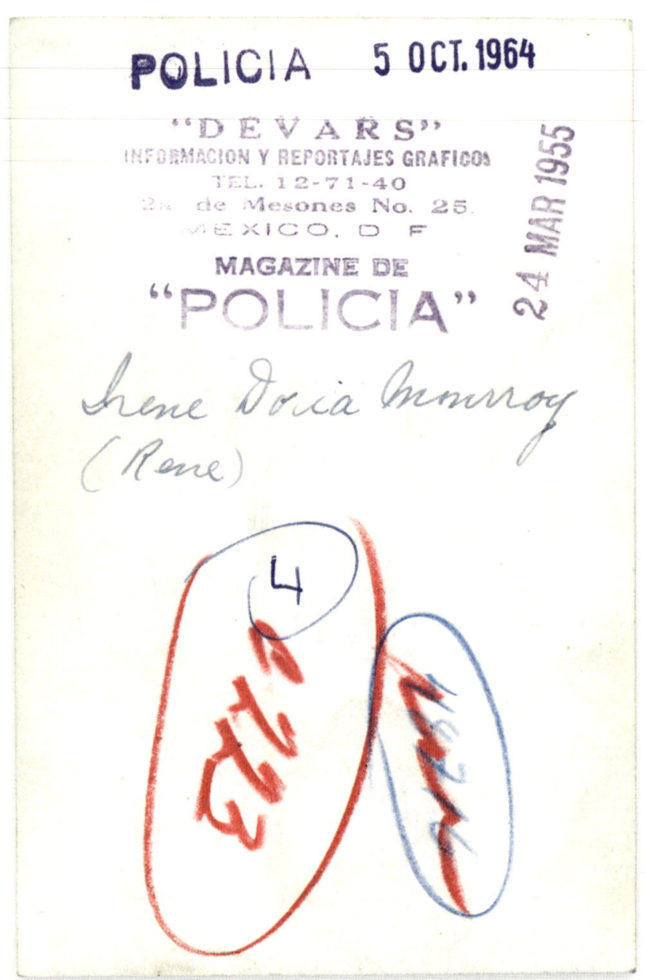

Over the course of more than three decades—from 1939 to the beginning of the 1970s—*Magazine de Policía* and, for a shorter period of time, *Suplemento de Policía* hit the streets at prices within all budgets, offering first-hand information about criminal activity in Mexico City: the metropolis that, from time immemorial, had been the center of both the secular and religious powers of the Mexican republic. The *Magazine de Policía*'s colophon declared the motto "To call out society's ulcers is to serve it," while also announcing that this printed material was "completely unaffiliated with public security bodies." In keeping with that denunciatory mandate, the magazine combined reportage, photographic images, comic strips, photomontages, shocking titles and captions, prejudiced affirmations, and moralizing precepts. The distancing from official guardians of order seems more like a rhetorical declaration if one considers that the majority of the information published in the pages of *Magazine de Policía* and its supplement came from environs that were under the control of the police and judicial authorities.

From the first issue until the mid-1960s, Adrián Devars, Jr. was the principal photographer credited with the majority of the images in *Magazine de Policía* and *Suplemento de Policía*. These images showcased Devars's skills as a reporter—his ability to be present at crime scenes, to photograph victims and murderers, and to move freely between police stations, morgues, and prisons—as well as his talent for setting up staged and fictional photographs, such as the photographic comics published on the back page of *Magazine de Policía*. Researcher Miguel Ángel Morales has followed the trail of this photographer who served as an example for other police-blotter photojournalists. One such reporter was Enrique Metinides, whose work is now published and exhibited internationally. He made a name for himself for his coverage in the newspaper La Prensa. Metinides had the opportunity to see Devars at work in Lecumberri Prison, where he converted the forensics department into a studio and would prepare cadavers—cleaning them up, combing their hair, dressing them, and even going as far as to insert objects (a knife in a wound, a brick to prop up a head) to add dramatic flair to his images.

In his early career, Devars was director and publisher, from 1926 to 1934, of the weekly paper *Vida alegre*, a role he gave up to become a photographer and to test his luck in pornographic films. From 1937 to 1939, he belonged to the staff of the magazine *Vea*, the epitome of erotic publications in Mexico in the last century, in whose pages he demonstrated an inclination toward the sinister and the gruesome. After being a star photographer for *Magazine de Policía* and *Suplemento de Policía*, Devars ended his career as a photojournalist working for *Alerta*, another weekly paper devoted to the police blotter.

The journalists with whom Devars shared the pages of *Magazine de Policía* and *Suplemento de Policía*—Rosa Vega, Renato Alanís, R. Lara, Lauro Vélez de Dargast, and Comandante Masuski, among others—practiced a kind of crime reporting that involved conducting fieldwork and collecting testimonies, but with a particular emphasis on the morbid and the scandalous. Mexico City proved an inexhaustible source for their stories. The metropolis had undergone rapid growth in an utterly disorganized way. It had turned into a cultural melting pot and a mesmerizing showcase of transformation, modernization, commercial exchanges, and new fashions. As the researcher Gabriela Pulido Llano has observed, one can clearly see the contradictions and tensions of Mexican modernity in these publications: their records of violence, crime, and debauchery reveal the dark side of mid-twentieth-century life in Mexico City.

While *Magazine de Policía* published accusations against beneficiaries of female prostitution, proprietors of hole-in-the-wall nightclubs, and corrupt police officers, they also made note of men of "wrongful habits," those who did not fit within heterosexual normativity and who chose to identify as women. Merely appearing

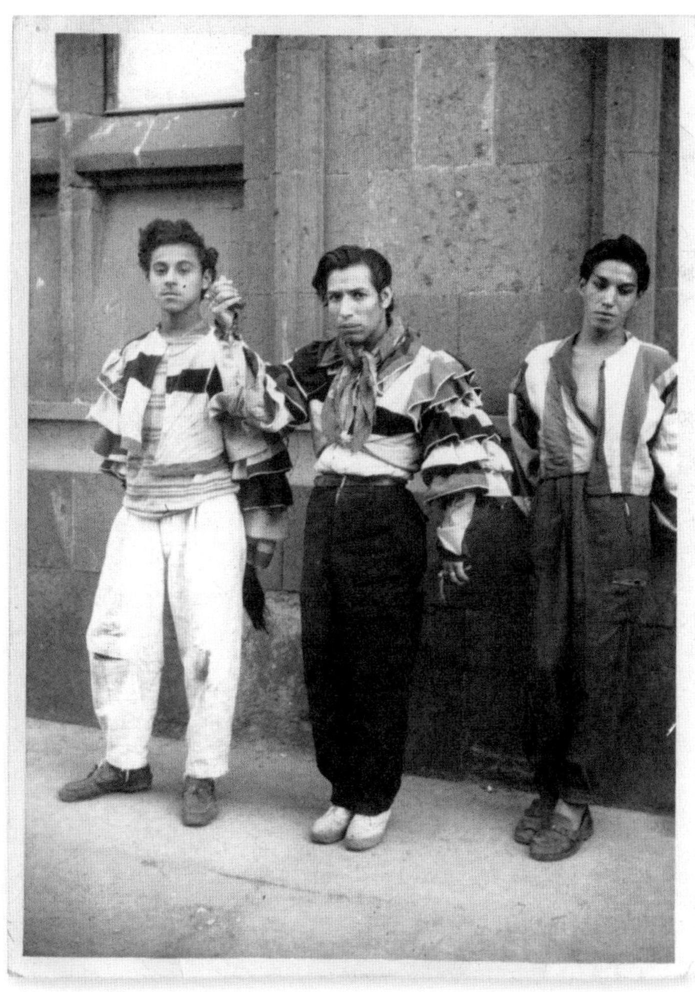

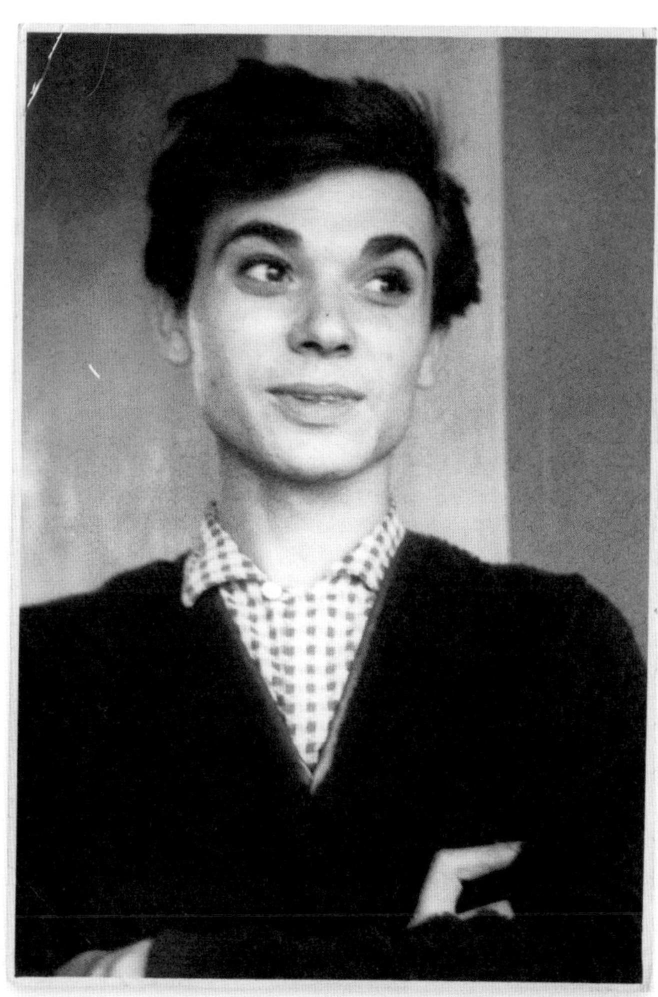

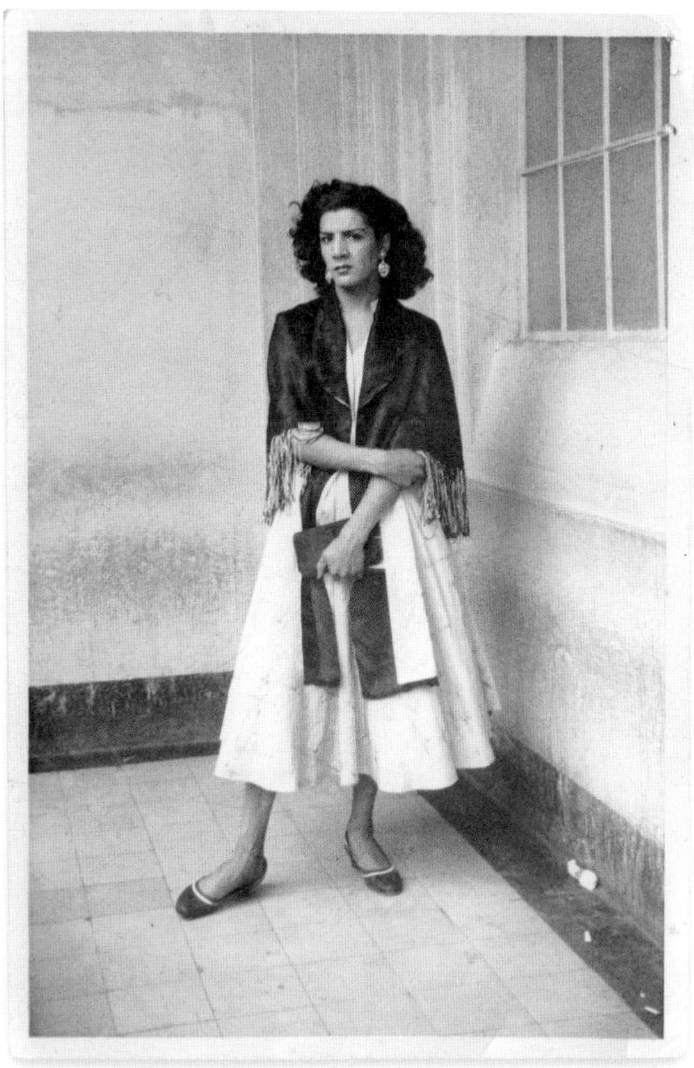

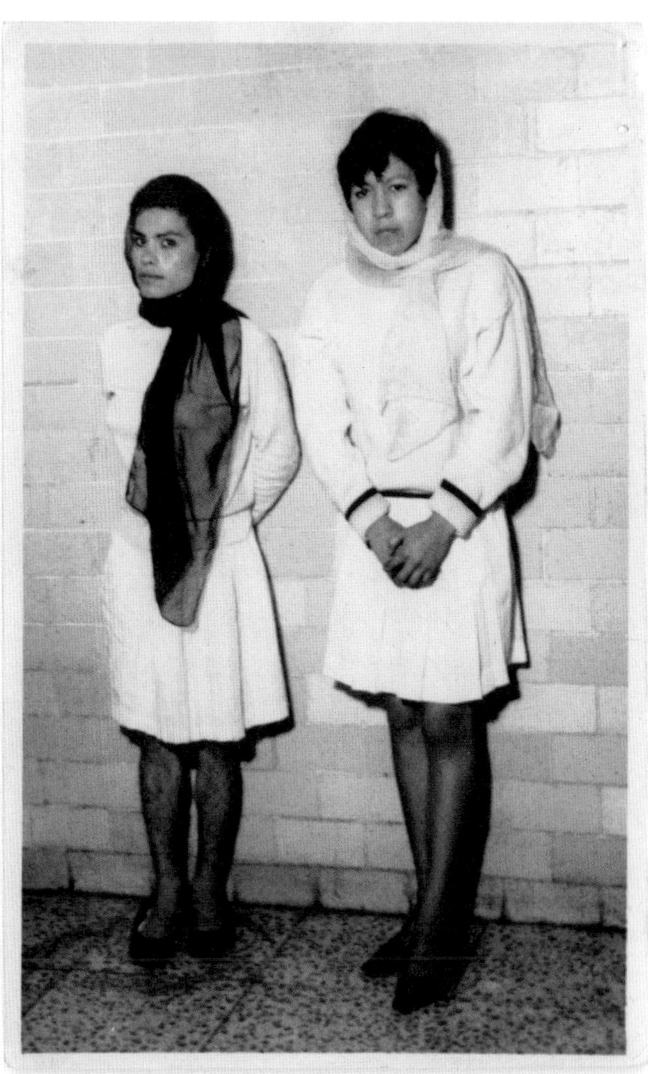

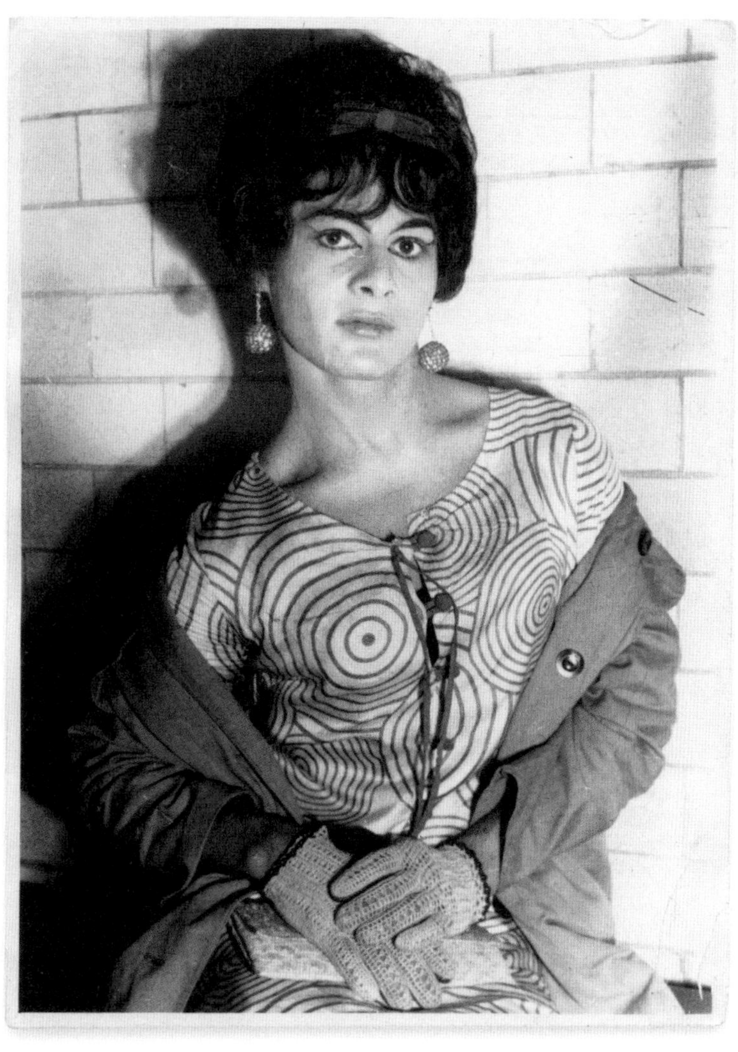
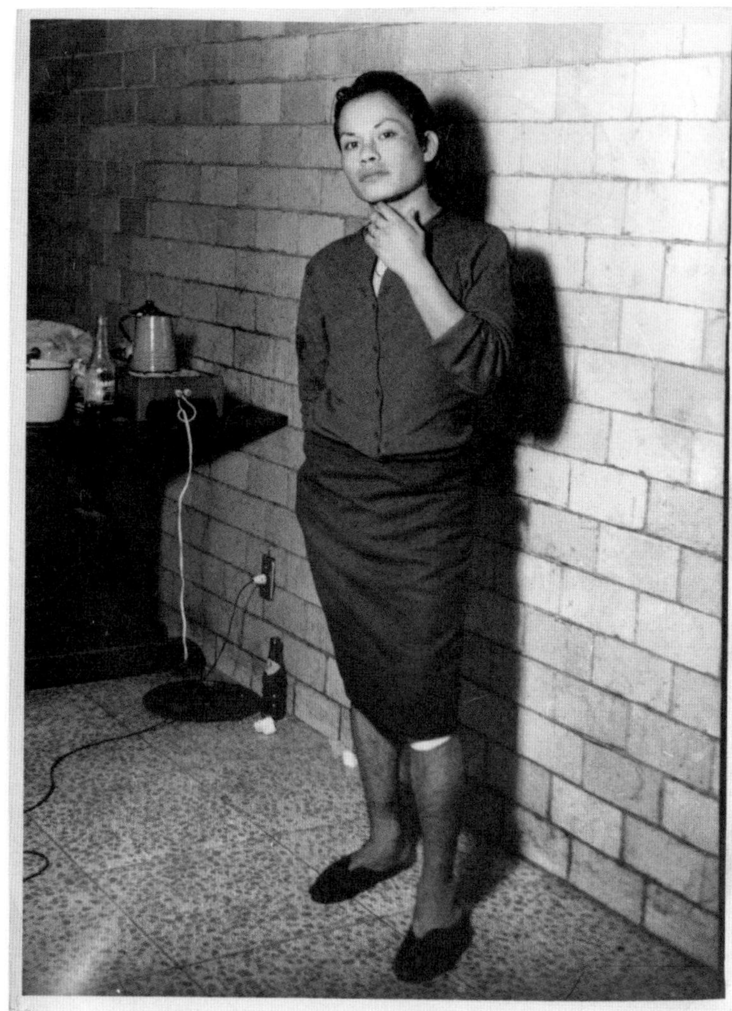
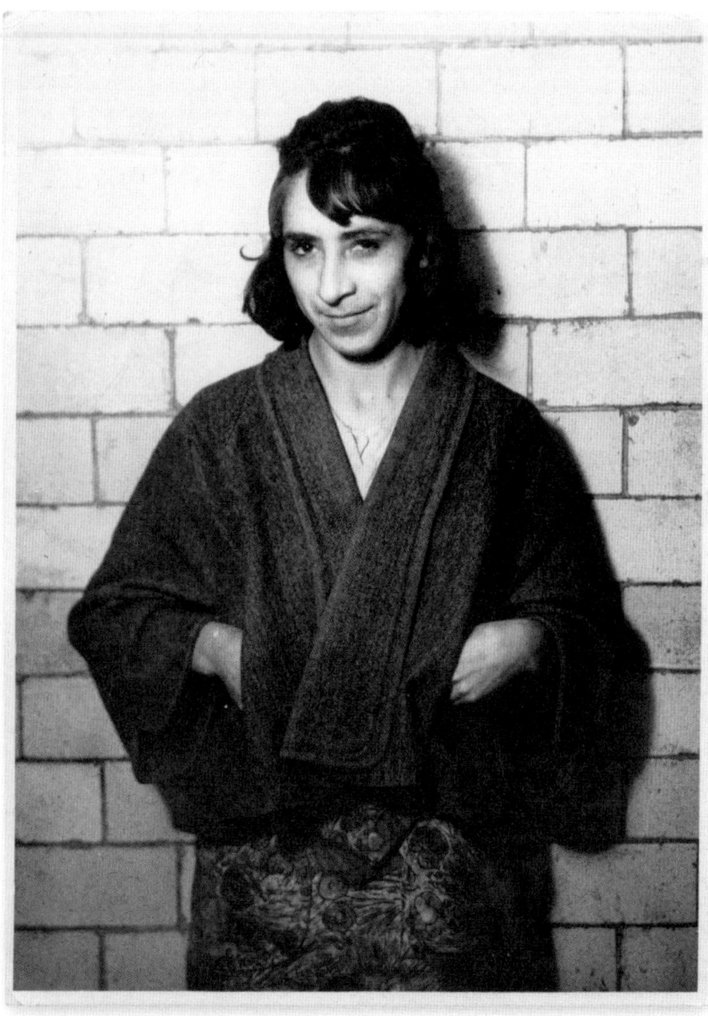
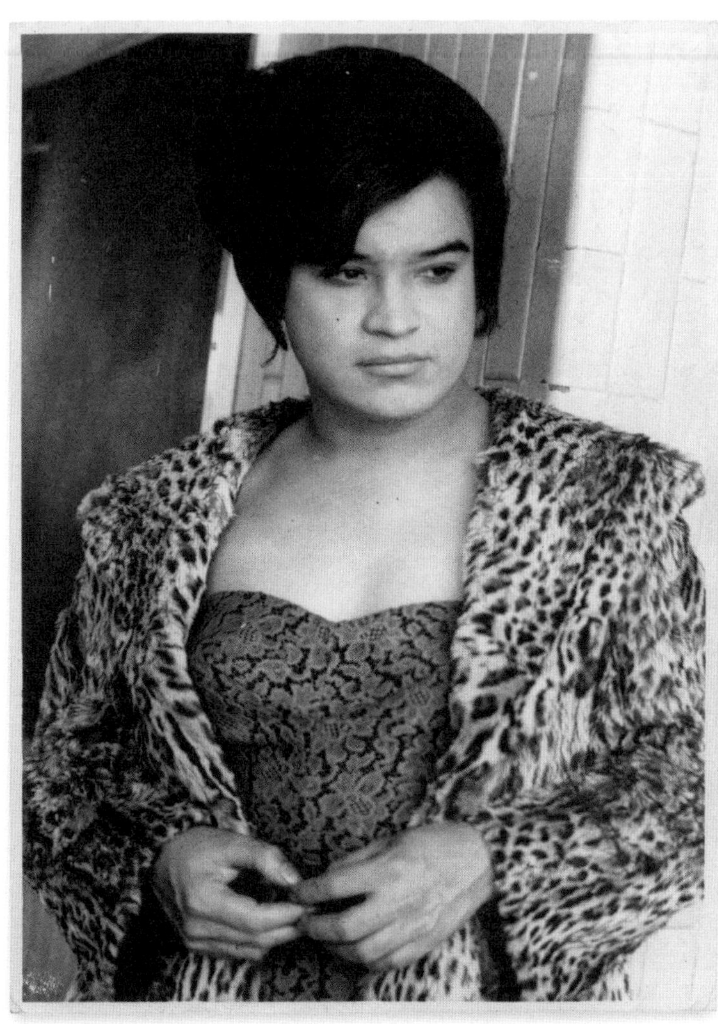

feminine raised suspicion toward these "*lilos*," "queers," and "effeminates," who were often victims of extortion and imprisonment, especially if they dared to walk through the streets offering up their charms for sale. The magazine's texts and images ridiculing *los travestis* (transvestites) revealed not only the authoritarian reflection of a macho mentality, but also the not-so-hidden fascination with people who blurred traditional gender boundaries. Proof of the latter lies in the stories of supposed deceit that befell certain male wooers, including police officers who boasted Don Juan prowess, who discovered to their surprise, in moments of intimacy, that "she" was in fact a "he."

The portraits of transvestites taken by Devars for *Magazine de Policía* are extensions of the police bookings where the personal data and infractions of the detained were recorded. Nevertheless, in spite of the weight of the investigative and derogatory gaze cast upon these people with the aim of exposing their rarity and grotesqueness, the subjects of Devars's photographs—at least to a certain degree—reclaim their capacity for self-representation and declare their own defiant presence. Individuals unjustly punished for their sexual preferences pose as if on an imaginary catwalk in the bleak and depressing police precinct interior, affirming the boldness of their manifold identities and the right, as expressed by one subject, to dress "however she may please, so long as the Constitution allowed it."

This confrontation between a classifying typology and individual agency is on display in the set of portraits by Devars that are found in the photographic archive of the late writer Carlos Monsiváis, one of the most influential Mexican intellectuals of the twentieth century. It remains unclear whether the prolific essayist and journalist—who chose not to reveal his own homosexuality though he was a tireless defender of sexual rights—ever planned to do something specific with these images. His writings that reference transvestites reveal some reservations with regard to what he viewed as a proclivity toward dramatization and subservience to stereotypes. However, these are characteristics that Monsiváis greatly admired in the 1977 Canadian film *Outrageous!* starring the drag queen Craig Russell, for which Monsiváis wrote the Spanish subtitles. His most empathic work about *las vestidas* (cross-dressers) can be found in an article about a performance by the artist Xóchitl during Carnival in the Port of Veracruz. In this 1984 piece, for *Su Otro Yo* magazine, Monsiváis writes: "A transvestite is the joke made in seriousness and the parody of seriousness … someone who doesn't care to comply with patrolled boundaries between *masculinity* and *femininity* and who, lacking a theory in that regard, receives what they are told and quickly transforms into the being as described by its own critics (and into the reduction, taken to the absurd, of the critics' description)."

These portraits, bearing Devars's and the *Magazine de Policía*'s stamps on the back, were first displayed in the exhibition *Pasado venidero* (Forseeable past), in 2015, at the Museo del Estanquillo in Mexico City. Founded in 2006, the museum is charged with caring for and disseminating Monsiváis's collections of sculptures, paintings, prints, comics, photographs, books, and magazines. If the literary and journalistic work of Monsiváis left no subject untouched—from poetry of the highest order to expressions of popular culture, from the ups and downs of politics to the vibrant chaos of street life—as a collector he was no less omnivorous. He gave shape to an archive that has value as cultural memory while also serving as a faithful portrait of his interests and obsessions. For this celebrated author of *Días de guardar* (Days to remember) and *Amor perdido* (Lost love), photography was a subject for investigation, a source of inspiration, and a creative resource. Monsiváis not only utilized photographs by referencing them in his essays, but he also integrated images into his style of writing, a quality that earned him the role of innovator of Mexican literature.

Page 109, clockwise from top left:
Eduardo Pérez del Ángel, Mario Ruíz González, and Roberto Calderón Bello, "three subjects in incorrect clothing, arrested by the police for dancing in a public street," 1952; La Güera or La Chabela (Manuel Álvarez Treviño), "an effeminate who was on the go in the vicinity of Plaza Garibaldi, in search of someone to make love to," 1969; Rosa (Carlos Acuña Rodríguez) and Carmen (Eduardo Ramírez García), who "were walking down the street when an undercover police car arrested them and took them in to headquarters as suspects, where it was then made clear that they were not women, but men," 1963; María Mac Clios Silva (Miguel Martínez Silva), who was detained by undercover police in Intime cabaret, Roma, Mexico City, 1955

Opposite, clockwise from top left:
Maribel (Alberto del Valle Galindo), accused of "practicing prostitution," 1968; Carmen Reyes Pérez (Guillermo Acosta González), who was taken in for "causing a ruckus at a hotel," 1964; Susana (Víctor Manuel Mejía González), who confessed to dressing as a woman for eight years and to being a dancer in theaters and nightclubs in border towns on the outskirts of Mexico City, 1964; Amapola (Alfredo Rodríguez Gutiérrez), arrested "when he was selling his charms on Juan de la Granja Street," 1965

All photographs by Adrián Devars Jr. and published in *Magazine de Policía* Collection of Carlos Monsiváis/Mueso del Estanquillo

Alfonso Morales Carrillo is Editor of *Luna Córnea*. The publication's forthcoming issue will be dedicated to the photography collections of Carlos Monsiváis.

Translated from the Spanish by Elianna Kan.

In 1972, in a commercial space in the Cacho neighborhood of Tijuana, my parents founded Venegas Fine Photography. Their studio offered novel services such as color photography made with a medium-format Hasselblad camera and, eventually, the delivery of a wedding album that chronicled the milestone event in its entirety. For all these innovations, my father's brand became a form of identification for Tijuana's nascent upper-middle class.

Years before, my mother, Julia Edith, had encouraged my father, José Luis, to study photography by correspondence through the Famous Photographers School, where Alfred Eisenstaedt, Richard Avedon, and Irving Penn taught. A key part of the school's philosophy was that students pay for the course through their photographic work. My parents moved from Tijuana to Los Angeles in 1967, and José Luis began to work for Alfred & Fabris Studio, where he learned a method of documenting weddings through twenty-five pivotal moments, from the bride's final preparations before the mirror to the newlyweds driving off, leaving the celebration behind.

The Tijuana subjects seen in my parents' archive—much like my father himself—collectively believed in and bestowed power on ritual, placing love as the linchpin of their coming together. But their identity was being formed by what destiny had given them: they were a community coming into their own on the border of the United States. Tijuana citizens were having their children on the other side; men and women were marrying people from the United States. My parents bought materials, developed their film, and printed their work in California. They emulated the poses and tropes of wedding documentation that had been taught to them by a U.S. company.

Now, as I work with these photographs in my Mexico City studio, I see how this archive excludes one of the most essential aspects of any border experience: vulnerability. The line between skill and error is a latent space, where things transpire that fit neither of the two extremes, but that are also a part of the story. Ambiguity, unplanned gestures, strained bodies in the process of understanding themselves as spectacle: all speak of a border identity. Given this, I believe it is essential to reformulate my parents' archive to allow the more vulnerable moments their due attention, salvaging the images that weren't ultimately used in the official wedding albums. The essential function of photographs has always been to preserve one's image for posterity's sake. Expressions of our fragility, or that which makes us perishable, lend something important to the way we are depicted.

The J. L. Venegas Archive

Yvonne Venegas

Yvonne Venegas is an artist based in Mexico City.

Translated from the Spanish by Elianna Kan.

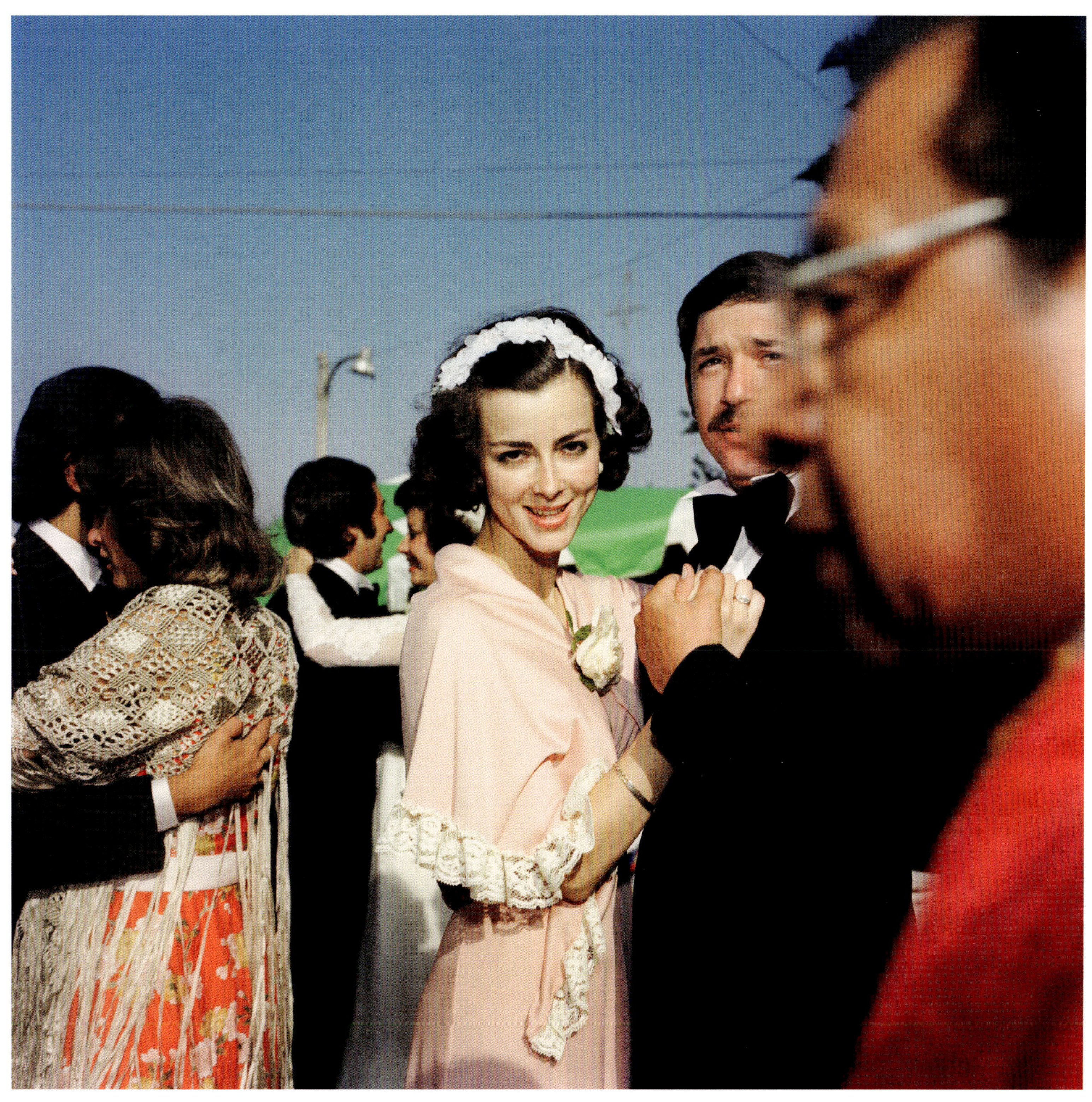

Polianna Appel dancing,
1974

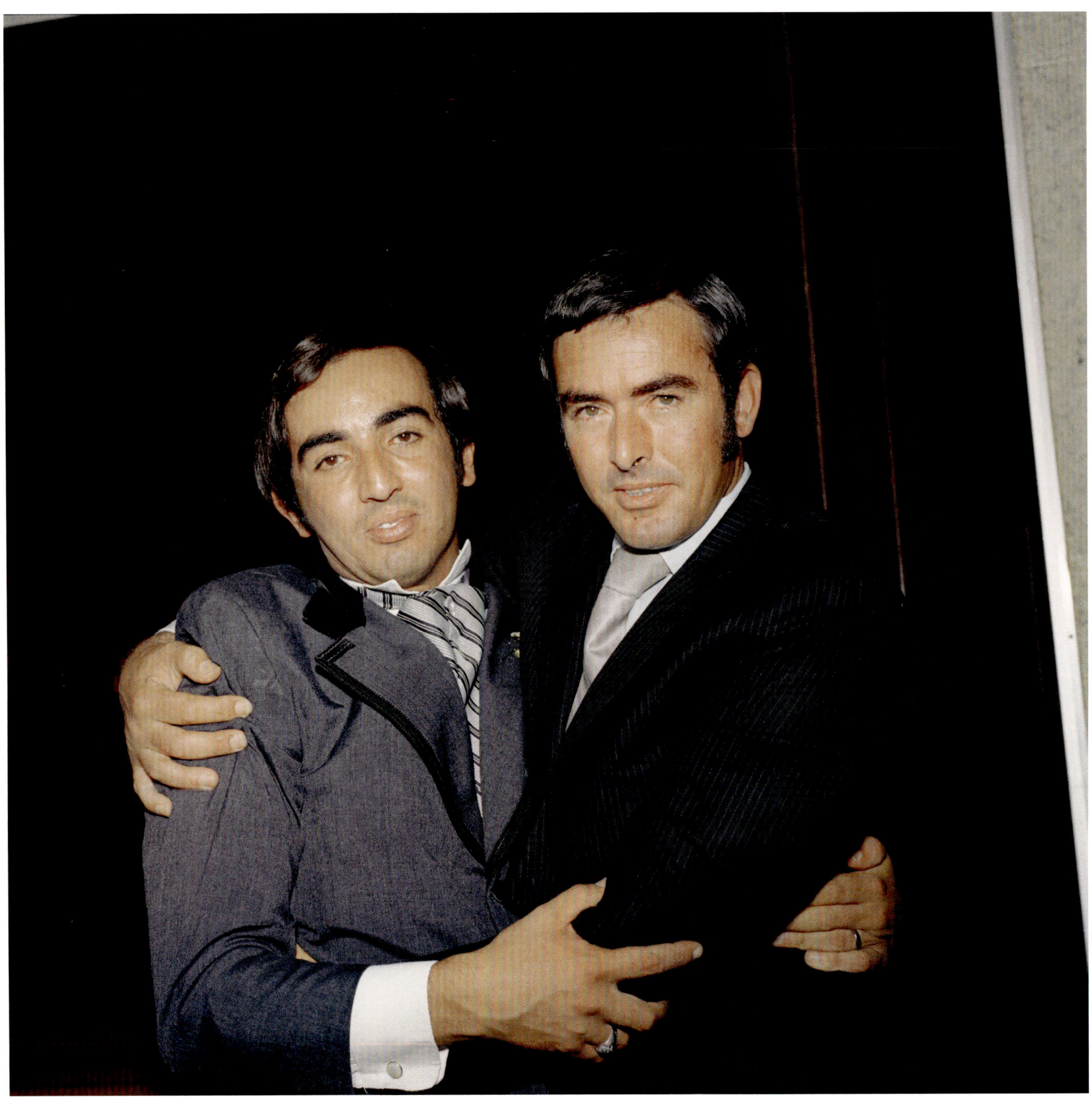

Hermanos (Brothers), 1973

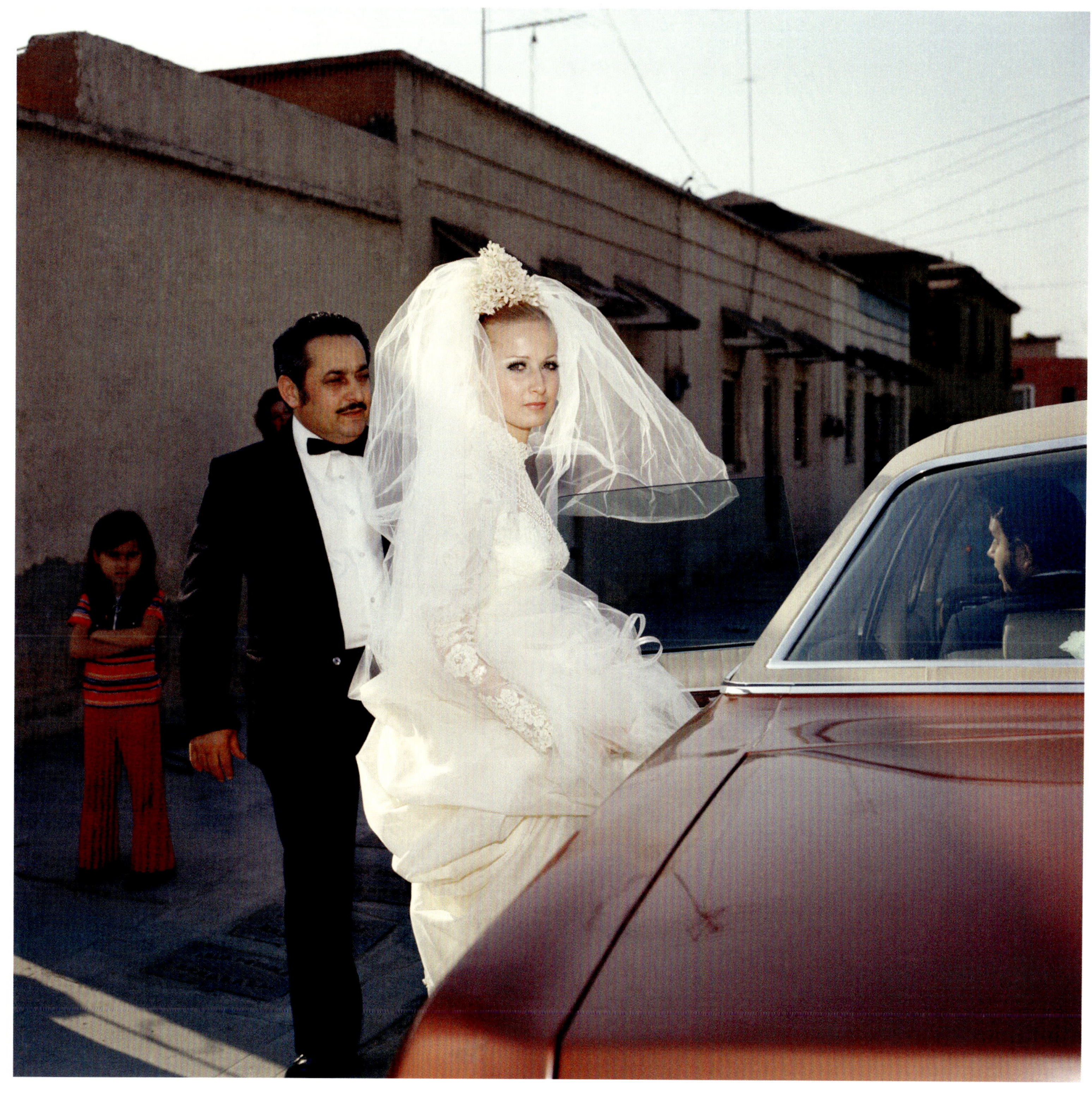

Malof-González, 1973

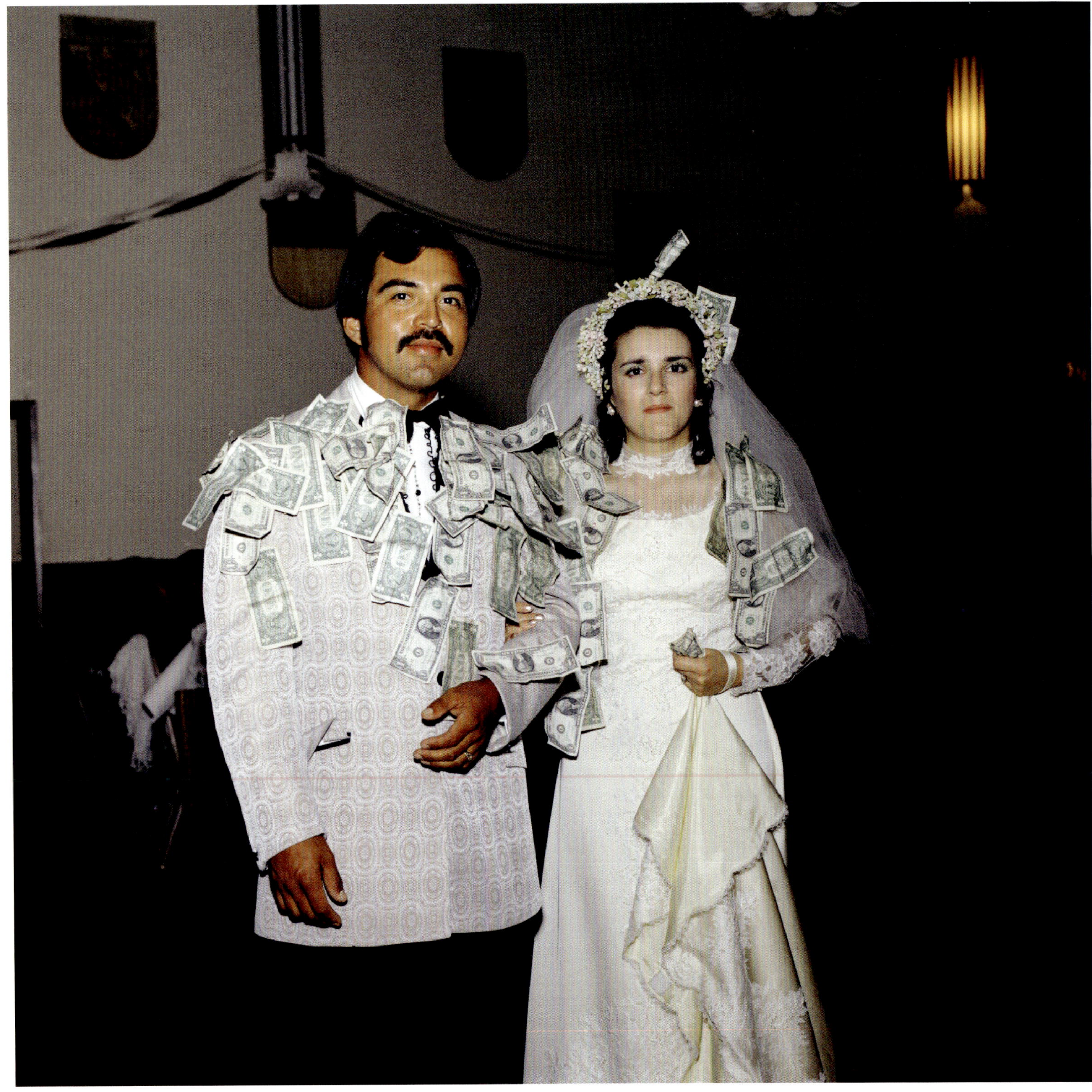

Sosa, 1972

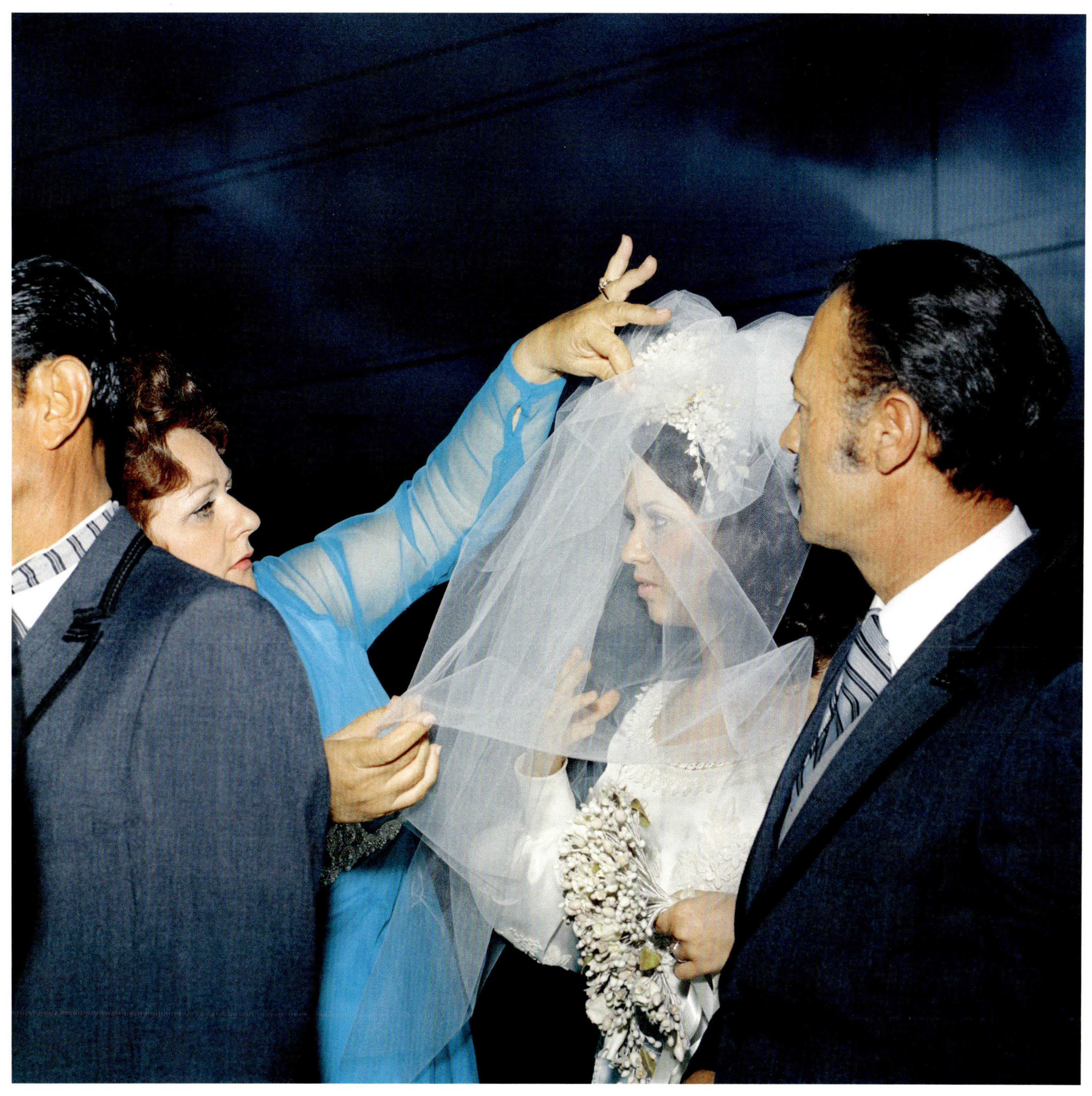

Castillo-Salinas, 1972

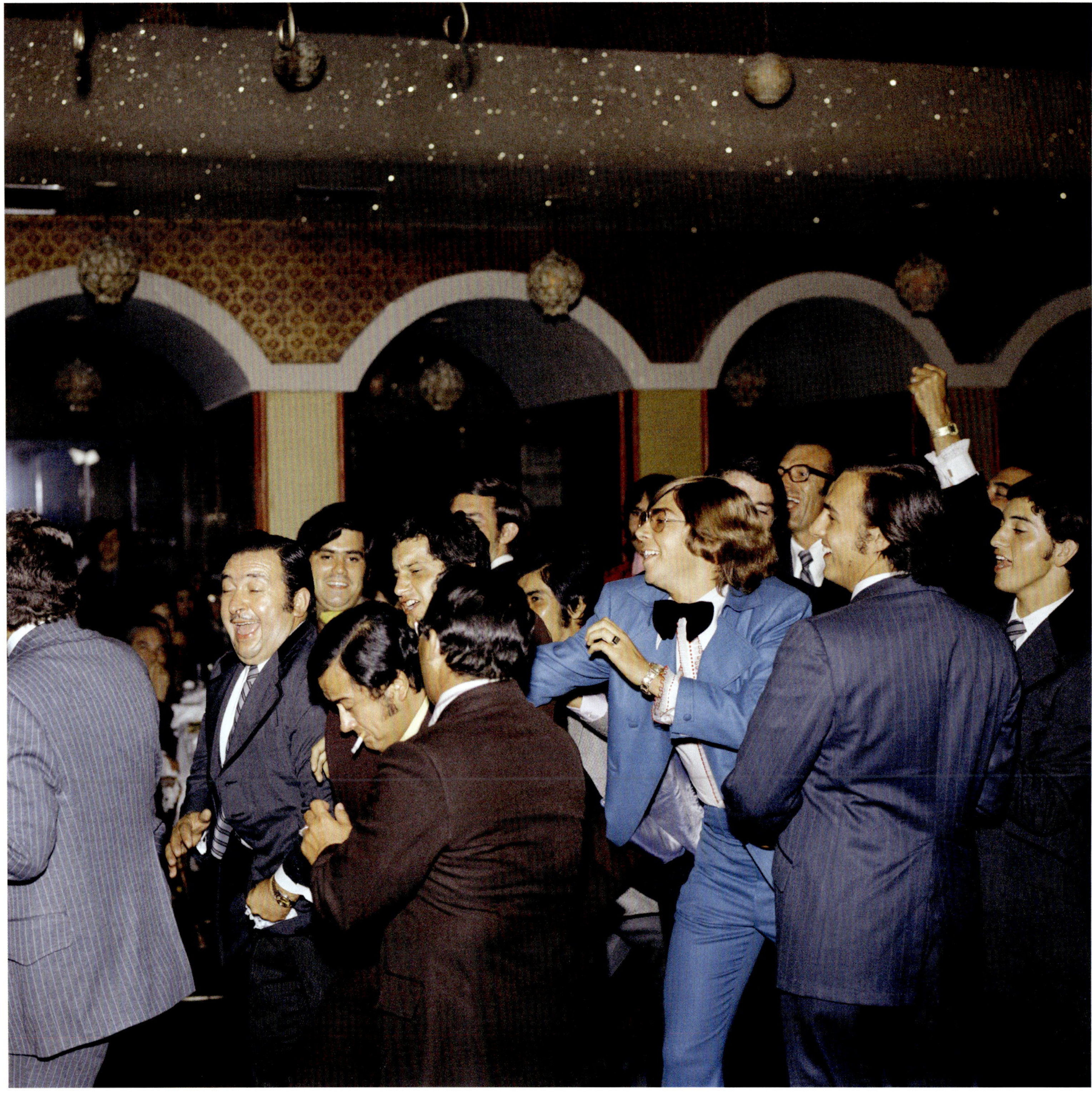

Fajardo-Duarte, 1972

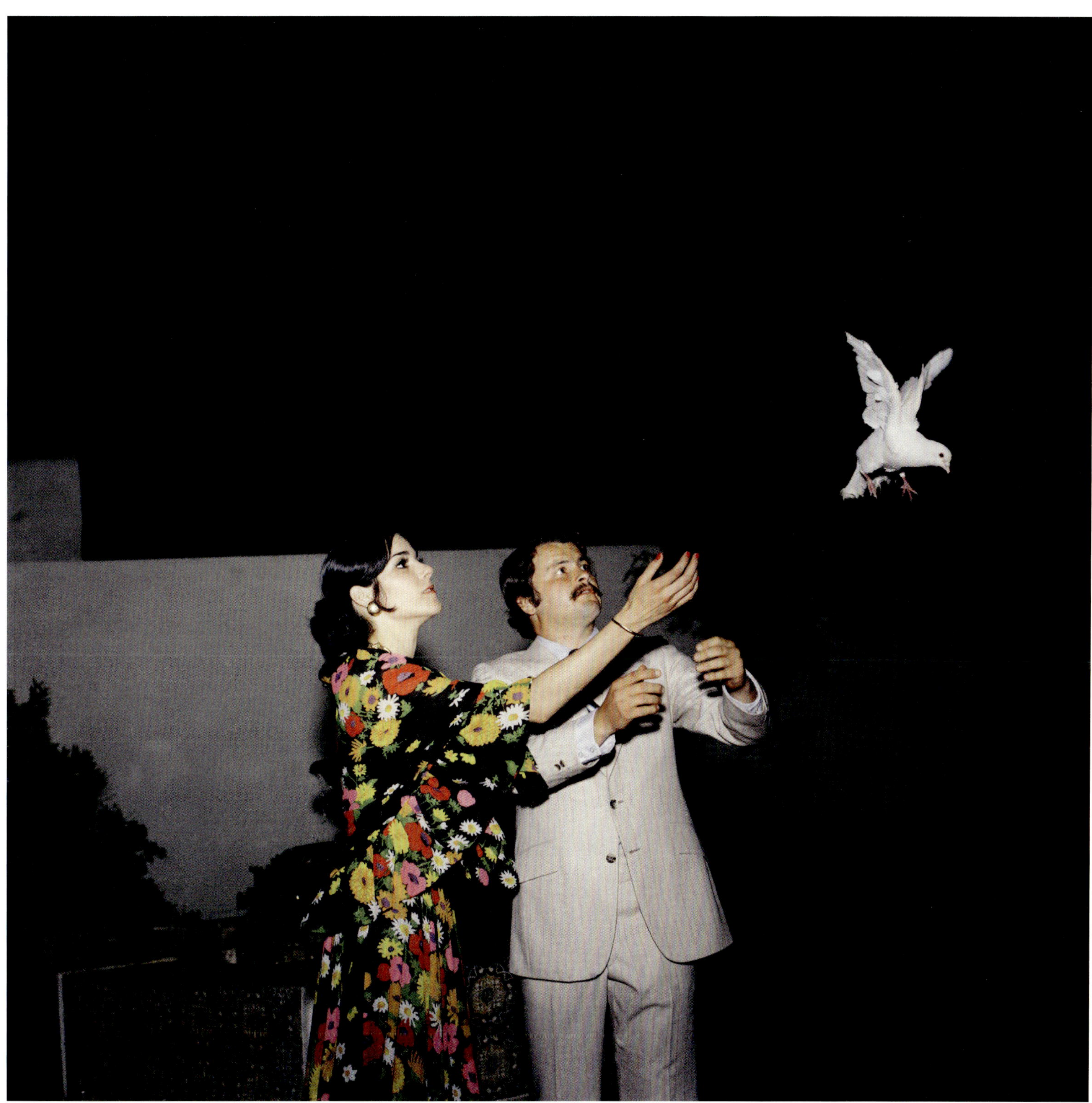

Castellanos-Martínez, 1973

All photographs from the archive of J. L. Venegas. Edited by Yvonne Venegas, 2019

Courtesy Yvonne Venegas

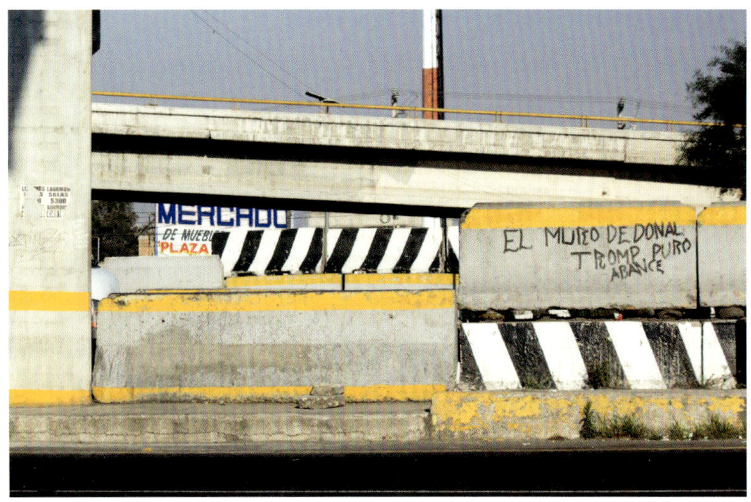
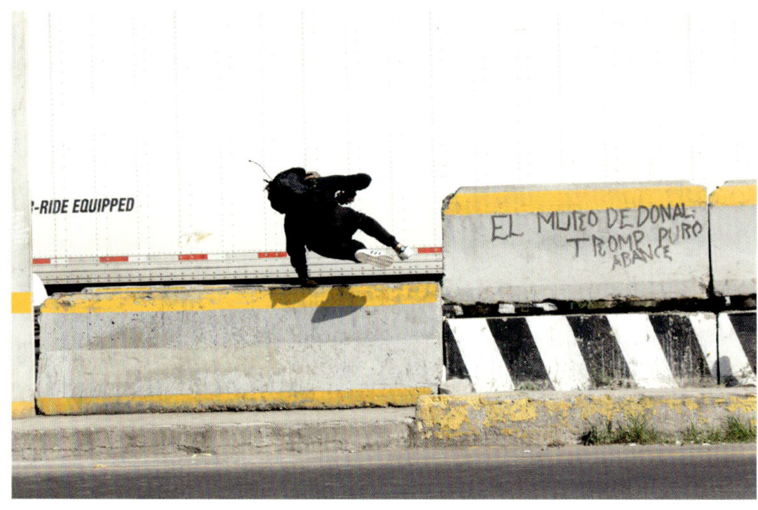
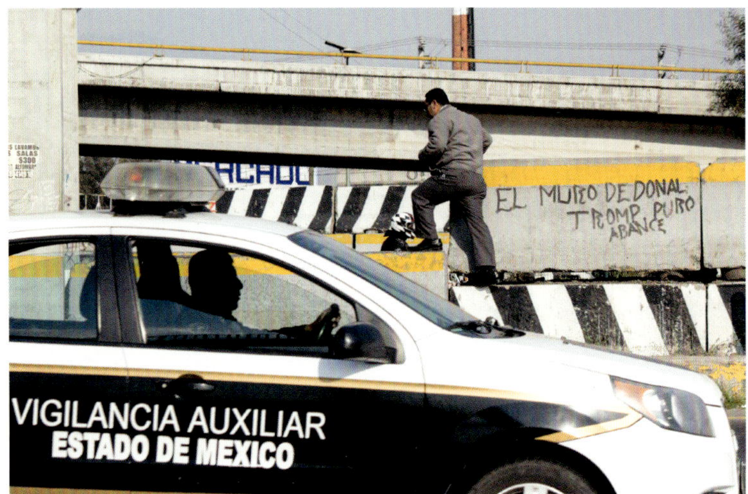
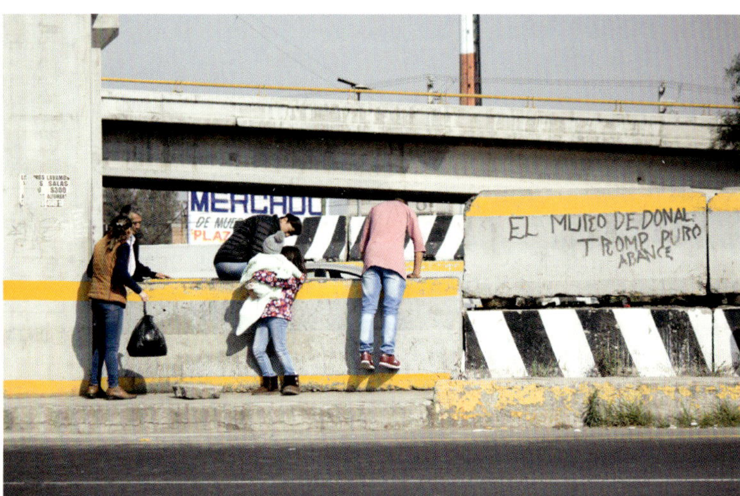

Sonia Madrigal

Yxta Maya Murray

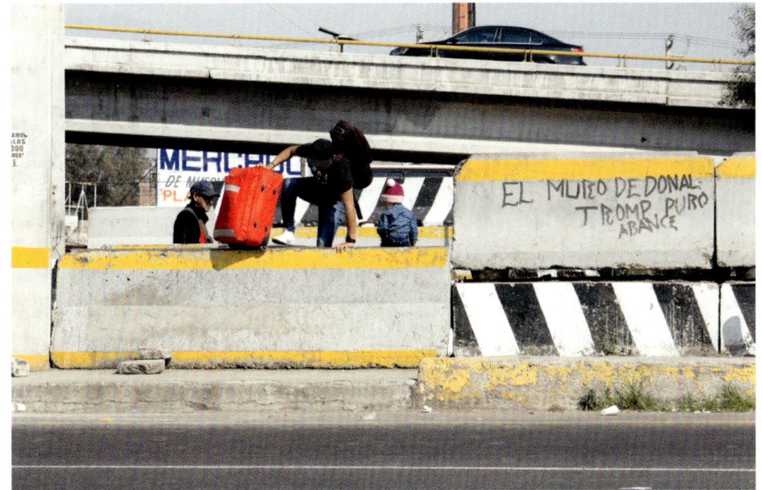 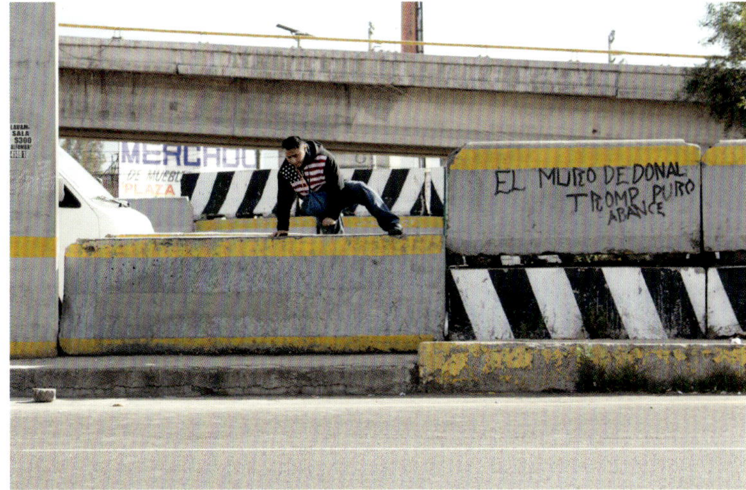

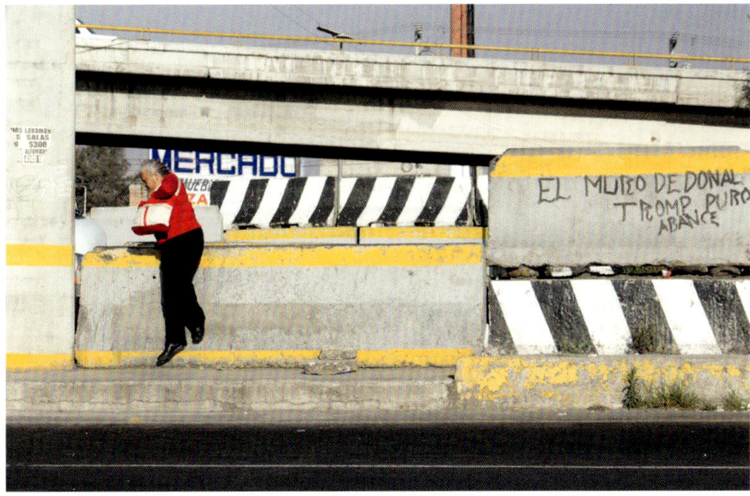 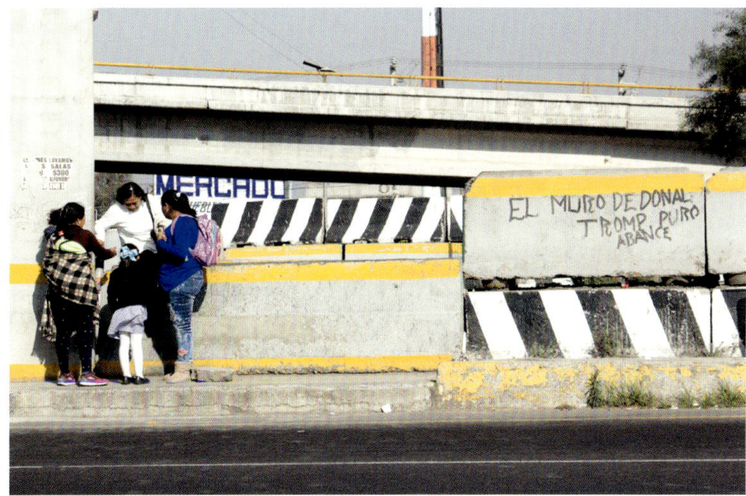

Sonia Madrigal's galvanizing photographs of Mexican residents leaping over a concrete retaining wall of the Chalco–Ixtapaluca expressway recall the tales of desperate treks that repeat through myth and history. In her seventy-one-image series *El Abance, Estado de México* (The advance, State of Mexico, 2018), she reveals men and women hurtling themselves over this barrier to gain access to public transportation, as the area does not have a footbridge where people can walk to the buses that form part of their daily commute. She often catches them midair, their hair flying, their bodies akimbo. Or she'll capture them as they grasp their children, foodstuffs, and other supplies to make their unsteady journeys over the bulwark.

The barricade is spray-painted with the phrase EL MURO DE DONAL TROMP PURO ABANCE (DONAL TROMP'S WALL UTTER PROGRESS), which inserts the current corrosive political moment into our readings of these odysseys. But the images resonate also with older stories of dangerous crossings during catastrophic times. In Virgil's *The Aeneid*, for example, Aeneas migrates over the death-filled River Acheron to visit with the spirit of his father, who assures him of the future of their kin. In the biblical book of Joshua, the Israelites cross the perilous River Jordan aided by their belief in God.

Madrigal reveals her subjects to be both family-focused Aeneases as well as steadfast wayfarers. In a particularly striking image, a cluster of five people, all deeply attentive to each other, clamber over the barricade while engaged in conversation—one of the women, wearing a pink floral top, hoists a child wrapped in a fluffy, green blanket while a second woman, seated on the edge of the wall and wrapped in a puffy, black jacket, half turns to look at the baby. In another picture, a woman wearing slim, dark jeans and a bright-pink backpack straddles the partition while carrying a little boy, who curls up his legs, cocks his left arm, and makes a tight fist. This tableau is mirrored in the photograph showing a dark-garbed man lifting a little girl dressed in a turquoise sweatshirt and pink-and-white sneakers, who casts a shadow of tiny, dangling feet onto the concrete. Yet another possible mother figure, wearing a white sweatshirt and with her hair tied into a ponytail, totters over the barrier while juggling an unwieldy paper bag and plastic bags full of group-size groceries.

Do any of these travelers pray before jumping toward the oncoming cars? Or do they simply own a steely conviction, born of economic hardship, that they can survive the mad scramble? Whatever well they draw from, such leaps of faith can be found in the specter of a man wearing a black-and-white patterned vest and a large, black backpack as he pushes off the wall with one brown-shod foot, looking as if he were tossing himself off a cliff. The most kinetic image shows a figure, of indeterminate sex, dressed all in black but for bright-white sneakers; placing one hand on the divider, this person levitates sideways and almost appears to be running—straight into an approaching red-and-white eighteen-wheeler.

Yxta Maya Murray is Professor of Law at Loyola Law School, Los Angeles, and the author of the forthcoming novel *Art Is Everything*.

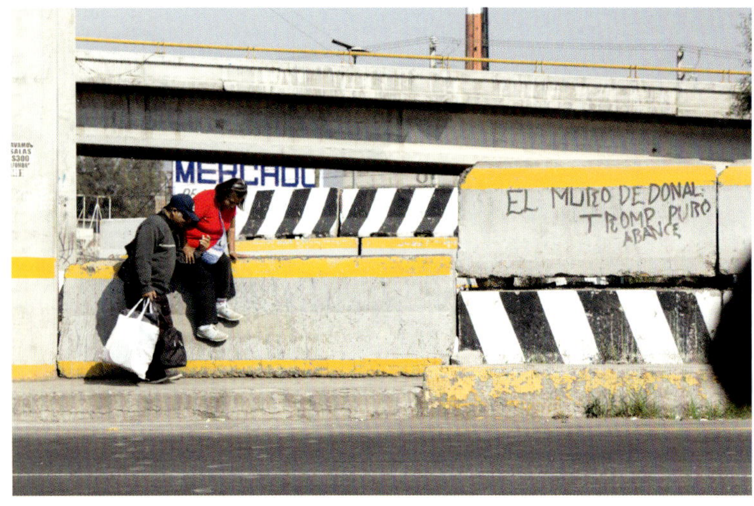
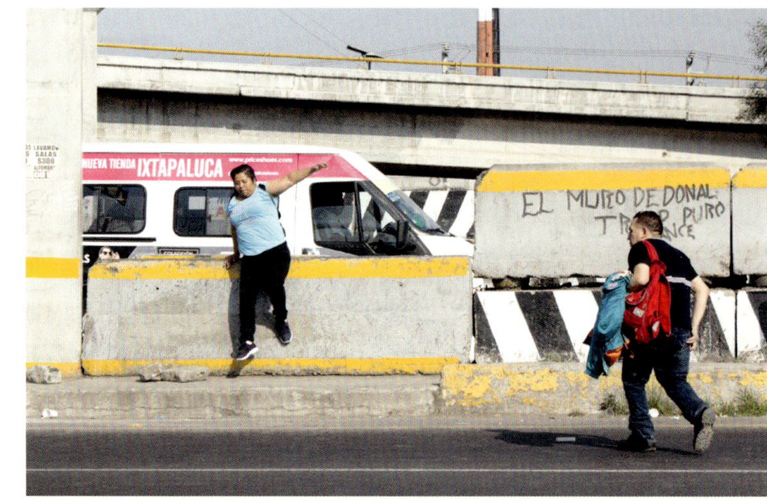
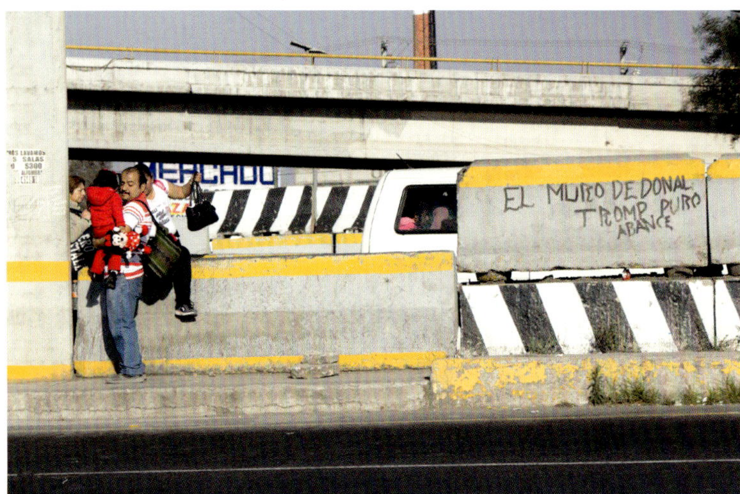
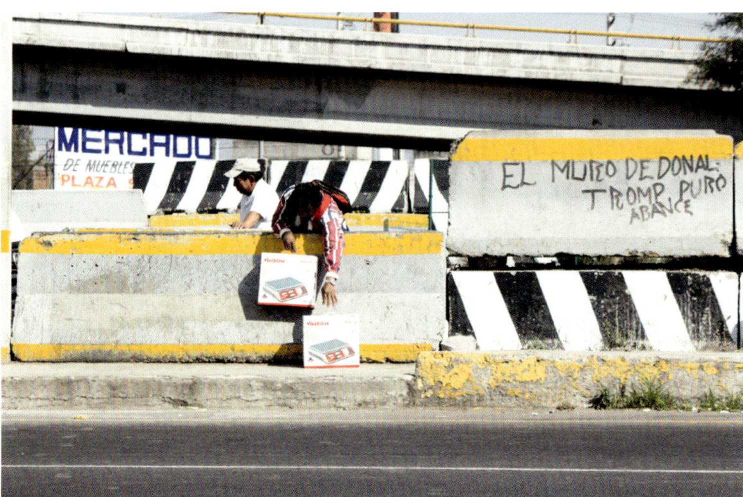
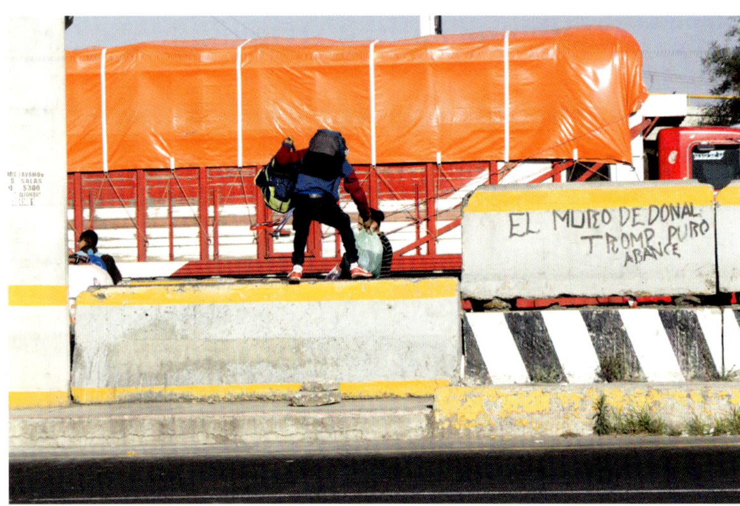
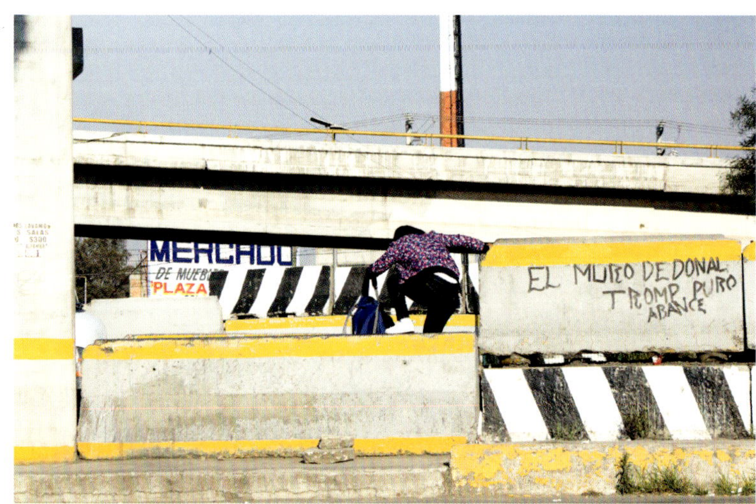
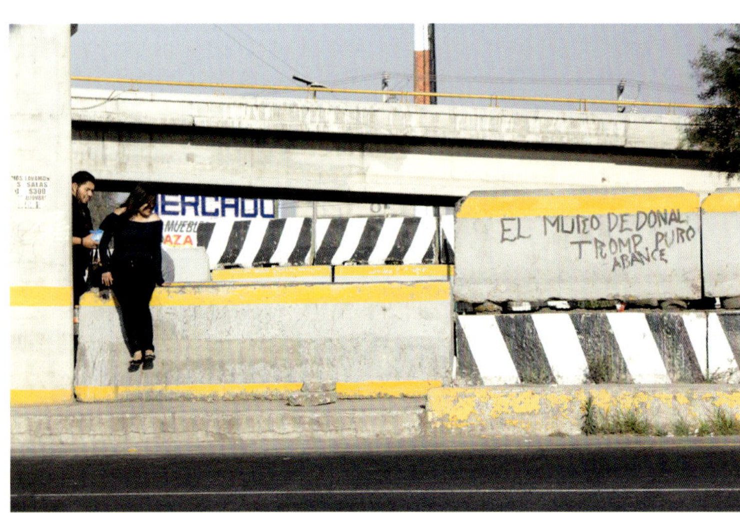
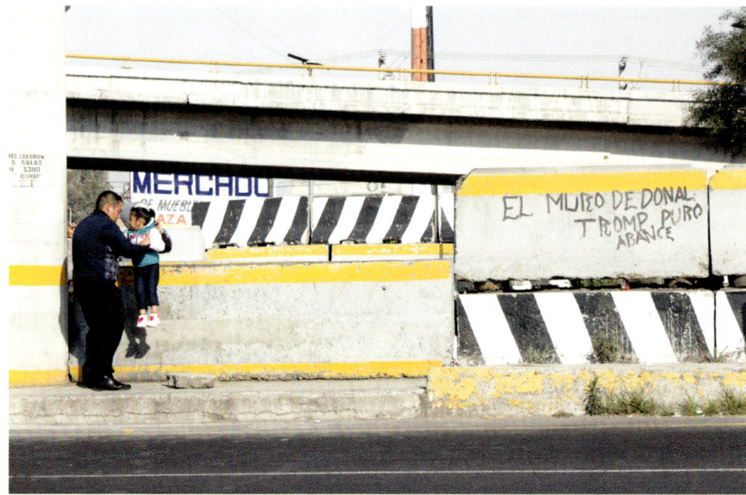

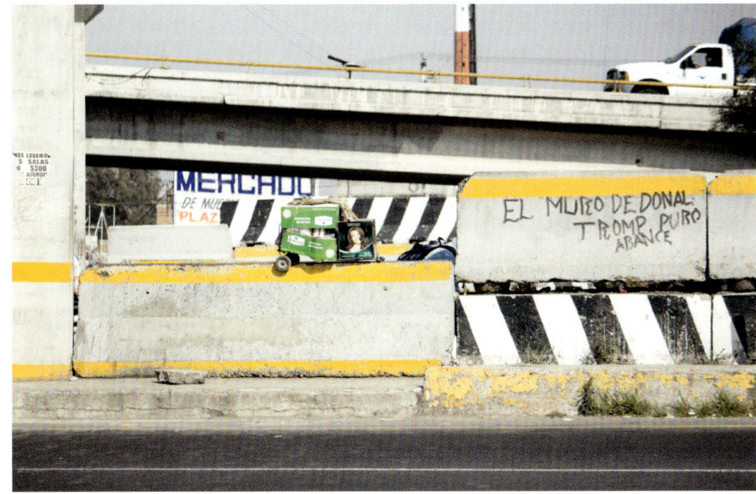
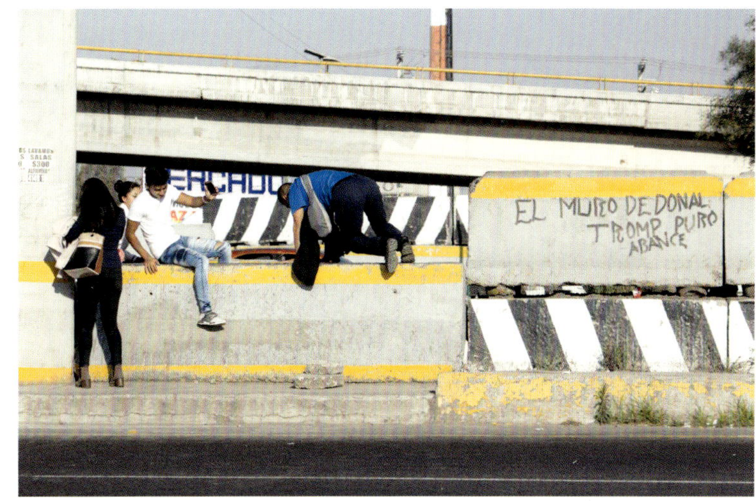
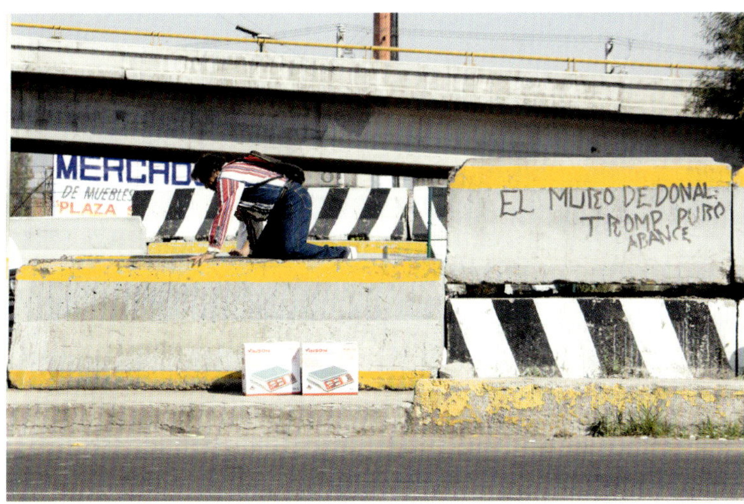
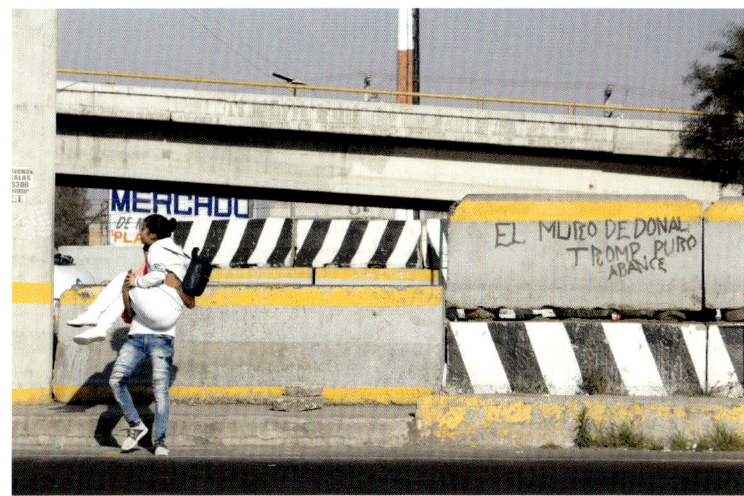
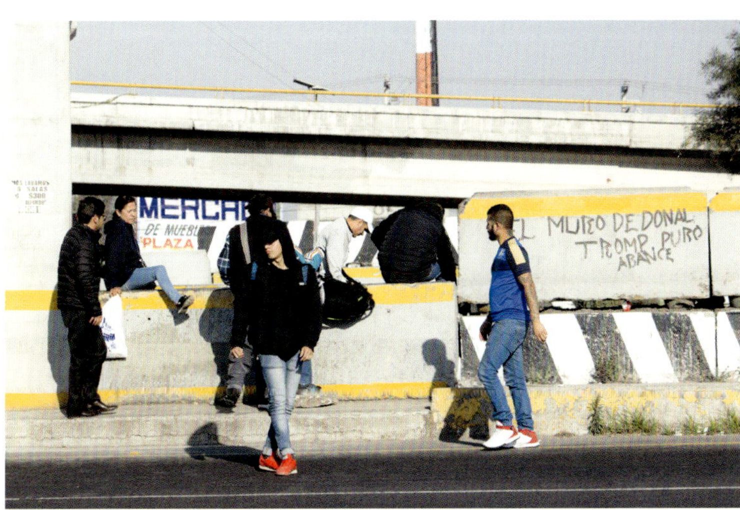
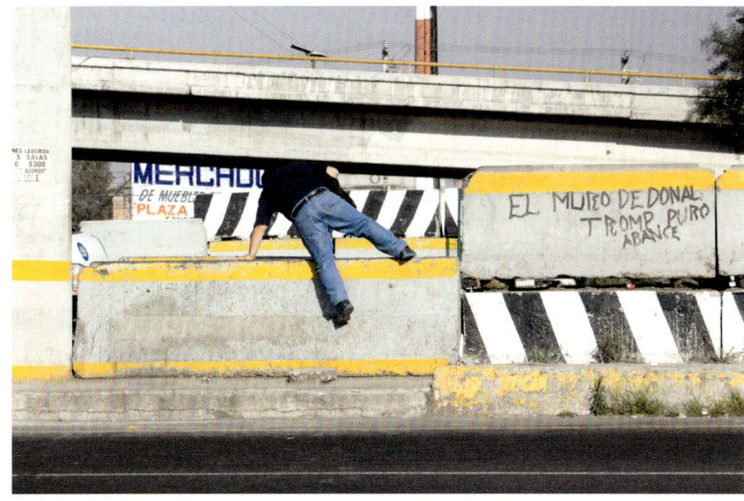
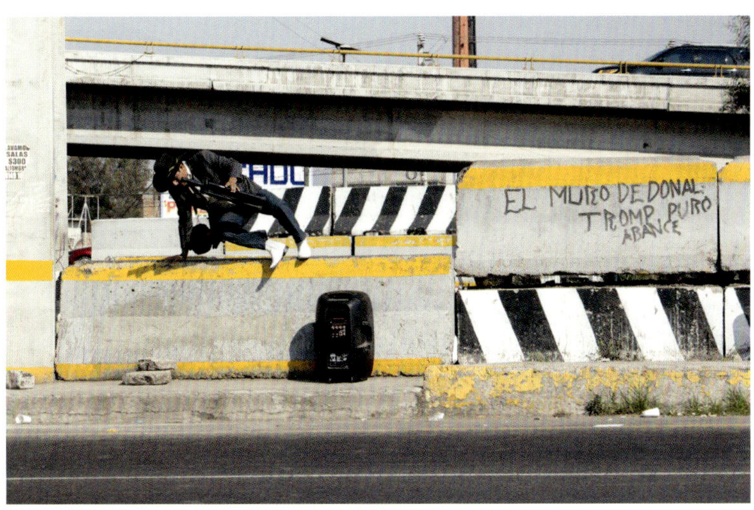
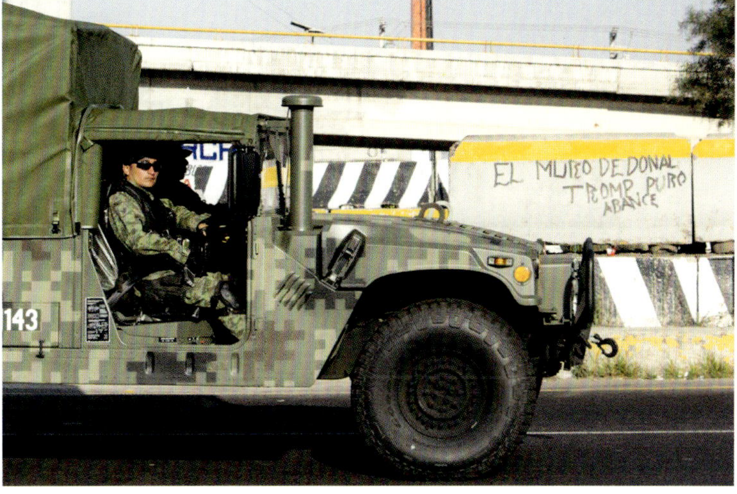

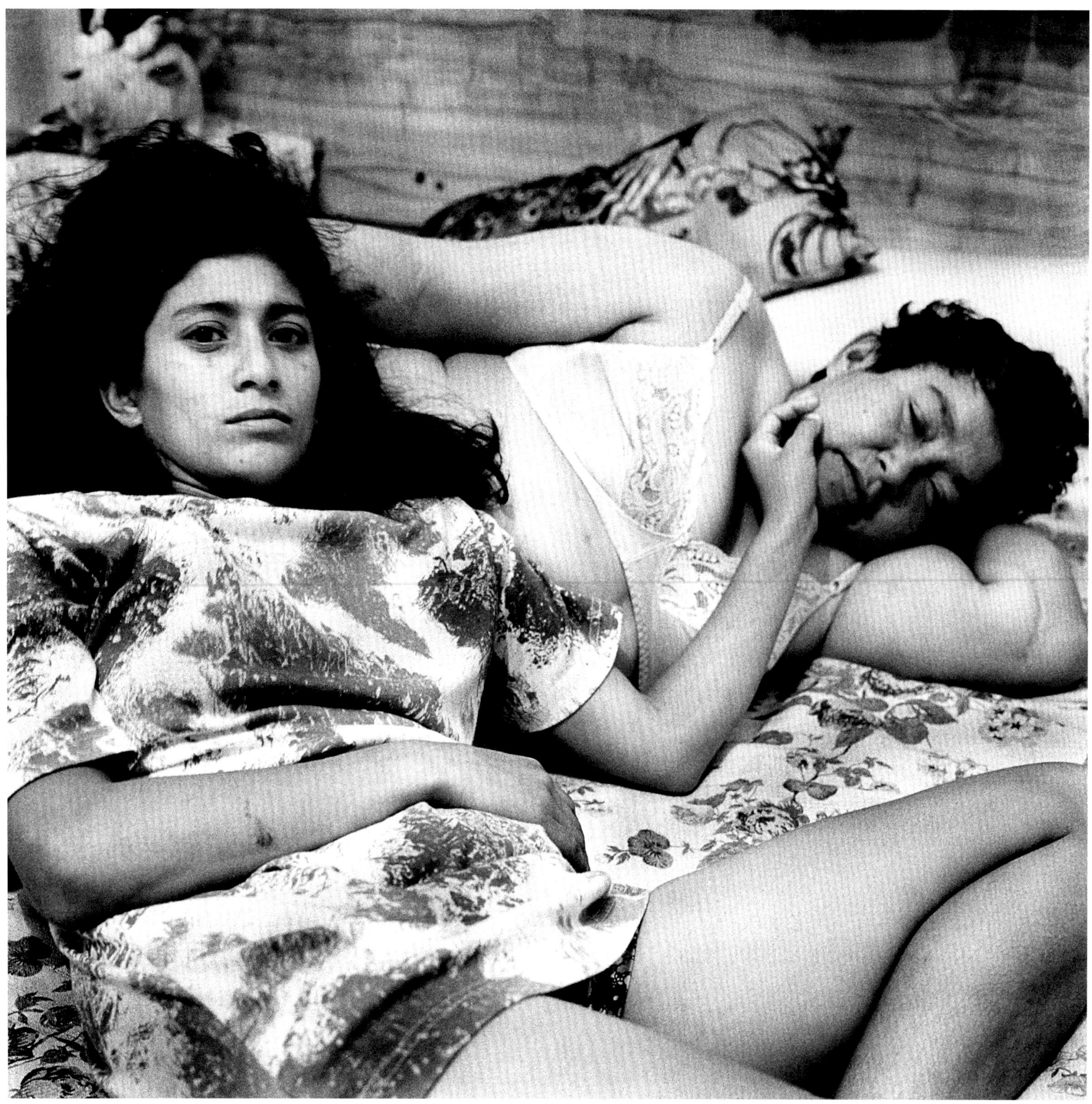

Maya Goded, Marcela
and Paty, two sex workers,
at the motel where
Marcela's children live,
1999, from the series
Plaza de la Soledad

A History of Violence

Maya Goded and Mayra Martell in Conversation with Marcela Turati

Maya Goded and Mayra Martell are two Mexico City–based photographers who chronicle the stories of families whose daughters have been murdered or disappeared in Ciudad Juárez. Martell has worked her whole life—first in Juárez, her hometown, and then across Latin America—on the identities and vestiges of young women who are absent, yet present in the places they used to inhabit. She has also documented those affected by other forms of violence, such as the mothers of people murdered by the Colombian Army or the everyday nature of drug culture in Sinaloa.

In turn, Goded's work has been, as she describes it herself, "exploring the subjects of female sexuality, prostitution, and gender violence in a society in which the role of women is narrowly defined and femininity is shrouded in myths of chastity, fragility, and motherhood." Goded has done so by photographing sex workers in Mexico City and on the U.S.-Mexico border, Afro-Mexican communities, and traditional Indigenous healers defending their territory.

In this conversation, Goded and Martell speak with Mexican journalist Marcela Turati about their work portraying the violence suffered by women, how they deal with the pain they photograph, their hesitations and lessons learned, and the conflicts surrounding their lives in Mexico, a country where people continue to disappear—more than forty thousand in the past twelve years.

Marcela Turati: **Maya, how did you discover and decide to explore violence against women? And Mayra, how did you decide to go deeper and explore the same issue in your hometown, having grown up in Ciudad Juárez?**

Mayra Martell: I am the daughter of a single mother of two, who juggled two jobs. It was very hard to see how the rest of the family and our environment treated her. I noticed violence right then. In Ciudad Juárez, I learned how to treat people very lovingly because you never know what others might be going through.

Maya Goded: When you are out there taking photographs, you are also carrying around your own story. That defines what you are going to look at and what your eyes will prioritize. I grew up with women who also broke through that structure: a grandmother who had to flee her own country, at the age of nineteen, during the Spanish Civil War, never to see her parents again. She reinvented herself and fought on her own.

My mother also left home at the age of nineteen, running away from domestic violence. From the United States, she migrated to Mexico, to study anthropology. Both of them decided to act against the violence they were going through. They moved on. They sought healing. Every time I am out there photographing women, I think of them.

Within excluded communities, women suffered from further exclusion. I started to photograph this normalization of violence. I was interested in women who fought to break patterns and reject whatever society expected from them.

MT: **Maya, in a previous interview you mentioned that you were scared of being a mother yourself. What were you scared of? And what were you looking for when you went to Mexico City's La Merced neighborhood?**

MG: I refused to be part of this classification of being a good or a bad woman, that Christian moral judgment implying women must sacrifice themselves for the sake of children and their household, not being allowed to live with unrestrained sexuality. With motherhood, I was terrified of losing the freedom that I had fought for all my life. I carried those narratives of guilt. I gravitated toward La Merced. When I arrived in Plaza Loreto, that square seemed like a microcosm. It condensed the different types of violence experienced by women and the solidarity established among them. I saw how men divide women and how violence unites them.

MT: **Mayra, how did you make it into the homes of disappeared women? How did you present yourself, and how did you start portraying their absence?**

MM: One day, I dialed one of the numbers written on the missing-women posters that covered the city center. I knew that that poster had been put up by the missing girl's mother. The first call led me to Hortensia, the mother of Erika Carrillo. I told her I was a photographer, and that I wanted to interview her. It was obvious that I had no idea of what I would do, and she immediately noticed my clumsiness. She reacted lovingly, invited me to her home, and that's where it all began. I guess she felt nostalgic when looking at me. I was as old as her daughter back then, and she would ask about what I had done in the past years, where I had been, what I had studied. It was a very weird relationship. Two strangers establishing a close bond where the only meeting point was a person who was not there. I tried to solve the problem of her absence with her presence. I photographed everything that proved that girl's existence: her room, her letters, her clothes, her photographs.

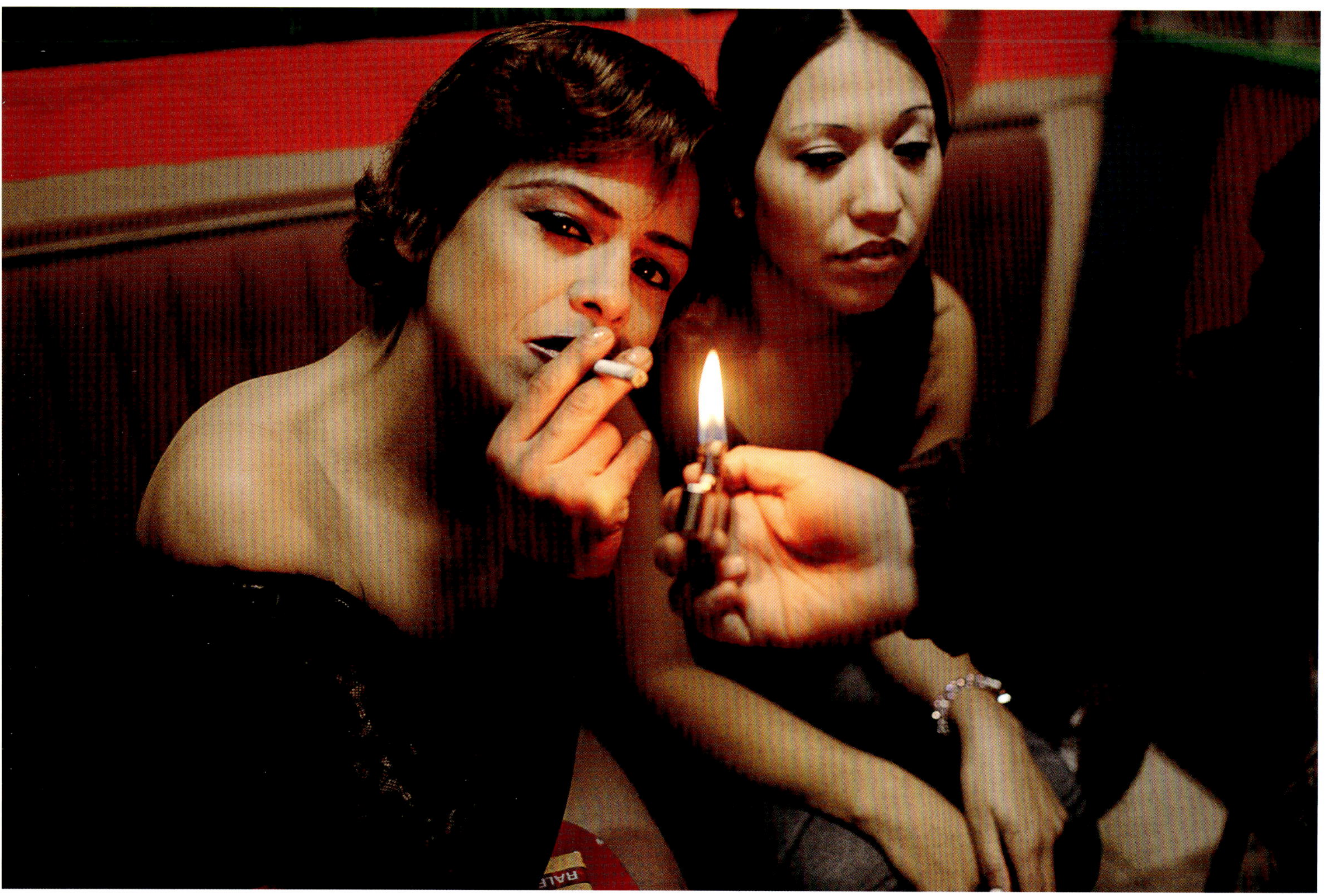

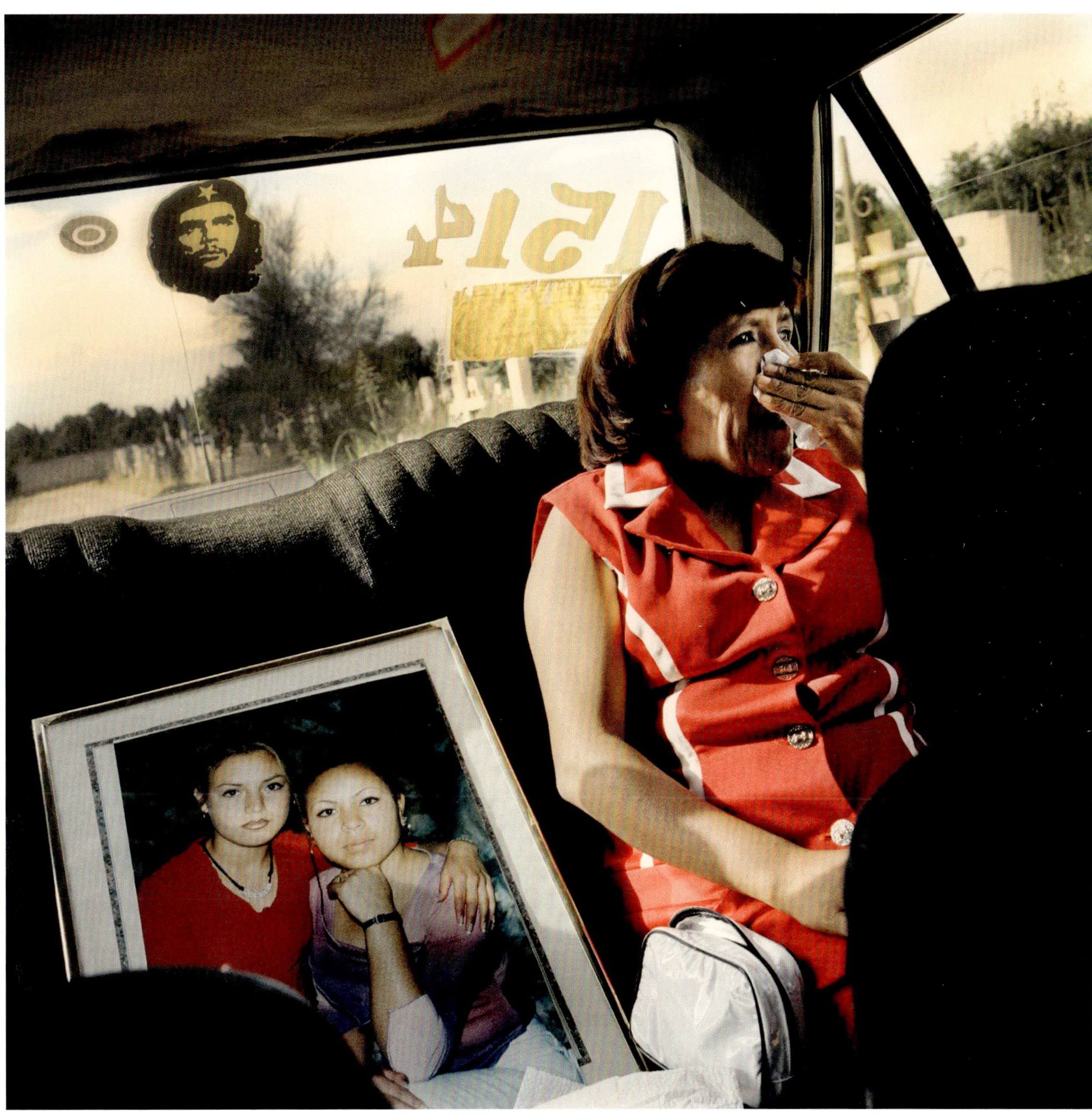

MT: **Mayra, did the fact of experiencing the intimacy of the victims, those rooms that seem to be memorials, make you feel any sort of commitment?**

MM: It was a situation full of sensations. In some rooms, I could still perceive the smell of the person. At times, I even felt observed by them. I have always known that everything is energy, and that, one way or another, in death or in life, we all share this space. On other occasions, I did not feel anything, as if her spiritual energy was also gone. Of all the cases I have documented, no one has ever returned home.

The only thing I know how to do is to record the situation family members are going through as a way to embrace them and accompany them through the hardships they are living, from which they will never recover.

MT: **Maya, you went from La Merced to Juárez in order to accompany other women, mothers of victims of femicide. Why did you think it was important to bring a camera with you?**

MG: One day, a young, Indigenous, unknown girl was killed at the busiest hotel around La Merced in broad daylight, strangled with her own pantyhose. I followed the case during that whole day. The girl was going to the mass grave. A man said he knew her.

Afterward, rumors spread that he was her pimp. I was shocked to see how many girls have their papers, their identities, their names, their birth certificates changed. As we learned about the disappearance of women in Ciudad Juárez, I was sent there to do a report for a magazine.

Ciudad Juárez was the place where I had fallen in love with my husband. Back then, I had traveled with him to that border town in order to attend a film festival, and we did not stop dancing for three or four days. It was a place full of life. But this time, everything had changed. I discovered women were being kidnapped, victims of human trafficking. Then I began to investigate who those girls were: young, poor, most of them without children. The government said they deserved it because they ran around wearing miniskirts and went out at night, and condemned them for breaking the rules. It was very frustrating to talk about women who are no longer there, about the violence that you do not see but that manifests itself in many other ways.

I am not quite sure whether I like this series. It was a hard one. I've always fallen short when addressing Juárez. Even though I've returned, I always feel powerless. I went back several times in order to work on it by means of different formats—photography, video installations of the children and sisters of disappeared women, and a video of one of the sisters of a disappeared girl, which was subsequently used as part of an experiential theater production.

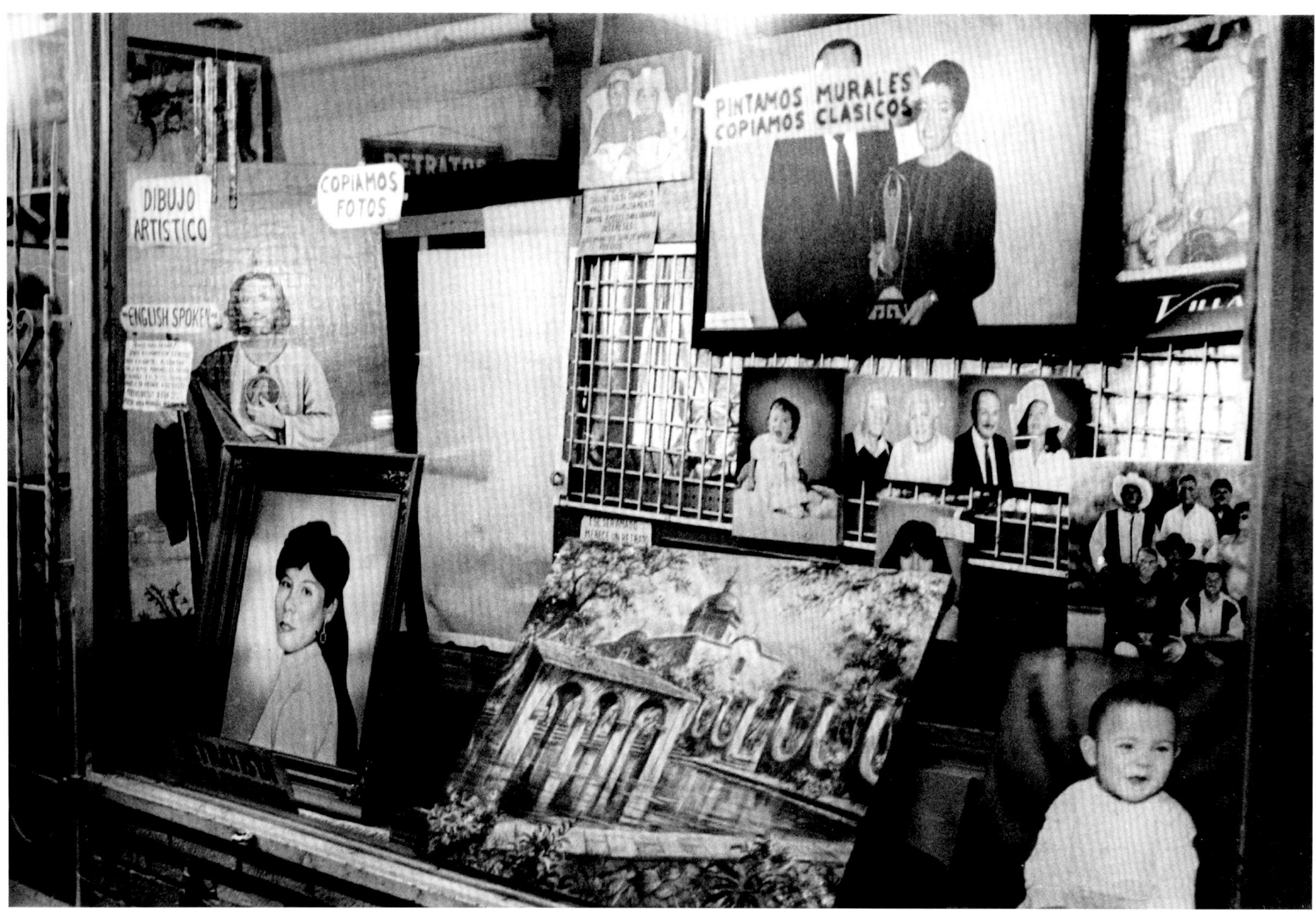

MT: **Mayra, how did your portrayal of the absences in Juárez mutate into your subsequent work on the types of violence suffered by women? For instance, the case of women in Sinaloa, violence experienced by *ficheras* [ballroom escorts who are paid to dance, often to live music, with their partners] in Mexico City, or by the mothers of individuals murdered by the Colombian Army?**

MM: Every project is new to me. I put aside every prejudice, start from scratch, and decide what to do in the course of the project. Ciudad Juárez was a real emotional challenge. I came in contact with situations I was not used to dealing with: funerals, interviews with alleged murderers, the monitoring of the *nota roja* [local newspapers that exclusively publish cases of murder, rape, and other violent crimes]. I would attend trials, accompany mothers to identify bodies that might belong to their daughters. Very painful situations in which I often had to hold back my tears. Now I know that if I had not gone through all those experiences, I would have never emotionally stood the projects that came afterward.

MT: **Maya, when you introduce yourself to a sex worker from La Merced or to a mother who has lost a daughter or a migrant whose newborn son has been taken away, how do you explain that you want to photograph them? What do you do to be accepted?**

MG: You have to be as honest as possible with your intentions, otherwise you will generate false expectations or come across as something you are not. It is hard. You keep on questioning what is ethical. When I started taking photographs, it was very frustrating to realize that you are not going to change anything, that you are a witness, and how uncomfortable it is to be nothing but a witness. Then, over time, you can become involved in activism as a consequence.

MT: **Could you say more about this inner struggle between being a photographer-witness against the impulse to do something in the face of difficult realities. Is this something you have solved, or something you are still trying to solve?**

MG: The inner struggle of being a photographer-witness has changed what I am. In pursuit of topics for my projects, I intend to explore and record all those stories of resilience and self-reconstruction, which often originate in the personal and collective realms, away from the political sphere. My current quest relates to healing, not only on the legal level—which is very important—but also spiritually and bodily, in our connection to the earth, the water. After having captured such hard realities, I want to dedicate my work and energy to documenting small drivers of change, such as the alleviation of pain, which have become a tool of resistance. This fight energizes me.

MT: **What are your ethical conflicts as a photographer, Mayra?**

MM: I have been in conflict with a number of things. The first was having to interview alleged murderers. I struggled not to judge and to carry out the interviews as objectively and humanely as possible.

MT: **How did you manage to stay calm?**

MM: I think what caused me the greatest distress was when I had to leave Ciudad Juárez, because I lived surrounded by mothers who protected me and listened to me, and suddenly I had to turn my life around in a matter of days. From that moment on, I haven't stopped feeling lonely. It was like a big wave that swept away my whole life and took everything I had. I work through it by doing my job, which is the only way I have to feel present.

MT: What happened to you? Is this something you can talk about?

MM: I left Ciudad Juárez at the end of 2009 because I was kidnapped. In those situations, the government appoints security guards to protect you for four days so that you can pack your stuff and leave. In the end, I left after two days because they tried to kidnap me again, and the people who were in charge of protecting me had to take me directly to the airport. My partner at that time met me there, brought along a piece of luggage, and the rest of my things were shipped afterward.

MT: That is horrifying. Was it because of your work?

MM: Things got pretty heavy when [President Felipe] Calderón declared a war on drugs. The city became a mess, so it also became easier to disappear people.

MT: What types of violence have you suffered as women photographers? Do you have to take care of yourselves in a different way than a man would in a certain kind of place? Are you more vulnerable in this country where it is dangerous to be a woman?

MM: I am not aware of having suffered violence in my projects for being a woman. As I grew up in Ciudad Juárez, where being a woman, a girl, a boy, a teenager is dangerous, I learned to move around and act discretely when I am being stared at. I am some sort of spy who knows how to respond to each situation: I change my way of dressing, of speaking, and that has always kept me safe wherever I work. I am very much aware of what it could mean to be a woman in these kinds of environments.

MG: I imagine that all women photographers have gone through situations of violence and normalized them as if they were part of being a woman photographer and traveling alone. This is why I love #MeToo and that the new generation's questioning it all. The way I take care of myself is by being close to other women. They warn me about any problems or threats. I increasingly look for that solidarity that has protected me so that I can do my work. This is a country riddled with violence and, based on the topics you address, you might become a threat to the state—even without realizing. It is dangerous to both women and men, but danger is always gender differentiated and particularly latent for women in this country. There is always fear in the air.

MT: What do you do with violence that permeates your skin, that stays in your body when you see it so close and live around these realities for so long?

MM: I have never actually recovered from all this because, at the end of the day, things keep on happening. Therefore, I believe I will never stop working on denouncing. I have seen horrible things. People who were close to me have been murdered; mothers of disappeared or murdered women are dying; I've lost my own personal life so many times that I can't even remember who I used to be. I don't quite know where my life ends or starts since I had to flee Ciudad Juárez. I haven't been able to become emotionally grounded because whatever is happening in that city is beyond my

I am very much aware of what it could mean to be a woman in these kinds of environments.

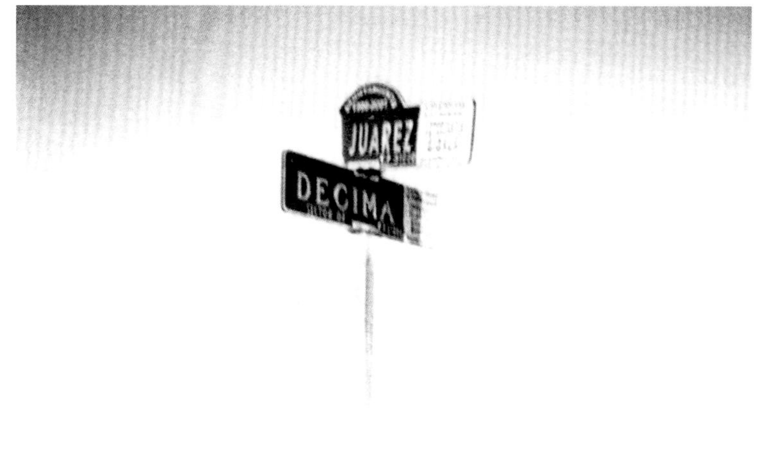

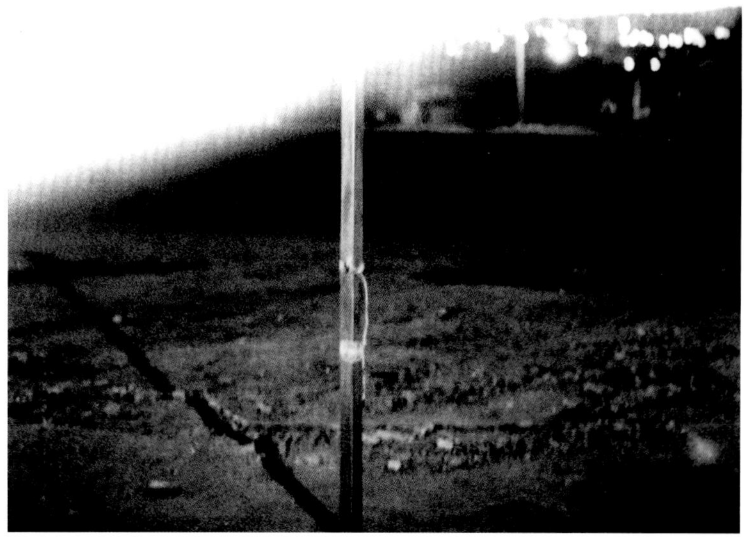

understanding. However, what helps me when I am feeling really bad is to think that, while I might be feeling sad, the mothers of those women and girls must be feeling a thousand times worse, and that pushes me to get up and get down to work. It is necessary to accompany those who are suffering such situations.

MG: When I was working with cases of disappeared women and then went to Chiapas to do a report, I was very scared by some things that happened to me while photographing. Sadness and horror invaded my body. I couldn't sleep. One day, when my daughter was thirteen, I did not want to let her go out because I was scared; and she, wise as she's always been, said, "Mom, those are your ghosts, not mine. Work them through." I realized I was not allowing myself to say: I am scared, I am feeling sadness, I am disappointed. I stopped taking photographs. I was not traveling on my own as I used to. I did not see the point of photography anymore. I got into psychoanalysis and explored other ways of healing and understanding pain, focusing on the kinds of pain that remain in the body.

I started photographing women who do witchcraft, in the north of Mexico, as well as doing research on Spanish and Indigenous women from the 1700s who healed with plants, were accused of witchcraft, and burned at the stake. I started to heal that pain by learning about them. My current quest began there.

I also went deeper into sacred plants, around which this country has a great tradition, and started working with healers to understand that, even though justice heals, you also have to heal at the energy level, honoring both your ancestors and future generations. Coming from a rather rational family, this has made me question my views and forced me to try to see things from another perspective.

MT: Mayra, what thought or sensation overtakes you when you realize this is not only about Ciudad Juárez, but that we live in a country where mothers with missing sons and daughters march every May 10, or that the very places you photographed continue seeing the disappearance of young women?

MM: There is a book, *Juárez: The Laboratory of Our Future* (1998) by Charles Bowden, with texts by Noam Chomsky and Eduardo Galeano, as well as images by press photographers from Ciudad Juárez, that explains very well the situation of Juárez and Mexico. It elaborates on the social decomposition none of us can escape. In Juárez, there were many warning signs around us, which nobody paid attention to because it was always about the neighbor, the poor fellow, the girl from the *maquiladora* [foreign-owned factory]. Nobody understood that if things were happening to people across the street, it would someday reach their homes too. Violence is expandable.

MT: Maya, what advice would you give, if you could meet your younger self—that photographer who was only starting to capture the violence in La Merced or in Juárez?

MG: That she should study philosophy, read about culture in general, because technique is learned quickly, but, in the end, photography is enriched by life and knowledge.

MT: Mayra, what would you advise a younger Mayra who was just starting?

MM: I'd hug myself so tight that I'd cast a spell of protection to last for years. I haven't changed that much—it's just that the little flame in my heart has been extinguished several times. But it always lights up again. And I would say to myself, I love you. That would have helped me in a lot of personal situations.

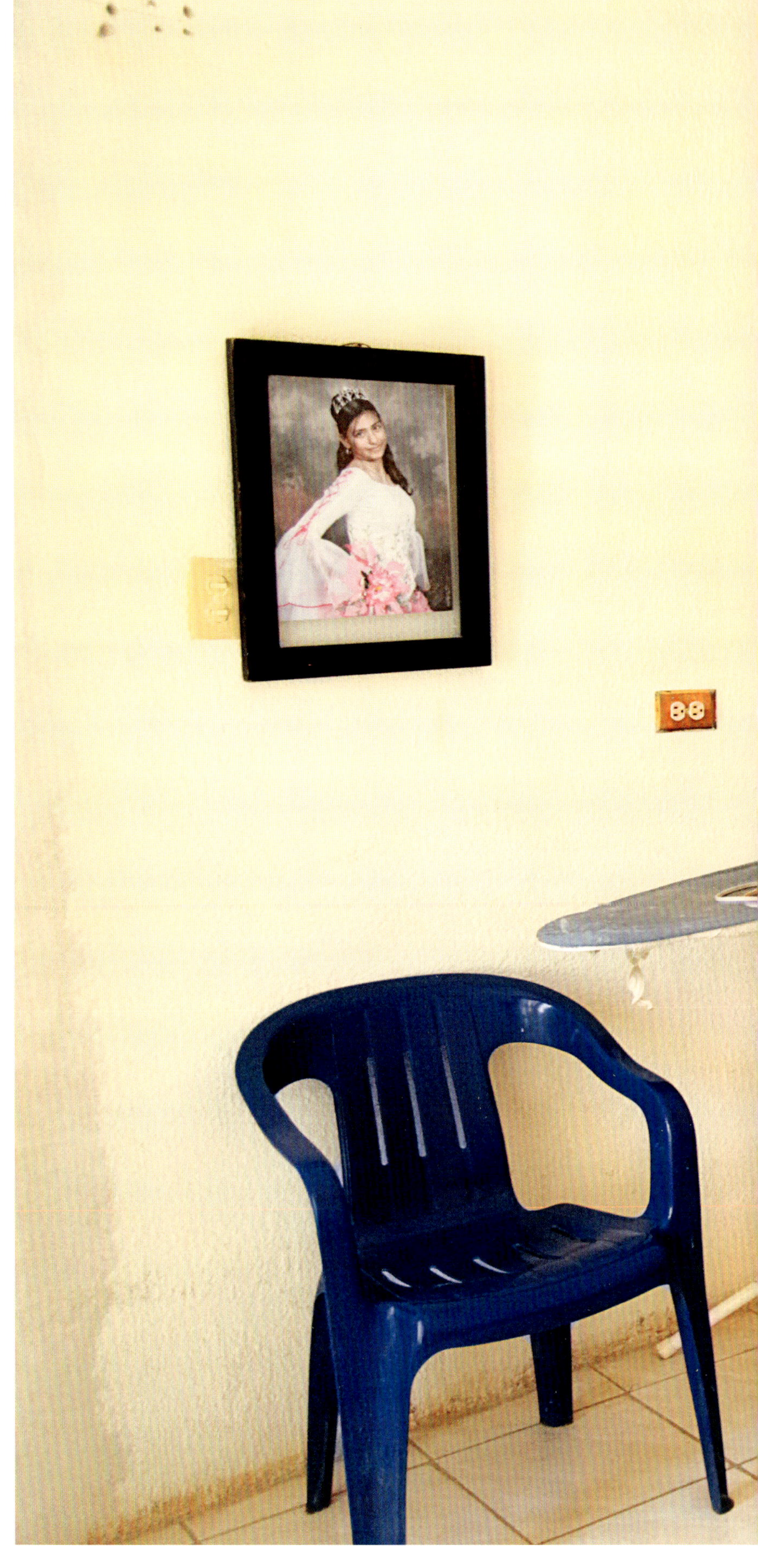

Mayra Martell, Yanira Fraire, 15 years old. On June 10, 2010 she went to pay her tuition at a bank located downtown and never returned. She was a junior in high school. In January 2012, her remains were found in the city's outskirts. She was one of the twenty-six victims of the human trafficking organization that operated at the Hotel Verde in the downtown of Ciudad Juárez, 2013
All photographs courtesy the artists

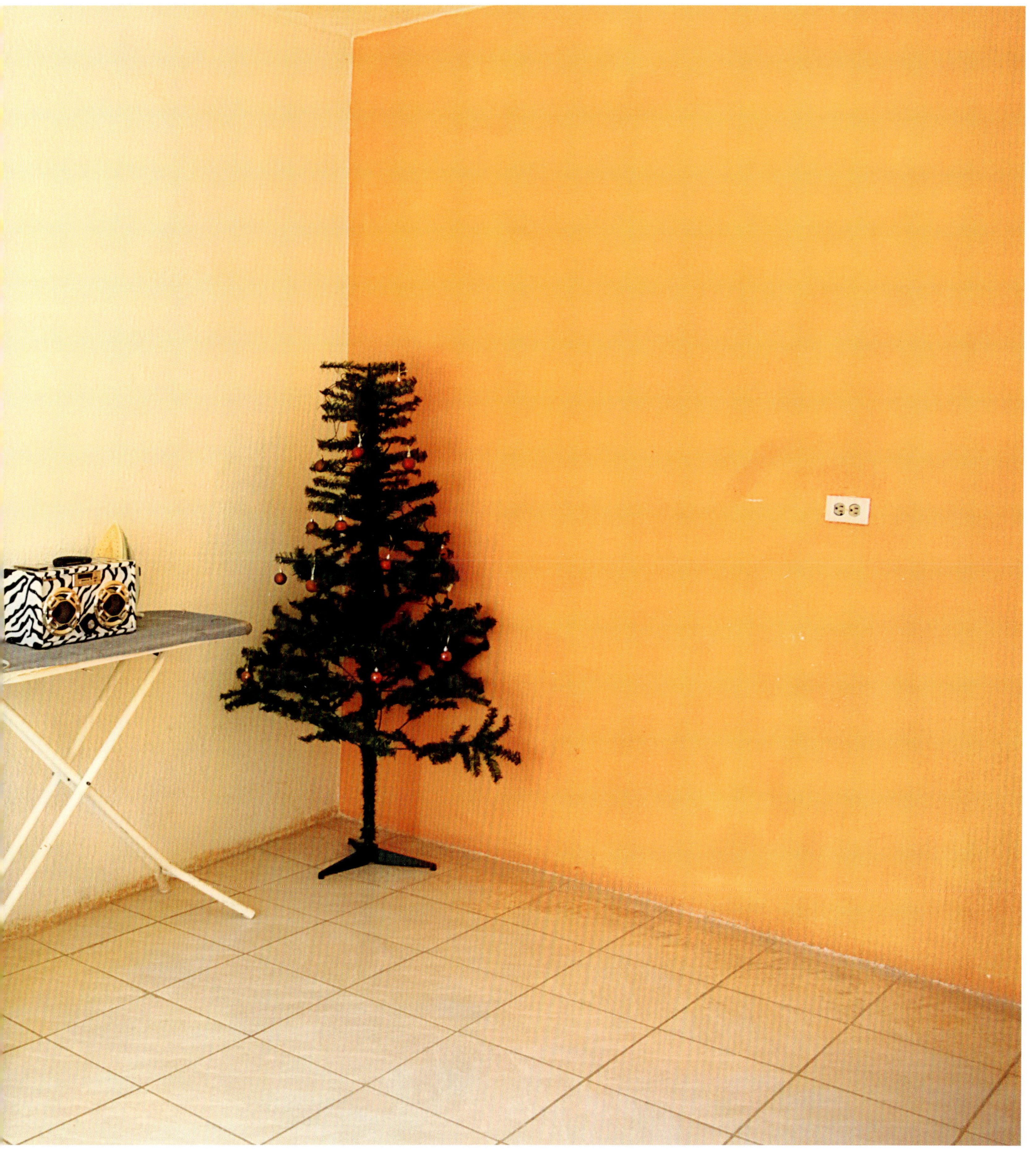

Marcela Turati is an investigative journalist based in Mexico. She is the author of *Fuego Cruzado: Las víctimas atrapadas en la guerra del narco* (Crossfire: Victims trapped in the war on drugs, 2011).

Translated from the Spanish by Enrique Pérez Rosiles.

"But beyond time and space is the empire of the Night," the German poet Novalis wrote in his *Hymns to the Night*. The photography of Jesús León seems to be based on this poetic intuition. What transpires at night, plucked from time and space, radiates like a fiction, a myth: an ecstatic face, a moment of vulnerability, a truth that flickers briefly before becoming submerged once more in the tempestuous waters of the party and debauchery. León's lens captures these atypical moments in which a person, upon shedding various masks, embodies the Dionysian spirit of the night and the city.

Born in Mexico City in the 1970s, José de Jesús León Hernández grew up in Colonia Doctores, a central, working-class neighborhood where he still lives today. Since the 1990s, he has been dedicated to chronicling, with absolute aesthetic consistency, the nightlife of this "terminally ill city," as he calls it. His universe stretches from Doctores, to the historic center, to La Condesa, but in this small cross-section of the world, he has found more than enough material to develop a complex metonymy for contemporary metropolises: "I enjoy photographing the details of things and, from there, explaining something like the city, constructing a story about the place where I live."

His interest in the night and its creatures transcends merely documenting the party. León rummages through garbage, through remnants, like a crime reporter who reconstructs the scene of the murder or an anthropologist who imagines a strange civilization based on its remains. There is plenty of film noir in his gaze, and a great amount of Catholic aesthetics, as well: his portraits are full of Saint Teresas in alcoholic ecstasy and Saint Sebastians martyred by the glorious arrow of cocaine.

He began, more than two decades ago, by photographing art-world gatherings: openings, cocktail parties, the transition from fake smiles and 10 p.m. calculations to the carefree frenzy at dawn. León has a series of some twenty photographs that documents the gradual withering of a rose, step by step. His approach to the nightlife scene employs a similar strategy: there is a narrative that tells the story of a decomposition— or, at the very least, of a transformation. At the same time, this account is a dance: "I went out one night. Three days later I was looking at what I had photographed, and I pieced it all together. I like to create a story, and a choreography as well."

But the work of the photographer goes beyond the intuition to capture this choreography. León is a tireless editor who lives submerged in the universe that he has been creating for decades: "Now I spend much of my time revisiting my archives. I never got rid of anything. I have nearly two million images." The result of this accumulation is *Vida*, a photobook published in 2018, which has given León a well-deserved international reputation as a "savage detective" of the streets and the clandestine bars of Mexico. Within that singular and recognizable world, the queer community occupies a prominent place, and Léon has become, over the years, their visual historian.

"Vast and anguished city with room for dogs / misery and homosexuals, / whores and the famous melancholy of poets, / prayers and Christian orations," wrote Efraín Huerta in one of his most famous poems, "Declaration of Hatred," precisely dedicated to Mexico City. That is the metropolis depicted by León: a world in which people from far-flung origins coexist, wrapped in a blanket of peculiarity.

Jesús León

Daniel Saldaña París

All photographs
Untitled, from the series
Tenochtitlan, 2000/2019
Courtesy the artist, Carlos
Mérigo, and ALMANAQUE
fotográfica, Mexico City

Daniel Saldaña París is a writer based in Mexico City and the author of the novel *Among Strange Victims* (2016).

Translated from the Spanish by Elianna Kan.

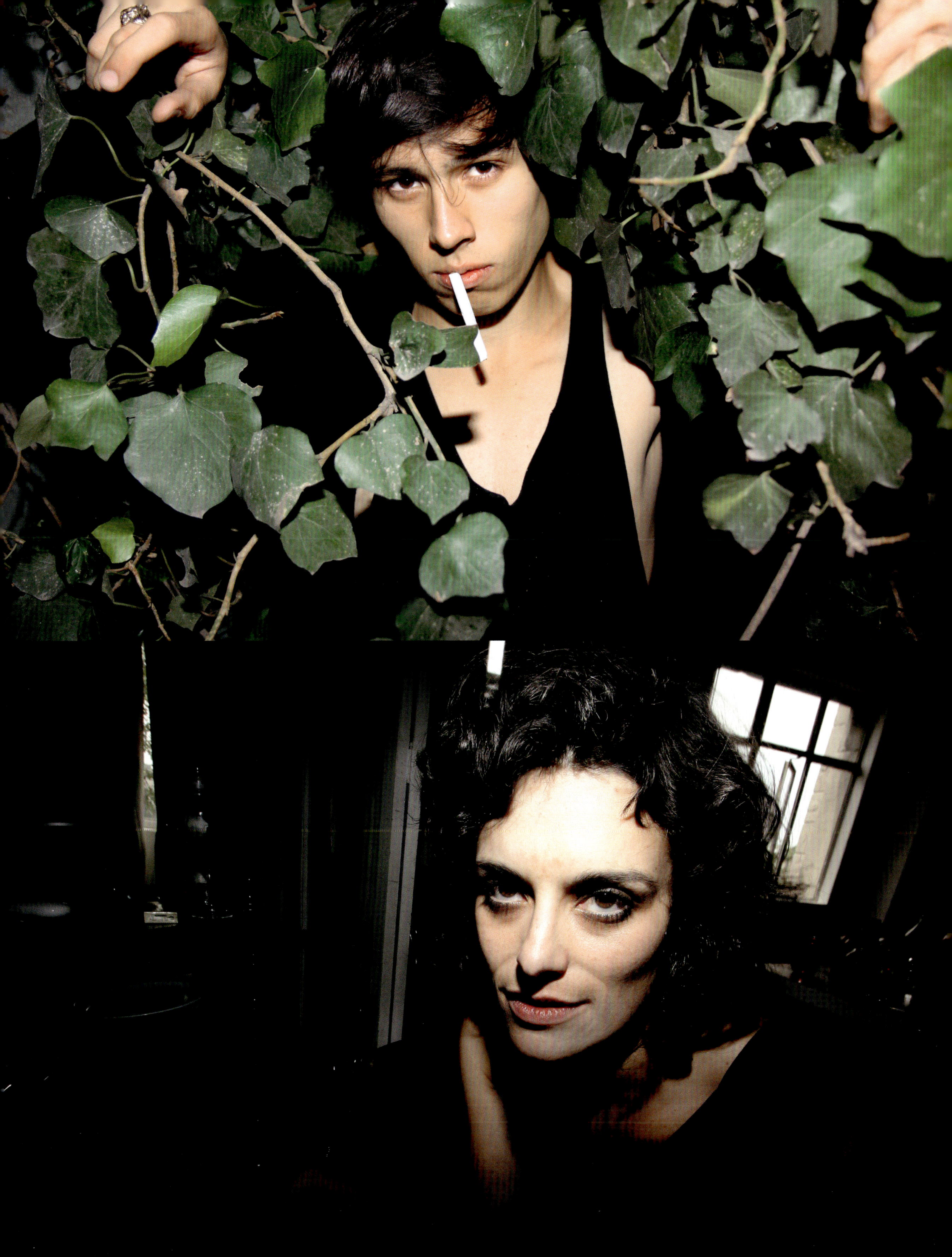

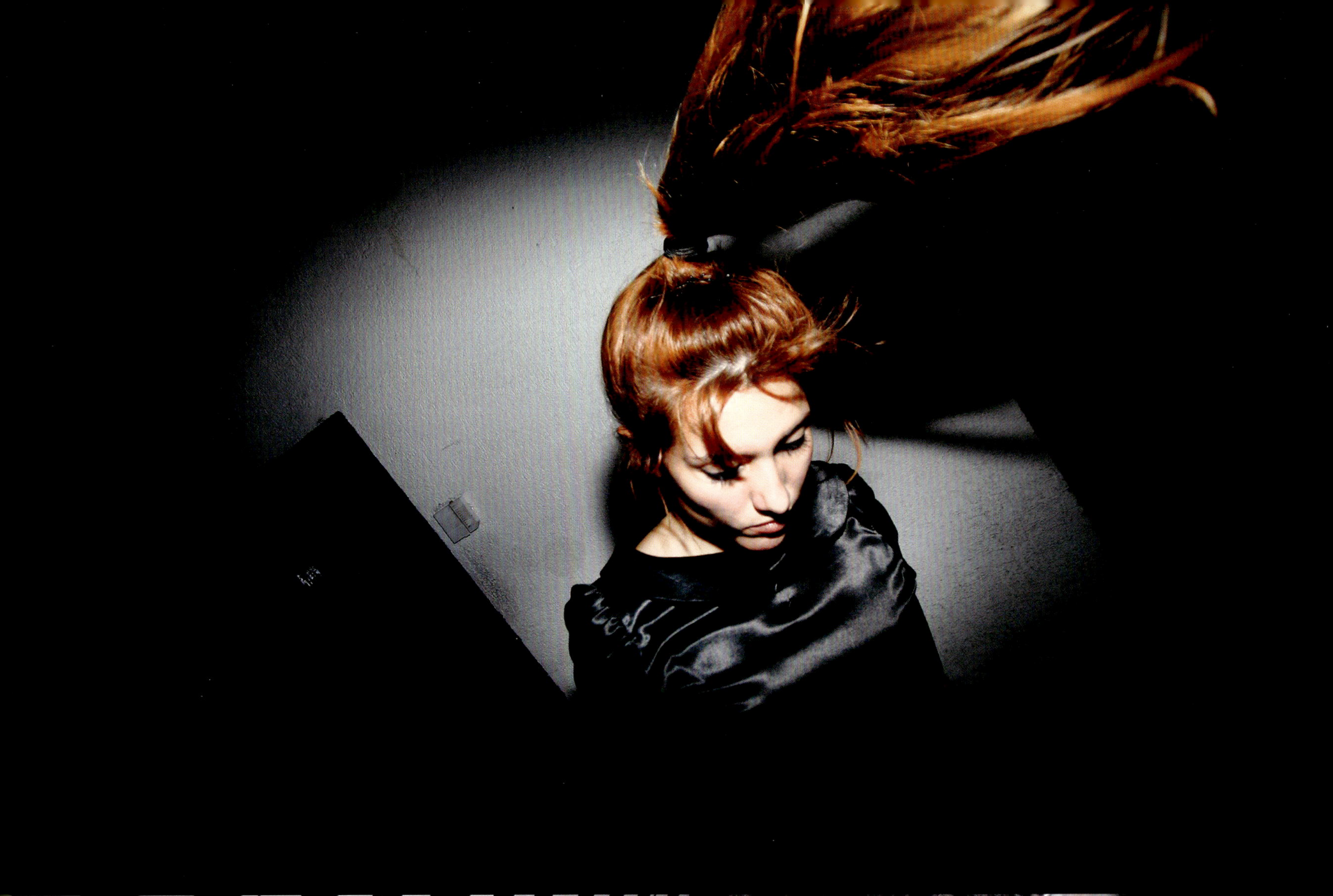

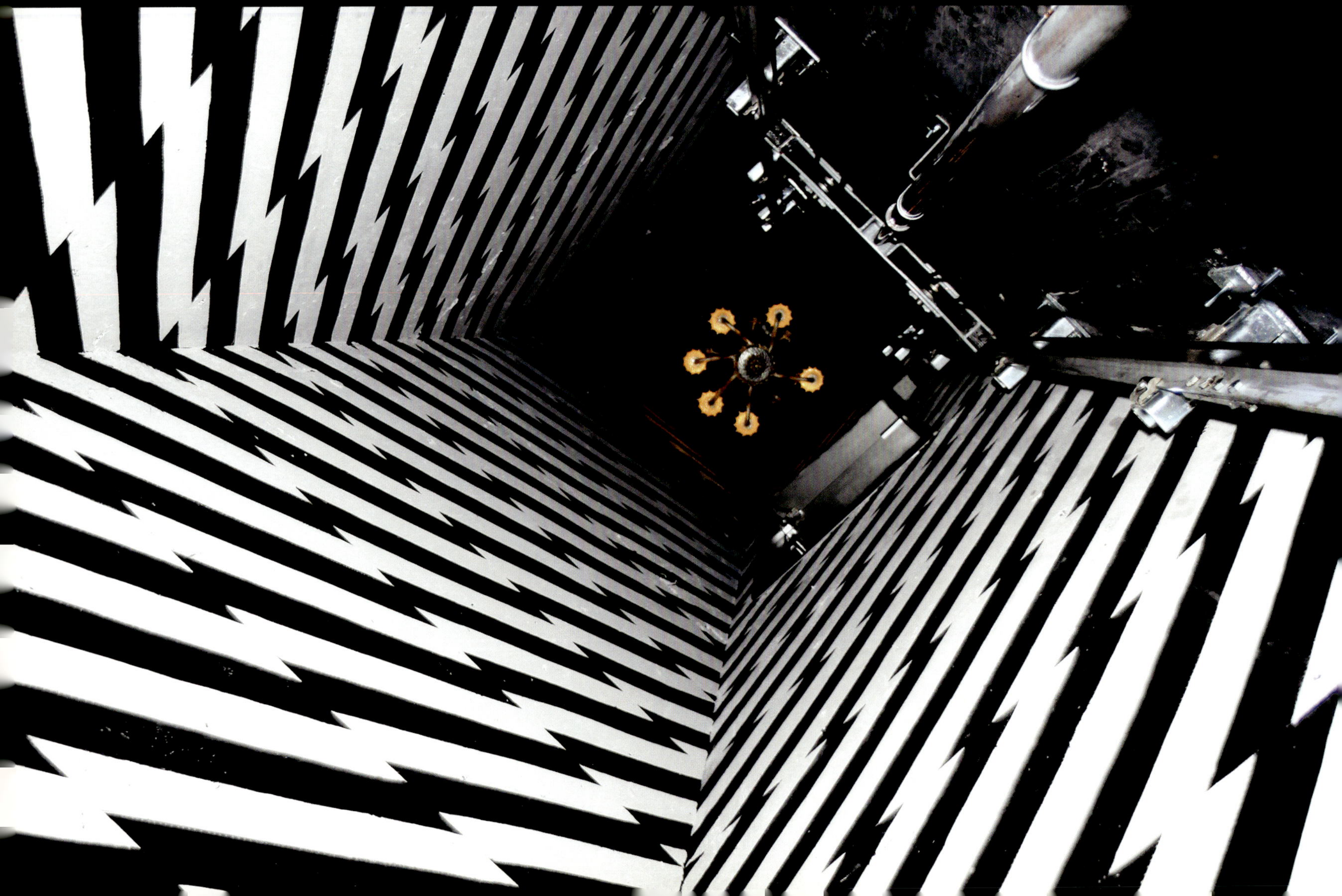

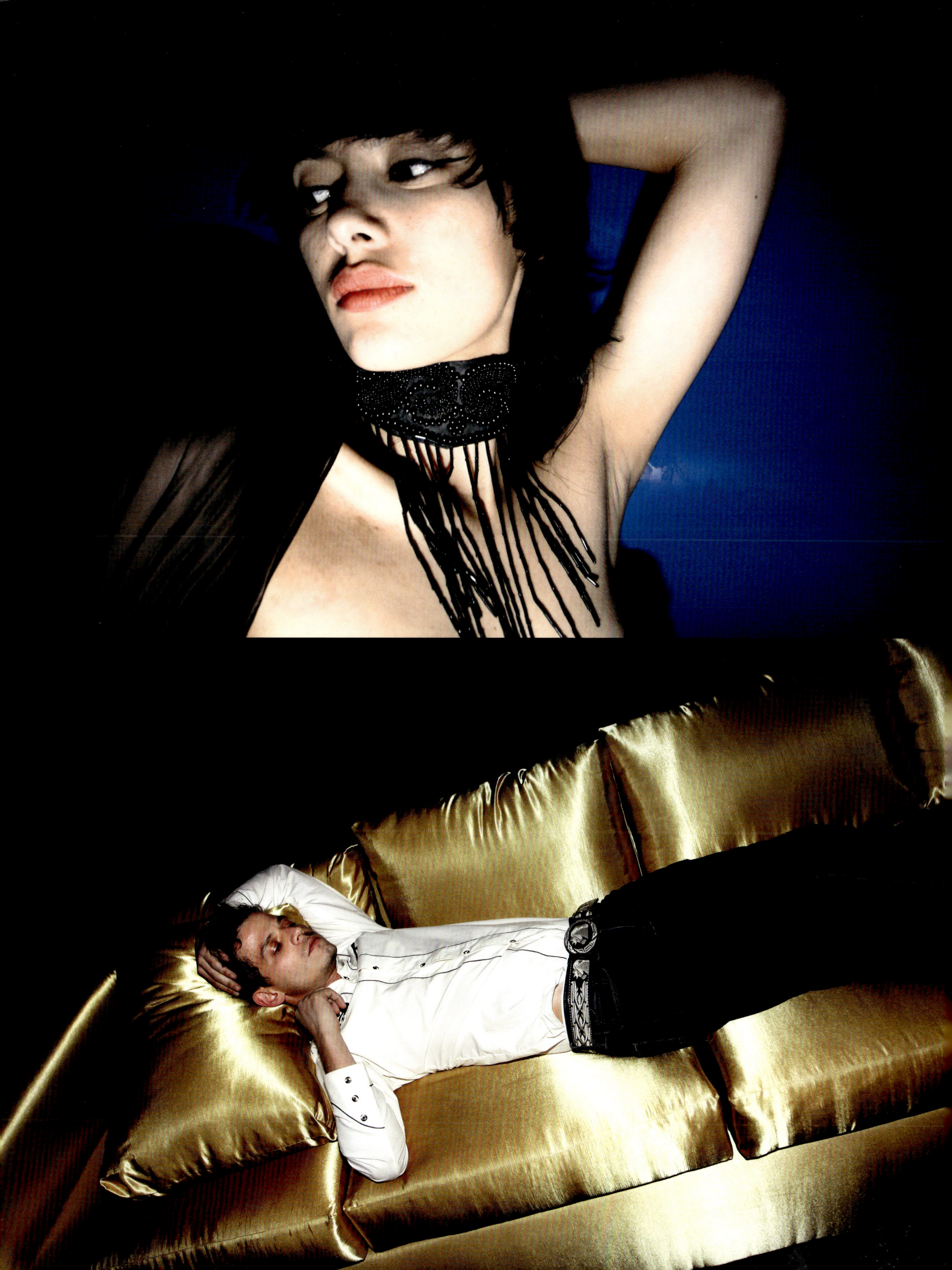

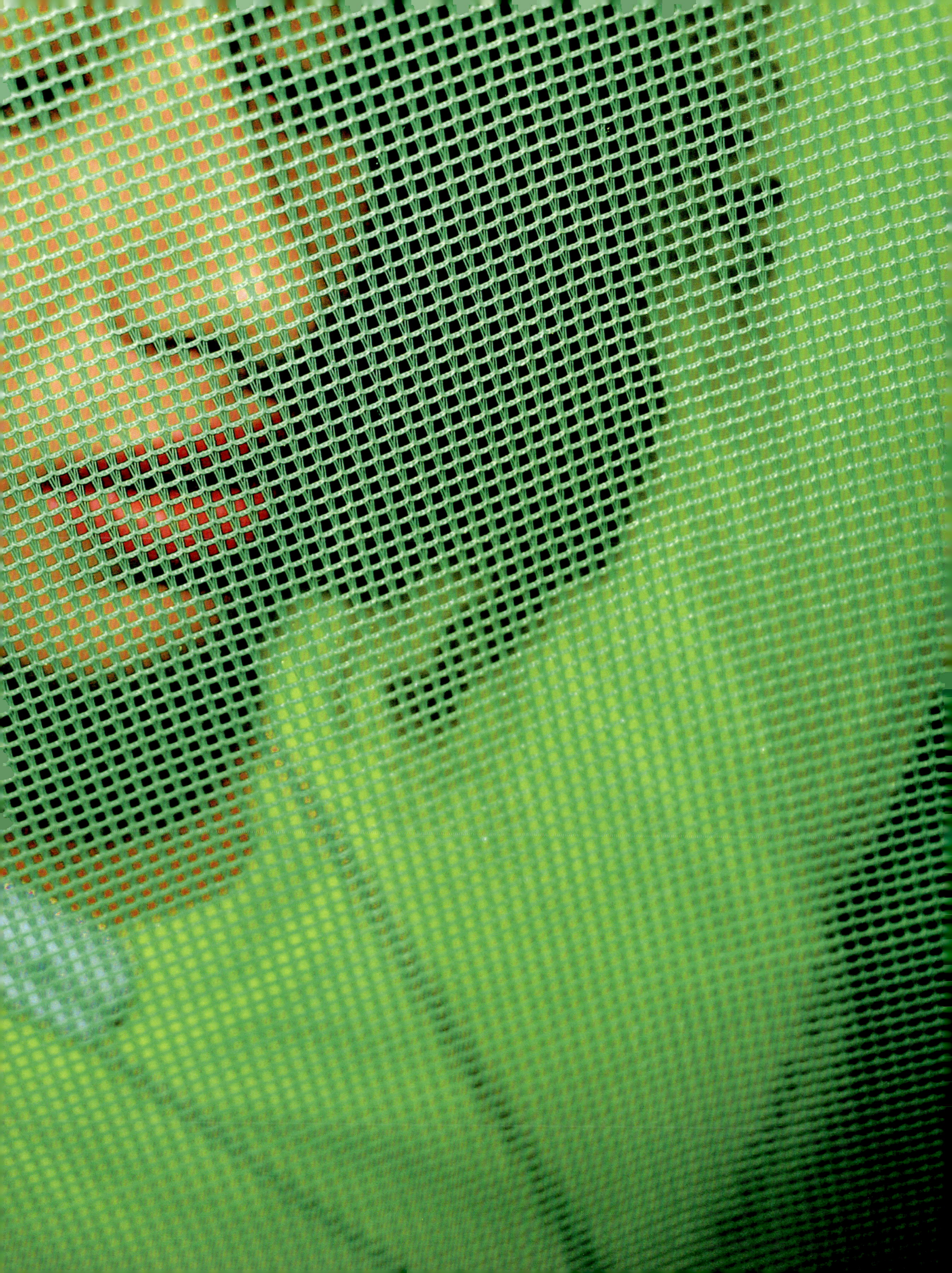

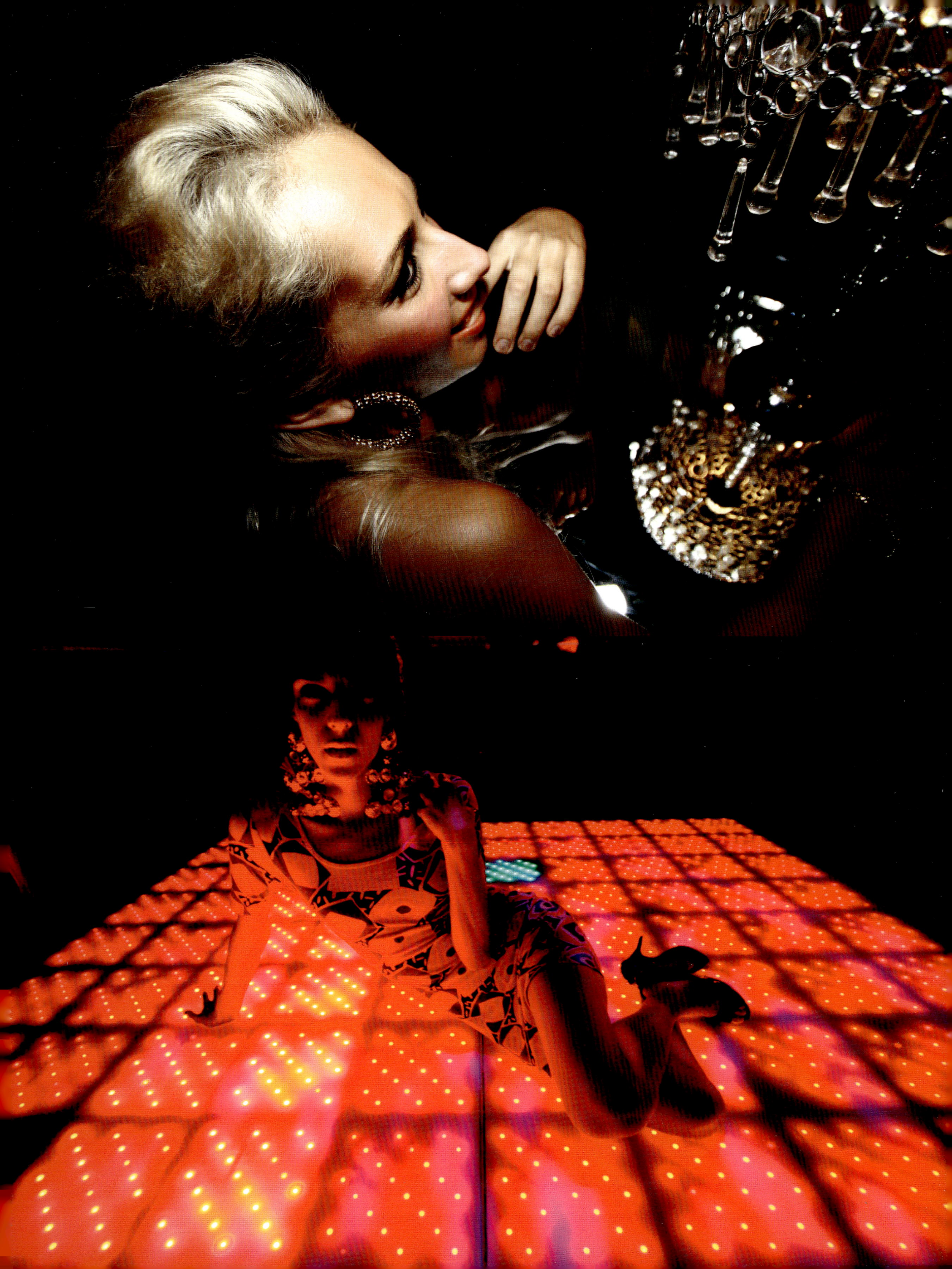

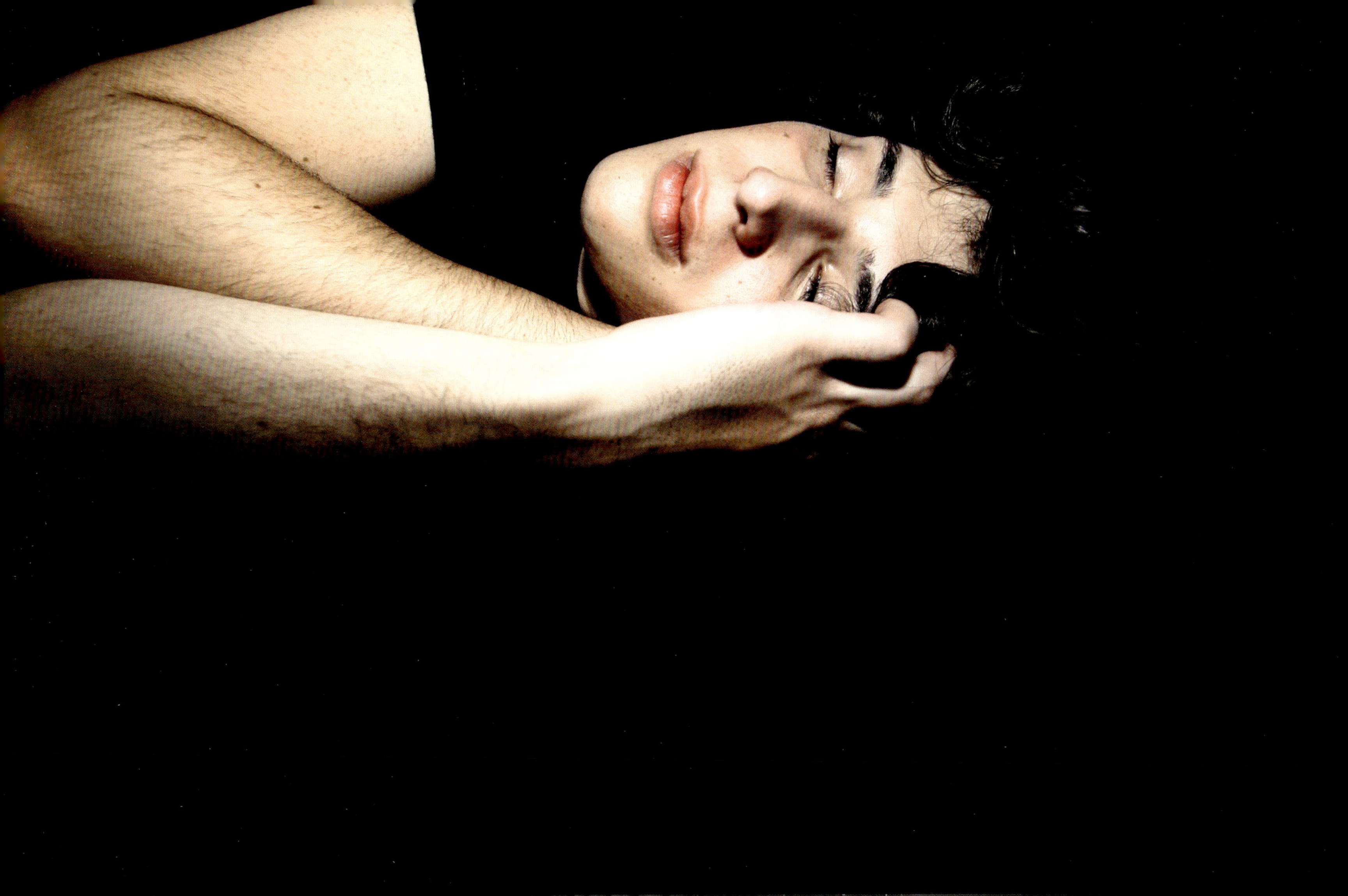

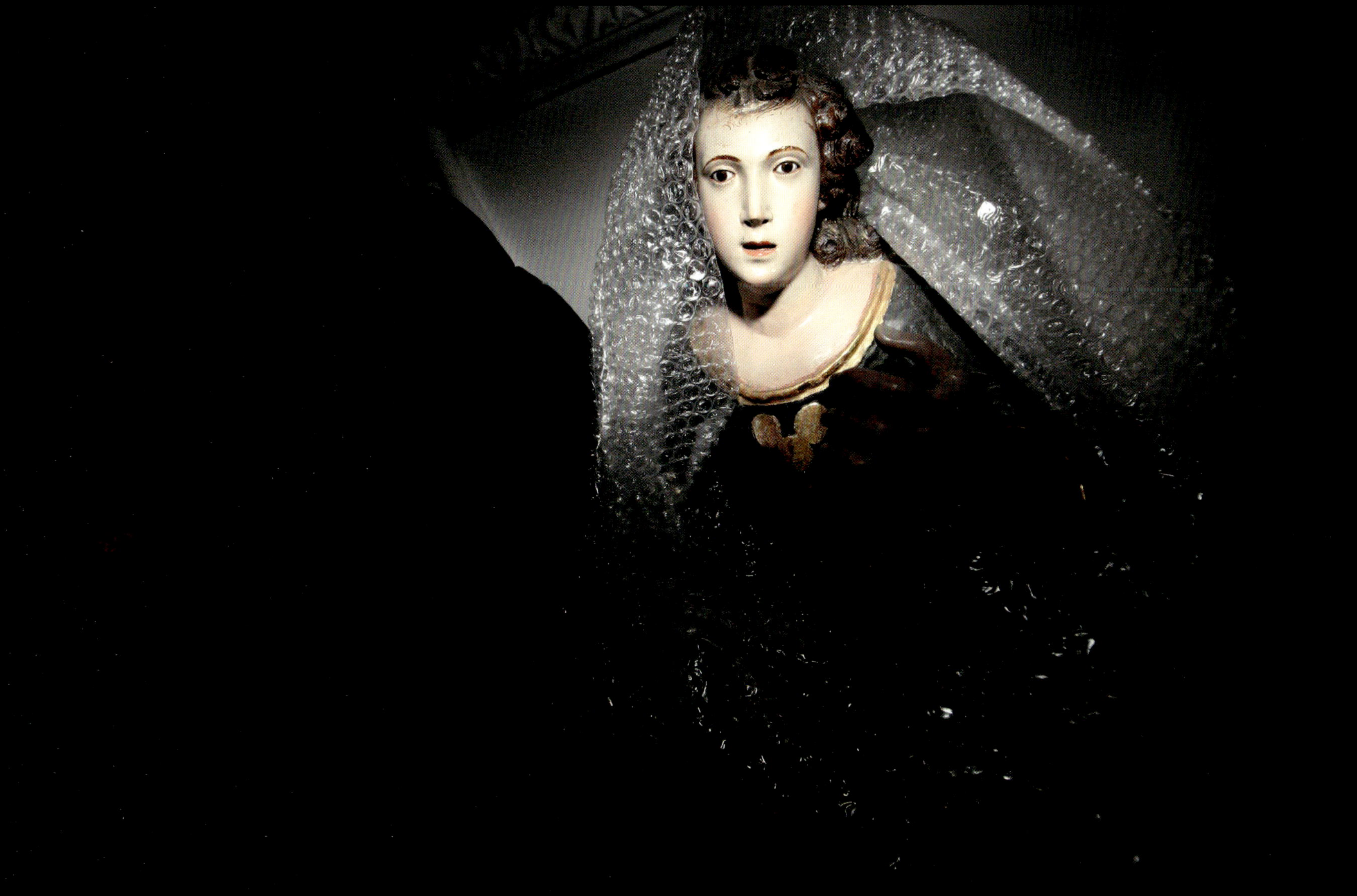

Many of Tania Franco Klein's photographs depict female figures who seem lost in the vastness of an inhospitable landscape or in a moment of contemplation, the edges of the self contained within those of a geometrical interior. Her images are bathed in a warm cinematic light, boudoir red, and suffused with a Lynchian sense of menace—they resemble film stills taken midnarrative, though it's unclear whether the climactic moment has yet taken place.

For her newest series, *Mercado de Sonora* (2019), Franco Klein focuses her gaze for the first time, after many photographic projects abroad, on her native Mexico. In the past, she has often donned a wig and turned the camera on herself; in this body of work, her mother and grandmother become the models in an extended form of self-portraiture that captures the ways in which beliefs are passed from generation to generation.

The Mercado de Sonora, a vast traditional market in southeast Mexico City, is a space, Franco Klein explains, where class boundaries dissolve: a cross-section of society, from the house servant to the industrialist's wife, comes here to find esoteric cures. The politics of the marketplace are evident in its gender distribution: women sell spells, men sell animals. For alongside the stalls of abracadabra and Santa Muerte figurines is a squirming menagerie of trafficked wildlife, a vast array of fauna crammed into cages, heaped on one another, struggling for air and space. Around 70 percent of creatures transported to the market die en route, and those that survive often meet their end in a gruesome Santeria ritual or, in the case of the more exotic species, as pets to narco juniors. For decades, authorities have turned a blind eye toward this lucrative hub of illegal trafficking.

Because of the rampant criminal activity, photography at the market is strictly forbidden. Franco Klein decided to shift the context and bring the spells, the promises being sold, into a more private realm, in order to explore what happens once these products are taken home. In doing so, she has created spaces of longing and atmospheric ambiguity, where every detail is freighted with forensic significance. Over and over, the viewer is invited to imagine the psychodrama unfolding within.

In one disquieting photograph, a hand appears to hold down the shoulder of a woman in a silky dress and black wig, while the other hand runs an egg over her head as part of a limpia, or spiritual cleansing, the negative energy extracted condensing into shadow. Elsewhere, the components of an abandoned magic spell are strewn across a carpeted floor in a palette of dusky reds and greens—a small voodoo doll, a lock of hair, a burnt candle. Nearby, the feet of a woman soak in a green bowl; it's unclear whether this is part of the ritual. Another photograph shows three perfume bottles, one resting on a two-hundred-peso note, on a linoleum floor; meeting them head-on is the white shoe of a woman. Both images suggest a schism between the magical product and the human subject, an abyss between expectation and fulfillment.

Animals, the most troubling "items" for sale at the Mercado de Sonora, feature in the two darkest photographs. A piglet perches on a table covered by a red cloth; it stares at the camera, accompanied only by its shadow, like a stage prop missing its magician. In the other, a green velvet sofa is juxtaposed with the curled tail of a (presumably dead) crocodile. Torn from their habitats, these animals, decontextualized in the marketplace, appear now even further estranged from nature.

The most hopeful composition—should faith be correlative to levels of brightness—shows a green soap and its box, which bears the words *Ven a mi* (Come to me), resting on a bathroom shelf alongside a plastic green comb and a bright red dustpan. The playful primary color scheme, set against a blue-tiled wall, evokes an optimism absent from the murky incertitude elsewhere.

Throughout this series of lyrical and unsettling mise-en-scènes, Franco Klein deconstructs the human subject and the magic charm. Female figures—defamiliarized by wigs or disembodied—interact with spells that have also, in some way, become fragmented. In our Mexico, a country beset by violence, poverty, and environmental crisis, these images depict an unshakable belief in enchantment, however tenuous its promise.

Tania Franco Klein

Chloe Aridjis

All photographs from the
series *Mercado de Sonora*,
2019, for *Aperture*
Courtesy the artist

Chloe Aridjis is a Mexican writer based
in London and the author, most recently,
of the novel *Sea Monsters* (2019).

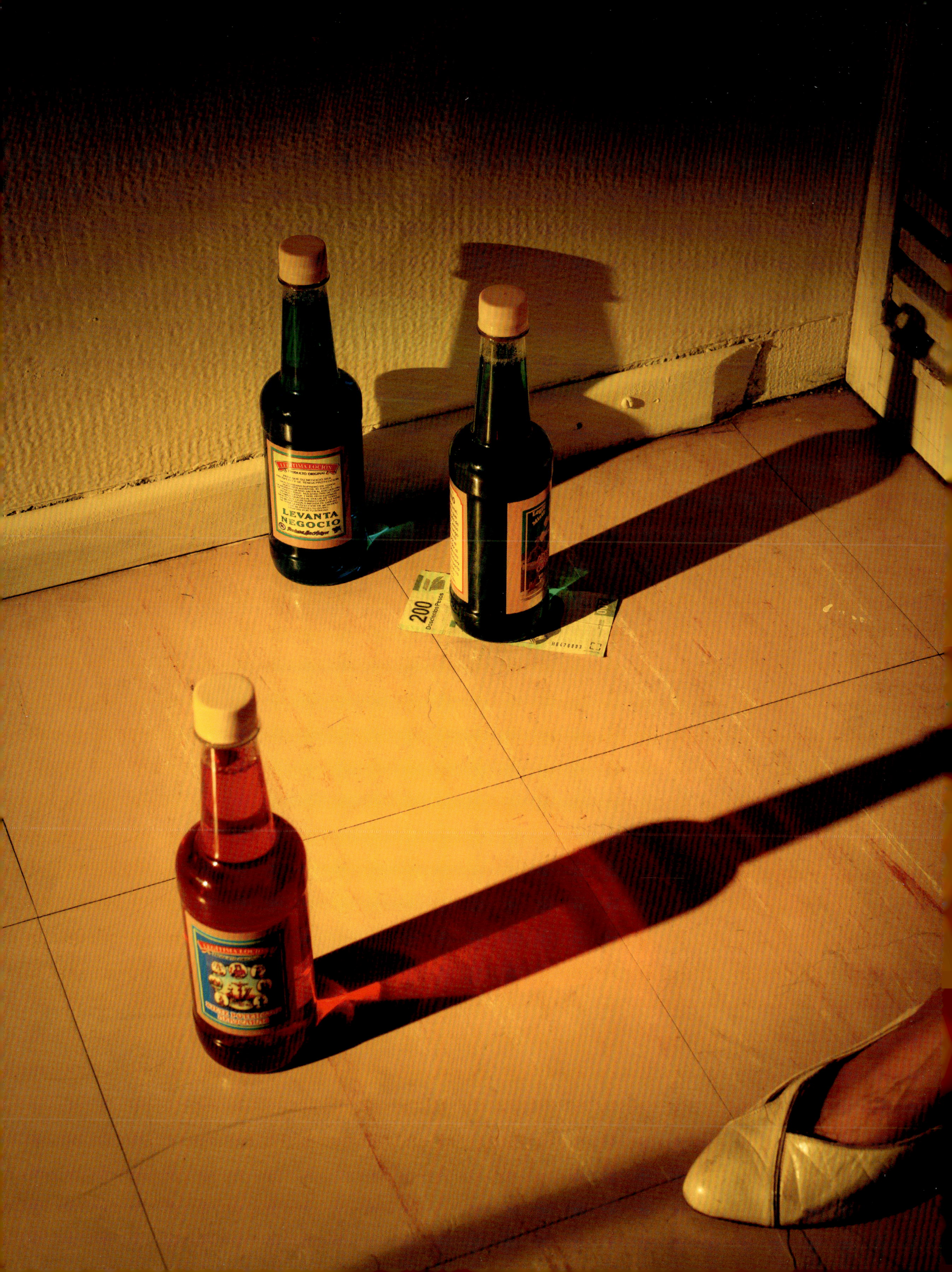
LEGITIMA LOCIÓN
PRODUCTO ORIGINAL
LEVANTA
NEGOCIO
200

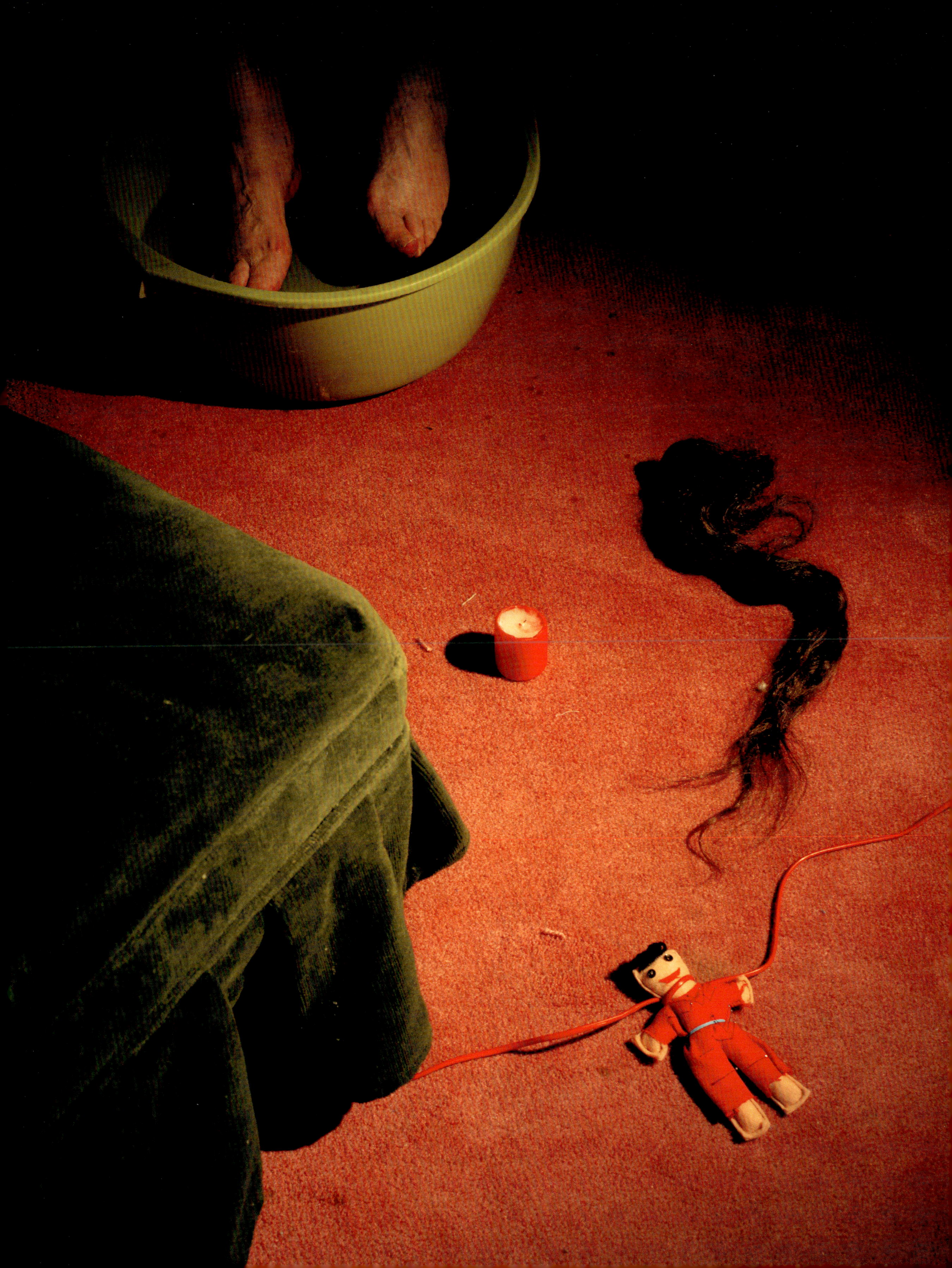

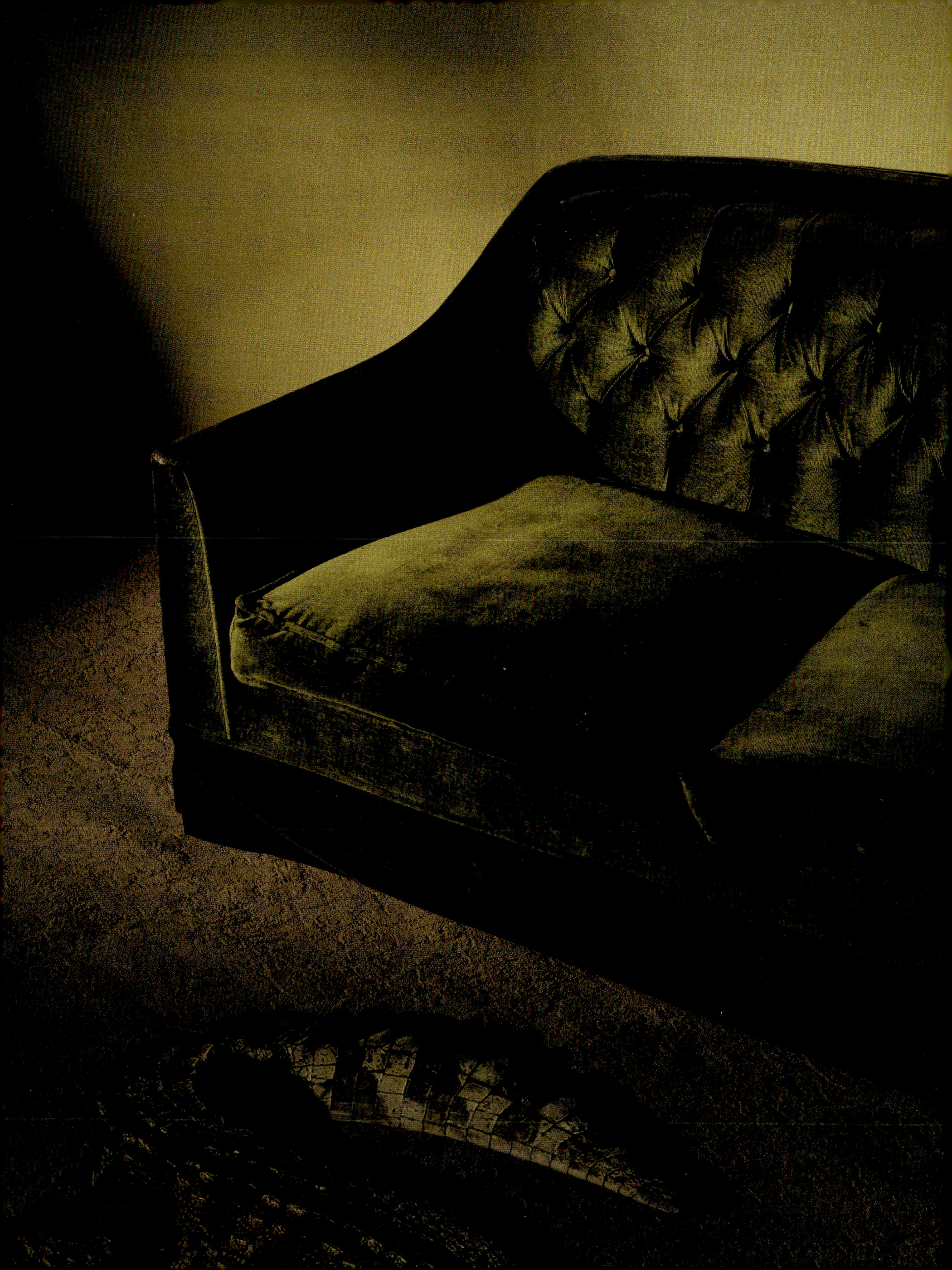

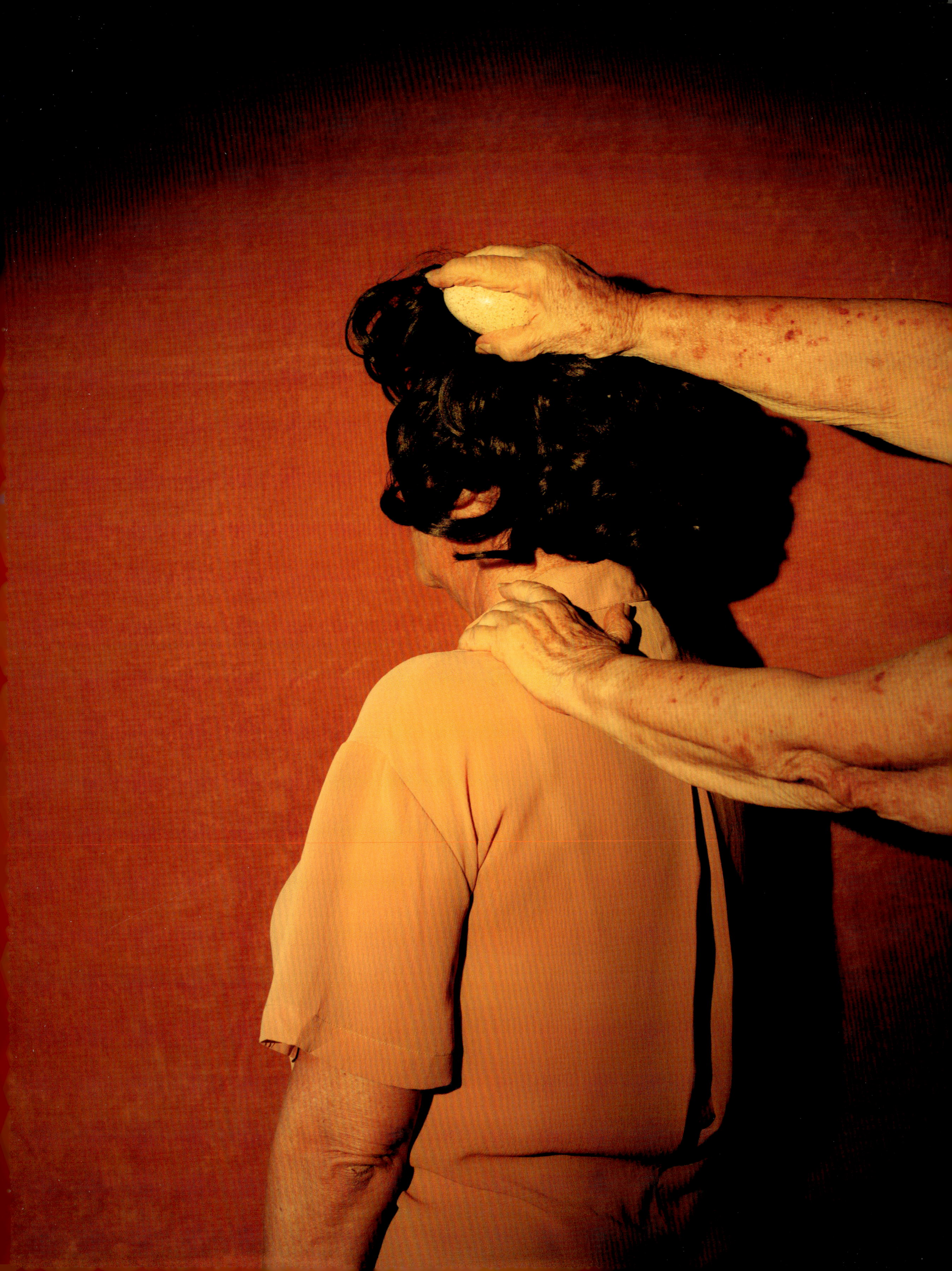